MW01156871

Argument Realization

The relationship between verbs and their arguments is a widely debated topic in linguistics. This comprehensive survey provides an up-to-date overview of this important area of research, exploring current theories of how a verb's semantics can determine the morphosyntactic realization of its arguments. Assuming a close connection between verb meaning and syntactic structure, it provides a bridge between lexical semantic and syntactic research, synthesizing the results of work from a range of linguistic subdisciplines and in a variety of theoretical frameworks.

The first four chapters survey leading theories about event structure and conceptualization. The fifth and sixth chapters focus on the mapping from lexical semantics to morphosyntax, and include a detailed discussion of the thematic hierarchy. The seventh chapter reviews treatments of multiple argument realization. With useful bibliographic references and clear definitions of relevant terms, this book will be invaluable to students and researchers in syntax and semantics, as well as those in related fields.

Beth Levin is William H. Bonsall Professor in the Humanities at the Department of Linguistics, Stanford University. She has held positions at the MIT Center for Cognitive Science and the Department of Linguistics at Northwestern University. She is the author of *English Verb Classes and Alternations: A Preliminary Investigation* (1993) and co-author of *Unaccusativity: At the Syntax–Lexical Semantics Interface* (with Malka Rappaport Hovav, 1995).

Malka Rappaport Hovav is Professor in the Department of English, the Hebrew University of Jerusalem. She has held positions at the MIT Center for Cognitive Science and Bar Ilan University, Israel. She is the co-author of *Unaccusativity: At the Syntax–Lexical Semantics Interface* (with Beth Levin, 1995).

Research Surveys in Linguistics

In large domains of theoretical and empirical linguistics, scholarly communication needs are directly comparable to those in analytical and natural sciences. Conspicuously lacking in the inventory of publications for linguists, compared to those in the sciences, are concise, single-authored, non-textbook reviews of rapidly evolving areas of inquiry. Research Surveys in Linguistics is intended to fill this gap. It consists of well-indexed volumes that survey topics of significant theoretical interest on which there has been a proliferation of research in the last two decades. The goal is to provide an efficent overview of, and entry into, the primary literature for linguists – both advanced students and researchers – who wish to move into, or stay literate in, the areas covered. Series authors are recognized authorities on the subject matter, as well as clear, highly organized writers. Each book offers the reader relatively tight structuring in sections and subsections and a detailed index for ease of orientation.

Previously published in this series

A Thematic Guide to Optimality Theory, John J. McCarthy
ISBN 0 52179194 4 hardback
ISBN 0 52179644 X paperback

The Phonology of Tone and Intonation, Carlos Gussenhoven
ISBN 0 521 81265 8 hardback
ISBN 0 521 01200 7 paperback

Argument Realization

BETH LEVIN

Stanford University

MALKA RAPPAPORT HOVAV

The Hebrew University of Jerusalem

CAMBRIDGE UNIVERSITY PRESS

Cambridge, New York, Melbourne, Madrid, Cape Town, Singapore, São Paulo

CAMBRIDGE UNIVERSITY PRESS
The Edinburgh Building, Cambridge CB2 2RU, UK

Published in the United States of America by Cambridge University Press, New York

http://www.cambridge.org
Information on this title: www.cambridge.org/9780521663311

© Beth Levin and Malka Rappaport Hovav, 2005

This book is in copyright. Subject to statutory exception
and to the provisions of relevant collective licensing agreements,
no reproduction of any part may take place without
the written permission of Cambridge University Press.

First published 2005

Printed in the United Kingdom at the University Press, Cambridge

Typeface Times 10/12pt. *System* LaTeX 2ε

A catalogue record for this book is available from the British Library

ISBN-13 978-0-521-66331-1 hardback
ISBN-10 0-521-66331-8 hardback
ISBN-13 978-0-521-66376-2 paperback
ISBN-10 0-521-66376-8 paperback

Cambridge University Press has no responsibility for the persistence or accuracy of
URLs for external or third-party internet websites referred to in this book, and does not
guarantee that any content on such websites is, or will remain, accurate or appropriate.

Contents

Acknowledgments

This book had its origins in an unpublished manuscript entitled "From Lexical Semantics to Argument Structure." We thank Hagit Borer for providing us with the impetus to write this paper. Christine Bartels suggested that with some work this paper might find a home in the Research Surveys in Linguistics series at Cambridge University Press. We agreed that this seemed like a good match and set about expanding the paper into this book. We did not anticipate that this process would take so long, in part because the rewriting process turned out to be an intellectual odyssey. We hope that we manage to convey the richness of the phenomena we deal with and their centrality to linguistic theory to those who read and use this book.

Four anonymous reviewers provided comments which proved extremely helpful as we turned the paper into a book. Our students forced us to think deeply about the issues here, and we have benefited considerably from their questions and comments. The material on thematic hierarchies was presented at the Stanford Semantics Fest in March 2000, IATL 16 at Tel Aviv University in June 2000, and the Conference on Semantic Role Universals at the Max Planck Institute of Cognitive Neuroscience in December 2002. We thank Christine Bartels, Bill Croft, Mari Olsen, Grace Song, and Carol Tenny for their comments on the original paper. We also thank John Beavers, Liz Coppock, Hana Filip, Kate Kearns, Anita Mittwoch, Masha Polinsky, Ivan Sag, Peter Sells, and Ivy Sichel for helpful comments and for discussions of parts of this book. We are indebted to Shiao Wei Tham for giving the whole manuscript a once over and catching the numerous inconsistencies and infelicities we could no longer see.

This work would not have been possible without the unstinting help of the staff of Northwestern University's Inter-Library Loan service and the librarians at the Center for Advanced Study in the Behavioral Sciences. We thank them all for their efforts to track down obscure and not so obscure materials. For bibliographic and editorial assistance, we also thank Victoria Gelfand, April Leininger, and especially Olivia Chang and Lena Goretsky.

The preparation of this book was supported in part by US National Science Foundation grants DBS-9221993, SBR-9616453, and SBC-0096036 to Levin and by Israel Science Foundation grants 832–00 and 806–03 to Rappaport Hovav. This book was partially prepared while Levin and Rappaport Hovav were Fellows at the Center for Advanced Study in the Behavioral Sciences. Financial support for Levin's stay at the Center was provided by the Center's general funds and for Rappaport Hovav's stay by the Andrew W. Mellon Foundation Grant 29800639. We are grateful to the Center for providing us with the opportunity to work in this uniquely stimulating and congenial environment.

We dedicate this book to the memory of Ken Hale, who was a major force in bringing the issues discussed in this book to the attention of the generative linguistics community. He was instrumental in formulating the central questions and in defining the major challenges in the area of argument realization.

Finally, our deepest appreciation goes to our families for their love and support during the time we have spent on our latest and longest trans-Atlantic collaboration.

Beth Levin and Malka Rappaport Hovav

Introduction

A boy throws a ball, which hits a window and breaks it. This scene can be described using either sentence in (1), the first with *break* and the second with *hit*.

(1) a. The boy broke the window with a ball.
    b. The boy hit the window with a ball.

The participants in this scene – the boy, the window, and the ball – are expressed in a parallel fashion in both sentences: *the boy* is the subject, *the window* is the object, and *the ball* is the object of the preposition *with*. However, *break* can be used to describe a part of the same scene in another way, an option not available to *hit*.

(2) a. The window broke.
    b. *The window hit.

Such puzzles are at the heart of the area of linguistics called ARGUMENT REALIZATION: the study of the possible syntactic expressions of the arguments of a verb. In the *hit/break* example, the challenge is to explain why two verbs show divergent behavior and why the divergences take the forms that they do. This example, drawn from Fillmore's well-known study, "The Grammar of *Hitting* and *Breaking*" (1970), is particularly apt because both verbs in their basic, nonidiomatic uses are commonly characterized as "agent-act-on-patient" verbs, and linguists often assume that much of what needs to be said about argument realization can be summarized with a simple statement correlating agents with subjects and patients – roughly, affected entities – with objects. Needless to say, such simple statements do not go far in helping to understand the basis for the difference between these two verbs.

It has long been known that verbs fall into semantically identifiable classes, which are the basis for generalizations concerning argument realization. Fillmore (1970) points out that in terms of their linguistic behavior, *break*

1

and *hit* are each representative of a larger set of verbs, including those listed in (3). Each set shows semantic coherence: verbs patterning like *break* involve a change of state in an entity, while those patterning like *hit* involve contact, often forceful, with an entity, without entailing any change of state in that entity (e.g., *The rocks hit the window, but luckily it wasn't damaged*).

(3) a. *Break* verbs: bend, fold, shatter, crack   (Fillmore 1970: 125, (15))
    b. *Hit* verbs: slap, strike, bump, stroke   (Fillmore 1970: 125, (16))

All verbs in the *break* class – and none in the *hit* class – show the two argument realization options in (1) and (2), which together constitute the CAUSATIVE ALTERNATION (also known as the "anticausative" or "causative/inchoative" alternation). This alternation is characterized by verbs with transitive and intransitive uses, such that the transitive use of a verb V means roughly 'cause to V-intransitive'; see B. Levin (1993) for discussion and references. More generally, both the *break* verbs and the *hit* verbs show a range of characteristic argument realization possibilities, going well beyond those just illustrated. As Fillmore (1970: 126) discusses, *The window was broken* allows both eventive and stative readings, while the comparable *The window was hit* allows only a stative reading. He also points out that *hit* permits alternate expressions of the possessor of a body part, while *break* does not.

(4) a. I broke his leg./*I broke him on the leg.
    b. I hit his leg./I hit him on the leg.   (Fillmore 1970: 126, (23)–(26))

Furthermore, in a later paper, Fillmore (1977a: 74–78) points out that the sentences in the pair in (5) are not paraphrases, though those in (6) are.

(5) a. Perry broke the fence with the stick.
    b. Perry broke the stick against the fence.
(6) a. Perry hit the fence with the stick.
    b. Perry hit the stick against the fence.

The fact that classes of verbs with similar meanings show characteristic argument realization patterns suggests that these patterns can be attributed to the semantic properties of each class. In fact, two comparable classes of verbs, again with distinct behavioral patterns, can be identified in other languages, such as Lhasa Tibetan (DeLancey 1995), Berber, Warlpiri, and Winnebago (Guerssel et al. 1985).

One goal of a theory of argument realization is the isolation of the relevant components of meaning and the explication of their connection to the range of argument realization options. Groundbreaking studies exploring such regularities in the realization of arguments within the framework of generative grammar include Carter (1976, 1977, 1988 [1976]), Fillmore (1968, 1971b), and Ostler (1979). Over the years many argument realization regularities have been uncovered, and recently several general theories of argument realization have been developed (Ackerman and Moore 2001; Baker 1996a, 1997, 2001; Croft 1991, 1998; Davis 2001; Davis and Koenig 2000; Dowty 1991; Hale and Keyser 1992, 1993, 1994, 1996, 1997a, 1997b, 1998, 1999, 2002; Jackendoff 1987, 1990b; Joppen and Wunderlich 1995; Rappaport Hovav and B. Levin 1998a; Schlesinger 1995; Van Valin 1993b; Van Valin and LaPolla 1997; Wechsler 1995; Wunderlich 1997a, 1997b, 2000; among others). This book aims to provide an overview and synthesis of the results of current research on argument realization, to highlight questions which remain open, and to lay out the challenges such phenomena present for linguistic theory.

Throughout this book we illustrate the richness and complexity of the phenomena falling under the rubric "argument realization." As we use it, this term encompasses all facets of the syntactic expression of arguments of verbs, including the entire range of options for the grammatical relation they may bear, their syntactic category, and their surface morphosyntactic expression. The term "linking" has also been used in this connection. This term appears to have originated in Richard Carter's unpublished 1976 paper, "Some Linking Regularities" (eventually published in 1988), where he uses the phrase "linking regularities" (1988: 3) for the regularities in the syntactic realization – i.e., the syntactic category and grammatical relation – of a verb's arguments. Since the term "linking" does not transparently reflect the full range of phenomena we are concerned with and has other uses in other areas of linguistics, we adopt the term "argument realization" instead.

A complete theory of argument realization has to address five major questions: (i) Which facets of the meanings of verbs are relevant for the mapping from lexical semantics to syntax? (ii) What is the nature of a lexical semantic representation that encompasses these components of meaning? That is, what are the primitives of this representation and the principles for combining these primitives into representations of specific verb meanings? (iii) What is the nature of the algorithm which derives the syntactic expression of arguments? (iv) To what extent do nonsemantic factors such as information structure and heaviness govern argument realization? (v) To what extent are the semantic determinants of argument realization lexical and to what extent can some of them be shown to be nonlexical? This book is devoted to an exploration of these issues, laying out and comparing different theories which address them.

These issues have become important to linguistic theory because many current theories of grammar assume that the syntactic realization of arguments is predictable to a large extent from the meaning of their verbs. Our goal in this book is to provide a bridge between the line of syntactic research that presupposes a tight connection between verb meaning and syntactic structure and lexical semantic research into verb meanings. Syntacticians are most often interested in sweeping generalizations concerning argument realization and formulate theories without sufficiently delving into the lexical semantic notions that enter into argument realization. On the other hand, lexical semanticists – including formal semanticists dealing with lexical semantic questions – facing the task of articulating lexical semantic representations of verbs are not always adequately versed in the syntactic issues impinging on the choice of representation. Furthermore, the lexical semantics of verbs has been explored from a wide range of theoretical perspectives, a fact which hinders the pooling of important insights. In this book we attempt to provide a synthesis and evaluation of these strands of work, placing them in a unified perspective. Our goal is not to develop a comprehensive theory, but rather to present research results which must be taken into consideration within any theoretical framework.

In the first part of the book we investigate the nature of a lexical semantic representation that can encode the grammatically relevant facets of verb meaning and, thus, can serve as a foundation for a theory of argument realization. We review various forms of lexical semantic representation and explore how each fulfills the basic requirements of a theory of argument realization. We focus both on the nature of the representation itself and on the appropriate characterization of the relevant components of meaning, since existing discussions present overlapping, but distinct characterizations. We begin in chapter 2 with SEMANTIC ROLE LISTS, one of the simplest – and, possibly, most commonly adopted – forms of lexical semantic representation, although, as we review, a form that also suffers from severe drawbacks. In chapter 3 we look at a more sophisticated version of semantic roles, GENERALIZED SEMANTIC ROLES, which overcomes some, but not all, of these drawbacks. In this chapter we also introduce a second form of lexical semantic representation, PREDICATE DECOMPOSITION, in which the meaning of a verb is represented in terms of some of its basic grammatically relevant elements of meaning. These representations are often called EVENT STRUCTURES, as they represent the linguistically relevant event types. Event structures have two properties that make them particularly effective: they encode a distinction between simple and complex events – a distinction which has repercussions for argument realization – and they make a distinction between the core meaning of a verb – its root – and the components of meaning that identify the verb's event type.

Since verbs are predicates of events, a characterization of the components of verb meaning relevant to argument realization must be couched within a theory of EVENT CONCEPTUALIZATION – a theory about which facets of events are encoded in event structures. In chapter 4 we review three approaches to event conceptualization; they differ as to whether they take events to be conceptualized in terms of notions of motion and location, in terms of their causal structure, or in terms of their aspectual structure. Each one, then, takes a different cognitively salient facet of events as relevant to argument realization. We focus on the last two approaches, as they have the most significant contributions to make to the understanding of argument realization. We conclude that it is not possible to isolate a single semantic factor which determines either subject or object selection, and attempt to tease apart and assess the relative contribution of both causal and aspectual notions. We further show that sentience, which cannot always be subsumed under causal notions and lacks a natural place in the aspectual approach, is sometimes implicated in argument realization.

With this background, we turn in two subsequent chapters to questions of argument realization. In chapter 5 we address general properties of theories of the mapping from lexical semantics to syntax. The various accounts of this mapping which we review take as one of their goals the preservation of facets of the event structure in the syntax. We identify two hypotheses about which facets of event structure are preserved: some approaches assume that the mapping to syntax preserves equivalence classes of arguments or predicates, while others assume that the mapping preserves prominence relations in the event structure. Concomitantly, we show that the actual mapping algorithms are designed to be consistent with these hypotheses.

In chapter 6 we explore the use of a theoretical construct, a hierarchy of semantic roles or THEMATIC HIERARCHY, that has figured prominently in a wide range of approaches to argument realization. We underscore one reason for its prevalence: a thematic hierarchy facilitates the formulation of a mapping algorithm that ensures that prominence relations in the event structure are preserved in the syntax. Not all researchers, however, share this conception of the thematic hierarchy. We also identify a second conception: the thematic hierarchy provides a way of recognizing priorities among meaning components relevant to argument realization that fall outside the structure of event structure. Thus, the exploration of thematic hierarchies allows us to further weigh the ways in which different facets of a lexical semantic representation contribute to argument realization, buttressing the results in chapter 4. We also extensively consider the question of why there are so many different formulations of the thematic hierarchy in the literature.

As the discussion of *break* and *hit* revealed, verbs may show ARGUMENT ALTERNATIONS – alternate expressions of their arguments – as illustrated with the causative alternation. Argument alternations represent one instantiation of the larger phenomenon of MULTIPLE ARGUMENT REALIZATION – the ability of most verbs to appear in a variety of syntactic contexts. We devote chapter 7 to this phenomenon, though many of the issues discussed are touched on in earlier chapters as well. We review various treatments of multiple argument realization, showing that some alternations appear to be meaning driven (i.e., are a by-product of verbal polysemy), while others are not. We show that when two alternate argument realizations are truth-conditionally equivalent, the choice between them is governed by nonsemantic factors, such as the information status and heaviness of a verb's arguments. Perhaps one of the most vexed issues is the distribution of verbs across alternations. Verbs that are similar in meaning do not always show the same alternations, yet despite this apparent idiosyncrasy, argument alternations can be extended to new verbs. We conclude that a verb's root has a major part to play in determining which forms of multiple argument realization it might show.

Finally, chapter 8 offers a brief conclusion, summarizing the results of our study in the context of the five questions about argument realization we laid out above and pulling together the insights emerging in earlier chapters.

Although this book focuses on the relationship between verb meaning and argument realization, it is important to acknowledge right at its outset that some researchers (Borer 1994, 1998, 2003a, 2003b, in press a, in press b; Erteschik-Shir and Rapoport 1996; Ghomeshi and Massam 1995; Goldberg 1995; Hoekstra 1992; Jackendoff 1997; Kay 2000; Ritter and S. T. Rosen 1996, 1998) have recently espoused the position that most of the determinants of argument realization are not strictly lexical; rather, they suggest that certain syntactic configurations are themselves the bearers and determiners of certain meaning components; see section 7.1 for discussion. Nevertheless, the basic point still holds: the semantic determinants of argument realization – be they lexical or not – need to be studied seriously in order for a theory of argument realization to be firmly grounded. Therefore, the issues we deal with and the results we report are relevant even if the semantic determinants of argument realization turn out to be extralexical. Although at several points in the book we argue that there is much to be learned from paying attention to the lexical core of verb meaning, we do not take an explicit position on the larger question of how much is lexical and how much is extralexical. We usually refer to lexical semantic properties and lexical semantic representations, but most of the discussion can be recast in terms which are not strictly lexical.

1

Challenges for theories of argument realization

In this chapter we set out the broad descriptive generalizations which emerge from investigations of argument realization and its lexical semantic underpinnings, as well as the methodological issues which a comprehensive theory of argument realization must address. These constitute the major challenges for a theory of lexical semantic representation and a theory of argument realization that dovetails with it.

1.1 Taking lexical semantic representations seriously

Since the 1980s, many theories of grammar have been built on the assumption that the syntactic realization of arguments – their category type and their grammatical function – is largely predictable from the meaning of their verbs. Such theories take many facets of the syntactic structure of a sentence to be projections of the lexical properties of its predicator – its verb or argument-taking lexical item;[1] see Wasow (1985) for discussion. To ensure this, these theories incorporate conditions requiring that the arguments of the verb are appropriately represented in the syntactic representation of its clause.[2] Such principles include the Principles and Parameters framework's Projection Principle (Chomsky 1981: 29, 38), Lexical-Functional Grammar's Completeness and Coherence Conditions (Kaplan and Bresnan 1982: 211–12), and Role and Reference Grammar's (RRG's) Completeness Constraint (Foley and Van Valin 1984: 183; Van Valin 1993b: 74–75; Van Valin and LaPolla 1997: 325–26).[3] The successful implementation of the program of deriving the syntactic properties of verbs from facets of their meaning depends on the existence of both an articulated theory of the lexical semantic representation of verbs and a theory of the mapping between this representation and the relevant syntactic representation. Syntacticians often appeal to principles such as the Projection Principle, which presuppose a lexical semantic representation, without seriously considering the

7

nature of the lexical semantic representations on which they are meant to operate and without taking into account the full range of empirical generalizations concerning argument realizations which these representations are meant to help account for. We illustrate these shortcomings through a review of some relevant discussions, devoting the rest of this chapter to setting out the generalizations that need to be taken into account.

In the past two decades, claims have often been made to the effect that a lexical entry needs to register s(emantic)-selection, the semantic selectional properties of verbs, and not c(onstituent)-selection, the morphosyntactic properties of the arguments of verbs (Chomsky 1986; Pesetsky 1982; Stowell 1981). Implicit in this line of work seems to be the assumption that s-selection takes the form of a list of arguments, identified by their semantic roles. Chomsky (1986: 86), for example, suggests that part of the semantic description of the verb *hit* is a specification that it selects arguments bearing the semantic roles agent and patient. He suggests that the syntactic type and grammatical relation of each argument (c-selection) can be derived from s-selection via general principles, so that subcategorization frames can be dispensed with altogether. In particular, the fact that this verb is transitive, taking an NP subject and an NP direct object, follows from the fact that the verb selects two "things" as arguments (rather than, for example, a "thing" and a "proposition"), and "things" are realized syntactically as NPs (cf. Grimshaw's [1981] notion of canonical structural realization). The fact that the NP denoting the hitter is the subject and the NP denoting the contacted object is the direct object follows from the classification of the former as agent and the latter as patient, and the fact that universally agents and patients are realized, respectively, as subjects and direct objects.[4]

As already mentioned, lexical entries with agent and patient arguments have been attributed to *break* and *hit*. A similar entry is also proposed for *eat* (Pesetsky 1995: 4) and even for *see* (Rothstein 1983: 23). Again, this lexical entry is supposed to explain these verbs' choice of subject and object. However, *break, hit, eat,* and *see* turn out to diverge in systematic and fundamental ways when their argument realization options are examined more fully. As already shown, *hit* differs from *break* in English. Moreover, although verbs like *break* are consistently transitive across languages, verbs like *hit* are not, but rather in some languages they are intransitives with an oblique complement; see section 1.6. The verb *eat* differs from *break* in still other ways. Like *hit*, it does not show an intransitive use whose subject is the transitive use's object (**The cookie ate*), but it does allow the omission of its object (*The boy ate*), unlike *break* and other change-of-state verbs (Rappaport Hovav and B. Levin 2002) and *hit*. Furthermore, *eat* and other verbs of consumption show some unique properties in other languages. For instance, they may causativize differently from other transitive verbs in certain languages, including Amharic (Amberber 2002a, 2002b: 37–38), Berber (Alalou and Farrell 1993: 165–66; Guerssel 1986: 36ff), Kannada (Fried 1992: 175–78), Tariana (Aikhenvald

2000: 157–58), and various Indo-Aryan languages (Alsina and Joshi 1991: 6–7, 12–13; Masica 1976: 46; Ramchand 1997: 182–87). The perception verb *see* shows yet another pattern: it can appear without an object, although this use receives a definite interpretation, contrasting with the comparable use of *eat*, which receives an indefinite interpretation (Fillmore 1986). Such examples show that the program of deriving a verb's argument realization options from its meaning must be firmly grounded in the relevant empirical facts, and the range of facts goes well beyond those that syntacticians usually cite.

A basic understanding of what is involved in formulating a lexical semantic representation is also a prerequisite for the application of certain principles often invoked by syntacticians. For example, many syntactic analyses are motivated using Baker's (1988: 46, 1997) Uniformity of Theta Assignment Hypothesis, which states that NPs bearing identical semantic roles to a verb have to be realized in the same syntactic relation to that verb. Invoking this hypothesis without an understanding of when two NPs bear the same semantic relation to a verb deprives it of much of its power, since it is never clear whether it is being applied appropriately. As we discuss in chapter 7, this question surfaces in the analysis of the dative alternation, exemplified by near-paraphrase sentence pairs, such as *Terry gave a watch to Sam/Terry gave Sam a watch*. The question of whether the two VP-internal arguments bear the same semantic roles in both sentences is crucial to this hypothesis and, hence, to the larger analysis of the alternation. Most of the recent well-articulated theories of argument realization take semantic roles to be convenient labels for referring to arguments, derived from more basic components of lexical semantic representations, as we discuss extensively in chapter 2. Although lip service is usually paid to the nonprimitive status of semantic roles, most syntacticians still ignore the complicated issues involved in determining a comprehensive analysis of particular roles, and, hence, rarely adequately motivate particular semantic analyses, including those apparently dictated by Baker's hypothesis.

1.2   Identifying grammatically relevant facets of meaning

Given the complex and multifaceted nature of word meaning (Aitchison 1994; Bolinger 1965; Ullmann 1962), it is no small task to provide words with a structured lexical semantic representation which provides a basis for argument realization. Two methodological choices have facilitated this task. The first involves the nature of the evidence used to posit a lexical semantic representation and the second involves the types of semantic elements relevant to the lexical semantic representation.

Lexical semantic representations have been proposed on the basis of various types of evidence. Some evidence is purely linguistic in nature, while other evidence reflects language acquisition, cognitive, and philosophical considerations. As our focus is on the mapping from lexical semantics to syntax, we follow Dowty (1991: 560–62) and take as our primary criterion for developing a lexical semantic representation the ability to formulate a perspicuous theory of argument realization. Any semantic distinction that affects argument realization is relevant to the design of a lexical semantic representation, while any others are to be ignored. This methodological choice is prompted by a lack of certainty that the lexical semantic elements relevant to argument realization are also relevant to other linguistic or nonlinguistic concerns. However, as B. Levin and Pinker (1991: 3–4) note, there is considerable convergence in the facets of meaning that various types of evidence home in on, so that the use of one type of evidence is likely to lead to a representation pertinent to other concerns.

Having discussed acceptable forms of evidence, we devote the remainder of this section to the second methodological choice pertinent to choosing the elements of a lexical semantic representation.

It is commonly assumed that only certain facets of word meaning are relevant to argument realization (Davis 2001; Grimshaw 1993; Jackendoff 1990b; B. Levin 1999; Pinker 1989; T. Mohanan and K. P. Mohanan 1999; Rappaport Hovav and B. Levin 1998a; among others).[5] One of the most explicit statements of this hypothesis is made by Pinker: "Perhaps there is a set of semantic elements and relations that is much smaller than the set of cognitively available and culturally salient distinctions, and verb meanings are organized around them" (1989: 166). These grammatically relevant components of verb meaning are usually isolated through an examination of the common semantic denominator of verbs exhibiting the same range of argument realization options.

A few examples will help clarify what is meant by grammatically relevant. Although the notion of color may be cognitively salient, Grimshaw (1993: 3) points out that there are no grammatical processes or generalizations about the morphosyntactic realization of arguments which are restricted to verbs having to do with color (e.g., *paint, color, bleach, redden, stain*). Similarly, Pesetsky (1995: 14) writes that the distinction between verbs of loud speech (e.g., *bellow, holler, shout*) and verbs of soft speech (e.g., *murmur, whisper*) is not relevant to the syntax. Such observations should not be taken as denying the importance of these particular meaning elements; they simply do not figure in linguistic generalizations. In contrast, as Pesetsky (1995: 14) points out, the distinction between verbs of manner of speaking, such as *holler* and *whisper*, and verbs of content of speaking, such as *say* and *propose*, is grammatically relevant. Pesetsky supports this point by making reference to particular grammatical properties of these classes of verbs. We do not present his examples as they involve sentential complements, which we do not discuss in this book, but instead present comparable examples involving verbs of sound emission, drawing on the discussions in B. Levin, Song, and Atkins (1997) and Song (1996).

English has a large class of verbs of emission, which can be subdivided according to the nature of the emitted element: light, sound, smell, or substance (B. Levin 1993). Verbs of sound emission display a wide range of argument realization options, some of which are apparently restricted to a subset of these verbs. All take an argument denoting the sound emitter, but some, including *clatter* and *rattle*, allow transitive, causative uses with the emitter as object and an entity or natural force that causes the sound emission as subject.

(1) a. The truck rumbled.
    b. *Peter rumbled the truck.
(2) a. The tea kettle whistled.
    b. *The boiling water whistled the tea kettle.
(3) a. The teacups clattered.
    b. I clattered the teacups as I loaded the dishwasher.
(4) a. The windows rattled.
    b. The storm rattled the windows.

Consistent with what Pesetsky (1995: 14) notes in his discussion of verbs of speaking, the volume, pitch, resonance, and duration of the relevant sound apparently play no part in determining whether a verb of sound has a causative use. Instead, what is critical is the mode of sound production. Some sounds are produced internal to the sound emitter (e.g., *babble, gurgle, holler, rumble*), while others are produced external to it (e.g., *clatter, jingle, rattle*). Still others may be produced in either way, depending on the emitter (e.g., *buzz, squeak, squeal, whistle*); for instance, a squeal can be produced internally via the vocal tract, as when a baby squeals, or externally due to friction between two surfaces, as when tires squeal. The verbs of sound with causative uses are associated with externally produced sounds (B. Levin, Song and Atkins 1997; Song 1996).

B. Levin, Song, and Atkins (1997) argue, however, that it is not mode of sound production which determines a verb's behavior, but rather, whether the verb lexicalizes an internally caused event or an externally caused event. The internally vs. externally caused event distinction is introduced by B. Levin and Rappaport Hovav (1995: 90–98), drawing on Smith (1970), to characterize which verbs have transitive causative uses; see also Croft (1990, 1991), Haspelmath (1993), van Voorst (1995). An externally caused event is conceptualized as brought about by an external cause with immediate control over the event. The core verbs lexicalizing externally caused events are change-of-state verbs, such as *break, open*, or *cool*, which describe an external force or entity bringing about an effect on a second entity. Such verbs always have transitive uses, as in *The wind opened the door*, but they often have intransitive uses which do not make the external cause explicit, as in *The door opened*; these verbs, then, participate in the causative alternation. In contrast, an internally caused event is conceptualized as arising from inherent properties of the entity participating in this event. These properties are "responsible" for the event; no external force is required. The prototypical verbs lexicalizing internally caused events, such as *sing* and *dance*, have an agentive argument with a self-controlled body acting volitionally. Less prototypical internally caused verbs include those associated with actions which arise from within the entity denoted by their argument or from some property inherent to it. For example, the events associated with the verbs *shiver* and *yawn*, while usually not volitional, can only arise from within the entity shivering or yawning. Other internally caused events result from inherent properties of the entity denoted by their argument; instances of light emission, such as shining and glistening, require that their emitters have certain properties so that they may shine or glisten. Since internally caused events involve only one argument and this argument cannot be externally controlled, verbs denoting such events are intransitive and do not regularly show the causative alternation.

Returning to the verbs of sound emission, B. Levin, Song, and Atkins (1997) show that mode of sound production correlates with the distinction between externally and internally caused events. Verbs describing sounds produced internal to the sound emitter, such as *groan* and *holler*, are conceived of as internally caused, and those describing sounds produced external to the emitter, such as *jingle* and *rattle*, are conceived of as externally caused. Verbs describing sounds that can be produced either internally or externally, according to the choice of emitter, are open to either an internally or an externally caused classification, depending on the mode of sound production. This result is welcome since the distinction between an internally and an externally caused event cuts across a larger swath of the lexicon than a distinction based on mode of sound production.

What emerges, then, is that although verbs of color, verbs of communication, and verbs of sound emission constitute semantically coherent classes of verbs, they do not constitute GRAMMATICALLY RELEVANT classes. As the examples in (1)–(4) suggest, verbs of sound emission belong to at least two distinct grammatically relevant semantic classes and probably crossclassify into others. The study of the argument realization options available to verbs in various semantic classes can be used to isolate the grammatically relevant aspects of meaning, as discussed in B. Levin (1993) and Pinker (1989), among others.

Failure to classify verbs in terms of the appropriate semantic elements may give rise to spurious problems regarding the lexical semantics–syntax interface. A case in point involves the distribution of verbs of bodily process with respect to auxiliary selection in Italian (C. Rosen 1981: 64–65; B. Levin and Rappaport Hovav 1995: 9, 159–60). In Italian some intransitive verbs are found with the auxiliary *essere* 'be' and others with the auxiliary *avere* 'have.' This nonuniform behavior has been understood in the context of Perlmutter's (1978) Unaccusative Hypothesis, which posits two syntactically distinct subclasses of intransitive verbs: UNACCUSATIVE verbs, whose surface subject is an underlying object, and UNERGATIVE verbs, whose surface subject is an underlying subject; see also Burzio (1986), Grimshaw (1987), B. Levin and Rappaport Hovav (1995), Perlmutter (1989), Pullum (1988), and C. Rosen (1981), among others. Auxiliary selection has been linked to unaccusativity: unaccusative verbs are said to select *essere* 'be' and unergative verbs *avere* 'have' (Burzio 1986; Perlmutter 1978, 1989; C. Rosen 1981). A verb's classification as unaccusative or unergative is itself said to be semantically determined (Perlmutter 1978; Perlmutter and Postal 1984), so in some sense auxiliary selection reflects semantic considerations.

The first accounts of the classification of verbs as unaccusative or unergative (Perlmutter 1978) made reference to specific semantic classes of verbs. Verbs of bodily process, such as *cough, snore*, and *yawn*, were included among the unergative verbs. As expected given this classification, these verbs take the auxiliary *avere* 'have' in Italian, with one exception: the Italian verb *arrossire*, glossed as 'blush,' takes the auxiliary *essere* 'be.' Furthermore, as C. Rosen (1984) notes, some members of this semantic class in other languages also could be considered unaccusative. Such examples have led Rosen and others to argue that unaccusativity is not fully semantically determined after all. However, McClure (1990) and others argue that the semantic notion "verb of bodily process" is not appropriate for generalizations concerning the lexical semantics–syntax interface. Instead, McClure suggests that activity verbs take *avere* 'have'[6] and achievement verbs – which are largely change-of-state verbs – take *essere* 'be.' Since most verbs of bodily process are activity verbs, it might appear that this class figures in the auxiliary selection generalization, but, in fact, the Italian verb *arrossire* is the exception that proves that the right rule involves the notion of change of state. This Italian verb, which is based on the adjective *rosso* 'red,' literally means 'become red'; thus, it is a change-of-state verb and takes the appropriate auxiliary, *essere* 'be.' Once the relevant facets of meaning are isolated, the behavior of these verbs turns out to be more regular and rule-governed than previously assumed.

As this Italian example shows, there is more than one way of semantically characterizing most verbs, and it is not always a priori obvious which characterization is appropriate for argument realization. Certainly, concepts with greater generality such as "change of state" or "activity" are preferable in principle to more specific concepts such as "verb of bodily process." However, certain verbs can receive multiple characterizations even in terms of general semantic notions because of overlaps and interdependencies between them. It is necessary to look for verbs that satisfy only one semantic characterization in order to identify which one matters to a given phenomenon. This point can be illustrated with the notions "agentivity" and "stativity." Many of the stativity tests identified by Lakoff (1966) turn out to be agentivity tests, but this mischaracterization only becomes apparent when it is shown that nonagentive nonstatives also fail the tests (Lakoff 1966: I-12–I-13; Lee 1971: L7–L15; B. Levin and Rappaport Hovav 1995; also see section 4.2.1). Thus, based on contrasts such as **My mother persuaded me to know French* vs. *My mother persuaded me to learn French*, Lakoff argues that only nonstatives can be complements of *persuade*; however, the unacceptability of **My mother persuaded the telephone to ring* shows that the real issue is agentivity. For discussion and exemplification of potential pitfalls in identifying semantic determinants of argument realization and methodological strategies for avoiding them, see the literature on unaccusativity, including B. Levin and Rappaport Hovav (1989, 1995), L. Levin (1986), and McClure (1990).

The consequences of misidentifying the relevant semantic determinants can be illustrated with verbs of psychological state or PSYCH-VERBS, as they are often referred to. Psych-verbs have a variety of distinctive properties. (See B. Levin 1993 for references on English psych-verbs and section 1.5 for discussion of psych-verbs across languages.) One striking property is the existence in English of psych-verb minimal pairs such as *fear* and *frighten* or *like* and *please*. These verbs are found in sentences that are near-paraphrases, as illustrated in (5) and (6), although the comparable arguments receive distinct expressions. For instance, all the verbs are said to select an argument with the semantic role of experiencer, yet in the (a) sentences the experiencer is expressed as subject and in the (b) sentences as object.

(5) a. My children fear thunderstorms.
    b. Thunderstorms frighten my children.

(6) a. I like this solution to the problem.
    b. This solution to the problem pleases me.

In English this phenomenon is rarely observed outside the class of psych-verbs. Many early discussions of semantic roles cite minimal pairs as in (5) and (6) to illustrate that semantic roles themselves are not sufficient for determining the syntactic expression of arguments. However, these sentences only pose a problem if the facet of meaning they share is indeed what determines argument realization.

The apparent paraphrase relation between sentences with verb pairs such as *fear* and *frighten* or *like* and *please* was initially taken to indicate that the subject of *fear* and the object of *frighten* bear the same semantic role and that the object of *fear* and the subject of *frighten* likewise bear the same semantic role, though one distinct from the other argument. For example, Belletti and Rizzi (1988) and Grimshaw (1990) analyze these verbs as taking experiencer and theme arguments. The assignment of an experiencer role to one argument reflects the meaning of these verbs, but it is unclear what motivates the assignment of the theme role to their second argument. "Theme" is usually defined as the role of an entity whose movement, location, state, or change of state is specified by the verb (Gruber 1965, 1976; Jackendoff 1972, 1976, 1983, 1987). As this characterization does not fit the second argument, there seems to be little reason for assigning it this role, beyond a general tendency to treat theme as a default role; see section 2.4. The assumption that the verbs in each pair have the same lexical semantic representation leads to syntactic analyses in which these verbs are found in very similar, if not identical, underlying syntactic representations (Belletti and Rizzi 1988; Postal 1971), as they should be if Baker's Uniformity of Theta Assignment Hypothesis is correct. Furthermore, these analyses are extended to other psych-verbs since *fear* and *like*, on the one hand, and *frighten* and *please*, on the other, are representative of two larger classes of psych-verbs in English. Also patterning like *fear* are *adore, detest,* and *esteem*, while *astonish, disturb,* and *shock* are among the approximately two hundred verbs patterning like *frighten* (B. Levin 1993).

However, problems with maintaining parallel underlying syntactic analyses for *fear* and *frighten* psych-verbs emerged (Arad 1998, 1999, 2002; Bouchard 1995; Croft 1993; Grimshaw 1990; Koenig and Davis 2001; Pesetsky 1987, 1995; Reinhart 2000, 2001, 2002; among others). Concomitantly, semantic differences between verbs like *fear* and verbs like *frighten* were discovered; see Allen (1986, 1995), Bouchard (1995), Croft (1993), Grimshaw (1990), Koenig and Davis (2001), Pesetsky (1987, 1995), Pylkkänen (2000), Reinhart (2000, 2001, 2002), Wechsler (1995). Grimshaw (1990) characterizes verbs like *frighten* as causative and verbs like *fear* as stative. Therefore, the subject of *frighten* is analyzed as a cause, while the subject of *fear* is not. Although all *fear* verbs are stative, some *frighten* verbs, such as *concern*, are also stative, and others, such as *bother*, can be stative or nonstative; therefore stativity is not relevant. Rather, the notion of cause is probably implicated in the difference between the two verb types. Pesetsky (1995) points out that the nonexperiencer argument of *fear* verbs must denote the actual stimulus of the psychological state, but this is not true of the nonexperiencer argument of the *frighten* verbs. If Terry fears war, it is the contemplation of war itself which evokes fear in Terry, but if a newspaper article frightens Terry, the article may have been the cause of his fear, but the fear may be of something discussed or reported in the article, such as the possibility of war. This unspecified association between a cause and a result is typical of causative verbs (B. Levin and Rappaport Hovav 1995; Vendler 1984). Therefore, the *frighten* verbs are causative – whether or not they are stative – and their nonexperiencer argument is analyzed as some kind of cause. In contrast, the *fear* verbs are noncausative; the semantic role of their nonexperiencer argument is a matter of debate, but the semantic role "stimulus" suggested by Talmy (1985) is often used, and the role "target" and "subject matter" introduced by Pesetsky (1987, 1995) have also gained some currency. These suggestions for the appropriate label for the nonexperiencer argument can be evaluated only in the context of a full theory of argument realization, which is not tailored to psych-verbs alone. However, the fact that only one type of nonexperiencer argument is analyzed as a cause is sufficient in certain theories to account for the difference in mapping (Dowty 1991; Pesetsky 1995); see section 3.1.1 for discussion. We return to psych-verbs in section 1.5, reconsidering them in a crosslinguistic context.

To conclude, the isolation of the meaning components appropriate to the characterization of verbs in a particular semantic class presents a real challenge. The most obvious components of meaning may not be the actual semantic determinants of syntactic behavior. A failure to identify such elements may impede the formulation of a perspicuous theory of argument realization.

1.3   The crossclassification of verbs and the status of verb classes

As we have shown, certain patterns of argument realization point to the existence of semantically coherent classes of verbs. However, other generalizations
pick out sets of verbs that are larger, smaller, or even partially overlapping
with these classes. Such data lead to the conclusion that it is the elements of
meaning that define verb classes that are most important, and that verb classes
themselves are epiphenomenal – a point also stressed by S. T. Rosen (1996) –
even if they might be useful in the statement of certain generalizations. Therefore, advances in the understanding of argument realization regularities require
isolating those semantic components which ultimately determine them. We
reinforce this point by further examining the two classes of verbs of communication mentioned in section 1.2 – verbs of manner of speaking and verbs of
content of speaking. Although both types of verbs can express the addressee in
a PP headed by *to* and can take an indirect speech complement, as in (7), verbs
of manner of speaking allow the addressee to be expressed in a PP headed
by *at* and the content to be expressed in a PP headed by *about*, but verbs of
content of speaking do not, as shown in (8) and (9).

(7) a. Evelyn screamed (to Marilyn) to go.
     b. Evelyn said (to Marilyn) to go.

(8) a. Evelyn screamed at Marilyn.
     b. *Evelyn said at Marilyn.

(9) a. Claudia screamed about the new management.
     b. *Claudia said about the new management.

However, it seems that the relevant argument realization generalizations
should not make explicit reference to either verbs of manner of speaking or
verbs of content of speaking. Mufwene (1978) demonstrates that the many
distinctive properties of verbs of manner of speaking laid out in Zwicky (1971)
are not unique to these verbs, but are also manifested by verbs of other semantic
types. For instance, Mufwene (1978: 282) points out that, as Zwicky himself
observes, verbs like *chat, complain, speak*, and *talk*, like manner-of-speaking
verbs, allow *about* phrases, as illustrated in (10).

(10) Claudia complained/spoke/talked about the new management.

Thus, these verbs must have some semantic property in common with verbs of
manner of speaking, which gives rise to their partially shared behavior, and, if
so, as Mufwene points out, it does not make sense to associate properties such
as selecting *about* phrases with a class of verbs of manner of speaking. The
differences in argument realization options that distinguish verbs of manner of
speaking from verbs of content of speaking arise from elements of meaning
which are not exclusively associated with the members of these two individual

classes; rather they are shared with other classes. (Of course, further investigation is needed to identify the conjunction of semantic properties that is the source of the constellation of behavioral properties that first led Zwicky to identify a class of manner-of-speaking verbs.)

The finer elements of meaning that crosscut recognized verb classes result in an intricate system of verb crossclassification. We illustrate this crossclassification by examining the argument realization options of several subclasses of verbs of putting. Many verbs, including these, have more than one argument realization option and may show one or more alternations in the expression of the same set of arguments, participating in one or more ARGUMENT (or diathesis) ALTERNATIONS, such as the causative alternation. A subset of verbs of putting, including *spray* and *smear*, exhibit what is now known as the LOCATIVE ALTERNATION – an alternation instantiated not only in English, but in a range of other languages (B. Levin 1993 and references cited therein; for more recent work see Baker 1997, Basilico 1998, Brinkmann 1997, Dimitrova-Vulchanova 1998, Laffut 1997, 1998, 1999, Stroik 1996). Locative alternation verbs may express either the transferred stuff or the surface as direct object, as in (11a) and (11b), respectively. The first argument realization pattern is characteristic of verbs like *put* and *pour* and the second of verbs like *cover* and *fill*; however, neither verbs like *put* or *pour*, nor verbs like *cover* or *fill* show both options for argument realization.

(11) a. Pat sprayed paint on the wall.
      b. Pat sprayed the wall with paint.

(12) a. Pat put paint on the wall.
      b. *Pat put the wall with paint.

(13) a. *Pat covered paint on the wall.
      b. Pat covered the wall with paint.

Yet, even locative alternation verbs do not share all options for argument realization. For example, *splash* shows the transitive and intransitive uses characteristic of the causative alternation, while *smear* does not (Hale and Keyser 1993: 89–95, 1997b: 53–55, 1999: 60–63; Kiparsky 1997: 494, 496).

(14) a. The pigs splashed mud on the wall.
      b. Mud splashed on the wall.   (Hale and Keyser 1993: 89, (63))

(15) a. We smeared mud on the wall.
      b. *Mud smeared on the wall.   (Hale and Keyser 1993: 89, (67))

As discussed in section 1.2, this alternation is shown predominantly by verbs of change of state, but it is also characteristic of certain verbs which, like *splash*, involve a change of location (e.g., *move, roll, spin*) (Smith 1970). Furthermore, most verbs found in the causative alternation do not show the locative alternation, so whatever element of meaning determines *splash*'s participation in this alternation, it is different from the element of meaning that determines its participation in the locative alternation. These observations reinforce the proposals that verb classes themselves are epiphenomenal and that there are more basic elements of meaning which determine argument realization.

A theory of lexical semantic representation should be rich enough to express what the locative alternation verbs *splash* and *smear* have in common with the nonalternating verbs *cover* and *pour* by virtue of which they share the argument realizations of *cover* and *pour*, and also what sets each of these verb types apart from the others, by virtue of which they, but not verbs like *cover* and *pour*, can alternate. Precisely delineating the class of verbs showing a particular argument alternation presents a real challenge, which we take up in chapter 7.[7] In addition to identifying the facets of meaning which *splash* and *smear* have in common, those which set them apart must also be identified (see section 3.2), as these are responsible for their distinct behavior with respect to the causative alternation. In this respect, verb classes are similar in status to natural classes of sounds in phonology, and the elements of meaning which serve to distinguish among the classes of verbs are similar in status to phonology's distinctive features. Furthermore, since these grammatically relevant facets of meaning are viewed as constituting the interface between a full-fledged representation of meaning and the syntax, most researchers have assumed that, like the set of distinctive features, the set of such meaning elements is both universal and relatively small in size. Despite these parallels, however, feature notations may not be the appropriate means for representing semantic elements (see section 2.2.1).

A full analysis of these phenomena cannot afford to ignore the variations in meaning that often accompany argument alternations. These variations are often illustrated with the locative alternation. As discussed in numerous studies (see chapter 7 for references), sentence pairs such as *Avery loaded grapes on the wagon* and *Avery loaded the wagon with grapes* are not truth-conditionally equivalent: the first sentence can describe a scenario in which a significant part of the wagon is still empty, but the second sentence cannot describe such a scenario. As we illustrate extensively in chapter 7, a wide range of verbs show argument alternations, and these alternations represent one instantiation of the larger phenomenon of MULTIPLE ARGUMENT REALIZATION – the ability of most verbs to appear in a variety of syntactic contexts. The variation in meaning that accompanies many argument alternations has led a number of researchers to conclude that the program of deriving the syntactic contexts a verb is found in directly from its meaning (see section 1.1) – what we refer to as the PROJECTIONIST approach – is misguided. Instead, they argue for a CONSTRUCTIONAL approach, where meaning resides in the syntactic context. We discuss these two approaches more extensively in chapter 7. Here we simply note an important point of convergence that the comparison of both types of approaches reveals: proponents of both approaches agree to a large extent on what the elements of meaning are – be they lexical or extralexical – which determine the realization of arguments, and so the identification of these elements of meaning can be considered a real achievement of research into argument realization.

1.4   Verb meanings represent construals of events

In order to identify the grammatically relevant facets of verb meaning, it is crucial to recognize that verb meanings represent construals of events rather than the events themselves. (A related point is made by Krifka [1998], who stresses that telicity is a property of event descriptions, not of events themselves.) Happenings in the world, unlike most physical objects, do not come perceptually individuated (Clark 1978; Croft 1991; Gentner 1981, 1982); rather, they are individuated via language. Verbs lexicalize properties of happenings in the world; we use the term EVENT for happenings whose properties are lexicalized by verbs. Verbs, then, are predicates of events (Parsons 1990) and phrases containing verbs can be considered "event descriptions." Since a particular happening in the world has many properties associated with it, different verbs, which lexicalize different subsets of these properties, may be applicable to the very same happening. The result is that certain happenings can be construed as events by languages in more than one way. Verbs used to describe such a happening will not have precisely the same meaning if they lexicalize distinct, though largely overlapping, sets of properties. Such verbs will have distinct truth conditions, though this may not always be apparent, because in most instances these verbs can be used to describe the same happening. As discussed in section 1.2, in the English–Italian pair *blush/arrossire*, the same happening is construed as a process in English, but as a change of state in Italian, so that the English and Italian verbs do not present identical descriptions of a single happening. As Hale and Keyser write, "There is no guarantee, or necessity, that languages should agree in their conventional descriptions of entities, events, conditions, and states – where these are understood as something outside language, related to language only by the names they are given …" (1998: 95). When alternate construals are possible and involve different grammatically relevant aspects of meaning, the result can be pairs of near-synonyms within or across languages showing different argument realization options.

Many purported counterexamples to the claim that argument realization is determined by meaning reflect a failure to recognize this. Those who raise such counterexamples sometimes commit what DeLancey (1991) terms "the objectivist error." This error involves "trying to incorporate into the semantic representation of the clause inferences which, however legitimate they may be, are not in fact part of the event representation of the clause" (DeLancey 1991: 349). To exemplify this, DeLancey (1991: 339) recounts how students asked to provide a semantic analysis of *John threw the ball through the window* chose the window and not the ball as the entity that changed. The reason, they said, was that they imagined a scenario with a closed window. The objectivist error arises when a lexical semantic representation is based on what DeLancey describes as an "imagined 'real world'" (1991: 347), rather than on the linguistic construal of a happening as an event.

The objectivist error perhaps underlies some premature conclusions that certain pairs of verbs that can name the same event arbitrarily represent distinct "lexicalizations." Psych-verb doublets such as *fear* and *frighten* have been taken to represent arbitrariness in argument realization (Dowty 1991), but more likely these verbs represent different construals of the same happening as events. As discussed in section 1.2, *fear* represents a psychological state holding of the experiencer and *frighten* represents the bringing about of a psychological state in the experiencer.[8] The claim that argument realization is arbitrary is sometimes supported by reference to the verbs *buy* and *sell*, which can describe the same commercial transaction. Some researchers describe *sell* as presenting a particular event from the perspective of the seller and *buy* as presenting it from the perspective of the buyer (e.g., Dixon 1979: 104; Fillmore 1977b: 102–09). That is, they take these verbs to provide different "viewpoints" on the same transaction and assume that there is no truth-conditional difference in the descriptions of a commercial transaction provided by these verbs. In fact, Van Valin (1999: 387–88) presents data suggesting that *buy* and *sell* represent different construals of a happening, and may differ in truth conditions; see also Shopen (1972: 343–44). He notes that in various languages the verb meaning *sell* is morphologically derived from the verb meaning *buy*, often via a causative morpheme, e.g., German *kaufen* 'buy'/*verkaufen* 'sell,' Lakhota *ophéthu* 'buy'/*iyópheya* 'sell,' and Tagalog *bili* 'buy'/*mag-bili* 'sell,' but the verb meaning *buy* is never the causative of the verb meaning *sell*, surely not an accident. More importantly, there are certain happenings which can be described using one verb, but not the other, as the following pair exemplifies: *Chris bought a pack of cigarettes from the vending machine in the hall* vs. **The vending machine in the hall sold Chris a pack of cigarettes* (Van Valin 1999: 388). Jointly these facts about *buy* and *sell* indicate that buying is in some sense more basic than selling and that *buy*'s meaning is perhaps properly contained in *sell*'s. If *sell* is causative, while *buy* is not, then it is not an accident that the seller is realized as *sell*'s subject. As we discuss in section 4.1.2.2, arguments analyzed as causes are subjects regardless of the semantic properties of other arguments; thus, the seller, since it would be properly analyzed as a cause, would be *sell*'s subject, notwithstanding whatever principle determines the subjecthood of the buyer argument with *buy*. Argument realization, then, is not as arbitrary as certain verb pairs might suggest, but appreciating the regularity can require a careful examination of word meaning and an awareness that these meanings represent linguistic construals of happenings and, thus, may pick up on only certain facets of these happenings in the world.

1.5   Uniformity and variation in argument realization

Theories of lexical semantic representation and argument realization must also be developed keeping in mind patterns of variation in argument realization. Verbs in some semantic classes show uniformity in argument realization within a given language, and these tend to be the same verbs whose options for argument realization come close to being uniform across languages. Verbs in other classes tend to show variation in argument realization both within and across languages. These patterns of variation and uniformity form another testbed for the isolation of grammatically relevant aspects of meaning. If the appropriate elements of meaning are chosen, verbs whose classification is clearcut with respect to these elements of meaning should have stable argument realization patterns, while those whose classification is less clearcut are expected to show wider variation.

As has been pointed out repeatedly and confirmed in a variety of typological studies (Andrews 1985: 68; Croft 1990; DeLancey 1984; Dixon 1979: 103, 1994: 114–18; Hopper and Thompson 1980; B. Levin 1999; Nichols 1975; Tsunoda 1985; among others), verbs which denote events in which an animate agent acts on and causes a change in a patient, such as *crush, destroy*, or *kill*, are transitive in all languages, with the agent being expressed as the subject and the patient as the direct object (though see note 4). Both within and across languages, there is hardly any departure from this pattern of argument realization for such AGENT–PATIENT VERBS. On the other hand, classes of two-argument verbs which do not fit this mold exhibit crosslinguistic variation in the way their arguments are expressed (Blume 1998; Dezsö 1982; Nichols 1975; Testelec 1998; Tsunoda 1985), and these same classes tend to exhibit less uniformity in the expression of their arguments within a given language (B. Levin 1999). For example, in Russian, many verbs of authority, ruling, and disposition, including those in (16), take instrumental complements, though their English counterparts are transitive (Dezsö 1982: 58–59; Fowler 1996: 521; Nichols 1975: 346–47, 1984: 201; Wierzbicka 1980: 160–61, n. 15).

(16) *rukovodit'* 'rule, direct, manage,' *upravljat'* 'govern,' *komandovat'* 'command,' *zavedovat'* 'manage, be in charge,' *ovladevat'* 'master,' *vladet'* 'rule, own,' *dirižirovat'* 'conduct (an orchestra),' *verxovodit'* 'lord it over'

Even within English, such verbs do not show uniformity in argument realization. Although some are transitive (e.g., *command, direct, govern, manage*), others are intransitive, expressing their second argument as the object of the preposition *over* (e.g., *preside, reign*), and *rule* and *tyrannize*, at least, allow both options. If two-argument verbs that do not fit the agent–patient mold receive a different lexical semantic representation than those that do, then argument realization rules could be sensitive to this difference, resulting in such verbs showing distinctive argument realization options. A challenge, however, is to predict that change-of-state verbs all show the same argument realization options, while verbs in certain other classes may not all show the same argument realization.

A second example is provided by *hit* and other surface-contact verbs, including *kick, kiss*, and *slap*. These verbs number among the English transitive verbs whose counterparts in other languages are not necessarily simple transitive verbs (Tsunoda 1985). In Lhasa Tibetan, although the counterparts of verbs such as *break, cut*, and *kill* are obligatorily transitive, the counterpart of *hit* is not; the argument denoting the surface contacted obligatorily takes a locative marker, as (17) shows (DeLancey 1995).

(17) shing*(-la) sta=re-s gzhus-pa
     tree-LOC   axe-ERG hit
     'hit the tree with an axe'   (DeLancey 1995: (18))

The concepts expressed by certain other English surface-contact verbs are expressed in Tibetan using verb–noun combinations, as in (18).

(18) nga-s blo=bzang=la rdog=rdyag gzhus-pa yin
     I-ERG Lobsang-LOC   kick$_N$ hit/throw-PERF/CONJUNCT
     'I kicked Lobsang.'   (DeLancey 1995: (20))

This option is reminiscent of the English paraphrase *I gave Lobsang a kick* for *I kicked Lobsang* – an option not available to English change-of-state verbs (**I gave the window a break*). Ingush also uses verb–noun combinations to express the counterparts of certain English surface-contact verbs (Nichols 1982: 447, 1984: 188); thus, the noun *tuop* 'rifle' in combination with the verb *tuoxan* 'hit' means 'shoot' and not 'beat with a rifle' (Nichols 1984: 189). Again, as in Tibetan, the surface contacted is expressed in an oblique case – a case-marking pattern which according to Nichols (1984: 188) is common across Caucasian languages. The same verb classes whose members tend to show variation in argument realization options within and across languages also may allow individual members to show a range of argument realization options. For example, in English and some other languages, some surface-contact verbs show a flexibility in argument realization that agent–patient verbs lack (Fillmore 1970, 1977a; Rappaport Hovav and B. Levin 1998a). These verbs allow either the surface which the agent contacts or the instrument the agent uses as their object, as in (19) and (20).

(19) a. Lindsay hit the stick against the fence.
     b. Lindsay hit the fence with a stick.
(20) a. Taylor beat his fists against the wall.
     b. Taylor beat the wall with his fists.

Interestingly, the pattern in (19a) and (20a) could be considered the English analogue of what Nichols (1982: 447, 1984: 188) identifies as the most common Caucasian argument realization pattern for surface-contact verbs.

Another example is presented by psych-verbs, which display striking crosslinguistic variability in argument realization options. Overall, verbs like *frighten* do not show much crosslinguistic variation: they are consistently experiencer–object verbs (Croft 1993). This consistency is perhaps not surprising since these verbs describe the causation of a psychological state in the experiencer, and they often even take animate, agentive subjects, making them close to prototypical transitive verbs. The major departure from the agent–patient mold, then, is that their object is animate rather than inanimate. Italian *frighten* verbs, for example, are transitive verbs just like their English counterparts.

(21) Questo preoccupa Gianni.
      this   worries   Gianni
      'This worries Gianni.'   (Belletti and Rizzi 1988: 292, (2))

However, there is a fair amount of crosslinguistic variation in the counterparts of the *fear* verbs, that is, the psych-verbs that are inherently noncausative (see section 1.2). Italian, for instance, has verbs which are semantically *fear* verbs and which express their arguments precisely as the English *fear* verbs do.

(22) Gianni teme questo.
      Gianni fears this
      'Gianni fears this.'   (Belletti and Rizzi 1988: 292, (1))

In many languages, however, these verbs show a pattern of argument realization that is rarely available in English: the experiencer is in the dative case and the stimulus in the nominative case (absolutive in ergative languages) (Belletti and Rizzi 1988; Croft 1991, 1993; Dziwirek 1994; Harris 1984a, 1984b; Hermon 1986; Klaiman 1980; Masica 1976; Massey 1992; Moore and Perlmutter 2000; Nichols 1975; Perlmutter 1978, 1984; C. Rosen and Wali 1989; Sridhar 1979; Talmy 1985; Tsunoda 1985; Verma and K. P. Mohanan 1990; among many others). In the Italian example in (23), the dative preposition *a* introduces the experiencer, while the stimulus is nominative. (Although Italian *piacere* is translated in English with what appears to be a *frighten* verb, it does not pattern syntactically like these verbs, nor does it have a causative meaning.)

(23) Questo piace   a Gianni.
      this   pleases to Gianni
      'This pleases Gianni.'   (Belletti and Rizzi 1988: 292, (3b))

English has very few examples of this kind; one possibility is *This rug appeals to me*; see B. Levin (1993). Furthermore, languages showing this pattern differ as to how so-called subject properties are distributed over the experiencer and stimulus arguments. According to Hermon, for example, in Kannada it is the dative NP that is replaced by PRO in a control structure (1986: 202), while in Hebrew it is the nominative NP (1986: 209).

Any theory of argument realization taken together with a well-motivated theory of lexical semantic representation should allow researchers to predict which semantic classes of verbs will be stable and uniform in their argument realization options, in and across languages, and which will not. Croft (1993) explicitly points out that there is variation within and across languages in the expression of the arguments of noncausative, but not causative, psych-verbs. According to him, the reason is that the causative psych-verbs unambiguously fit the semantic mold of core transitive verbs, while the noncausative psych-verbs do not; rather, the noncausative psych-verbs can be "coerced" into either of two semantic molds, each of which gives rise to its own argument realization (see also section 4.3). A theory of argument realization should, furthermore, account for why the verbs which allow variation show this variation within strict limits. B. Levin (1999) presents an effort along these lines for two-argument verbs that do not fit the agent–patient mold. We return to this question in chapter 2, where the implications of the patterns of argument realization of psych-verbs for the nature of semantic roles is discussed, in chapter 4, where we suggest that argument realization considerations can help choose between different theories of the semantic determinants of argument realization, and, yet again, in chapter 7, which is devoted to systematic patterns of multiple argument realization associated with certain verbs.

1.6   When subjects are not agents and objects are not patients

Since agent–patient verbs constitute a significant part of the class of transitive verbs of every language and are so uniform in their argument realization, many theories of argument realization make direct reference to the semantic roles agent and patient – or its relative theme (see section 2.4) – and have rules which explicitly realize agents as subjects and patients as objects. However, these simple statements are misleading for two reasons. First, "agent" and "patient" are not the only semantic notions associated with subject and object. Second, subject and object often have multiple morphosyntactic realizations, and a complete theory of argument realization needs to take this into consideration. As we show, deviations from the agent and patient prototypes are sometimes, but not always, associated with deviations from the prototypical morphosyntactic realizations of subject and object.

Although agents of two-argument verbs are always subjects, some languages also allow a range of nonagents as subjects. These include various kinds of nonagentive causes, experiencers, and emitters (Fillmore 1968; Hawkins 1985; B. Levin and Rappaport Hovav 1995; Schlesinger 1995), as we illustrate with data from English in (24) and Hebrew in (25).

(24) a. The storm destroyed the crop.
     b. The bulldozer flattened the hovels.
     c. The child hated the spinach.
     d. The old machine spews smoke.

(25) a. Ha-se'ara harsa   et   ha-yevul.
        the-storm destroyed ACC the-crop
        'The storm destroyed the crop.'
     b. Ha-daxpor   maxac   et   ha-biktot
        the-bulldozer flattened ACC the-hovels
        'The bulldozer flattened the hovels.'

   c. Ha-yeled sana et ha-tered.
     the-child hated ACC the-spinach
     'The child hated the spinach.'
   d. Ha-mexona ha-yeSana poletet aSan.
     the-machine the-old   spews smoke
     'The old machine spews smoke.'

In English the range of subjects can be even wider, as noted by Hawkins (1985), citing Rohdenburg (1974), and Perlmutter and Postal (1984). The examples in (26) might be said to have location and measure subjects, though the natural Hebrew translations of these sentences do not maintain the same subjects.

(26) a. This room sleeps five people.
     b. This edition of the text book had added a new chapter.
     c. A dollar won't buy a cup of coffee any more.

Principles of argument realization for subject, then, should be formulated so that agents are always subjects, but other kinds of arguments can be subjects as well. (There is an additional wrinkle: although the preverbal NPs in the sentences in (26) are subjects by virtue of determining verbal agreement, these sentences do not have corresponding verbal passives.) Furthermore, these principles should allow languages to differ as to what nonagent arguments may be subjects (DeLancey 1985; Dixon 1979: 105–06; Guilfoyle 1995, 2000; Hawkins 1981, 1982, 1985, 1995; van Voorst 1996). Across languages, these nonagent arguments tend to be those that are semantically "close" to agents, including natural forces, experiencers, instruments, and even emitters, as in the examples in (24), with many fewer languages allowing the types of subjects that are even further removed semantically from the concept of "agent" illustrated in (26). Some languages, such as Irish (Guilfoyle 1995, 2000) and Jacaltec (Craig 1976: 108–09), do not allow even the semantically "closer" arguments to be subjects. In fact, many languages may be as restrictive in their choice of subjects as these two, though confirmation is needed from a systematic crosslinguistic exploration.

    The picture is, in fact, even more complicated. In English the nonpatient arguments that are not prototypical agents need not be expressed as subjects; for example, they may be obliques, as in (27)–(30), an alternative usually not open to true agent arguments, as shown in (31) and (32).

(27) a. Pneumonia killed his uncle.
     b. His uncle died from/of pneumonia.
(28) a. The sun melted the chocolate.
     b. The chocolate melted in the sun.
(29) a. That old machine spews smoke.
     b. Smoke spews from that old machine.

(30) a. This room sleeps five people.
    b. Five people can sleep in this room.

(31) a. Brutus killed Caesar.
    b. *Caesar died from/of Brutus.

(32) a. I melted the chocolate.
    b. *The chocolate melted in/from me.

Therefore, it seems that the factors that determine subjecthood are quite different from those that determine expression as an oblique; the latter involve much finer-grained semantic distinctions than the former.

Two additional considerations pose a challenge for the algorithm determining the subject. First, patients which are expressible as direct objects of transitive verbs can sometimes be expressed as subjects of the intransitive uses of the same verbs, as in (33) and (34), or of semantically related intransitive verbs, as in (35) and (36). In each pair, the patient is a direct object in the (a) sentence and a subject in the (b) sentence.

(33) a. Mallory opened the window.
    b. The window opened.

(34) a. Mark cracked the plate.
    b. The plate cracked.

(35) a. The lumberjack felled the tree.
    b. The tree fell.

(36) a. Pneumonia killed his uncle.
    b. His uncle died from pneumonia.

Second, languages often have one or more morphosyntactic processes which create subjects from objects, with passive being the most widely cited.

(37) a. Mallory opened the window.
    b. The window was opened by Mallory.

The analysis of patient subjects depends on the basic assumptions adopted concerning the nature of the mapping between lexical semantics and syntax. A theory that adopts Baker's (1988) Uniformity of Theta Assignment Hypothesis (see section 1.1) necessarily maps the patient argument in (37) to direct object in passive as well as active sentences; its realization as subject in passive sentences is accomplished by a syntactic "promotion" – most often, movement. Such analyses are typical of multistratal theories of syntax, including the Principles and Parameters framework and its descendants and Relational Grammar. Monostratal theories deal with such phenomena in other ways. They may impose a more sophisticated organization over the semantic roles themselves, as in Role and Reference Grammar (Foley and Van Valin 1984; Van Valin and LaPolla 1997), or they may introduce another level of analysis which is not necessarily syntactic in nature, as in Lexical-Functional Grammar's Lexical Mapping Theory (Bresnan 2001: 302–21; Bresnan and Kanerva 1989). The ways in which theories deal with these phenomena are briefly discussed in section 5.1; see also Sadler and Spencer (1998).

Some of the data discussed in this section also have implications for the design of a lexical semantic representation. Data such as (24) indicate that the label "agent–patient verb" is not entirely accurate for many of the verbs taken to be prototypical agent–patient verbs, since they have two-argument uses with subjects that need not be agents in the strictest sense. For example, in "The Grammar of *Hitting* and *Breaking*," Fillmore (1970) uses the verb *break* to represent a verb which selects an agent argument; however, as DeLancey (1984), Van Valin and D. Wilkins (1996), and even Fillmore (1970) note, this verb is not necessarily agentive, even when it takes an animate subject, as (38) shows.

(38) The boy broke the window (accidentally).

(Van Valin and D. Wilkins 1996: 307, (4a))

Van Valin and D. Wilkins (1996) further show that *kill*, another verb commonly taken to be agentive, does not require an agent argument, contrasting with the verb *murder*, which does require one.

(39) a. Larry killed the deer.
    b. Larry intentionally killed the deer.
    c. Larry accidentally killed the deer.
    d. The explosion killed the deer.

(Van Valin and D. Wilkins 1996: 309, (9);
adapted from Holisky (1987: 118, (15))

(40) a. Larry murdered his neighbor.
    b. *Larry inadvertently murdered his neighbor.
    c. *The explosion murdered Larry's neighbor.

(Van Valin and D. Wilkins 1996: 310, (10))

As Van Valin and D. Wilkins point out, elaborating on Holisky (1987: 118–19), verbs which require agents as subjects such as *murder* are much rarer than those which allow agents as subjects, but also allow various nonagentive cause subjects, such as *kill*. This important point is rarely recognized, but it has significant implications for the characterization and analysis of argument realization regularities. We discuss solutions to these problems throughout this book.

The issues which arise with the notion of agent and the semantic underpinnings of subjecthood also arise with respect to the notion of patient and the semantic underpinnings of direct objecthood. All languages realize patients – and themes, if these are distinguished from patients – as objects, but some languages allow various types of nonpatients as objects as well. English is particularly liberal in this regard, as the following examples strikingly illustrate.

(41) The engineer cracked the bridge. (patient)
      The engineer destroyed the bridge. (patient/consumed object)
      The engineer painted the bridge. (incremental theme; Dowty 1991)
      The engineer moved the bridge. (theme)
      The engineer built the bridge. (effected object/factitive; Fillmore 1968)
      The engineer washed the bridge. (location/surface)
      The engineer hit the bridge. (location; Fillmore 1970)
      The engineer crossed the bridge. (path)
      The engineer reached the bridge. (goal)
      The engineer left the bridge. (source)
      The engineer saw the bridge. (stimulus/object of perception)
      The engineer hated the bridge. (stimulus/target or object of emotion)
                                                      (B. Levin 1999: 224, (1))

Even these examples do not capture the full semantic breadth of the notion
"object" in English, largely because they all have inanimate objects. The
frighten psych-verbs have been characterized as taking experiencer objects.
The objects of transitive verbs of authority, ruling, and disposition in English
do not fit neatly under any of the traditional semantic roles, though as noted
in section 1.5, these verbs are not necessarily transitive in all languages.
Just as English allows a broader semantic range of subjects, so it allows a
broader semantic range of objects (Hawkins 1985; Plank 1985; Tsunoda 1985;
Schlesinger 1995; Van Voorst 1996). For example, Blume (1998) documents
several languages in which what she calls "interaction verbs" – a somewhat
loosely defined class of verbs with two animate arguments – take a subject
and an oblique; these include German, Hungarian, Maori, Rumanian, Samoan,
and Tongan. Yet, these same verbs are almost all transitive in English. English
also permits various path, goal, and source arguments as objects, as in some
examples in (41), though not all languages do (Schlesinger 1995: 174).

Furthermore, just as there are objects said to be "advanced" to subject, so
there are obliques that are said to be "advanced" to object. That is, certain
sentence pairs with the same verb have a particular argument expressed as an
oblique in one sentence, but as an object in the second. Usually, the expression
as an object is accompanied by the affixation of what is known as an "applicative" morpheme on the verb. This phenomenon is particularly well represented
in Bantu languages and illustrated in (42) with an example from Chicheŵa;
the *kwa*-marked argument in (42a) occurs as the first object in (42b), with the
verb showing the applicative morpheme *–er–*.

(42) a. Mbidzi zi-na-perek-a   msampha *kwa* nkhandwe.
         zebras SP-PAST-hand-ASP trap   *to*   fox
         'The zebras handed the trap to the fox.'   (Baker 1988: 229, (2a))
      b. Mbidzi zi-na-perek-*er*-a   nkhandwe msampha.
         zebras SP-PAST-hand-APPL-ASP fox   trap
         'The zebras handed the fox the trap.'   (Baker 1988: 229, (3a))

As with passives, a theory adopting the Uniformity of Theta Assignment Hypothesis will have a rule "promoting" an oblique to object in applicative constructions to maintain a uniform assignment of semantic roles to grammatical relations in both applicative and nonapplicative constructions (Baker 1988). In contrast, a theory that does not adopt this hypothesis deals with the relation between these two in other ways. Lexical-Functional Grammar's Lexical Mapping Theory, for instance, associates semantic roles with partially specified characterizations of argument realization options that give rise to one realization when a morphological rule operates, as in (42b), and another otherwise, as in (42a) (Alsina and Mchombo 1993; Bresnan and Moshi 1990).

The special status of subject and object is also shared by the first or "inner" object in a double object construction in English and other languages that have such a construction and by the dative case-marked argument in languages that have such a case marker; the first object and dative case-marked argument are sometimes both included together under the label "indirect object." The prototypical first object in the double object construction is probably best characterized semantically as a recipient, the animate goal in an event that involves a physical or abstract transfer of possession (Goldberg 1995; Shibatani 1996), as in (43a) and (43b), respectively, but the first object can also realize a beneficiary, as in (43c), and in a few instances a source, as in (43d), or a possessor that is not construable as a recipient, as in (43e). The different semantic characterizations are emphasized by the distinct paraphrases available to some of these examples; the sentence/paraphrase pairs together constitute instances of the "dative alternation," as in (43a) and (43b), or the "benefactive alternation," as in (43c).

(43) a. My cousin sold me this car.
   (cf. My cousin sold this car to me.)
   b. His sister told him the answer.
   (cf. His sister told the answer to him.)
   c. Our grandmother baked us a pie.
   (cf. Our grandmother baked a pie for us.)
   d. The police fined him $50.
   e. Kelly envied Kerry her good fortune.

There are also some crosslinguistic differences; in some languages, including French, German, and Korean, though not English, the indirect object in a broad sense – that is, the first of two objects or a dative NP with a three-argument verb – can quite regularly realize the animate "source" in negative transfer of possession events of the type denoted by the verb *take* (Maling 2001: 430–31, 433). Furthermore, as Shibatani (1996: 169–70) illustrates, a wider range of verbs may have benefactive indirect objects than in English.

The issues that arise for subjects and direct objects surface again for indirect objects. The distinct paraphrases in (43) suggest that even if a rule mapping to indirect object could make reference to a rather coarse-grained, but unified semantic notion, other partially overlapping semantic notions must be identified to give rise to the various oblique realizations found in the paraphrases of the sentences in (43). So once again, the mapping process needs to make reference to overlapping semantic notions at different levels of specificity.

Just as many semantic roles can be associated with a given grammatical relation, each grammatical relation can have one or more morphosyntactic realizations. Every language has a prototypical morphosyntactic realization for its subjects and objects, through word order, morphological case, verb agreement, or a combination of these; nevertheless, languages often have what are apparently subjects or objects whose morphosyntactic expression deviates from this morphosyntactic prototype. In the many languages with a nominative–accusative case system, for example, subjects are typically nominative and objects accusative, yet such languages can show deviations from these case/grammatical relation associations. So-called "dative subjects" – dative case NPs that share certain properties with the more "regular" nominative NPs – are not uncommon crosslinguistically, and "subjects" marked for other oblique cases are found as well. As discussed in section 1.5, some languages express the experiencer of some psych-verbs in the dative case and the stimulus in the nominative (or absolutive) case, yet it is the dative experiencer which shows "essential" properties of subjects. Thus, in the French example (44), it is the dative experiencer – and not the nominative stimulus – which controls the subject of the gerund clause.

(44) Ayant étudié toute sa vie, l'ignorance   lui   déplait.
     having studied all   his life, ignorance.NOM him.DAT displeases.
     'Having studied all his life, he hates ignorance.'
                                          (Legendre 1989: 774, (50d))

Furthermore, although direct objects are most commonly marked with the accusative case in nominative–accusative languages, "oblique objects" are also sometimes found in these languages; these are NPs marked for an oblique case that pattern in certain respects like objects. The instrumental second argument of Russian verbs of authority, ruling, and disposition mentioned in section 1.5, for example, may qualify as an oblique object in that it is expressed as the nominative subject of the corresponding passive verb (Fowler 1996).

(45) a. Borisov   upravljaet   fabrikoj.
        Borisov.NOM manage.PRES3s factory.INST
        'Borisov manages the factory.'
     b. Fabrika   upravljaet-sja   Borisovym.
        factory.NOM manage.PRES3s-REFL/PASS Borisov.INST
        'The factory is managed by Borisov.'   (Fowler 1996: 519, (1))

The existence of oblique case marking on what might otherwise be considered a subject or an object raises a number of questions. First, the status of the oblique case-marked argument as a "true" subject or object must be established. Verifying this is not always easy, and there is a longstanding debate about the subjecthood of oblique case-marked experiencer NPs. The issues were first clearly articulated in the Relational Grammar literature, but their investigation continues (Harris 1984a, 1984b; Moore and Perlmutter 2000; Perlmutter 1984; Shibatani 1999; Sridhar 1979; Ura 2000; Verma and K. P. Mohanan 1990; among others). The larger issues regarding what it means for an NP to be a subject are brought to the fore in Keenan's influential paper "Towards a Universal Definition of 'Subject'" (1976), which demonstrates that certain purported criteria for subjecthood do not consistently isolate the same NP in a sentence either within or across languages. Particularly important here is the distinction introduced by Keenan (1976) between "behavioral" properties and "coding" properties of subjects. The coding properties involve the most surface manifestation of subjects, that is, their morphosyntactic expression, via word order, agreement, and case marking. In English, for example, a subject is coded by its preverbal position, and, if a pronoun, by nominative case. The behavioral properties are grammatical properties, such as the ability to be the antecedent of a reflexive pronoun, the ability to control the nonexpressed subject of various types of adjunct clauses and the ability to be controlled when in an infinitival complement to a verb like *try*. Therefore, the notion of subject as a grammatical relation needs to be distinguished from its morphosyntactic instantiation. In most instances arguments that show the behavioral properties of subjects also show their coding properties; however, in some instances, what is behaviorally a subject does not show the coding most often associated with a subject.[9]

Certain NPs with oblique case, such as dative experiencers of psych-verbs or instrumental arguments of Russian verbs of authority, ruling, and disposition, nevertheless pattern like subjects or objects with respect to behavioral properties. Conversely, certain NPs that show the typical coding properties of subject or object in a language may lack some behavioral properties of the relevant grammatical relation. Thus, as discussed in section 1.5, in some languages there is a class of psych-verbs whose stimulus is typically in the nominative case – the typical subject case – even though the experiencer, which is marked for dative case, shows behavorial properties of subjects. Maling (2001: 439, 445–46) shows that in German the accusative case-marked arguments of the verbs *bitten* 'ask,' *bedienen* 'serve,' and *unterrichten* 'instruct' pattern like dative case-marked NPs in not becoming the subjects of middle verbs or hosts of depictive predicates, rather than like typical accusative objects; these problematic NPs are all semantically closer to goals than to patients. Comparable issues arise with respect to the double object construction in English and other languages. Some theories of syntax, such as Lexical-Functional Grammar (Alsina and Mchombo 1993; Bresnan 2001; Bresnan and Moshi 1990) and Relational Grammar (Perlmutter and Postal 1983a, 1983b), take the first object to be a direct object on a par with the direct object of a transitive verb. The reason is that the first object shares certain properties with direct objects of transitives; most obviously, both appear postverbally and both correspond to the subject of a related passive. Other studies, however, point out that the first object does not pattern like a transitive direct object in all respects, suggesting the two should not be subsumed under the same grammatical relation (Baker 1997; Hudson 1992; B. Levin and Rappaport Hovav 2002; Maling 2001; Polinsky 1996; Ziv and Sheintuch 1979). Some studies also suggest that a more apt comparison is with the dative case-marked argument of a three-argument verb in languages with dative case (B. Levin and Rappaport Hovav 2002; Siewierska 1998), supporting the identification of a broad notion of indirect object.

Given that there are deviations from the prototypical morphosyntactic expressions of subject and object, another question arises: what semantic properties of arguments govern these deviations?[10] In some instances, belonging to a particular semantic class of verbs, such as the Russian verbs of authority, ruling, and disposition, seems to be a necessary condition. In other instances, the variation seems to depend on properties of the NP bearing a particular grammatical relation. For instance, accusative/partitive case alternations in some languages, such as Finnish or Estonian (Kiparsky 1998; Ackerman and Moore 2001), depend on the contribution of the case-marked NP in determining the time course of the event. In still other instances, the animacy or the specificity of the NP bearing a particular grammatical relation determines its morphosyntactic expression, giving rise to phenomena such as case-marking splits (Silverstein 1976), inverse agreement (Aissen 1999), and differential object marking (Aissen 2003; Bossong 1991, 1998). There is some indication, as we discuss in sections 4.2.3 and 6.4.2, that a different range of semantic notions is involved in some of these deviations than in the basic choice of subject and object. Despite the pervasiveness of the agent–subject and patient–object associations, the bottom line is that there are also many other rich empirical generalizations underlying the association of semantic roles with their morphosyntactic realizations.

1.7   Conclusion

This chapter has outlined major challenges that must be confronted in developing a theory of argument realization and a related theory of lexical semantic representation. We reviewed possible strategies for isolating the semantic determinants of argument realization, as well as potential pitfalls that might be encountered in carrying out this task. In this context, we pointed out the importance of recognizing that verb meanings represent linguistic construals of happenings in the world and, thus, may pick up on only certain facets of these happenings. We also stressed that theories of lexical semantic representation and argument realization must be designed to accommodate patterns of variation and uniformity in argument realization. Finally, we illustrated the variety and complexity found in the association of semantic roles with their morphosyntactic realizations, showing that argument realization involves much more than the commonly assumed agent–subject, patient–object associations. Building on this background, the next three chapters turn to the nature of lexical semantic representation, providing the foundation for subsequent chapters, which are devoted to questions of argument realization.

Notes

1 Verbs are the prototypical predicators, that is, argument-taking words. Since this book deals almost exclusively with the realization of the arguments of verbs, we refer to verbs throughout this discussion. A complete theory of argument realization must, however, also deal with the morphosyntactic realization of the arguments of predicators in other lexical categories.

2 The Projection Principle conflates two separate claims: (i) verbs have structured lexical entries which register the number and types of arguments they take and (ii) these lexical properties are configurationally represented at all levels of syntactic representation. The second claim of the Projection Principle, namely, that lexical properties are configurationally encoded at all levels of syntactic representation, is no longer recognized in the Minimalist Program (Chomsky 1995: 188–89), and it is explicitly denied in Lexical-Functional Grammar's Lexical Mapping Theory (Bresnan and Kanerva 1989) and Role and Reference Grammar. However, all these theories are still "projectionist" in the sense of claim (i).

3 The specification of the syntactic realization of arguments depends on the larger theoretical framework adopted; possibilities include grammatical relations, configurationally defined positions within structures generated by X'-Theory, positions in an argument structure, or morphological cases. Since this book discusses issues that are applicable across theories of syntactic representation, we generally refer to syntactic representations in terms of grammatical relations, since these notions have analogues in most theories of syntactic representation, even when they are not treated as primitives of the theory. We make reference to the notions of subject, direct object, and oblique, as well as first and second object in discussions of double object constructions.

4 The exception may be certain ergative languages. Some researchers (Dixon 1972, 1979, 1994; B. Levin 1983; Marantz 1984; Mel'čuk 1979) have argued that at least some ergative languages show a reversal in the association of agent and patient with the grammatical relations subject and object, but the validity of such an analysis is a matter of debate; for example, Baker (1997: 123) argues that such languages are impossible. For recent discussions of ergativity see Bittner and Hale (1996), Bobaljik (1992), Dixon (1994), Johns (1992, 1997), Manning (1994), and Murasugi (1992). What matters here is that even in languages with ergative case-marking, agents and patients are privileged in being associated with "core" grammatical relations, and, furthermore, their morphosyntactic expression is consistent and predictable.

5 See Taylor (1996) for the alternative point of view – that a verb's meaning cannot be carved up according to whether or not it is grammatically relevant – and Jackendoff (1996a) for a rebuttal.

6 More accurately, activity and semelfactive verbs take the auxiliary *avere* 'have.' Semelfactives and activities are often confused due to their similar behavior; see B. Levin (1999), Olsen (1994, 1997), and Smith (1991) for discussion.

7 Since we are focusing on larger questions about argument alternations, we do not return to the question of why some verbs, including *splash, smear,* and *load,* show the locative alternation, while some apparently similar ones, such as *fill* and *pour,* do not. Pinker (1989) offers a solution, but there is still more work to be done since, as Kim (1999) documents, in some languages, including Korean, verbs like *fill* show the locative alternation, though those like *pour* still do not; see also S. T. Rosen (1996).

8 The frequency with which the verb pairs *fear/frighten* and *like/please* are cited might suggest there are numerous comparable pairs of morphologically simple English psych-verbs; actually, there are not, despite the fair number of psych-verbs patterning like *fear* and the very large number patterning like *frighten.* Assuming that each psych-verb type instantiates a distinct kind of event, an explanation for this observation might lie in the inherent connection between the particular psychological state associated with a verb and the event type it is most naturally associated with. For instance, Pylkkänen (2000) notes that the *frighten* verbs, unlike the *fear* verbs, are necessarily stage-level; therefore, a psychological state which can only be construed as being individual-level must be lexicalized by a *fear* verb. We leave this important question for further research.

9 The fact that not all diagnostics for subjecthood and objecthood pick out the same NPs both in and across languages has prompted researchers in some theoretical frameworks to question the validity of the notions "subject" and "object" altogether. For example, in Role and Reference Grammar (Van Valin and LaPolla 1997), there is no unified notion of subject, and the same holds for Head-Driven Phrase Structure Grammar (Pollard and Sag 1987). We do not enter into these issues and simply point out that however this question is resolved, in laying out a theory of argument realization it is necessary to distinguish behavioral and coding properties.

10 Sometimes tense, mood, and aspect considerations affect the morphosyntactic realization of arguments; we will not be concerned with these phenomena.

2

Semantic role lists

One of the most widely adopted forms of lexical semantic representation is what we term a SEMANTIC ROLE LIST, also known as a "case frame" (Fillmore 1968) or a "theta-grid" (Stowell 1981). The best-known instantiations of this approach are Fillmore's Case Grammar (1968) and Gruber and Jackendoff's thematic relations (Gruber 1965; Jackendoff 1972, 1976), but such representations have a long history, going back to the Sanskrit grammarian Pāṇini. The modern interest in semantic role lists originated in Fillmore's work, especially as presented in "The Case for Case" (1968).[1] In a semantic role list, grammatically relevant facets of a verb's meaning are represented by a list of labels identifying the role that each of the verb's arguments plays in the event it denotes. For example, the verbs *break* and *put* might be associated with the semantic role lists "Agent, Patient" and "Agent, Theme, Location," respectively.

Rather than comparing and contrasting the myriad proposals for semantic role list representations, this chapter provides a critical discussion of these approaches. First, in section 2.1 we present the essential properties of semantic role lists. Then, in section 2.2 we discuss their most fundamental limitations. In section 2.3 we review some attempts aimed at overcoming these shortcomings, while maintaining many basic assumptions underlying such approaches.

2.1 The properties common to semantic role list approaches

The components of a semantic role list are a predetermined set of labels that identify arguments according to the semantic relation they bear to their verb; each verb is associated with the relevant list of semantic roles. As noted by Croft (1991: 156), several fundamental assumptions are implicit in at least the earliest semantic role list approaches: (i) the semantic roles are taken to be semantically unanalyzable, (ii) the semantic roles are defined independently of the meaning of the verb, and (iii) the set of semantic roles is small in size.

The composition and size of the set of semantic roles is a matter of debate, but the set in (1), from one of Fillmore's papers, is typical. (This set includes two roles that are not often encountered, counter-agent and result; the latter is often subsumed under a broader interpretation of the object role – i.e., what is known more commonly as a "patient.")

(1) a. Agent (A), the instigator of the event
   b. Counter-Agent (C), the force or resistance against which the action is carried out
   c. Object (O), the entity that moves or changes or whose position or existence is in consideration
   d. Result (R), the entity that comes into existence as a result of the action
   e. Instrument (I), the stimulus or immediate physical cause of an event
   f. Source (S), the place from which something moves
   g. Goal (G), the place to which something moves
   h. Experiencer (E), the entity which receives or accepts or experiences or undergoes the effect of an action ...   (Fillmore 1971b: 376)

Semantic role assignments are meant to bring out similarities and differences in verb meaning that are reflected in argument expression. Each semantic role defines a natural class of arguments, with members of this natural class usually having a common semantic relation to their verbs and shared options for their morphosyntactic expression. Semantic roles, then, can be viewed as labels for equivalence classes of arguments, and the goal of a theory of semantic roles is the identification of a set of semantic roles that is applicable to any argument of any verb.

In a sense, the use of semantic roles is analogous to the use of features in phonology. Phonological features distill from the wide range of phonetic detail those aspects of sounds which are phonologically relevant. Semantic roles distill from the perhaps even wider range of semantic detail those facets of meaning which are grammatically relevant. The choice of features or roles is justified to the extent that they define equivalence classes which recur in rules of phonology or morphosyntax. Phonological features, however, generally appear in clusters defining particular phonemes, and, in addition, define natural classes of phonemes, while semantic roles, as they were initially used, are taken to be atomic elements. As we discuss in section 2.3.1, there have been moves to define semantic roles in terms of more basic semantic elements, which could be viewed as the real analogues to phonological features.

To illustrate how semantic role lists can fulfill the requirements of a lexical semantic representation, we return to Fillmore's (1970) study of the verbs *break* and *hit*, first presented in the introduction. Fillmore points out that both can appear in two different transitive syntactic contexts, as in (2) and (3), although when a wider range of contexts is examined, it becomes apparent that the behavior of these verbs diverges, as in (4)–(7).

(2) a. John broke the window with a rock.
    b. A rock broke the window.

(3) a. John hit the fence with a stick.
    b. A stick hit the fence.

(4) a. The window broke.
    b. *The fence hit.

(5) a. The window was broken. (eventive and stative readings available)
    b. The fence was hit. (only eventive reading available)

(6) a. I broke his leg./*I broke him on the leg.
    b. I hit his leg./I hit him on the leg.   (Fillmore 1970: 126, (23)–(26))

(7) a. John broke the rock against the window.
        (does not paraphrase (2a))
    b. John hit the stick against the fence. (paraphrases (3a))

And as already noted, these two patterns of behavior are even more deserving
of explanation since the behavior of *break* is representative of a whole class
of verbs, as is that of *hit*. Other verbs patterning like each of these verbs are
listed in (8).

(8) a. *Break* Verbs: bend, fold, shatter, crack   (Fillmore 1970: 125, (15))
    b. *Hit* Verbs: slap, strike, bump, stroke   (Fillmore 1970: 125, (16))

In order to explain the differences between the two types of verbs, Fillmore
(1970) proposes distinct semantic role lists for the *break* verbs and the *hit*
verbs. (We have simplified Fillmore's representations by omitting information
concerning the optional or obligatory status of each element in the list.)

(9) a. *break*: Agent, Instrument, Object
    b. *hit*: Agent, Instrument, Place

Each class of verbs, then, is characterized by the number of participants associated with its members, as well as their semantic roles. Fillmore also proposes
rules of subject selection and object selection that take as their starting point
semantic role labels. For a given verb, the choice of subject and object depends
on its associated semantic role list. If this list contains an agent, then the participant with the agent role is chosen as subject. If there is an instrument in the
list, then it too can be chosen as subject, but only in the absence of an agent.[2]
The similarities between the *hit* verbs and the *break* verbs follow because
verbs of both types select arguments bearing the roles agent and instrument,
while the differences follow because verbs in one class select an object (i.e.,
patient) as their second argument, while those in the other class select a place
(i.e., location). Of course, the identification of semantic roles which distinguish
between the classes does not in itself constitute an explanation of the divergent
behavior of *hit* and *break* verbs. Mapping rules such as Fillmore's rule of

subject selection are a first step in this direction; however, a full explanation of
the divergent behavior of the *hit* and *break* verbs requires a full-fledged theory
of mapping from lexical semantic representation to syntax; this is the topic of
chapter 5.

2.2   Problems for semantic role list approaches

Semantic role list approaches have received abundant and typically well-merited
criticism. In this section we review some of the most serious criticisms, and then
consider some attempts to overcome them in the next section. For other recent
discussions of the problems with semantic role-based approaches see Croft
(1991: 155–58, 1998: 27–34), Davis (2001: 20–25), Dowty (1991: 553–59),
and Parsons (1995: 637 47).

2.2.1   Problems of definition and grain-size

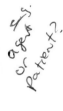

The use of semantic roles has been criticized because it is difficult to find
reliable diagnostics for isolating precisely those arguments bearing a particular
role. There do not seem to be diagnostic tests which can be consistently applied
to an argument with relatively uncontroversial results to determine whether that
argument bears a particular role in the way that there are tests for, say, lexical
and syntactic categories. Fillmore's use of the term "Case" for what we term
"semantic role" reflects the existence of correlations between certain morphological cases, prepositions, or grammatical relations and certain semantic roles,
but such grammatical markers do not prove to be adequate indicators of the
semantic roles of the NPs. If they did, there would be no reason to distinguish
between semantic roles and their morphosyntactic encoding. For example, the
preposition *with* can signal instruments (*cut with a knife*), comitatives (*work
with Pat*), themes (*spray a wall with paint*), causes (*shiver with cold*), and
manners (*agree with enthusiasm*). A variety of heuristics intended to identify
instances of particular roles have been proposed in the literature, but they
invariably break down under closer scrutiny; see McKercher (2001), Nilsen
(1973), Schlesinger (1979, 1989, 1995), and Schütze (1995) for comprehensive
discussions of proposed tests for instruments.

Some of the problems that plague attempts to provide precise definitions
for individual semantic roles can be avoided. The key is recognizing that
semantic roles are actually defined relative to the verbs which select them.
The current dominant approach to semantic roles takes them to be defined by
recurring sets of lexical entailments or, perhaps, presuppositions imposed by
verbs on their arguments (Dowty 1989, 1991: 552–53), what Dowty (1989: 77)
calls L-thematic roles. Every verb specifies certain entailments that hold of its
arguments (e.g., *murder* entails that its subject acts volitionally). A verb might
also presuppose certain properties of its arguments (Dowty 1991: 552; Primus,

1999: 34) though, as Dowty (1991: 552) suggests, presuppositions can be hard to distinguish from entailments. Since in most instances, this distinction is unimportant, we follow Dowty and refer to these lexical properties of arguments as entailments. Natural classes of arguments result when arguments of a number of verbs share certain lexical entailments. The commonly cited semantic roles can be viewed as labels for certain good-sized natural classes of entailments that are relevant to linguistic generalizations.[3]

Establishing what semantic role an argument of a verb bears, then, requires a careful examination of the meaning of the verb and, in particular, the identification of the lexical entailments which the verb specifies for that argument. This approach, however, also faces serious problems. Clearly, a set of shared entailments on arguments deserves to fall under the rubric of a recognized semantic role only if such a semantic role enters into significant generalizations in argument realization. However, it is difficult to decide on a fixed set of roles with just this property. One of the best-known problems in the identification and definition of semantic roles is what Dowty calls "role fragmentation" (1991: 553–55): the subdivision of a single role into multiple roles as a result of additional semantic and syntactic investigations. Dowty cites studies of the agent role to exemplify this. Cruse (1973), for instance, after a careful study of the syntactic properties of agentive verbs in English, concludes that there are four distinct agent-like roles – volitive, effective, initiative, and agentive – with each displaying distinctive behavior. Nilsen (1972), in an extended study of the instrument role, also ends up subdividing this role into four roles. Several studies of instruments, drawing on the observation that some instruments can be expressed as subjects as well as in *with* phrases, while others cannot, make a distinction between "intermediary" instruments and "facilitating" or "enabling" instruments (Marantz 1984: 247; McKercher 2001: 52–54; Ono 1992; Wojcik 1976: 165); the former, unlike the latter, are able to perform the action independently, as reflected in their occurrence as subjects.

(10) a. The cook opened the jar with the new gadget.
      b. The new gadget opened the jar.

(11) a. Shelly ate the sliced banana with a fork.
      b. *The fork ate the sliced banana.

The source of the problem appears to be determining the right "grain-size" to use in the definition of semantic roles. For certain argument expression generalizations coarse-grained lexical semantic analyses are suitable; however, others call for finer-grained analyses. For example, B. Levin and Rappaport Hovav (1995: 135) formulate a rule which realizes the "immediate cause" of an event as the subject in English. They argue at length for this statement of the rule, positing a notion of immediate cause, which is broader than the notion of agent, since it also subsumes many nonagentive animate arguments, for example, the emitter arguments of verbs of sound and light emission such as *rumble* or *sparkle*; see Van Valin and D. Wilkins (1996) for discussion of the related notion "effector." This argument realization generalization, then, refers to a large class of arguments; however, there are other generalizations that pick out various subclasses of immediate causes. As discussed in section 1.6, although both agents and other causes can be expressed as subjects, natural causes can also be expressed in *from* phrases, while agents cannot, as shown in (12)–(13), repeated from this earlier discussion.

> (12) a. His uncle died from/of pneumonia.
>   b. Pneumonia killed his uncle.

> (13) a. Brutus killed Caesar.
>   b. *Caesar died from/of Brutus.

As these examples suggest, in some languages the different kinds of immediate causes receive different morphosyntactic realizations; see DeLancey (1984) and van Voorst (1996) for further discussion and exemplification. Canonical agents – causes that are animate and have volition and control over their actions – are always expressed as subjects, while other types of immediate causes may show several realizations (see section 1.6) or in some languages may be precluded from being realized like canonical agents (e.g., see Guilfoyle [1995] on Irish). And, as noted above, certain grammatical generalizations make distinctions among different kinds of agents as well. Thus, the grain-size appropriate for the sweeping generalization concerning subject selection is not appropriate for other generalizations.

There are some verbs which require analyses that are fine-grained in the extreme, since they have one or more arguments that cannot be characterized in terms of typically posited semantic roles. For instance, what roles do the objects of *contemplate, facilitate, require*, or *confirm* bear? Such verbs appear to have arguments requiring an individually tailored semantic role. Positing such individualized roles could result in a staggering number of roles; furthermore, little is gained by introducing them since many would not enter into any significant linguistic generalizations. However, generalizing the semantic characterization of some roles to include such arguments is no less problematic since overly general semantic roles tend to have little predictive power. Yet many researchers apply the label theme or patient to almost any NP expressible as an object, perhaps in an attempt to formulate a single object selection rule. This strategy may reflect a desire to avoid role fragmentation and even a hope that there is a unified semantic basis for objecthood. It is possible that researchers are resistant to positing role fragmentation where objects are concerned because the potential fragmentation associated with objects is much more severe than with subjects; with subjects it can be constrained to a handful of roles, such as agent, experiencer, instrument, and natural force. Even if there are reasons that the broad application of certain semantic roles might be desirable in the abstract, the question is whether such uses are empirically supported. For instance, the assignment of the theme or patient role to just about all objects reflects a failure to appreciate differences in the behavior of the objects of various verbs. There is no empirical basis for such a wide application of one of these terms, as demonstrated in section 1.1 via an examination of the objects of *break, hit, eat,* and *see.*

2.2.2 Problems reflecting cross-role generalizations

Having discussed complications that arise because some generalizations refer to a grain-size smaller than the "average" semantic role, we now examine difficulties posed by generalizations that cut across "average"-size semantic roles. The first type of problem leads to role fragmentation, while the second suggests that "average"-size semantic roles fall into natural classes. Both suggest that semantic roles themselves cannot be unanalyzable notions if certain generalizations are to be perspicuously expressed.

The problems we discuss arise because the typical semantic role inventory lacks internal structure. If each semantic role is taken to be discrete and unanalyzable, generalizations holding over more than one semantic role are not expected. For example, there is no reason to expect that a patient might have more in common with a goal than with an agent, or that an instrument might have more in common with an agent than with an experiencer. Yet, there is evidence that this is so: patients and recipients, for example, have the same morphological expression in languages with double object constructions, and agents and instruments have the same morphological case in many ergative languages of Australia (Blake 1977: 44). There are also languages where goals and benefactives (Blake 1977: 35; Croft 1991) or instruments and comitatives (Croft 1991; Stolz 1996) are assigned the same morphological case or are signaled by the same preposition. In English, for example, *with* indicates both instruments and comitatives.

(14) a. Tracy washed the car with an enormous sponge.
      b. Tracy washed the car with Stacy.

Similarly, as discussed in section 1.6, the first object in the double object construction can indicate either a goal or a benefactive. Thus, there are both partial similarities and partial divergences in the expression of arguments of verbs bearing particular roles, giving rise to complex patterns of crossclassification, such as those reflected in these syncretisms in morphosyntactic expression. These suggest that there is organization imposed over the semantic roles in the typical inventory.

Further evidence suggesting that the semantic role inventory has internal organization comes from Jackendoff's (1983) discussion of verbs of motion. As the examples in (15) illustrate, a simple motion verb such as *come* can appear with a variety of complements.

(15) a. Pat came to the library.
     b. Pat came from the cafeteria.
     c. Pat came from the cafeteria to the library.
     d. Pat came towards us.
     e. Pat came through the woods.

On a semantic role list approach, these different uses of *come* have the verb
appearing with a goal, as in (a), a source, as in (b), both a source and a goal,
as in (c), what Jackendoff (1983: 165) calls a direction, as in (d), and what he
calls a route, as in (e). Source and goal figure in most semantic role inventories.
Direction and route are not typically included in such inventories, but that in
itself is not a problem. There is nothing in the various semantic role lists which
unifies these different uses of *come*, though, as Jackendoff points out, there is
a simple underlying generalization: the verb *come* can appear with a path, but
there are a number of different types of paths.

The root of these problems is the assumption that semantic roles are
taken to be discrete and unanalyzable; see Croft (1991: 156–58) for additional discussion. Given this, it is not possible to impose any structure over
the set of semantic roles that can account for similarities in patterning or
dependencies in cooccurrence. The small set of unanalyzed roles that characterizes an ideal semantic role approach, then, is incompatible with linguistic
reality.

2.2.3   Problems of one-to-one correspondence

Fillmore's Case Grammar (1968) and its descendants make the assumptions
that there may be at most one instance of each semantic role per clause and that
each argument bears one and only one role; see also Starosta (1978). However,
potential deviations from these assumptions are frequently cited. Gruber (1965,
1976) and Jackendoff (1972, 1976, 1983) present sentences with verbs of
motion and verbs of transfer of possession where a single NP apparently bears
two semantic roles. For instance, they claim that the subject of *run* in *Kelly ran
across the field* is both an agent and a theme – in the sense of an entity that
moves or is located. The potential for dual role assignment is identified as the
source of the ambiguity in *Kelly rolled down the hill*. Here *Kelly* is necessarily
understood as the theme, but there is also a reading available where *Kelly* is
understood to be the agent, as well. On the reading where *Kelly* is only theme,
the rolling down the hill is unintentional, and on the other where *Kelly* receives
two semantic roles, the rolling is intentional.

Dual semantic role assignment is especially useful in distinguishing between
certain verbs of transfer of possession. For instance, it can be used to differen-
tiate the sentences in (16). *Phil* is source, *Mira* goal, and *the yacht* theme, in
both sentences; in addition, *Phil* is also agent in the (a) sentence and *Mira* is
also agent in the (b) sentence.

(16) a. Phil sold the yacht to Mira.

   b. Mira bought the yacht from Phil.

Gruber and Jackendoff take examples such as those just discussed as support for dispensing with the assumption that an NP can bear only one semantic role. If this assumption is dropped, new questions arise: which pairs of semantic roles be assigned to an NP, and if only some of the possible pairings are attested, what prevents the others?[4]

Equally problematic for attempts to constrain the associations of semantic roles with arguments are verbs which appear to have two arguments bearing the same role; see Dowty (1991: 556), Huddleston (1970: 510), Starosta (1978: 468–70), among others for discussion. Various examples are cited, with *resemble* being representative. This verb's two arguments are said to bear the same role because sentences such as *Pat resembles Lee* and *Lee resembles Pat* are paraphrases. In fact, purported instances of two-NPs-with-the-same-role may be less problematic than purported instances of one-NP-with-two-roles. Closer examination reveals that the two arguments of *resemble* do not have precisely the same role. Rather, one is the standard of comparison and the other is the object being compared with this standard, as shown by the contrast between the unexceptionable *Dorothy resembles the Mona Lisa* and the somewhat odd *The Mona Lisa resembles Dorothy* (Fillmore 1971a: 39; Gleitman et al. 1996; Parsons 1995: 645–46; Starosta 1978; among others). Nevertheless, verbs such as *resemble* remain problematic as their analysis involves introducing a role, "standard of comparison," that is not otherwise typically posited – a label introduced specifically for this particular class of verbs. Furthermore, this role is what Dowty (1991: 562–66) calls "perspective dependent": it is assigned based on a speaker's notion of what is discourse prominent rather than based on properties of the event itself, like typical semantic roles.

2.2.4 Overall explanatory effectiveness

Finally, an unstructured list of semantic roles, whatever its effectiveness, remains fundamentally unexplanatory in a number of ways.

First, as discussed by Rappaport and B. Levin (1988), a lexical semantic representation which consists solely of an unstructured list of semantic roles has no way of distinguishing a possible set of roles that can be associated with a single verb from an impossible one. Although many verbs are associated with the semantic role lists "Agent, Patient, Instrument" (e.g., *break, cut, mix*) or "Theme, Source, Goal" (e.g., *run, swim, walk*), a list of the form "Location, Experiencer, Patient" seems decidedly unnatural. Yet, there is no way of allowing the natural groups of semantic roles and disallowing the unnatural ones. Second, there are no constraints on the number of roles which may be associated with a given verb, yet crosslinguistically, verbs are at most triadic. (The exception, perhaps, are verbs of commercial transfer such as *buy* and *sell*, which involve a buyer, a seller, the merchandise, and the payment; see Carter [1976, 1977]; Croft, Taoka, and Wood [2001].) A similar point is made in Davis and Koenig (2000: 59).

Third, an unstructured list of semantic roles does not give any insight into why semantic roles figure in argument expression in just the way they do. For example, as already mentioned, agents in all languages – possibly putting aside some ergative languages – are always expressed as subjects. This observation can be captured with a stipulation that agents are always subjects, but surely there is a reason for this generalization. Many other broad generalizations concerning the morphosyntactic expression of arguments bearing particular semantic roles can be formulated, but a simple list of semantic roles gives no insight into why just these generalizations are valid.

2.3   Attempted solutions

There have been various attempts to circumvent the problems most often attributed to semantic role list approaches, while still maintaining the basic nature of semantic role lists as a lexical semantic representation. One solution is to define each semantic role in terms of a small set of binary features; a second is to allow a structured form of dual role assignment, known as a TIER MODEL, using roles drawn from two different sets. These two solutions, however, meet with mixed success.

2.3.1   Feature decomposition

Some researchers have suggested that the problems of crossclassification and grain-size can be solved once the assumption that semantic roles are unanalyzable is rejected, and semantic roles are provided with definitions in terms of a small set of semantic features. This approach is adopted by J. M. Anderson (1971, 1977), Ostler (1979), Reinhart (1996, 2000, 2001, 2002), and Rozwadowska (1988, 1989), among others. This approach strengthens the parallel between semantic roles and phonemes, with both being characterized in terms of distinctive features.

Feature decomposition approaches can deal with the problems of crossclassification by making reference to a feature shared across a set of semantic roles. Rozwadowska (1988: 157, 1989: 117–18) provides an analysis of restrictions on the syntactic expression of arguments in derived nominals based on the decomposition of semantic roles into bundles of features. She points out that a single generalization covers experiencers and patients in the nominalization of English transitive verbs. She considers derived nominals based on transitive verbs which express only one of their arguments, with this argument being expressed in prenominal position (e.g., *the building's demolition*). If one of the two arguments of the transitive base verb is either an experiencer or a patient, this argument is necessarily the one expressed. This generalization is intended to account for the examples in (17). In (17a), *John* must be understood as the experiencer, as in *John loves Mary*, and not as the stimulus. In (17b) *the movie* cannot be understood as the stimulus, as in *The movie shocked the censors*, and (17c) cannot have a reading where *the barbarians* are understood as the agent, as in *The barbarians destroyed Rome*, but only the reading where *the barbarians* is understood as the patient, as in *The Romans destroyed the barbarians*.

(17) a. John's love   (Rozwadowska 1989: 117, (11a))
    b. *the movie's shock
    c. the barbarians' destruction   (Rozwadowska 1989: 117, (10d))

According to Rozwadowska (1988: 158, 1989: 119) experiencers and patients share the feature [+change], which is associated with arguments that "are affected physically or psychologically in the course of action, process, or state" and the appropriate generalization, whatever its origin or explanation, can be formulated in terms of this feature. However, Rozwadowska (1988: 159, 1989: 127) points out that experiencers have more in common with agents with respect to certain other grammatical generalizations, and she accounts for this commonality by assigning experiencers the additional feature [+sentient], which is shared by agents. This analysis captures the dual character of experiencers.

Since natural classes of semantic roles can be defined through the use of shared features, the range of attested morphological case syncretisms, mentioned in section 2.2, might be accounted for in terms of these shared features. For example, to account for the fact that agents and instruments share certain grammatical properties, they can both be assigned a common feature, say Rozwadowska's feature [+cause] (1988: 159), and an additional feature [+control], indicating control over the execution of an action, could be assigned to agents, but not to instruments (cf. the discussion of agents and instruments in DeLancey 1984).[5] Patients and recipients (i.e., the goals found with transfer of possession verbs such as *give* or *sell*) might be said to share a feature [+affected] – a relative of Rozwadowska's feature [+change]. The basis for this proposal is that both can be objects, and Jackendoff (1990b: 135–37), for example, attributes this to their being affected by the action. Rozwadowska's feature [+sentient] – sometimes presented as [+animate], though see section 4.4 – might then distinguish possessional goals from patients.

Furthermore, generalizations which are apparently stated with respect to semantic roles of different grain-sizes can be accommodated by referring to feature specifications of greater or lesser generality. For example, the broad generalization concerning mapping to subject discussed in section 1.6 may be sensitive to a feature [+immediate cause], while other language-specific generalizations may make reference to features that distinguish among immediate causes, such as [+volitional], [+animate], or [+sentient].

Another attempt to cover a wide range of argument realization phenomena along similar lines is pursued by Reinhart (1996, 2000, 2001, 2002), who also defines semantic roles in terms of binary features. She introduces two features, [c], for "cause change" and [m] for "mental state," for this purpose. Coarse-grained roles are those left unspecified for one feature. For example, the role cause is represented simply as [+c], being unspecified for the feature [m]. Roles defined by a single feature may have varying contextual interpretations, so that a cause – i.e., [+c] – argument may be realized as an agent – a [+c, +m] argument – or an instrument – a [+c, −m] argument – since both their definitions are compatible with the single feature [+c]. As in other semantic role list approaches, classes of verbs can then be defined in terms of the semantic roles of their arguments, though for Reinhart, these roles are defined in terms of feature clusters.

The use of underspecified feature clusters solves the problem of grain-size. It is natural for some verbs to allow agent, cause, or instrument subjects – these are precisely the verbs that select for a [+c] subject – and for others to require an agent subject – these are the verbs that select for a [+c, +m] subject. Furthermore, the fact that agents, causes, and instruments can all be subjects follows if [+c] arguments can be subjects; there is no need to have a subject selection rule that explicitly lists the possibilities.

Rozwadowska and Reinhart's feature decompositions have somewhat different motivations: Rozwadowska is concerned with the interaction of argument structure and derivational morphology, while Reinhart is interested in explaining the argument expression options of verbs, particularly psych-verbs, as well as patterns of lexical causativization. Nevertheless, the features that the two posit largely overlap. This overlap reflects an emerging consensus regarding the semantic determinants of argument realization that need to be incorporated into any lexical semantic representation, the topic of chapter 4.

However, as discussed by Rappaport and B. Levin (1988), approaches based on feature decomposition are not unproblematic. They still do not provide any insight into what constitutes a natural set of semantic roles which can be associated with an individual verb. Furthermore, unless the number of features is small, as in Reinhart's and Rozwadowska's work, the number of attested feature combinations is usually less than the number of possible combinations, so that these approaches give rise to uninstantiated roles. This problem can be quite severe, as Kisala (1985) demonstrates. She points out that Ostler (1979) makes use of 48 roles, which he defines in terms of eight features, yet eight features are sufficient to distinguish 256 roles – over 200 more roles than Ostler uses. To account for these discrepancies between predicted and existing roles, a theory of the features that define semantic roles must be supplemented with a theory that predicts the possible combinations of these features. However, as Rappaport and B. Levin write, "Considering the care that Ostler takes in motivating this set of features and the wide range of phenomena he attempts to deal with, it is doubtful that other attempts at defining comprehensive feature systems will meet with much more success" (1988: 33).

Feature analyses are appealing because they provide a way of defining and making reference to natural classes of semantic roles. It is important to recognize, however, that there are two ways in which semantic roles fall into natural classes and that feature analyses are only relevant to one of the two. First, semantic roles can fall into natural classes in that they pattern together with respect to argument realization options. These classes are typically the ones that are implicated in issues of crossclassification and grain-size. Second, semantic roles can form natural classes in that they may cooccur as the arguments of particular types of verbs. Although feature approaches provide a way of dealing with the first type of natural class, they do not offer insight into natural classes of cooccurring semantic roles. Understanding these natural classes requires a theory of possible events, since the nature of an event determines its participants; chapter 4 introduces theories of event conceptualization intended to address this problem.

2.3.2 Dual semantic role assignments and tier models

Some researchers relax the assumption that each argument bears one and only one semantic role. Certain arguments, then, may be assigned more than one role, and this dual role assignment allows for some degree of crossclassification. The best-known instantiation of this approach is the system of thematic relations introduced by Gruber (1965) and Jackendoff (1972); it was exemplified with the verbs *roll, buy,* and *sell* in section 2.2.3 and is discussed further in section 4.1. Jackendoff explicitly reviews the advantages of allowing dual role assignments. A challenge for such approaches, however, is that only certain combinations of roles seem to be viable. The allowable combinations are easy to describe, but an explanation is necessary for why only particular combinations are possible.

To deal with this problem, some instantiations of this approach impose additional organization on the set of roles. Culicover and W. Wilkins (1984) propose there are two sets of roles, with dual role assignments always involving one role from each set. These two sets of roles are referred to as the extensional or perceptual roles and the intensional or action roles. The perceptual or extensional roles are so-named because they can be assigned to arguments of a verb by looking at the event in the world that is being described; these roles are source, goal, location, and theme in the Gruber/Jackendoff sense (see also section 4.1). The action or intensional roles are agent, patient, instrument, and benefactive; these roles "categorize objects according to their status as actors in an action" (Culicover and W. Wilkins 1984: 212). They are referred to as intensional roles because, unlike the perceptual roles, they must be assigned "based on our natural theories of human action" (Culicover and W. Wilkins 1984: 212). As discussed in section 4.1, Jackendoff (1990b) takes this idea further, proposing that the lexical semantic representation involves two distinct dimensions, his "thematic" and "action" tiers (1987, 1990b), corresponding roughly to Culicover and Wilkins' perceptual and action roles, respectively.

Although Jackendoff's tiers are cast in predicate decomposition terms, they incorporate a notion of dual role assignment since a single argument may play a part in both tiers. Grimshaw (1990) also adopts the idea that there are two representations, proposing an aspectual dimension, which is a projection of the event structure of predicates, as well as a thematic dimension, which is inspired by Jackendoff's thematic tier. In fact, these are perhaps the most recent instantiations of an idea that keeps recurring in the semantic role literature, having made one of its earliest appearances in Grimes (1975: 133–38). Most noteworthy is that the two dimensions identified in these approaches foreshadow two distinct perspectives on event conceptualization, each relevant to argument expression; these are discussed in chapter 4.

2.4   Conclusion

In this chapter we presented lexical semantic representations that take the form of semantic role lists, surveying the severe problems that such representations face. We reviewed attempts to overcome these problems by rejecting the assumption that semantic roles are unanalyzable, while still maintaining the assumptions that semantic roles are indeed an appropriate basis for a lexical semantic representation and that, even if analyzable, they are definable by a set of necessary and sufficient properties. These revised approaches, however, are only partially successful. The next chapter considers further developments in the theory of lexical semantic representation designed to overcome the fundamental limitations of semantic role lists. These developments are incorporated into most current theories of lexical semantic representation.

We end this chapter on a methodological note. Due to the many problems facing theories of semantic roles, existing semantic role labels are often "reappropriated" by researchers: some semantic role labels are used in various, possibly incommensurable, ways. Nowhere is this more evident than with two of the most often cited semantic roles, "theme" and "patient." These two roles, which are most often associated with arguments realized as direct objects, are neither defined, nor used consistently. For instance, many researchers have assigned theme or patient to almost any NP expressible as an object, perhaps in an attempt to formulate a unified object selection rule (see section 2.2.1). Other researchers use these notions as if they were interchangeable, while still others refer to a "patient/theme" role, without making any commitment as to whether there is one role or two. Such uses most likely stem from statements by Gruber (1965) and Jackendoff (1972) that every sentence must have a theme (see section 4.1), which has led to a tendency to treat this role as a "wastebasket," assigning it to all objects. However, there are researchers who recognize a well-defined difference between the patient and theme roles. The notion "patient" goes back to traditional literature on transitivity, and in its narrowest sense is applied to the entity that is affected in an event, though "affectedness" itself is not so easily defined. On a narrow interpretation it means an entity that changes state, but often it is used in a looser sense, so that the objects of *hit* and *wipe* qualify as affected, and, hence, patients (Jackendoff 1987, 1990b; see section 4.2.4). The notion "theme" is introduced by Gruber (1965, 1976; Jackendoff 1972, 1976, 1983, 1987) to refer to the moving entity in a motion event or a located entity in a location event and then extended to the entity that changes state in a change-of-state event; this notion is then adopted and elaborated by Jackendoff (1972, 1976, 1983; see section 4.1). In later work, Jackendoff (1987: 394; 1990b: 125–30) recognizes a notion of patient as affected entity, in addition to a notion of theme, seeing each notion as relevant to distinct facets of a lexical semantic representation (see section 4.1). Finally, some researchers give precedence to the notion "theme": they define it as the role of an entity that changes state, and then apply the label patient to entities that might qualify as "affected" in a broad sense, but that do not fall under their notion "theme" (Marantz 2003). For these researchers, the objects of *hit* and *wipe* are patients, while the objects of *break* and *open* are themes. This use of "patient," then, diverges considerably from the more traditional use.

These different understandings of "theme" and "patient" reflect both the difficulties in defining semantic roles and the efforts to give them more effective definitions. In the following chapters we address the various semantic notions that figure in the many definitions of these terms. Here we simply address the terminological consequences of this plethora of uses for this book. Since our goal is to review and synthesize work in lexical semantics and argument realization, we usually use the term patient/theme as it is typically used, that is, to refer to the semantic range of arguments that are expressed as direct object. Where reference to a narrower notion is critical, as in discussions of semantic generalizations stated in terms of theme or patient, we will make clear precisely what is meant through a fuller specification, such as "the entity which undergoes a change of state."

Notes

1 The "Case for Case Reopened" (1977a) presents Fillmore's views on semantic roles close to ten years after his seminal paper "The Case for Case" and includes his responses to some common criticisms of semantic role approaches. For an extensive survey of major semantic role list approaches, which also reviews the various stages in Fillmore's work, see Cook (1989). For a shorter survey with somewhat different coverage, see chapter 3 of Blake (2001).
2 English sentences with instrument subjects describe a more circumscribed set of events than the corresponding sentences with an overt agent and the instrument expressed in a *with* phrase. As DeLancey (1984: 203) points out, *The axe broke the window* can describe an axe falling off a shelf onto a window, but without considerable context it is unlikely to describe a window breaking because someone deliberately strikes it with an axe. These limitations on the use of instrument subject sentences were not appreciated when Fillmore wrote his Case Grammar papers.

3   Not all researchers take semantic roles to be defined in terms of lexical entailments. Jackendoff (1972, 1976) and Talmy (1975, 1985), among others, allow NPs to be assigned different semantic roles, even if they do not differ in their entailments, but rather differ in their pragmatic or information-structure status.

4   Examples such as (16) are sometimes considered to be problems for Chomsky's (1981) Theta-Criterion; however, as noted by Chomsky (1981: 139, n. 14), and stressed in Rappaport and B. Levin (1988), the uses to which the Theta-Criterion is put in the Principles and Parameters framework, are not affected if the Theta-Criterion needs to be modified to allow for the kinds of examples which Gruber and Jackendoff cite.

5   This use of the feature [control], which we introduce solely for illustrative purposes, diverges from Rozwadowska's use of a feature with the same name. She assigns her feature [control] to instruments as well as agents because of other considerations raised by the particular phenomena she is exploring.

3

Current approaches to lexical semantic representation

As we discussed in the last chapter, a general consensus has emerged that semantic roles, to the extent that they do figure in argument realization, cannot be considered unanalyzable notions. We reviewed two approaches to overcoming this problem: unpackaging the content of semantic roles in terms of bundles of binary features and allowing arguments to be assigned more than one semantic role. In this chapter, we survey two other widely adopted solutions. The first involves introducing what Van Valin (1999) calls "generalized semantic roles." On this approach the content of traditional semantic roles is unpackaged into more basic components, as in the feature decomposition approach, but these components do not constitute a set of jointly necessary and sufficient conditions on any given role. The second involves introducing a more structured lexical semantic representation known as a predicate decomposition. The most sophisticated of the current theories of argument realization build on generalized semantic roles, predicate decompositions, or both. Section 3.1 introduces generalized semantic roles, while section 3.2 introduces predicate decompositions.

3.1 Generalized semantic roles

The difficulties that arise in identifying a semantic role inventory and in assigning semantic roles to certain NPs have led some researchers to reject the traditional assumption that the semantic roles relevant for argument realization are characterized by a set of jointly necessary and sufficient conditions. In so doing, they are able to posit semantic roles that lump together arguments that pattern in the same way with respect to morphosyntax, without requiring that they have a single common semantic ingredient. Consequently, they can make use of semantic roles that encompass a wider range of arguments than traditional semantic roles, yet are not simply more coarsely defined roles, but rather are defined in terms of relatively specific semantic criteria. Van Valin

(1999) refers to such semantic roles as "generalized semantic roles," while Croft (1998: 22) characterizes them as "super-roles."

As discussed in section 1.6, the notions of subject and object are different from other morphosyntactic expressions available to arguments, in that both can be associated with a particularly wide range of semantic roles, and there are morphosyntactic processes which alter the assignment of arguments to these expressions. As a result, it has proven difficult to associate semantic roles with these grammatical relations, and a key motivation for the use of generalized semantic roles is their potential to overcome this difficulty. For this reason, generalized semantic role approaches usually posit only two such roles: one associated with subject and a second with object. Primus (1999), however, posits a third generalized semantic role, which is associated with the first object in a double object construction. Her proposal is based on parallels between the first object and the grammatical relations, subject and direct object (see section 1.6).

The seeds for generalized semantic roles were most likely sown in Dixon's (1972: 59, 1979: 60, 102–07, 1994: 6–8) work on ergativity, which introduces the labels "A" and "O" to refer to the semantic classes of arguments of transitive verbs that are realized as subject and direct object, respectively, in a language like English with a nominative–accusative case system. Dixon himself sees these labels as "syntactic-semantic primitives" (1979: 60; 1994: 6) in the sense that they have a semantic basis, but are used in the definition of grammatical relations such as "subject" and "object." These labels have been widely adopted for use in statements about the morphosyntactic realization of arguments in work on a broad range of languages, particularly work with a typological cast. The core exemplars of A and O are prototypical agents and patients, respectively, but the labels are intended to encompass other arguments that share the morphosyntactic realization of agents and patients. Thus, not only is the agent of prototypical agent–patient verbs an A, but so is the perceiver for verbs of perception (Dixon 1994: 8, 1991). This last idea underlies generalized semantic role approaches: classes of arguments with a range of semantic properties pattern together in terms of morphosyntactic realization, and there may be no semantic property common to the whole set of arguments. Members of these classes are said to share a generalized semantic role label, allowing rules of argument realization to make direct reference to just these classes of arguments. This general approach obviates the need to propose that the patient has a vague definition that covers the entire semantic spectrum of possible direct objects – the type of definition that prompts some researchers to characterize this as a "wastebasket" role.

In this section we review two approaches to generalized semantic roles. The first is Dowty's (1991) proto-role approach, which we briefly compare with a similar approach developed by Schlesinger (1995). We then review another perspective on generalized semantic roles developed within Role and Reference Grammar (RRG) by Van Valin (1990, 1993b; Foley and Van Valin 1984;

Van Valin and LaPolla 1997). Both approaches take generalized semantic roles not to be defined by a set of jointly necessary and sufficient conditions, and both appeal to many of the same semantic ingredients in defining these roles, but, as the comparison in section 3.1.2 shows, the actual part generalized semantic roles play in the overall theory of grammar is quite different.

3.1.1 Dowty's proto-roles

Dowty (1991) suggests that many of the problems inherent in developing a viable system of semantic roles can be overcome if semantic roles are viewed as cluster concepts or prototypes, which bring together related notions without imposing jointly necessary and sufficient conditions for membership in a category.[1] In presenting the prototype approach to semantic roles we focus primarily on Dowty's (1991) theory since it has been widely discussed and adopted. We also briefly discuss the work of Schlesinger (1995) in order to emphasize the potential benefits of a prototype approach, while highlighting points of contrast in implementation.

3.1.1.1 An overview of the proto-role approach

Dowty (1991) introduces two prototype-based generalized semantic roles, which he calls the AGENT PROTO-ROLE and the PATIENT PROTO-ROLE. His starting point is the assumption, developed in earlier work (Dowty 1989; Ladusaw and Dowty 1988), that arguments are associated with lexical entailments (or presuppositions) imposed on them by their verbs, and that semantic roles are best understood as names for recurring clusters of lexical entailments imposed by groups of predicates on one of their arguments. Semantic roles, then, are second-order properties – properties of predicates. Such clusters of entailments deserve a semantic role label only to the extent that they enter into significant linguistic generalizations – they are what he calls "L-thematic roles" (1989: 77).[2] Dowty argues that with respect to argument selection, only two such roles need be recognized, an Agent Proto-role and a Patient Proto-role. He associates these two proto-roles with the properties given below.

(1) Contributing properties for the Agent Proto-Role:
   – volitional involvement in the event or state
   – sentience (and/or perception)
   – causing an event or change of state in another participant
   – movement (relative to the position of another participant)
   – (exists independently of the event named by the verb)

(Dowty 1991: 572, (27))

(2) Contributing properties for the Patient Proto-Role:
   – undergoes change of state
   – incremental theme

– causally affected by another participant
– stationary relative to movement of another participant
– (does not exist independently of the event, or not at all)

(Dowty 1991: 572, (28))

Dowty (1991: 572) writes that the last, parenthesized entailment in each set – the entailment involving independent existence or the lack thereof – has its origins in the lists of subject properties in Keenan (1976, 1984). Dowty parenthesizes these entailments since he is unsure whether they belong to the discourse dimension of subjecthood rather than the semantic dimension. Polinsky (1996) further discusses the presupposition of existence with respect to the recipient and theme arguments of dative verbs. She associates it with the semantic characterization of certain arguments, while proposing that it is important to establishing a link between the semantic and discourse characterizations of the arguments of dative verbs.

Not unexpectedly, the components of meaning that enter into the proto-roles overlap significantly with those proposed in previous discussions of the agent and patient roles; these same notions also figure in the more structured lexical semantic representations that are introduced in the next section. The only notion that does not figure in work on semantic roles is "incremental theme," an aspectually based notion, which is discussed in section 4.2.1. The main innovation, then, is not in the content of the semantic components which enter into the definition of the proto-roles, but rather in the fact that these components contribute to the degree to which an argument can be taken to be an agent or a patient without being jointly necessary and sufficient in defining either of these notions. Concomitantly, there is no longer any reason to provide an exhaustive analysis of all arguments in a given sentence in terms of recognized semantic roles. This, too, is a major departure from earlier semantic role approaches.

The basic idea is that there is no invariant entailment or set of entailments which determines access to subjecthood or objecthood. Dowty illustrates this by presenting examples satisfying only one of the relevant entailments of each proto-role to the exclusion of the others. For example, the subject of *John sees/fears Mary* only possesses the Agent Proto-role entailment of sentience (Dowty 1991: 572, (29b)), while the object of *John erased the error* only possesses the change-of-state Patient Proto-role entailment (Dowty 1991: 572, (30a)). Thus, any given argument does not have to meet all of the criteria associated with a particular proto-role. Moreover, there are pairs of subject NPs or object NPs with no shared proto-role entailments at all. Obviously, an NP that meets all the criteria for either the Agent or the Patient Proto-role corresponds to what would be considered a good – or prototypical – example of the relevant role, as in *Brutus assassinated Caesar*. In fact, the most uncontroversial examples of the agent role in the literature tend to be those that have most, if not all, of the Agent Proto-role entailments, and the same holds for the most uncontroversial – or best – patients. The result is that arguments may be agent-like or patient-like to greater or lesser degrees, according to the number of Agent or Patient Proto-role entailments they are associated with. In this sense, the subject of *assassinate* is a more prototypical agent than the subject of *see*. The existence of more and less central exemplars of a category is a defining characteristic of a prototype category (Rosch 1973).

A single NP may even have some Agent Proto-role and some Patient Proto-role entailments. For example, when *frighten* psych-verbs have a change-of-state interpretation, their objects possess the Agent Proto-role entailment of sentience and the Patient Proto-role entailment of undergoing a change of state (Dowty 1991: 579–80). We return to these examples below. Finally, an argument of a verb need not be associated with any of these entailments. Although presumably every argument of a verb is associated with some entailment or presupposition imposed by its verb, Dowty stresses that there is no evidence that each such semantic restriction be associated with a recognized semantic role – or "L-thematic role" in his terms – which enters into generalizations concerning argument realization.

The proto-role approach to semantic roles is consistent with the observation that most recognized roles have what Dowty has perspicuously termed "unclear boundaries." This approach also solves the problem of generalizations that need to be stated over semantic roles of different grain-size (see section 2.2.1). Natural classes of arguments can be picked out by making reference to shared entailments; depending on the number of shared entailments, broader or narrower sets of arguments are picked out. Although for the purposes of subject and object selection, Dowty argues that only the broad categories he labels the Agent and Patient Proto-roles need be recognized, languages have other generalizations involving argument realization which refer to narrower semantic categories.

Dowty's basic motivation for introducing proto-roles is providing subject and object selection rules that have wide coverage and that overcome some of the problems facing rules formulated in terms of regular semantic roles. Dowty (1991: 576, (31)) proposes that for a given verb, the argument with the largest number of Agent Proto-role entailments is realized as the subject, and the one with the largest number of Patient Proto-role entailments is realized as object (his Argument Selection Principle). Thus, in *Chris built a house*, the builder is the subject since it has the volition, sentience, causation, and movement Agent Proto-role entailments, but no Patient Proto-role entailments, while the building is the object as it has several Patient Proto-role entailments: change, causally affected, incremental theme, stationary, and dependent existence (1991: 577). This approach explains why arguments which meet all the criteria for agenthood are always, in all languages, expressed as subjects in nonpassive sentences. This solid and overarching generalization must be expressed by any theory of argument realization. With three-place predicates, the nonsubject argument with the greater number of Patient Proto-role entailments is the direct object and the one with fewer Patient Proto-role entailments is an oblique or a prepositional object (Dowty 1991: 576, (33)).

Although we have referred to subject and object selection rules, it is important to stress that for Dowty, these rules represent not a step in a derivation, but rather constraints "on what kind of lexical predicates may exist in natural language, out of many imaginable ones" (1991: 576). A particular verb may "lexicalize", or determine, a particular pairing of semantic argument types and grammatical relations, but these pairings must conform to the "constraints" defined by the subject and object selection rules. In some sense, then, these rules define a set of possible verbs.

Dowty argues that his subject and object selection rules have broad applicability by showing that they can handle many widely discussed examples, such as *fear/frighten* verb pairs, the locative alternation, and several other less familiar instances of variable argument realization, including those characteristic of verbs of surface contact and motion such as *hit* and *kick* and so-called "partially symmetric interactive" predicates such as *hug* and *kiss* (e.g., Gleitman 1965; Gleitman et al. 1996; Lakoff and Peters 1969). To illustrate how Dowty's approach confronts some of the challenges of subject and object selection, we review its application to psych-verbs and partially symmetric interactive predicates.

As discussed in section 1.2, psych-verbs fall into two classes: the experiencer–subject *fear* verbs and the experiencer–object *frighten* verbs. Dowty (1991: 579–80, 586–87) points out that verbs of both types have an Agent Proto-role entailment associated with both their stimulus and their experiencer arguments: the sentience entailment for the experiencer and the causation entailment for the stimulus. Since no other proto-role entailments distinguish between the arguments of these verbs (on their stative use), the subject and object selection rules do not unambiguously determine which argument is subject and which object. Either a pairing of the experiencer with subject and stimulus with object or a pairing of stimulus with subject and experiencer with object is compatible with these rules, so that the appropriate pairing is determined verb-by-verb or, possibly, language-by-language. Dowty's approach explains why just this class of verbs allows different choices as to how particular verbs lexicalize the projection of their arguments. A further property of psych-verbs is at least compatible with, if not explained by, Dowty's approach: most *frighten* verbs systematically show an additional, nonstative change-of-state reading (e.g., *The loud noise frightened me*), as well as the previously discussed stative meaning (e.g., *Ghosts frighten me*); this reading is found with the comparable class of psych-verbs in other languages, an observation Dowty attributes to Croft (1986) (see also Croft [1993]). But when the experiencer is entailed to undergo a change of state, it is associated with a Patient Proto-role entailment, creating an asymmetry between the experiencer and stimulus, which forces the experiencer to be selected as object. (The *fear* verbs are consistently stative and never show this ambiguity.) As Dowty himself points out, the *frighten* verbs (on their stative use) also show a well-known range of peculiar syntactic properties (e.g., Giorgi 1983–84; Pesetsky 1987, 1995; Postal 1971). These properties are often given a syntactic explanation which builds on the assumption that the subject of these verbs is syntactically derived. Since Dowty assumes a monostratal syntactic analysis, he suggests that perhaps these unusual semantic properties can be attributed to another unusual property of these verbs: their object has the Agent Proto-role entailment of sentience (1991: 580–81, n. 23).

Dowty also uses his subject selection rule to explain certain complex facts involving partially symmetric interactive predicates (1991: 583–86). Such predicates show two patterns of argument realization in English and many other languages: they may have a subject in the form of a conjoined or a collective NP or they may have both a subject and an object (or sometimes a prepositional complement typically headed by *with*). For certain predicates, like *debate* and *play chess*, the alternate argument realizations are truth-conditionally equivalent (e.g., *Smith and Jones debated; Smith debated Jones*). For others, this need not be so: *Kim hugged Sandy* is not truth-conditionally equivalent to *Kim and Sandy hugged*, since in the second, but not the first, Sandy must be "agentively" involved in the action of hugging. For the same reason, *The drunk embraced the lamppost* is acceptable, but **The drunk and the lamppost embraced*, an example Dowty (1991: 583) attributes to Chomsky, is not. However, the difference between the two argument realization options cannot always be characterized in terms of the traditional notion of agency. An asymmetry in truth conditions also surfaces with the verb *collide: Pat and Terry collided* entails that both Pat and Terry were in motion, but *Pat collided with Terry* entails only that Pat was in motion (though it is compatible with Terry also being in motion). Here the difference involves motion with respect to another participant – another of Dowty's Agent Proto-role entailments. Presumably, the same entailment explains why *The truck and the lamppost collided* is odd, except as a description of a scene where a lamppost came loose and rolled down a hill, crossing the path of a moving truck.

A single generalization covers the *hug* and *collide* examples: when the alternate argument realizations differ in entailments, there is always an Agent Proto-role entailment which the denotation of the object (or the prepositional object) can lack, but which must hold for all subject denotations in the conjoined NP version. Whether or not there *can* be a difference in entailments seems to depend on the kind of activity denoted by the verb itself, but if the meaning of the verb does not force both arguments in the two-argument option to have exactly the same set of entailments, then the argument with more Agent Proto-role entailments is the subject and the other is a nonsubject. What is important is that the generalization which covers both options does not make reference to agency per se, but to the entailments constituting the Agent Proto-role, which, when distributed differentially over the arguments of a predicate, determine the realization of one argument as subject. It is precisely this kind of generalization which Dowty's theory is designed to handle.

Although Dowty is primarily interested in transitive verbs, he briefly addresses how his approach could be applied to intransitive verbs as part of a discussion of unaccusativity (1991: 605–13). He suggests that subject selection for one-argument intransitive verbs is trivial: every one-argument verb would simply have a subject. Unaccusative verbs would then be distinguished from unergative verbs without recourse to distinct syntactic analyses: unergative verbs have an argument with predominantly Agent Proto-role entailments, while unaccusative verbs have an argument with predominantly Patient Proto-role entailments. The morphosyntactic repercussions associated with the unaccusative/unergative distinction would be a result of some of the Agent and Patient Proto-role entailments being grammaticalized in some languages.[3]

Baker (1997) takes advantage of the basic properties of proto-roles in order to handle variation in subject choice with a given verb. As we discuss more extensively in section 6.2, often an argument bearing a particular semantic role may be chosen as a subject only in the absence of an argument bearing some other role; for instance, an instrument is never the subject in the presence of an agent, as Fillmore (1968: 33) notes, nor is a recipient ever the subject in the presence of an agent. Baker (1997: 11) suggests that such patterns arise due to variability in the proto-role associated with a given argument. In the presence of an agent, a recipient will not be analyzed as having the Agent Proto-role, but in the absence of an agent it can be. According to Baker, "the prototype theory says that certain participants in an event are less prone to being seen as agents than others are, but the one seen as an agent is always the subject" (1997: 110); such an approach would be impossible with traditional semantic roles.

Schlesinger (1995) presents another approach to using prototype notions in the definition of semantic roles, building on his previous work (1979, 1989, 1992). He deals with a wider range of semantic relations of arguments to verbs than Dowty does, and only gives prototype characterizations to some of them; again, one of his motivations is the ability to express argument realization generalizations concisely. Specifically, he introduces what he calls the A-CASE, which subsumes agents, as well as certain instruments, and, in contradistinction to Dowty's Agent Proto-role, certain patients.[4] The subsumption of patients under the A-case reflects its association with subject position, and Schlesinger's desire to subsume under it the subjects of the following examples, which would be characterized variously as agents, as in (3), patients, as in (4), and instruments, as in (5). (Since Dowty's concern is subject selection for transitive verbs this issue does not arise, and his discussion of unaccusativity suggests that he still characterizes the subjects of verbs such as those in (4) as having Patient Proto-role entailments.)

(3) a. The little boy threw the ball.
     b. They pushed the chair to the table.
     c. The girl drank her coffee.   (Schlesinger 1995: 31, (5))

(4) a. The butter melted in the sun.

    b. My little dog remained indoors all day long.

    c. The guard is standing near the entrance.   (Schlesinger 1995: 31, (6))

(5) The knife cut the cake.   (Schlesinger 1995: 92, (1))

Arguments bearing the A-case are associated with one or more of the following three features: CAUSE, CONTROL, and CHANGE. These features are reminiscent of entailments in Dowty's Agent Proto-role list. As Schlesinger (1995: 32) writes, "Dowty's properties 'causing,' 'volitional,' and 'movement' seem to correspond roughly to CAUSE, CONTROL, and CHANGE, respectively." However, the relationship between Dowty's notion of movement and Schlesinger's CHANGE needs some clarification. For Dowty, movement with respect to another participant is an Agent Proto-role property only in the absence of a cause (1991: 574); otherwise, undergoing a change of state is a Patient Proto-role entailment. Schlesinger, in contrast, does not impose such a restriction since CHANGE is included as an A-case feature in order to allow for patients bearing the A-case. Interestingly, Schlesinger does not propose a counterpart to Dowty's Patient Proto-role; he feels no single semantic characterization of object selection is possible, and though he does not mention this, most likely the statement of a unified object selection rule is rendered even more difficult because some patients need to come under his subject selection rule, rather than an object selection rule.

3.1.1.2 *Extensions and limitations*

Dowty's proto-role approach has proven widely attractive and has been adopted by many researchers (e.g., Aissen 1999; Alsina 1996; Aranovich 2000; Asudeh 2001; Filip 1996; Joshi 1993; Singh 1992; Zaenen 1993), including some who have refined and extended it (Ackerman and Moore 1999, 2001; Blume 1998; Davis 2001; Davis and Koenig 2000; Primus 1999). In joint work, Dowty even extends the proto-role approach to nominals (Barker and Dowty 1993). However, Dowty's (1991) paper itself is rather modest in scope. It does not integrate the proto-role approach into a larger theory of grammar, and so hardly deals with any issues relating to syntax. It provides an analysis of basic verbs, but not those that are the output of morphosyntactic rules which change valence, voice, or grammatical relations. Moreover, it is mainly motivated by English data and so does not deal with argument realization in languages with richer morphosyntax, which raise additional questions about argument realization (see section 1.6). It does not even present a specific theory of lexical semantic representation, and Dowty stresses that his approach is compatible with many other approaches (1991: 553); he merely shows how certain aspects of meaning – which can be represented in a variety of ways – are input to argument selection. We now present ways in which Dowty's theory has been extended to widen its scope and discuss some of its most serious limitations – limitations which often reflect its very nature. For further discussion see Croft

(1998: 36–38), Davis (2001: 61–73), Davis and Koenig (2000: 74–76), Koenig and Davis (2001: 80–84), Newmeyer (2002: 67–71), Primus (1999: 33–47), Tenny (1992: 21–22, 1994: 101–05), and Van Valin (1999: 386–88).

A major limitation is that Dowty's formulation of the proto-role approach presupposes a partial solution to the argument realization problem. The subject and object selection rules apply to verbs that are known to be transitive; they simply determine which argument is the subject and which the object, as also noted by Davis (2001: 64), Davis and Koenig (2000: 74), and Primus (1999: 47). Yet, this assumption is significant. As reviewed in section 1.5, crosslinguistically, verbs that fit the agent-act-on-patient mold – verbs whose arguments meet most, if not all, of the Agent Proto-role and Patient Proto-role entailments – are necessarily transitive, while there is substantial crosslinguistic variation in the transitivity of verbs that do not fit this mold. Furthermore, Dowty does not extend his system beyond transitives to two-argument intransitives. Yet, as Davis (2001: 65–66) and Davis and Koenig (2000: 74–75) point out, among two-argument intransitive verbs, the argument with the most Agent Proto-role entailments is realized as the subject and the other argument is realized as an oblique (e.g., *The magician relies on sleight of hand*) and not vice versa (e.g., *Sleight of hand relies on/by/of/with the magician*; Davis 2001: 66, (54a); Davis and Koenig 2000: 74, (23a)). If Dowty's approach is intended to include constraints on possible lexicalizations, it should be able to account for these generalizations. In fact, as Davis and Koenig (2000: 75) have pointed out, the very same semantic notions which figure in Dowty's theory of argument selection for transitive verbs are implicated with two-argument intransitive verbs. Dowty also does not provide an account of object selection for verbs showing the dative alternation, although, as discussed below, Primus (1999) introduces a Recipient Proto-role to deal with such verbs.[5]

A different sort of problem arises because all the entailments entering into each proto-role carry equal weight, yet, as Dowty himself acknowledges, this assumption is not uncontroversial. As he points out, "causation has priority over movement for distinguishing agents from patients" since movement is an Agent Proto-role entailment only when it is not caused by another participant, as in *The cloud passed the tree* as opposed to *John threw the ball* (1991: 574). Schlesinger makes a similar point, noting that "CAUSE has more weight than CHANGE when these two features compete" (1995: 47). Regarding the more general issue, Schlesinger explicitly proposes that "assignment to the A-case is determined by three factors: (i) the relative strength of the features; (ii) their number; and (iii) their differential weights" (1995: 45), while Dowty writes "I also would not rule out the desirability of 'weighting' some entailments more than others for purposes of argument selection" (1991: 574), though he does not pursue this issue. Ackerman and Moore (2001: 51), Davis (2001: 66–72), and Davis and Koenig (2000: 75–76) point out the primacy of the cause entailment. When an agentive verb is causativized in languages which allow productive morphological causativization, the new cause argument invariably becomes the subject of the derived causative predicate, regardless of the number of Agent Proto-role entailments carried by the subject argument of the base verb. For example, the introduced cause is the subject, even if the base verb requires that its subject – the causee – be sentient, as in *The frosty weather made her cough* or, even sentient and volitional, as in *The cold weather made her run faster*. Generalizing, Koenig and Davis (2001: 82–83) suggest a ranking of certain Proto-Agent entailments with respect to subject selection:

> for all verbs that denote causal events, the only proto-agent entailment that we need to consider is whether the participant causally affects another participant in the event ... Similarly, among non-causative verbs, sentience is sufficient to ensure mapping to subject ... Volitional involvement in the event is also sufficient to ensure mapping to subject position in non-causative verbs. Finally, for all verbs for which being in motion counts as a proto-agent entailment, the NP denoting the moving object is mapped onto subject position.

Researchers have also reexamined the relative importance of the Patient Proto-role entailments to argument realization. For example, Jackendoff (1996b: 314–15) argues that the incremental theme Patient Proto-role entailment – an entailment intended to pick out arguments with a special role in determining the time course of an event – does not have a part to play. We defer a full discussion of the success of this notion until the larger discussion of aspectual determinants of argument realization in section 4.2.

The question of the relative priority of various semantic features in subject and object selection has been raised previously by Tsunoda (1985) in a critique of Hopper and Thompson's (1980) prototype approach to transitivity. He points out that the semantic components of transitivity they propose do not all count equally, with "affectedness" of the object being crucial, while "volitionality" of the subject apparently being irrelevant. Tsunoda's discussion, taken together with the discussion of Dowty's proto-role entailments, suggests that the factors contributing to argument realization in transitive verbs may well be ranked. This possibility is perhaps not surprising since the components of prototype concepts have been shown to be differentially ranked; see Murphy (2002) for recent discussion and references. If the semantic ingredients entering into subject and object selection are indeed ranked, then another question arises: what is the source of the ranking? The most obvious answer is that there may be more organization to a lexical semantic representation than the prototype approach allows for. This additional organization is assumed by most researchers to be grounded at least partially in a theory of event types.

Finally, Dowty's approach suggests that all the semantic determinants of argument realization derive from the lexical entailments which verbs impose on their arguments and that only these entailments enter into assignment of grammatical relations to argument. However, the picture is more complicated. First, there are semantic properties relevant to argument realization which derive from sources other than the lexical entailments of verbs. Second, some semantic properties may affect the morphosyntactic realization of a grammatical relation, rather than the choice of grammatical relation. We discuss these complications in turn.

Some of Dowty's proto-role entailments may have their source not in the lexical entailments that a verb imposes on a particular argument, but in the choice of "filler" for that argument. Consider, for example, the dative verb *send*. This verb selects three arguments: the sender, the thing sent, and the goal of transfer. The goal need not be animate, as illustrated in *The factory sent the goods to the warehouse*. However, the goal can be realized as the first object in a double object construction only if animate, as in *The factory sent the contractor the goods*, or, at least, interpretable as a potential possessor, as in *The factory sent London the goods*, where *London* is understood metonymically as 'the people in the London office.' Thus, even though *send* does not lexically entail an animate goal, it appears that the animacy of the goal, which is determined by the filler of this semantic role, influences its morphosyntactic realization. It is, of course, possible to argue that there are two verbs *send*, each associated with a distinct realization of arguments and each imposing a distinct set of entailments on the goal. This polysemy view of the dative alternation is widespread (see chapter 7), and, indeed, Ackerman and Moore (2001) develop a theory of argument realization in which all such alternations are taken to reflect differences in lexical entailments. However, the question of whether dative verbs are monosemous or polysemous is far from settled (see B. Levin and Rappaport Hovav [2002] for arguments against the polysemy approach). It is at least worth investigating whether some semantic determinants of argument realization are derived from the properties of the fillers of argument positions and not only from lexical entailments of predicates. This position, argued for in Evans (1997), connects to the second issue raised above. Ackerman and Moore (2001) argue that the proto-role entailments associated with a particular argument can influence not only its grammatical relation, but also the morphosyntactic expression of this grammatical relation. They support this claim by pointing to languages in which proto-role entailments determine the assignment of an oblique case to an argument which is clearly a syntactic object. Evans (1997), in turn, points out that the properties of an NP bearing a particular semantic role – particularly, its animacy – influence the morphosyntactic encoding of the associated grammatical relation, rather than the choice of this grammatical relation.

Just as the inventory of semantic roles and the definitions of particular roles have been a matter of debate, so have the characterizations of Dowty's Agent and Patient Proto-roles. There have been attempts both to refine and to enlarge the sets of Agent and Patient Proto-role entailments. The most controversial of the Patient Proto-role entailments is the previously mentioned incremental theme entailment. Due to its limitations as a predictor of argument realization, Ackerman and Moore (2001: 97) propose an additional "bounding entity"

Patient Proto-role entailment (called "telic entity" in Ackerman and Moore [1999]), which is also aspectually based, but which identifies a somewhat different set of arguments. Turning now to the Agent Proto-role entailments, Primus (1999: 36–37) sees many of them as being entailments of what she calls a "control" relation, which is a reformulation of Dowty's volitionality entailment; see also Davis and Koenig (2000: 73). Davis and Koenig (2000: 72) propose an entailment "has a notion or perception of other participant(s) in event"; this entailment, which is inspired by the work of Wechsler (1995: 35–40), apparently replaces Dowty's sentience entailment. They also propose an additional Agent Proto-role entailment "possesses an entity" (2000: 72). The notion of possession plays a part in Primus' (1999: 54–55) suggestion that an additional, Recipient Proto-role is necessary to deal with object selection with dative verbs. This proto-role, which would be associated with recipient, addressee, and benefactive arguments, shares certain entailments with the Agent Proto-role and others with the Patient Proto-role. Attempts to reformulate, refine, and expand the list of proto-roles are not unexpected given that Dowty leaves open the source of the particular lexical entailments which are relevant for the assignment of the proto-roles and does not explain why just these entailments matter for argument realization. Dowty (1991: 601–04) does propose that these notions might have cognitive roots, figuring in a theory of the ontology of events, and has begun to explore this idea in subsequent research (Dowty 1998). In the absence of such a theory there is room for debate, just as there is in semantic role approaches in general.

As pointed out by Tenny (1994: 103), as Dowty's theory stands, it is an accident that the sets of Agent and Patient Proto-role entailments are what they are. For instance, why couldn't the incremental theme entailment have been associated with the Agent Proto-role and the volitional involvement entailment with the Patient Proto-role? Furthermore, as many, including Koenig and Davis (2001: 83), Croft (1998: 37), Primus (1999: 52–53), and even Dowty himself (1991: 574), note, some Agent Proto-role and Patient Proto-role properties are paired, such as the Agent Proto-role entailment "causing an event or change of state in another participant" and the Patient Proto-role entailment "undergoes change of state." These paired entailments identify participants in a semantic relation, so that one participant in the relation cannot exist without the second. Yet, there is nothing that would predict such coocurrences, let alone enforce their consequences. That is, there could, in principle, be an argument that causes a change of state without there being one that undergoes a change of state, contrary to fact. As Primus (1999: 52) notes, these pairings shed light on the convergence of certain sets of entailments as Agent or Patient Proto-role entailments. She writes, "Proto-Agents and Proto-Patients are ... distinguished ... only by their dependency relative to each other" (1999: 52) and argues that in each instance of paired entailments the Patient Proto-role entailment is dependent on the Agent Proto-role entailment it is paired with. The clustering of entailments as

Agent or Patient Proto-role entailments, then, to a large extent reflects a larger generalization.

Many of the proto-role entailments pick up on notions that figure in two major perspectives on event conceptualization reviewed in the next chapter. Some approaches to lexical semantic representations are based on "causal chain" representations of events, an approach reflected in the entailments involving causation, volition, and affectedness (see section 4.3). Others are based on temporal representations, as reflected in the incremental theme entailment. Tenny (1992: 21–22), for instance, proposes that the clusters of proto-role entailments follow from her Aspectual Interface Hypothesis, which builds on an aspectual model of event conceptualization. She argues that the Patient Proto-role entailments can be reduced to her aspectual notion of measure (see section 4.2.1). The fact that the Agent and Patient Proto-roles include entailments relevant to both causal and aspectual approaches may explain why the proto-role approach has the wide coverage that makes it so attractive.

In closing this section, we point out an important property of Dowty's proto-roles which distinguishes them both from traditional semantic roles and from other types of generalized semantic roles. As Davis (2001: 66), Davis and Koenig (2000: 74), and Van Valin (1999: 386–87) point out, Dowty's proto-roles are not "reified"; that is, they are not present in the grammatical representation of a sentence, nor does any grammatical process refer to them. As in most current theories of semantic roles, proto-roles figure only in the mapping from lexical semantics to syntax, and, furthermore, are considered to be composite notions, derived from more primitive properties or entailments. However, Dowty breaks with tradition in assuming that the entailments a verb imposes on an argument enter directly into a counting algorithm used to determine whether that argument may be realized as subject or object; he does not assign semantic roles to arguments as an intermediate stage in the mapping. In contrast, on the traditional view the entailments a verb imposes on an argument are used to determine that argument's semantic role, and then mapping rules determine its realization on the basis of this role.

As mentioned, Dowty (1991: 601–04) takes the proto-roles to instantiate important conceptual categories, prominent in cognitive development, but lacking an explicit role in the grammar. Therefore, the components of proto-roles differ in nature from the components of grammatical categories. Although the prototype approach shares with the feature decomposition approach the idea that semantic roles are not atomic, but can be decomposed into more basic components, it differs crucially from the feature decomposition approach both in assuming that the components are not jointly necessary and sufficient and in not taking these components themselves to be binary and discrete, dividing the world into classes with clear boundaries. An argument is either a subject or not a subject, but it is an agent to a greater or lesser degree. As Dowty (1991: 575) points out, binary features defining discrete classes have their place in the coding systems of phonology, morphology, and syntax, but not in the system relevant to our capacity to categorize happenings in the world as events. In this respect, Dowty's approach to generalized semantic roles differs from a second one, which we now turn to.

3.1.2 Role and Reference Grammar's macroroles

A second conception of generalized semantic roles is used in Role and Reference Grammar (RRG; Van Valin 1990, 1993b; Foley and Van Valin 1984; Van Valin and LaPolla 1997), where they are referred to as MACRO-ROLES. Van Valin and LaPolla describe macroroles as groupings of arguments which are treated alike in the grammar: "generalizations across argument-types found with particular verbs which have significant grammatical consequences" (1997: 140). Macroroles figure prominently in subject and object selection, and, therefore, it is not surprising that, just as Dowty posits two proto-roles for this purpose, RRG posits two macroroles, known as ACTOR and UNDERGOER. Though RRG's macroroles share many of the properties of proto-roles, nonetheless, they have a somewhat different place in the grammar, as Van Valin (1990, 1999, in press) points out.

RRG takes macroroles to be semantic neutralizations of finer-grained semantic roles. If individual verbs are associated with verb-specific semantic roles, such as giver, runner, shiner, breaker, and singer, then most of the familiar semantic roles such as agent, experiencer, recipient, patient, and theme, can be seen as medium-grained roles that generalize across some of these verb-specific semantic roles. For instance, agent generalizes across roles such as runner, giver, and singer. The macroroles Actor and Undergoer are generalizations across sets of medium-grained semantic roles whose prototypes are agent and patient, respectively. Roles such as agent, experiencer, instrument, recipient, source, and force are subsumed under the Actor macrorole, while patient, theme, stimulus, recipient, and location are subsumed under the Undergoer macrorole. This lumping is evident in the range of semantic roles that can be associated with the subject – the typical expression of the Actor – and the direct object – the typical expression of the Undergoer. Thus, instead of choosing the subject and direct object of a sentence by applying an algorithm directly to semantic roles such as agent, experiencer, or patient, RRG postulates an intermediate level of semantic role assignment – the assignment of macroroles.

RRG's macroroles differ from Dowty's proto-roles not so much with respect to their semantic conception, but rather with respect to the part they play in the grammar. Although RRG takes macroroles to be semantic rather than syntactic notions, many rules of grammar refer to them. In many ways, Actor and Undergoer, respectively, correspond to the traditional notions of underlying subject and object used in multistratal syntactic theories, such as the Principles and Parameters framework and Relational Grammar. In fact, Van Valin (1993b: 43–44) justifies the use of macroroles in the same way that traditional transformational grammar justifies positing underlying grammatical relations.

Thus, since the same range of argument types can be the object of a transitive verb and the subject of the corresponding passive verb, they ought to be associated with a single category in order to avoid reference to the same disjunction of semantic roles in more than one place in the grammar. Transformational grammar avoids this by assigning the semantic role types to the category of underlying direct object; however, since RRG is monostratal, it must achieve this in another way, making crucial use of the notion "macrorole." RRG associates the relevant set of argument types with the generalized semantic role Undergoer, which is then mapped onto the relevant morphosyntactic expression: in English, the direct object of an active verb and the subject of a passive verb. However, while in the Principles and Parameters framework and Relational Grammar the notion of underlying direct object is syntactic, the RRG notion of Undergoer is considered semantic.

In contrast to Dowty's proto-roles which are not "reified" (Davis and Koenig 2000: 74), RRG's macroroles are actually assigned to a verb's arguments, allowing rules of grammar to refer to them. For the purposes of assigning macroroles to the arguments of a verb, the semantic roles available to arguments are arranged along a hierarchy, with the most agentive roles at one end of the hierarchy and the most patient-like roles at the other. In early work in RRG, this hierarchy consisted of explicit semantic roles, taking the form in (6).

(6) Agent > Effector > Experiencer > Location > Theme > Patient

(Van Valin 1990: 226)

In more recent work (Van Valin in press; Van Valin and LaPolla 1997: 126–27) the semantic roles themselves are redefined as positions in predicate decomposition substructures (see section 3.2) and the hierarchy itself is redefined in terms of such substructures.

(7) Revised hierarchy:

Arg of	>	1st arg of	>	1st arg of	>	2nd arg of	>	Arg of state
DO		$do'(x,...)$		$pred'(x, y)$		$pred'(x, y)$		$pred'(x)$

In general, a two-argument verb in the active voice has two macroroles, with the Actor macrorole being assigned to the argument with the semantic role highest on the hierarchy, and the Undergoer macrorole being assigned to the argument with the semantic role lowest on the hierarchy. The placement of agent and patient at opposite ends of the hierarchy in (6) captures the fact that an agent is the unmarked choice for Actor, while a patient is the unmarked choice for Undergoer. Van Valin and LaPolla (1997: 150–54) discuss in some detail how the number of macroroles associated with a given verb is determined. Typically, a two-argument verb will have two macroroles, as mentioned above, and a one-argument verb will have one, though some systematic deviations from this assumption are recognized. RRG, then, has an explicit algorithm for determining transitivity, and does not presuppose that certain argument realization rules apply to verbs that are known to be transitive, as Dowty's approach does (see section 3.1.1), though it still lacks explanations for the systematic exceptions to macrorole assignment.[6]

Unlike Dowty (1991), Van Valin and LaPolla (1997) do not characterize the arguments filling positions in their lexical semantic representations and, hence, bearing specific semantic roles, in terms of lexical entailments. However, their algorithm for assigning Actor and Undergoer to a verb's arguments can be rather straightforwardly shown to pick out the arguments bearing the most Agent and Patient Proto-role entailments, respectively. As Dowty (1991: 578) notes in discussing a traditional thematic hierarchy, such as (6), the most highly ranked semantic roles have the most Agent Proto-role entailments, while the lowest-ranked roles have the most Patient Proto-role entailments. Specifically, all arguments in the hierarchy from experiencer up have some Agent Proto-role entailments, with the two most salient entailments being causation and sentience. The arguments below experiencer lack both these entailments. The patient has the most Patient Proto-role entailments, the most salient being causally affected and undergoing a change. (It also often has the incremental theme entailment.) In fact, Dowty (1991: 578) views the thematic hierarchy as an artifact of his proto-role approach precisely because of this distribution of entailments. Although Van Valin and LaPolla (1997) formulate the macrorole assignment algorithm in terms of positions in predicate decompositions, the positions in the decompositions reduce to the very same properties encoded in Dowty's proto-role entailments. The generalizations governing subject choice formulated by Koenig and Davis (2001: 82–83), which were mentioned in the previous section, can be recast in terms of positions in the revised RRG thematic hierarchy in (7). For example, the argument of DO and the first argument of **do**′ tend to be volitionally involved in the event or to be causes, while the first argument of **pred**′(x,y) tends to be sentient. Since the arguments of DO and **do**′ are the highest on the hierarchy, this captures the generalization that causation is the ultimate determinant of subject choice, with something akin to sentience determining choice of subject when causation does not enter into the picture.

RRG's macroroles, being reified, have a different status than Dowty's proto-roles. Van Valin and LaPolla integrate their theory of macroroles into a fully articulated theory of sentence structure and, concomitantly, show how the macroroles figure in a wide range of linguistic phenomena. They argue, for example, that in some languages, the relation between an anaphor and its antecedent should be formulated with reference to macroroles (1997: 279), that applicative constructions involve an alternate choice of Undergoer (1997: 337), and that many rules of case assignment make reference to the notions of Actor and Undergoer (1997: 352–76). Van Valin criticizes Dowty's proto-role approach for the status it assigns proto-roles: they are "simply generalizations about subject- and object-selection properties of verbs" (1999: 386) and are not notions that grammatical rules can make reference to. Therefore, the association of such a category with a given syntactic constituent can be indeterminate, following from the fuzzy nature of the category. In RRG, in contrast, this is not possible, as a macrorole must either be or not be associated with a constituent. As Van Valin himself points out, RRG differs from most other theories in this respect, since most other theories restrict the use of semantic roles to the mapping between lexical semantics and syntax, as an expression of autonomy of syntax, a notion which RRG explicitly rejects.

Macroroles are used to provide an interface between semantic notions and grammatical notions, though their status as syntactic or semantic entities needs further clarification. Van Valin and LaPolla (1997; Van Valin 2002) take the locative alternation and certain other well-known argument alternations to be semantic in nature. In RRG, most alternations are taken to arise from alternate choices of arguments as Undergoer, rather than, say, alternate assignments of grammatical relations to arguments. This position receives support from Dowty's recent work (2000, 2001), which draws attention to the semantic motivation behind the alternate argument realization options available to a single verb. Ironically, although RRG stresses the semantic nature of argument alternations, the same predicate decomposition underlies the alternate argument realization options of individual verbs (1997: 141). So locative alternation verbs have a single lexical semantic representation, and the different argument realizations reflect alternate choices of arguments in this representation as Undergoer (1997: 145). That is, the semantic content of each argument of an alternating verb remains constant since it is actually determined by its place in the predicate decomposition that constitutes the lexical semantic representation of the alternating verb (1997: 141).

In sum, RRG's macroroles are similar to Dowty's proto-roles in that both are derived notions with no invariant semantic entailments associated with them. What emerges as a consensus is that the individual semantic components associated with arguments are the ultimate determinants of argument realization. Dowty and Van Valin disagree as to whether or not there are composite categories such as Actor or Agent Proto-role and Undergoer or Patient Proto-role which, as categories, play a role either in the mapping to syntax or in other grammatical phenomena. The choice between these options depends on many assumptions in the larger approach to grammar.

3.2   Predicate decompositions and event structures

Some lexical semanticists have explored yet another way to surmount the problems and limitations of semantic roles. As in generalized semantic role approaches, they take the semantic determinants of argument realization to derive from verb meanings, but instead of decomposing semantic roles, the meanings of verbs themselves are decomposed into more basic elements, as assumed, for instance, in RRG. Such representations usually take the form of a

PREDICATE DECOMPOSITION – a representation of meaning formulated in terms of one or more primitive predicates chosen to represent components of meaning that recur across significant sets of verbs. For example, a primitive predicate CAUSE is often posited as the element common to the predicate decompositions of all lexically causative verbs, including transitive *break, open*, and *dry*.

The predicate decomposition approach is most extensively elaborated in the work of Jackendoff (1976, 1983, 1990b) and more recently in Role and Reference Grammar (Van Valin and LaPolla 1997) and in the work of Croft (1990, 1991, 1993, 1994, 1998); it is also discussed in Foley and Van Valin (1984), Rappaport and B. Levin (1988), Rappaport, B. Levin, and Laughren (1988), Rappaport Hovav and B. Levin (1998a), and Wunderlich (1997a, 1997b, 2000), among others. The idea that verb meanings can be decomposed into basic components is pursued by researchers working in various contexts. Generative semanticists (Lakoff 1968, 1970; McCawley 1968, 1971; Ross 1972) explicitly introduce primitive predicates into semantico-syntactic structures in order to capture various entailment relations, including relations between sets of sentences containing morphologically – and, thus, semantically – related words. For example, the facts that transitive/intransitive pairs such as *Marshall cooled the soup* and *The soup cooled* share the entailment 'The soup was cool' and that the same selectional restrictions hold for the object of the transitive verb and the subject of the intransitive verb are accounted for by positing a shared component of meaning, something like 'BE COOL.' This goal is adopted by others who propose predicate decompositions, among them Dowty (1979) and Jackendoff (1976). Another line of research, represented again by Dowty (1979) and also by Parsons (1990) and von Stechow (1995, 1996), exploits the primitive predicates of the generative semanticists, introducing them into the logical structure of sentences to account for interactions between event types and various tense operators and temporal adverbials. As we discuss in sections 4.2.2 and 5.1, more recently the elements of predicate decompositions have made their way back into syntactic structures, through the use of multiple so-called "VP-shells" (Larson 1988) – VPs whose heads correspond to the primitive predicates of lexical decompositions (Arad 1998, 1999, 2002; Hale and Keyser 1992, 1993, 1997a, 1997b, 1998, 2002; Erteschik-Shir and Rapoport 1996, 2004; Harley and Noyer 2000; Marantz 1997).

In most predicate decompositions, the primitive predicates are argument-taking functions, so that a verb's arguments are represented by the open argument positions associated with the predicates. This move allows semantic roles to be defined with respect to the argument positions of particular primitive predicates, making them explicitly derived notions, following a suggestion by Jackendoff (1972: 39). For example, assuming that the predicate CAUSE takes two arguments, an entity and an event brought about by that entity, the agent role is commonly defined as the first argument of this predicate (Jackendoff 1972: 39). Furthermore, rules of argument realization can be formulated in terms of the geometry of the predicate decomposition; that is, they might refer to the notion "first argument position of the predicate CAUSE" or even "first argument position of the predicate" rather than the semantic role "agent." As we discuss in chapters 5 and 6, there may be real advantages to formulating these rules in this way.

The number of commonly posited semantic roles is typically greater than the number of argument positions available in the most often postulated predicate decompositions. This discrepancy has two sources. First, certain semantic roles are actually associated with "adjuncts" and, thus, cannot be defined with respect to predicate decompositions, which are designed to be representations of verb meanings. Second, the argument positions in a predicate decomposition may actually correspond to semantic notions that are coarser in grain-size than the average semantic role. Although, as just mentioned, the notion "agent" is often defined in terms of the first argument position of CAUSE, this characterization may be too narrow. Only some verbs taking agent arguments are causative, and, conversely, the first argument of verbs whose decomposition is taken to include CAUSE need not be an agent in the narrow sense, but corresponds to a broader notion that encompasses not only agent, but also various types of causes and even certain instruments. Thus, this argument position of CAUSE is more like the "immediate cause" mentioned in section 2.2.1 or Van Valin and D. Wilkins' "effector", which they define as "the dynamic participant doing something in an event" (1996: 289). Certain more familiar, finer-grained roles can still be defined by referring to this position in combination with properties of its filler; for example, the agent role would be associated with this position when its filler is animate, sentient, and volitional. Assuming, then, that transitive *burn* is associated with a decomposition containing the predicate CAUSE, the agentivity of the subject in *Martha deliberately burned the chicken* would arise not from the decomposition representing the verb's own meaning, but from the nature of the NP which fills the first argument position of the predicate CAUSE. For other appropriately defined choices of filler, the same position would be the source of a cause or instrument role, as in *The intense heat burned the chicken* or *The malfunctioning oven burned the chicken*, respectively (Baker 1997: 109–10; Van Valin and D. Wilkins 1996). Other familiar semantic roles, such as experiencer or perceiver (Van Valin and LaPolla 1997), are labels for certain positions in predicate decompositions that share some other property – perhaps derived from some more narrowly defined facet of the meaning of verbs.

Since verbs individuate and name events (see section 1.4), theories of predicate decomposition are often taken to be theories of the basic event types. That is, such theories posit a limited inventory of linguistically relevant event types, which are available to speakers for describing happenings in the world. Two basic questions arise. First, what are the possible internal structures of EVENT STRUCTURES, as the representations developed in these theories are commonly called? Second, what semantic properties of events organize event types into grammatically relevant subclasses? These two questions are, in principle, independent. Two theories could agree on the structure of the lexical semantic representation, but disagree on the semantic properties defining the grammatically relevant event types, or, alternatively, they could agree on the event types, but not on the structure of the representation. Therefore, we consider these questions independently. We devote the remainder of this chapter to the first question. We provide an overview of those lexical semantic representations collectively called event structures, identifying the properties common to the various instantiations of these representations. The next chapter is devoted to the second question, which we address under the rubric of event conceptualization, because, as we discuss there, the most successful attempts to identify and delimit the grammatically relevant event types organize them around certain modes of conceptualizing happenings in the world as linguistic event types.

Early discussions of event structures focused on the primitive predicates that define the space of possible event structures, but event structure representations typically involve a second type of basic building block which represents the "idiosyncratic" element of a verb's meaning. Its function is best demonstrated with an example. Verbs of change of state in their causative use have predicate decompositions consisting of predicates representing the notions of cause and change; however, these verbs differ with respect to the specified state. One way to express this is to allow the predicate representing the change to take an argument representing the state, which can then be associated with distinct individual states. Representations for three causative change-of-state verbs are given in (8); the state relevant to each verb is given in capital italics and placed within angle brackets.

(8) a. *dry*: [[x ACT] CAUSE [y BECOME <*DRY*>]]
   b. *open*: [[x ACT] CAUSE [y BECOME <*OPEN*>]]
   c. *shorten*: [[x ACT] CAUSE [y BECOME <*SHORT*>]]

Individual verb meanings, then, are represented by primitive predicates together with an idiosyncratic element of meaning.

The idea that idiosyncratic information should be distinguished from the primitive predicates is now widely accepted, although it has been instantiated in somewhat different ways and the two components of meaning have been given various names. In earlier work we called the idiosyncratic element the "constant" since it is represented by a constant in a predicate decomposition (B. Levin and Rappaport Hovav 1995; Rappaport Hovav and B. Levin 1998a, 1998b; see also Hale and Keyser 1997b: 35); however, the accepted term is now "root," following Pesetsky (1995). Therefore, we use this term in the remainder of the book.

A root's most important property is its ontological type. There is a small set of these types, which include state, stuff, thing, place, manner, and instrument. Most roots have a single ontological type, though some may have more than one. As Rappaport Hovav and B. Levin (1998a) point out, a root's ontological type largely determines its basic association with an event structure type. These associations can be expressed using "canonical realization rules" (Rappaport Hovav and B. Levin 1998a), such as those in (9), which give rise to the event structures for *dry* in (10a) and *bottle* in (10b). In the event structure templates given to the right of the arrows in the canonical realization rules in (9), the ontological type of the associated root is indicated in angle brackets; it is filled by the actual root when these templates are instantiated for particular verbs, as in (10). (The representations in these examples are inspired by those in Rappaport Hovav and B. Levin [1998a], but other notations are possible.)

(9) a. externally caused state →

[[x ACT] CAUSE [y BECOME <*STATE*>]]

b. place →

[[x ACT] CAUSE [y BECOME IN <*PLACE*>]]

(10) a. *dry*: [[x ACT] CAUSE [y BECOME <*DRY*>]]

b. *bottle*: [[x ACT] CAUSE [y BECOME IN <*BOTTLE*>]]

Roots may be integrated into event structures in two ways. A root may fill an argument position associated with a primitive predicate; such roots appear in the appropriate position in the event structure, as in (10a) or (10b). Alternatively, a root may serve as a modifier of a predicate (Rappaport Hovav and B. Levin 1998a, 1998b); a modifier root is notated as a subscript to this predicate in the event structure, as in (11).

(11) *jog*: [x ACT$_{<JOG>}$]

What kind of verbs have modifier roots? As the example suggests, such roots might be appropriate for verbs of manner of motion, such as *walk, run, skip*, and *jog*, which differ in the manner in which the motion activity takes place. Since manners can be viewed as modifiers of activity predicates, a root of ontological type "manner" is represented as a modifier.[7] In fact, many modifier roots are of ontological type "manner."

Predicate decompositions are constructed so that verbs belonging to the same semantic class have decompositions with common substructures, with roots of the same ontological type filling the same position in these substructures. For example, manner of motion verbs all share the basic event structure template illustrated with *jog* in (11), consisting of the predicate ACT and a manner root. Broad semantic classes of verbs, then, are defined as those sharing a predicate decomposition. If the decompositions are chosen appropriately, the members of these classes will share syntactically salient properties, including those relevant for determining argument realization. The class of causative change-of-state verbs discussed above, for example, is a grammatically relevant semantic class since, as shown in numerous studies, these verbs share a range of grammatical properties (Fillmore 1970; Rappaport Hovav and B. Levin 1998a, 2002; see also sections 2.1 and 4.2.4). In this way, the substructures defined over the primitive predicates and pairings of substructures with roots of particular ontological types are instances of what in previous chapters we have called the "grammatically relevant aspects of meaning."

In much of the literature on event structure there is at least a tacit assumption that primitive predicates alone determine the grammatical behavior of predicates (Grimshaw 1993; K. P. Mohanan, T. Mohanan, and Wee 1999: 6–7; Pinker 1989: 166–67). However, it appears that this assumption is not correct. Consider, for example, the verbs *smear* and *splash*, mentioned in section 1.3. As reviewed there, Hale and Keyser (1993: 89, 1997b: 53–55, 1999: 60–63) point out that these two verbs presumably belong to the same broad class of verbs of causative change of location and, thus, should have the same predicate decomposition, yet only *splash* shows the causative alternation and *smear* does not.

(12) a. We splashed mud on the wall.
    b. Mud splashed on the wall.   (Hale and Keyser 1997: 53, (40))

(13) a. We smeared mud on the wall.
    b. *Mud smeared on the wall.   (Hale and Keyser 1997: 53, (41))

These verbs describe the placing of stuff on a surface, with individual verbs, differing in the manner in which the stuff is placed and in the resulting configuration of the stuff with respect to the surface (Dowty 1991; Pinker 1989). Hale and Keyser argue that the core meaning of *splash* imposes constraints on the nature of the stuff and the distribution of this stuff with respect to the surface; so its meaning only refers to the result state. In contrast, they argue that *smear* also describes something about the means or manner in which a certain type of stuff comes to be on the surface, and "that aspect of the event as a whole is attributed to the entity which carries out the action" (1997b: 54). Its meaning, then, further specifies the action of the agent leading up to the result state, and they attribute the infelicity of the causative alternation to a requirement that the agent's activity, and hence the agent, be expressed. This analysis fits into the more general picture which B. Levin and Rappaport Hovav (1995) draw with respect to verbs describing externally caused changes of state or location, such as *break* and *slide* (see section 1.2). Verbs in this class typically show the causative alternation; however, as discussed in B. Levin and Rappaport Hovav (1995), Smith (1970), and van Voorst (1995), some class members do not alternate, including *murder, assassinate, dent,* and *pasteurize* in the change-of-state class and *remove, stow,* and *immerse* in the change-of-location class. Presumably, these nonalternating verbs have largely the same event structure as *dry* or *break*, and it is the nature of their root that prevents "detransitivization," just as the nature of *smear*'s root prevents its detransitivization. This property may reflect a general requirement on the pairing of roots with event structures that the minimal elements of meaning encoded in the roots be given structural expression in the event structures (Rappaport and B. Levin 1988: 109). These examples represent just one instance of recent research which underscores the importance of studying the contribution of the root to the grammatical properties of verbs.

In what way are predicate decompositions superior to representations of verb meaning based on semantic roles?[8] There is an implicit assumption that it is easier to delimit a small set of grammatically relevant primitive predicates than it is to delimit a small set of grammatically relevant semantic roles. Indeed, relatively small sets of overlapping primitive predicates recur in various proposed systems of predicate decomposition, and the number of predicates is smaller than the number of semantic roles suggested in the literature. We have already shown how some traditional semantic roles can be defined with respect to argument positions associated with a primitive predicate, together with properties associated with the fillers of these positions. To the extent that argument realization is sensitive to the distinction between roles defined with respect to a primitive predicate alone and those whose definition also depends on properties of the fillers of the role as well, as we suggest it is in sections 4.2.3 and 6.4.2, then lexical semantic representations which make this distinction are preferable.

The primitive predicates which surface again and again include ACT/DO, CAUSE, BECOME, GO, BE, STAY, and LET. However, proposed sets of primitive predicates differ in size much more than is typically acknowledged. Although Jackendoff (1972) suggests that all verb meanings can be represented using just five predicates, later he (1990b) increases the number significantly, recognizing predicates such as ORIENT, EXTEND, EXCHANGE, REACT, MOVE, FORM, and CONFIGURE; furthermore, he augments many of these predicates with diacritics. Jackendoff introduces additional predicates because many classes of verbs which would be given similar decompositions if the set of predicates were limited, in fact, differ with respect to their syntactic properties and their potential extended meanings. Once predicates begin to proliferate, theories of predicate decompositions encounter the same problems as theories of semantic roles: identifying a small, well-motivated set of primitive elements (Carter 1976, 1978; Wilks 1987). Some of the distinctions which Jackendoff (1990b) tries to make by introducing additional predicates and annotating predicates with diacritics might be traced back to differences in the type of associated root, and the diacritics, at least, might be attributed to the roots. If so, differences among verbs in argument realization options could be traced to differences in the ways that their roots pair up with event structure types. In fact, Jackendoff's (1990b) own argument realization rules make reference to fewer distinctions than his decompositions allow. Positing an appropriate set of primitive predicates necessitates grounding the set within a theory of event conceptualization, the topic of the next chapter.

In what way are predicate decompositions superior to lexical semantic representations based on a set of undifferentiated lexical entailments of the sort employed in Dowty's proto-roles (1991)? Both types of representations derive the content of semantic roles from verb meanings, overcoming a major shortcoming of semantic roles. The semantic content of the primitive predicates can most likely be translated into entailments similar to those that Dowty associates with his proto-roles. However, there are differences. First, an approach that uses lexical entailments does not make a principled distinction between that part of a verb's meaning that falls under the notion "root" and that part that falls under the notion "event structure." To the extent that this distinction facilitates the statement of generalizations, the approach which makes this distinction is preferable. Second, predicate decompositions contain information which cannot be derived from a list of arguments classified in terms of lexical entailments. By their very nature predicate decompositions encode relations between arguments; therefore, they help explain why certain arguments coocur, while others do not, a problem raised in section 3.1.1.2. Finally, the function–argument form of a predicate decomposition represents the SUBEVENTUAL analysis of an event – it indicates the constituent subevents and their properties – and, in turn, defines relations among the arguments.[9] Proto-role analyses do not distinguish among the events denoted by verbs in terms of their internal complexity. In section 4.2.5 we review evidence that a subeventual analysis figures in argument realization generalizations, supporting a lexical semantic representation that allows for this added structure. Furthermore, as we discuss in sections 4.2.5, 5.2.2, and 6.4.1, the hierarchical relations among arguments which the subeventual analysis defines are appealed to in some theories of argument realization, yet such relations cannot be defined in a proto-role analysis which simply associates sets of entailments with arguments. If reference to this hierarchical organization is necessary, then a lexical semantic representation which defines the relevant structure is clearly preferable.

3.3 Conclusion

A consensus has emerged from research into grammatically relevant lexical semantic representations: to the extent that semantic roles figure in argument realization generalizations, they are to be considered both nonatomic and derived notions. There is also considerable agreement that grammatical relations cannot be associated in any simple manner with unified semantic notions. This chapter has reviewed two developments in the theory of lexical semantic representation which are meant to capture these insights: generalized semantic roles and predicate decompositions. Although these have been discussed separately, some approaches, such as Role and Reference Grammar and the work of Davis and Koenig (2000) within Head-Driven Phrase Structure Grammar, employ lexical semantic representations which make use of both predicate decompositions and generalized semantic roles.

The survey of types of lexical semantic representations in this chapter and the preceding one has also revealed that the semantic notions which figure in argument realization are derived largely from the properties of the events which verbs describe. Therefore, a theory of the semantic determinants of argument realization needs to be grounded in a theory of event conceptualization – the topic of the next chapter.

Notes

1 The pervasiveness and importance of prototype concepts is brought out in the extensive psychological studies on human categorization by Rosch and her associates (1973; Rosch and Mervis 1975). The idea of bringing prototype concepts into this area of linguistic description seems to have originated in Lakoff (1977). Lakoff specifies properties of prototypical sentences with agent–patient verbs, and many of the prototypical entailments of agents and patients adopted by Dowty (1991) derive directly from a Lakoff-style description of such sentences. Another early attempt at casting the semantic notions entering into argument realization in terms of prototypes is found in Hopper and Thompson's (1980) proposal that transitivity should be conceived of as a prototype notion; this proposal is accompanied by a listing of the semantic factors associated with a prototypical transitive sentence. In this spirit, Langacker (1990: 219–26, 1993: 486–97) explicitly recognizes "conceptual archetypes" which underlie the notions of subject and object of a transitive verb. (See Rice [1987a, 1987b] and Taylor [1989: 206–15] for further developments of this idea.) The type of complexity associated with the notions of patient and, particularly, agent that favors a prototype approach to semantic roles is brought out in the work of Cruse (1973), Fillmore (1977b: 102), and Grimes (1975).

2 Not all linguists who agree with Dowty that semantic roles are prototype notions agree with him that their source is in the lexical entailments of verbs. In approaches associated with cognitive grammar, a particular construal of a happening can determine the semantic role borne by an argument, even though different construals may not involve different lexical entailments.

3 The larger issue of whether unaccusativity should be treated semantically, as Dowty does, or syntactically is complicated; see Dowty (1991: 605–13), as well as B. Levin and Rappaport Hovav (1995), C. Rosen (1984), and Van Valin (1990) for extensive discussion.

4 Besides the A-case, Schlesinger (1989, 1995: 70–75) introduces the C-case, a proto-role which has no analogue in Dowty (1991). This role subsumes NPs that would traditionally be said to bear the instrument, comitative, or manner roles; these semantic roles are all expressed as objects of the preposition *with* in English. As far as we know, Schlesinger's C-case is the only generalized semantic role that is not motivated by the special status of subject and object. Nevertheless, the wide range of semantic notions expressed as objects of *with*, as well as the apparent use of this preposition to indicate noncanonically realized or "displaced" themes (Rappaport and B. Levin 1988), as in *spray the wall with paint*, make *with* objects not unlike subjects and objects.

5 Dowty (1991: 597, n.36) only briefly mentions the dative alternation, suggesting that the animacy of the recipient may be implicated in the availability of two possible argument realizations for dative verbs. There is no indication that he would handle this alternation by introducing a Recipient Proto-role, as Primus does.

6 In RRG, there are no grammatical relations corresponding to the traditional notions of "subject" and "object." The traditional properties of a subject are split between the argument analyzed as a "syntactic pivot" and a "syntactic controller," selected on a construction-specific and language-specific basis. In syntactically accusative languages, the Actor is the unmarked choice for the "privileged syntactic argument," which will be the pivot or controller in most constructions. Voice modulations can

alter the choice of pivot and controller, as when the passive forces the choice of Undergoer as pivot or controller.

7 In our event structure for an activity verb, a primitive predicate ACT is modified by a manner root, as in (11), an analysis which contrasts with Hale and Keyser's (1993, 2002) analysis of comparable verbs, which treats the root as the argument of a predicate DO, roughly comparable to ACT, as in [x DO <*JOG*>]. This other approach receives apparent support from Basque and some other languages, where the counterparts of activity verbs are expressed periphrastically using the verb meaning 'do' plus a noun (B. Levin 1989). We do not choose between approaches here, since additional investigation into the representation of such verbs is needed.

8 Predicate decompositions allow a solution to a problem raised in section 2.2.2: unifying the various instantiations of path found with motion verbs (e.g., *to the library, from the cafeteria, through the woods*), which are assigned distinct "traditional" semantic roles. In his predicate decompositions, Jackendoff (1983) recognizes a conceptual category of path, which consists of a path function and a reference object; since the path function has internal structure it provides a unified representation of all types of paths. Jackendoff then analyzes verbs of motion as based on a two-place primitive predicate GO, which takes theme and path arguments.

9 Much of the work which takes a mereological approach to aspectual classification (Hinrichs 1985; Krifka 1992, 1998) also assumes that verbs can denote events with subeventual structure (see section 4.2.1); however, this work is concerned with the analysis of the aspectual notion of telicity, rather than with argument realization.

4

Three conceptualizations
of events

In the previous chapter, we pointed out that the term "event structure" is now widely used to refer to the lexical semantic representation which determines argument realization. This term reflects a consensus that such representations encode properties of events. Nonetheless, there are fundamental differences among the representations that have been proposed. Many of these stem from alternative hypotheses about which semantic properties of events influence argument realization and, thus, are central to the organization of event structure. Our goal in this chapter is to delineate theories concerning these semantic properties. Semantic properties of events are shown to be relevant for the organization of event structure to the extent that the subclasses of events which they define share identifiable grammatical properties. We present a discussion of these properties under the rubric of theories of event conceptualization since a hypothesis about what facets of an event are grammatically relevant is a hypothesis about how language users conceptualize happenings in the world for linguistic encoding. It is reasonable to assume that those properties of events that are grammatically relevant are also cognitively salient in some pretheoretically intuitive way (B. Levin and Pinker 1991) and that such properties should find their way into semantic representations.

As we review in this chapter, broadly speaking, three ways of conceptualizing events have been proposed to be grammatically relevant; each focuses on a distinct cognitively salient facet of events. The first, the localist approach, highlights the notions of motion and location. The second, the aspectual approach, suggests that the temporal properties of events, including their mereological (part–whole) structure, are central. In the third, the causal approach, notions such as "causal chains" of event participants and "transmission of force" between these participants play a major role. We examine these proposals concerning event conceptualization and, for each one, illustrate the types of lexical semantic representations proposed to encode the relevant facets of an event. Although these representations are not always developed to account for argument realization, it is possible to compare how each fares in this respect. Our primary concern is how well each does in determining the subject and direct object of a verb, and, to a certain extent, the morphosyntactic expression of the subject and object. We briefly address predictions concerning the realization of arguments as obliques; for fuller studies in several theoretical frameworks of this question see Croft (1991), Jolly (1993), Markantonatou and Sadler (1995), and Wechsler (1995). We also consider how each approach deals with argument alternations. There are several versions of each approach, and as we cannot review all in detail, we focus on what is common to most instantiations of a particular approach, paying specific attention to those properties which have gained currency in recent research. Following the exposition of the three approaches, we conclude the chapter with a brief comparative evaluation.

4.1 The localist approach

An early attempt at introducing organizing principles to provide a logic underlying the assignment of semantic roles is found in the work of Gruber (1965), who develops an explicitly localist approach to the representation of events. The basic claims behind this approach are that events involving motion and location in space are central to the construal of all events and that the machinery used for representing motion and location events is harnessed for the description of events which are not obviously events of spatial motion and location. It is Jackendoff (1972, 1976, 1983, 1987, 1990b) who formalizes and most fully develops the localist approach to event structure representation, so we illustrate it with reference to his work, but see the work of J. M. Anderson (1971, 1977) for another localist approach, and van Voorst (1993) for an analysis which combines facets of the causal and localist approaches. Although Jackendoff's earliest work in this domain makes use of semantic role lists (1972), he early on adopted a predicate decomposition approach to lexical semantic representation, though the use of predicate decompositions is not necessary for the development of a localist approach. Indeed, Anderson's approach, which is more strictly localist than Jackendoff's, makes use of semantic role lists, using roles that are defined in terms of combinations of features.

As just stated, the notion of location is the central organizing concept in the localist approach. There are two major types of events: motion and location events; each type has its own set of participants. Location events involve a thing and a location (e.g., *The vase sat on the shelf*), while motion events involve a thing and the path that it travels along (e.g., *The truck went from the warehouse to the store*). The moving or located entity is known as the THEME (see section 2.4), and given the definition of the two event types, every event must have a theme. Jackendoff further distinguishes between two types of locational verbs: those which describe states (e.g., the verb *be* and all stative verbs) and those which, like motion verbs, are eventive (e.g., the verbs *remain* and *stay* when predicated of animates). The predicates GO, BE, and STAY, respectively, are used to represent motional verbs and the two types of locational verbs – stative and nonstative. Jackendoff also recognizes the existence of causative events that embed events of each of these three types. The (b) and (c) sentences in (1) are both causatives that embed the motion event in the (a) sentence.

(1) a. The rock fell from the roof to the ground.
    b. Linda lowered the rock from the roof to the ground.
    c. Linda dropped the rock from the roof to the ground.

(Jackendoff 1976: 104, (35))

Recognizing that the (b) and (c) sentences differ in the type of causation involved, Jackendoff proposes that the (b) and (c) sentences, respectively, exemplify what he calls causative and permissive agency; the former can be paraphrased with *make* or *cause* and the verb *fall* (e.g., 'Linda made the rock go down from the roof to the ground'), while the latter can be paraphrased with *let* and *fall* (e.g., 'Linda let the rock go down from the roof to the ground'). Consequently, Jackendoff introduces two distinct causative primitive predicates, CAUSE and LET. (See Jackendoff [1990b] for further refinements of the typology of causatives, building on Talmy's [1988] work on "force dynamics.")

The main claim of the localist approach is the Localist Hypothesis: all verbs are construable as verbs of motion or location. Specifically, Jackendoff proposes that even verbs that are not obviously verbs of motion or location can be construed as describing motion or location of an abstract type. In implementing this idea, Jackendoff recognizes a range of abstract semantic fields, setting up correspondences between the components of motion and location situations in what he calls the positional field – the field representing the most basic type of location, physical location – and the comparable components of more abstract fields. Jackendoff (1983) articulates this claim in his Thematic Relations Hypothesis (TRH), cited in (2).

(2) Thematic Relations Hypothesis:
    In any semantic field of events and states, the principal event, state, path, and place functions are a subset of those used for the analysis of spatial motion and location.
    Fields differ in only 3 possible ways:
    – what sorts of entities may appear as theme
    – what sorts of entities may appear as reference objects (i.e., locations)
    – what kind of relation assumes the role played by location in the field of spatial expressions.   (Jackendoff 1983: 188)

For example, the possessional field represents relations of possession, and in this field themes are possessed entities and locations are their possessors, so that the TRH is fulfilled as in (3).

(3) Alienable possession:
  a. [THINGS] appear as theme.
  b. [THINGS] appear as reference object.
  c. Being alienably possessed plays the role of location; that is "y has/possesses x" is the conceptual parallel to spatial "x is at y."

(Jackendoff 1983: 192, (10.9))

Other fields include the identificational and temporal fields. The identificational field is used in the description of states; in this field, themes are entities that can be in particular states and locations represent states. The temporal field is used to locate events in time: events and states appear as themes, and their time of occurrence is construed as an abstract location. The examples below illustrate BE, GO, and CAUSE verbs in several abstract fields.

(4) BE:
  a. Possessional:
     Beth has/possesses/owns a doll.
     The doll belongs to Beth.   (Jackendoff 1982: 192, (10.10a))
  b. Identificational:
     The light is red.   (Jackendoff 1983: 195, (10.14a))
     Elise is a pianist.   (Jackendoff 1983: 194, (10.12a))
  c. Temporal:
     The meeting is at 6:00.   (Jackendoff 1983: 190, (10.4a))
     My birthday is on Dec. 22.

(5) GO:
  a. Possessional:
     Beth received the doll.   (Jackendoff 1983: 192, (10.10b))
     Beth lost the doll.   (Jackendoff 1983: 192, (10.10c))
  b. Identificational:
     The pages yellowed.   (Jackendoff 1983: 195, (10.15a))
     The light changed from red to green.   (Jackendoff 1983: 195, (10.14b))
  c. Temporal:
     The meeting went from 2:00 to 4:00.

(6) CAUSE:
  a. Possessional:
     Amy gave the doll to Beth.   (Jackendoff 1983: 192, (10.10d))
     Beth obtained the doll.   (Jackendoff 1983: 192, (10.10g))
  b. Identificational:
     The flames blackened the building.   (Jackendoff 1983: 195, (10.15c))
     Sol made Gary a celebrity.   (Jackendoff 1983: 194, (10.12e))
  c. Temporal:
     We moved the meeting from Tuesday to Thursday.

(Jackendoff 1983:190, (10.4b))

Jackendoff's aim in articulating the TRH is not to account for argument realization, but rather to provide an account of certain instances of systematic polysemy. Jackendoff notes that in English there are many verbs which can be used to describe events which are very different from one another. Consider, for example the three uses of *keep* in (7).

(7) a. John kept the car in the garage.
    b. John kept the book.
    c. John kept Andy happy.

What unifies these uses, according to Jackendoff, is that they all involve the combination of the predicates CAUSE and STAY, each receiving a representation of the general form in (8).

(8) [CAUSE (x, (STAY y, z))]

What differentiates them is that each involves a different semantic field. As Jackendoff (1976) points out, many rules of inference hold across the different uses of the same verbs. For example, he writes that "if an event is caused, it takes place" (1976: 110), allowing the entailment *The car stayed in the garage* to be derived from (7a), the entailment *The book stayed with John* to be derived from (7b), and the entailment *Andy stayed happy* to be derived from (7c). The basic claim behind the TRH is that the existence of verbs showing this pattern of polysemy is both predicted and explained. To the extent that such polysemy is widespread in and across languages, the TRH has real explanatory force.

The TRH is also meant to account for a comparable phenomenon involving the distribution of prepositions. It is well known that individual prepositions show a wide range of uses. The claim is that for a certain class of prepositions the uses indicating aspects of physical motion and location are basic and that their extended uses can be understood only in the context of the TRH: the extension of notions of spatial motion and location to other semantic fields. Thus, the preposition *to* can be used to indicate not only a location that is the goal of physical motion, but also a possessor – a goal within the possessional field – as in *The reward went to Bill* or *Pat gave the ball to Terry* and the goal of a change of state in the identificational field, as in *The assassin shot him to death* or *The cook roasted the chicken to a golden brown.*

Does the TRH help overcome the problems inherent in the use of semantic roles mentioned in chapter 2? The TRH restricts the inventory of semantic roles (although, as we will discuss, it may restrict it too much), but there are still no real criteria for determining the assignment of particular roles to particular NPs. Often the evidence is post facto; that is, one decides that one argument of a verb is, say, a location and then finds that in one use of the verb a location-marking preposition surfaces with this argument. For example, Jackendoff (1972: 44) proposes that the verb *weigh* takes a location as its postverbal argument in a sentence such as *The champ weighed 654 pounds* because of the expression of the comparable argument in the near-paraphrase *The champ weighed in at 654 pounds*. However, there are verbs whose semantic analysis derives solely from intuition, with individual arguments not passing any established tests for the suggested roles. Furthermore, semantic roles are not established solely on the basis of lexical entailments, since two arguments may share the same entailments and still be assigned different semantic roles. An example often cited to support this point is Jackendoff's (1972, 1976) analysis of the verbs *contain* and *surround*. Jackendoff proposes that in *The circle contains the dot, the circle* is analyzed as a location (cf. *The dot is contained in the circle*), while in *The circle surrounds the dot, the circle* is analyzed as theme. Yet there are no lexical entailments in the sense of Dowty (1991) which distinguish the two sentences. Although lexical entailments are not sufficient for determining the assignment of semantic roles, it has never been made explicit in a systematic way what other factors enter into their determination and how.

The greatest drawback of the localist approach is that it lacks a natural analysis of a significant class of verbs which are nonstative, but cannot be taken to be verbs of motion along a path in any natural way. These include many of the verbs which are traditionally considered activity verbs on an aspectual analysis (see section 4.2); they include verbs such as *chew, cry, knead, juggle,* and *play*.[1] That is, even if it is possible that motion and location verbs can be taken as the starting point for the analysis of verbs of other kinds, it seems to be too stringent a requirement that EVERY verb in the language be analyzed as a verb of motion or location.

We now consider how well the localist semantic roles predict subject and object selection.[2] To our knowledge, the first attempt to use Jackendovian semantic roles in the prediction of argument realization is presented by S. R. Anderson (1977), who introduces what he calls an AGENT RULE and a THEME RULE. These rules, respectively, associate an agent with the subject position and a theme with the direct object position if the verb requires an agent and with the subject position if it does not. Indeed, the association of agent with subject and theme with direct object is widespread in the literature (e.g., Bresnan 1982b; Marantz 1984; Williams 1981). However, as J. M. Anderson (1977) points out, "agent" is not really a localist notion. In fact, in Jackendoff's decompositional representations, agents are the first argument of the predicate CAUSE, which is not a locational or motional predicate. As for the notion of theme, S. R. Anderson is not precise about the application of this term; he first reviews the Gruber–Jackendoff characterization of the term and then defines it vaguely as "logical topic" (1977: 367), providing no explicit criteria for determining when an NP is to be analyzed as bearing the role "theme."

The definition he does offer for "theme," which we quote below, is not cast entirely in localist terms.

> The theme of a clause ... is a central participant in the proposition the clause expresses ... with many transitive verbs it is the "patient" or entity that undergoes the action described ... In a sense, the Theme is the "logical topic" of the clause: the element that the clause is about, in a purely logical sense divorced from any particular use of the clause in discourse. This sort of logical topicality must be kept rigorously distinct from discourse topicality: thus, while a sentence such as "John took his books back to the library" could be used in discourse to make a statement about *John* ("Where did he go?"), the *books* ("What happened to the ones that were on this desk?"), the *library* ("Why are all its shelves full suddenly?"), or even some entity not mentioned at all explicitly ("Why is John's desk so clean?"), it is still a statement about the *books*, in a logical sense, whose motion or location are described independently of such discourse factors. (S. R. Anderson 1977: 367)

Although considerable effort has been devoted to the development of localist approaches, it appears that the spatially defined semantic roles theme, path (including goal and source), and location do not play a significant role in the selection of a verb's subject and object. A quick perusal of the examples in (4)–(6) illustrates this point. Even with simple BE verbs, the theme is sometimes the subject (e.g., *The scooter belongs to Taylor, Snow covers the ground*) and sometimes the object (e.g., *Taylor owns the scooter, The box contains cookies*). Some three-argument verbs have subjects that are sources (e.g., *Travis gave the scooter to Taylor*) and others have subjects that are goals (e.g., *Taylor obtained/borrowed a scooter*), while still others have subjects that are neither sources nor goals, but simply causes (e.g., *The assistant moved the meeting from 3:00pm to 3:30pm*).

Jackendoff himself presents a theory of argument realization in his book *Semantic Structures* (1990b), which also includes his most articulated and explicit analyses of verb meanings. In this book, Jackendoff moves away from a strictly localist approach, introducing many new primitive predicates in his lexical semantic representations which are not localist in nature and are not used in the representation of location and motion events. For example, he posits a new primitive INCH, reminiscent of "inchoative," to be used in the representation of change-of-state verbs, instead of the motion primitive GO, used in his earlier work. As a result, change-of-location verbs and change-of-state verbs are given distinct analyses, contrary to what is expected under the Localist Hypothesis. In fact, his lexical semantic representations include not only a dimension or "tier," which encodes localist notions, but also a second dimension, which Jackendoff calls the "action tier"; these were briefly mentioned in section 2.2 and are discussed further in section 4.3. The action tier encodes actor–patient relations, relations that are central to the causal approach to event structure to be outlined in section 4.3. It is significant that in Jackendoff's (1990b: 258) argument realization rules, the action tier is strongly implicated in subject and object selection. The roles in the action tier take precedence over those in the thematic tier for both subject and object selection. Furthermore, since most verbs take arguments with semantic roles drawn from the action tier, but there are many verbs having no arguments bearing roles from the thematic tier, the action tier determines subject and object selection in almost all instances. Jackendoff's work is motivated, in part, by the earlier work of Culicover and W. Wilkins (1984; W. Wilkins 1987), which distinguishes two sets of semantic roles, which correspond roughly to the semantic roles associated with Jackendoff's action and thematic tiers, and W. Wilkins (1987) comments that the roles associated with the thematic tier do not figure in generalizations concerning linguistic behavior, after suggesting that middle formation and *tough*-movement involve roles of the type associated with the action tier.

It appears, then, that although the localist approach accounts for certain aspects of event construal, it does not play an important part in subject and object selection. In fact, in current proto-role approaches, a range of semantic properties contributing to subject and object selection are identified, but these do not include localist notions among them; see section 3.1.1.[3] To the extent that the choice of morphological case or preposition for arguments realized as obliques is subsumed under argument realization, the localist approach does have an important contribution to make. In fact, Croft (1991: 192–98), although adopting the causal approach, acknowledges that motion and location have an important part to play in determining case marking. He presents three spatial metaphors that allow case-marking relations from the local domain to be transferred to the domain of causal relations that are central to his approach.

In contrast, J. M. Anderson (1971, 1977) and van Voorst (1993) present instantiations of the localist approach that, unlike Jackendoff's and Gruber's, cast the causal dimension of events in a localist perspective, and a similar approach is also extensively explored by DeLancey (1981, 1982, 1984). In purely localist analyses, agents are analyzed as sources. Yet, the notion of source does not figure as a semantic determinant of subject and object selection in any well-worked-out theory of the semantic determinants of argument realization. Evidence for the analysis of agent as source comes not from subject and object selection, but rather from the expression of agents as obliques. For example, Clark and Carpenter (1988, 1989) show that young children learning English sometimes use the preposition *from* to mark passive agents; see also Croft (1998: 40). Furthermore, Croft (1991: 193–97) points to the use of ablative cases and adpositions – the morphosyntactic indicators of spatial sources – to mark certain causes, such as the use of English *from* in *He died from exhaustion*, a use discussed in some detail by DeLancey (1984: 204–06). Although Croft uses such examples to argue that localist notions play an important part in morphological case systems, with cases used to marked local notions extended to mark nonlocal notions through the use of several metaphors, local notions are restricted to determining the realization of arguments as obliques only.

More generally, there are certain patterns of argument realization that are inconsistent with the fundamental consequences of the Localist Hypothesis. As mentioned above, Jackendoff (1990b) abandons the common localist analysis of change-of-state verbs and change-of-location verbs, analyzing the members of these two classes using different primitive predicates. With this move, much of what is gained by providing these classes with a common localist analysis is lost. Specifically, the instances of systematic polysemy characterized by shared inferences across different senses of a verb, illustrated in (4)–(6) with *keep*, no longer receive an explanation. However, this consequence may not be unwelcome since it is not clear that this type of systematic polysemy should receive the same account as the argument realization options. The reason is that change-of-state verbs and change-of-location verbs truly differ in the ways in which they realize their theme/patient argument.

Rappaport Hovav and B. Levin (2002) point out that with causative change-of-state verbs and causative change-of-location verbs the argument that undergoes the change shows strikingly different argument realization options, even though they are treated alike in localist approaches, differing only in the associated semantic field. Although an argument lexically entailed to undergo a change of state is restricted to being expressed as a direct object and a direct object only (see section 4.2.2), this restriction does not hold for an argument entailed to undergo a change of location. More generally, if verbs of motion and location provided the foundation for all argument realization, their argument realization options would be expected to be stable and consistent within individual languages. This expectation is not met, as Rappaport Hovav and B. Levin (2002) discuss. In English change-of-location verbs show several options for argument realization. In stark contrast, change-of-state verbs are remarkably stable and consistent in their argument realization options. These considerations seem to argue further against a localist approach to argument realization.

4.2   The aspectual approach

We have concluded that localist approaches to event conceptualization do not provide the appropriate semantic vocabulary for stating argument realization generalizations. An alternative approach, which has gained significant support since the mid-1980s, suggests that the internal temporal make-up of events provides the needed semantic vocabulary. On this approach, the temporal and mereological properties of predicates describing events are important for argument realization, with its various instantiations differing on the best characterization of these properties. This section introduces and evaluates this approach.

There is a long tradition in both linguistics and philosophy of classifying verbs according to lexical aspect (sometimes referred to as "aktionsart").

Such classifications distinguish among verbs – or, as we discuss below, the predicates they head – in terms of the internal temporal properties of the events they describe. Aspectual classes were introduced to account for a variety of linguistic phenomena. Initially, these phenomena did not include argument realization; rather, aspectual classes were appealed to in accounts of differences among verbs with respect to the interpretation of tense, the availability of the progressive, the distribution of various types of temporal adverbials, and the availability of certain entailments; see Dowty (1979: 60) for a summary. Aspectual classes were also developed to account for parallels between the denotational domains of nominal and verbal predicates and the interactions between the two (e.g., Bach 1981, 1986; Krifka 1986, 1989a, 1989b, 1992; Verkuyl 1972, 1993). Later, however, aspectual notions began to figure in accounts of phenomena involving argument realization.

In this section we review aspectual approaches to event conceptualization, highlighting those aspectual properties which have been implicated in argument realization, as well as reviewing debates over the best characterization of these properties and the way in which they figure in argument realization. The coverage of this section is governed by these considerations and does not try to do justice to the full richness and depth of the vast linguistic and philosophical literature on lexical aspect. We simply mention some of the many major linguistic studies of lexical aspect: Bach (1981, 1986), Binnick (1991), Brinton (1988), Dowty (1979), Filip (1999), Freed (1979), Krifka (1989a, 1989b, 1992, 1998), Moens and Steedman (1988), Mourelatos (1978), Smith (1991), Tenny (1994), Vendler (1957), and Verkuyl (1972, 1993, 1999). Syntacticians who appeal to aspect in studies of argument realization sometimes make reference to aspectual properties uncritically, often confusing aspectual with nonaspectual notions. Furthermore, not all semanticists working on aspect are aware of the full range of issues involved in the morphosyntactic realization of arguments. Therefore, this section attempts to provide a critical review of the relevant literature, to correct some misconceptions, and to bring research on the semantic foundations of aspectual notions together with that on the relevance of these notions to argument realization.

In section 4.2.1, we introduce the aspectual classes most commonly found in existing systems of aspectual classification and lay out the specific semantic properties which are said to be crucial in defining them. We focus on those aspectual properties which also figure in aspect-driven theories of argument realization. In section 4.2.2, we provide an overview of the properties which are common to most theories of argument realization which take aspect to be the dominant factor in argument realization. Section 4.2.3 lays out the evidence which is commonly taken to support the aspectual approach to argument realization and section 4.2.4 presents challenges to this approach. Finally, in section 4.2.5 we turn to a less traditional aspectually motivated perspective on the classification of events, which makes reference to whether or not an event is simple or complex.

4.2.1   Aspectual classifications and aspectual properties

Systems of lexical aspectual classification can be traced back to Aristotle, although perhaps the best-known system, which has also served as the foundation for most work in linguistics over the last forty years, is Zeno Vendler's (1957).[4] Vendler proposed four aspectual classes – activities, accomplishments, achievements, and states – and these continue to be the most widely identified classes. A variety of other aspectual class inventories have been proposed; however, they do not constitute radically different systems of aspectual classification. They either superimpose a different organization on the four aspectual classes proposed by Vendler or subdivide or collapse these classes somewhat (see Brinton 1988: 32–36 for some discussion); they may also refine the criteria used for defining these classes, as we discuss below. Thus, there is not the same degree of proliferation of aspectual classes as there is of semantic roles. Concomitantly, in contrast to the lack of agreed-upon tests for semantic roles, there are fairly well-established tests for determining aspectual classification. We do not provide an extensive review of the motivation for positing these classes, nor of the better-known diagnostics for them, which we will make free use of, as this is well-worn territory; see Dowty (1979), Kearns (2000), and Van Valin and LaPolla (1997) for a summary of these tests and Verkuyl (1993) for critical discussion of the diagnostics for aspectual classification and the various aspectual class taxonomies.

The most basic aspectual distinction is between states, such as *be in the garden, be tall, resemble one's mother, know the answer*, and *believe in witches*, which are stative, i.e., do not involve any change, and the other three aspectual classes, which are nonstative. (An alternative characterization of the distinction is in terms of nondynamic vs. dynamic predicates, as in Comrie [1976a].) Among the nonstative classes, accomplishments, such as *build a bridge, fix a sink, run to the store*, and *eat an apple*, and achievements, such as *realize your error, reach the summit*, and *discover the solution*, have an inherent temporal endpoint, variably called a TELOS, a BOUND, or a DELIMITER. Such predicates are often collectively referred to as TELIC (cf. Garey 1957: 106). Activities, such as *play the piano, run, laugh*, and *ride a bike*, in contrast, have no inherent temporal endpoint; they are ATELIC. Although achievements, like accomplishments, are telic, achievements, unlike accomplishments, lack duration and are close to punctual (Vendler 1967: 103; though see Kearns 2003). In addition, some researchers recognize a fifth class, the SEMELFACTIVES, such as *knock, kick, jump*, or *beep*, which are punctual and atelic in their noniterative uses (Engelberg 1999, 2000a; Smith 1991). Some researchers conflate semelfactives with achievements, since both are close to punctual; however, semelfactives are not telic with respect to the more precise definitions of telicity considered in section 4.2.1. In fact, B. Levin (1999) shows that in terms of argument realization, semelfactives pattern with activities – a property that supports distinguishing them from achievements.

Vendler intended his classes to be temporal in nature, defining each in terms of a temporal schema, but some classes overlap significantly with classes picked out by other commonly identified nontemporal semantic properties, particularly, agentivity and causativity. This overlap has been a source of both interest and confusion. Consider the notion of agentivity. Most statives are nonagentive, leading some researchers to identify what are actually agentivity tests as stativity tests (Lakoff 1966). Thus, some have proposed that if a predicate lacks an imperative form, then it is stative, as illustrated by the contrast between stative *know*, which cannot be used in the imperative, and nonstative *learn*, which can be. However, it is not stativity that is at issue, since nonagentive activity verbs also lack imperatives, as in *Roll down the hill, ball!* or *Babble, stream!*; see also section 1.2. Rather, the imperative is sensitive to agentivity. The same confusion arises with respect to certain diagnostics intended to separate achievements from accomplishments. Certain diagnostics purported to single out achievements actually turn out to be sensitive to agentivity, picking out achievements because they are typically nonagentive. For example, achievements have been said to contrast with accomplishments in not being found with adverbs such as *attentively* or *carefully* (Ryle 1949: 151), as in *My mother carefully noticed the spot* vs. *My mother carefully read the letter*. Once again, the determining factor is not aspect, but agentivity, as shown by the oddness of *The top carefully spun on the table*, which contains a nonagentive activity verb. In fact, as Dowty (1979: 183–84) convincingly illustrates, agentivity is orthogonal to aspectual classification, with agentive and nonagentive predicates being found in every aspectual class, once aspectual classes are purely temporally defined. See also Verkuyl (1989: 44–49) for another example of the confusion of agentivity with an aspectual diagnostic.

Also confounded with aspectual notions is the notion "causative," particularly in relation to accomplishments and achievements. The core accomplishments, such as transitive *cool, empty,* and *melt,* are indeed causative, and many achievements, such as *reach, die, lose,* and *notice,* are noncausative. Extrapolating, some researchers have suggested that all accomplishments are causatives (e.g., Erteschik-Shir and Rapoport 2004; Foley and Van Valin 1984; Slabakova 1998; Sybesma 1992; Van Valin 1990, 1993b); the aspectual classes, then, are taken to have a nontemporal definition, even though this goes against Vendler's original intention. However, the conflation of causation with aspectual classification cannot be correct. First, certain verbs, such as *break* and *explode,* have causative and noncausative uses, which are indistinguishable aspectually, since they are usually both punctual. Second, the intransitive uses of *break, cool, harden,* and *melt* are uniformly noncausative, yet these verbs vary in their aspectual properties, being necessarily telic (e.g., *break*) or either telic or atelic (e.g., *cool*) and durative (e.g., *cool*) or punctual (*break*). Furthermore, Pylkkänen (2000) argues in favor of recognizing a class of causative statives in Finnish. As McCawley (1976: 117) and Van Valin and LaPolla (1997: 97) point out, there are pairs consisting of semantically related causatives and non-causatives in all aspectual classes. Thus, the members of causative verb classes do not have uniform temporal properties, while the members of classes defined by temporal properties are not uniformly causative. Agentivity and causation, then, should not be included among the criteria for aspectual classification, as in the tripartite classification introduced by Mourelatos (1978) and Vlach (1981). This point is implicit, but not highlighted, in Dowty's discussion of aspectual classes (1979), and it is made explicit in Van Valin and LaPolla (1997). Furthermore, B. Levin and Rappaport Hovav (2004) and Rappaport Hovav and B. Levin (2002) show that the classes defined by temporal properties and the classes defined by causation are relevant to distinct sets of linguistic phenomena.

Initially, Vendler suggested that he was classifying verbs, but further studies made clear that aspectual classification really involves the event descriptions represented by linguistic expressions of various sizes. Event descriptions represent the construals of happenings discussed in section 1.4. Although a verb is typically associated with a particular aspectual class, all the material in the VP it heads – and even in its IP – can determine the aspectual classification of the event description (Declerck 1979; Dowty 1979; Mourelatos 1978; Verkuyl 1972; and subsequent work). It is for this reason that many of the examples we cited to illustrate the various aspectual classes were cited as VPs. Furthermore, researchers observed that there is a certain amount of systematicity in the way that the same verb can be part of event descriptions of more than one aspectual type, suggesting that the aspectual classes are related. Much of the research on aspect in linguistics and philosophy that followed Vendler's sought to bring out these interrelations, an effort that Vendler himself initiated. The relations between aspectual classes can be illustrated by the many verbs – *understand, see, hear,* and *recognize,* as well as *bloom* and *flower* – that can be found in sentences which are open to either state or achievement readings, as in (9).

(9) a. Ashley understands Maori. (state)
   b. Foster suddenly understood the letter's significance. (achievement)

More attention has been focused on the many verbs which are found in both activity and accomplishment event descriptions. The aspectual classification of sentences with certain verbs is determined by both the presence and the nature of their direct object as in (10).

(10) a. Morgan drank for five minutes/*in five minutes.
    b. Morgan drank lemonade for five minutes/*in five minutes.
    c. Morgan drank three glasses of lemonade in five minutes/*for five minutes.

When a sentence with the verb *drink* lacks a direct object, as in (10a), it shows the properties of having an atelic predicate: it cannot be modified by an *in* time adverbial, which sets a bound to the duration of the event, though it can be modified by a *for* time adverbial, which simply describes the duration of an event. When its direct object is a mass noun or an NP that is not specified for quantity, as in (10b), the sentence again manifests the hallmarks of having an atelic predicate, but when the direct object is specified for quantity, as in (10c), the sentence is telic. In some instances, material within the VP can give rise to a telic event description, as illustrated in (11) with an intransitive verb and in (12) with a transitive verb.

(11) a. Taylor ran *in an hour/for an hour.
     b. Taylor ran to the park in three minutes/*for three minutes.
     c. Taylor ran her Reeboks to tatters in three months/*for three months.

(12) a. Dana tugged the rope for a minute/in a minute.
     b. Dana tugged the boat to the shore *for twenty seconds/in twenty seconds flat.
     c. Dana tugged the rope loose *for twenty seconds/in twenty seconds flat.

Since activities and accomplishments are distinguished in terms of telicity and the telicity of such sentences is determined by material within the VP, such sentences are taken as evidence that telicity is often calculated compositionally (Hinrichs 1985; Krifka 1986, 1989a, 1989b, 1992; Platzack 1979; Verkuyl 1972, 1993, 1999; and much subsequent work). Because of systematic correspondences such as these, much effort has been devoted to developing representations of the various aspectual classes which give their members internal structure, making explicit the properties common to the various aspectual classes and the relations between them. A long-standing major challenge, first posed by Verkuyl (1972), has been to characterize precisely the set of verbs for which the choice of direct object or other complement can affect the telicity of the event description the verb participates in. This challenge arises because the choice of a quantized or nonquantized NP as direct object affects the classification of only some, but not all, verb–object combinations. Thus, it affects the classification of *drink*, as shown in (10). In contrast, it does not affect the classification of *pound*: both *pound the can* and *pound dough* are atelic, though one has a quantized NP as a direct object and the other does not.

Theories of argument realization rarely directly implicate aspectual classes in the mapping to syntax; more often, they make reference to properties involved in their definition. It is usually assumed that the properties which bring out the relationships between the aspectual classes and those which figure in argument realization are the same. As we discuss in section 4.2.3, the compositional building of telic from atelic predicates is used to motivate the relevance of aspectual notions – particularly those relating to telicity – to argument realization, especially as it involves the realization of arguments as objects. Since telicity figures prominently in aspectual theories of argument realization, we elaborate on its nature and its representation. Another, less traditional, quasi-aspectual notion, event complexity, is also implicated by some researchers in argument realization; we discuss it in section 4.2.5.

There are two major approaches to the representation of telicity;[5] one makes reference to a notion of result state, while the second makes reference to the mereological (i.e., part) structure of events, and in particular, whether an event has a proper subpart which could be described by the same event predicate. We review each in turn, though we leave the question of which is more appropriate open; however, see Kratzer (2004) for a view of telicity which makes use of elements of both approaches.

The first approach, which could be described as the result state or culmination perspective, is developed by Dowty (1979), based on insights from Kenny (1963), and then taken up by many others, including Higginbotham (2000), Kratzer (2004), Parsons (1990), Pustejovsky (1991b, 1995), Rothstein (2000), van Hout (1996), and Van Valin (1990; Van Valin and LaPolla 1997). Kenny (1963: 178) suggests that performances – his term for accomplishments and achievements – "must be ultimately the bringing about of a state or of an activity," and that, furthermore, "[o]ne performance differs from another in accordance with the differences between states of affairs brought about: performances are specified by their ends" (1963: 178). Building on this suggestion, Dowty (1979: 77–78) proposes that the endpoints of accomplishments and achievements, which determine their telicity, are represented as result states. As support for this perspective, Dowty points to triads based on English adjectives and verbs with a shared name, as exemplified with *cool* in (13), first discussed by Lakoff (1970).

(13) a. The soup was cool.
     b. The soup cooled.
     c. Alex cooled the soup.

The word *cool* can represent an adjective which describes an entity in a state, as in (13a), an intransitive inchoative verb describing the attainment of this state by an entity (an achievement), as in (13b), and a transitive causative verb describing a cause bringing about this state in an entity (an accomplishment), as in (13c). The systematic relation among these three uses of *cool* is evidenced by the shared selectional restrictions on their patient arguments and by the existence of entailment relations between the sentences. The relation between the different uses of the same predicate is captured by deriving the achievement from the state with the addition of the primitive predicate BECOME to the state's predicate decomposition, and the accomplishment from the achievement by the addition of the predicate CAUSE to the achievement's decomposition. In addition, the derivation of an accomplishment from an activity can be viewed as the addition of a result state to an activity. Certain instances of the English resultative construction demonstrate this clearly. *Brett swept the floor* is an activity, but adding the state *clean* yields the accomplishment *Brett swept the floor clean*. In this way, the result state or culmination view of telicity provides some insight into how telicity is calculated compositionally, since telic events are built directly on states.

However, this approach to telicity has some shortcomings. First, this way of representing telicity does not fare so well for the events described in *translate the poem* or *memorize the speech*, where it is difficult to characterize accurately what the result state is, although these events have a natural culmination, as also discussed in Dowty (1979: 186–87). At the very least, these examples suggest that an event can have a culmination without defining an obvious result state. This view of telicity also does not illuminate the way in which the nature of the direct object affects telicity or the way in which other kinds of expressions can affect telicity, such as the measure phrases in *Cameron ran a mile* or *Tyler pushed the stroller twenty feet*. Finally, it does not make explicit the relation between telic and atelic uses available to certain verbs of change of state, such as *cool*, as in *The soup cooled in ten minutes* (telic) and *The soup cooled for ten minutes* (atelic). Both uses are built on the same state of coolness (cf. the discussion of (13)).

A different basic insight underlies the second major approach to telicity: telic predicates are "indivisible," or "quantized," that is, they describe events which have no proper parts describable by the same predicate. The insight that this "subinterval property" characterizes these predicates is attributed to Kenny (1963: 172–73) by Dowty (1979: 57). The indivisibility of the event described by a predicate is attributed to the existence of an inherent terminal point. Since any subpart of the event does not include this terminal point, it cannot be described by the same telic predicate. In many instances, telic predicates have a designated argument, which plays a crucial part in determining whether the inherent terminal point has been attained. Instantiations of this approach to telicity concern themselves, among other things, with the ways in which telicity is compositionally calculated from the interaction between the lexical semantic properties of the verb itself and those of this distinguished argument; they differ, however, in the way in which they formalize the calculation of telicity. Versions of this approach are presented by Borer (in press b), Dowty (1991), Filip (1999), Hay, Kennedy, and B. Levin (1999), Hinrichs (1985), Kiparsky (1998, 2001), Krifka (1986, 1989a, 1989b, 1992, 1998), Ramchand (1997), Tenny (1987, 1994), and Verkuyl (1972, 1993, 1999), among others.

There are several related proposals about what makes the distinguished argument of a telic predicate special. Perhaps the best known is Krifka's (1986, 1989a, 1989b, 1992): this argument is involved in defining a homomorphism from the physical extent of its own referent to the temporal progress of the event described by the telic predicate. This theory capitalizes on the parallels between the part structure of the nominal domain and that of the event domain, first pointed out by Bach (1981, 1986). For example, in an event of eating an apple, every subpart of the apple that is eaten corresponds to a subpart (subinterval) of the event of eating that apple. Krifka calls such an argument a "gradual patient" (1992: 42; German "Sukzessiv-Patiens" in Krifka 1989b), though Dowty's (1991) term "incremental theme" is now typically used. A range of verbs have incremental theme arguments, including *destroy, mow, paint,* and *read,* as well as verbs of consumption, such as *eat* and *drink*, and verbs of creation, such as *build* or *write*. Dowty (1991: 568) also intends the term "incremental theme" to apply to the patient of change-of-state verbs, but this application of the term requires clarification. The sentence *Perry opened the shutter halfway* does not entail that half the shutter was open, but that the shutter was halfway open. Thus, the homomorphic mapping involves a property of the shutter and not the shutter's own physical extent. This type of analysis can be extended to verbs of motion, with the path of the moving object serving as the incremental theme, since parts of this path correspond to parts of the event. For instance, in *Mark jogged to the beach*, the event of Mark's jogging to the beach is half over, when half the path to the beach is traversed. In fact, Dowty (1991: 569) recognizes that the argument such a path is predicated of – the "theme" in the Gruber–Jackendoff localist sense – is not an incremental theme; he introduces the label HOLISTIC THEME for this argument. The three classes of verbs can be unified. The basic unifying insight is that patients of change-of-state verbs, traditional incremental themes, and holistic themes are all associated with some property – a scalar property of the object lexicalized by their verb for the first, the physical extent of the object for the second, and the path traversed by the theme for the third – which serves as a scale for determining the temporal progress of the entire event (Hay, Kennedy, and B. Levin 1999; Ramchand 1997).

A second proposal about the nature of the distinguished argument relevant to the determination of telicity was developed about the same time by Tenny (1987, 1992, 1994). She agrees that certain event types have such an argument, but she characterizes its aspectual role in a slightly different way. For her, the distinguished argument MEASURES OUT the event; however, telicity also depends on the presence of a temporal terminus or other delimiter for the event, which may or may not be provided by the distinguished argument. Precisely what measuring out means depends on the nature of the event itself. Tenny recognizes three classes of verbs, each describing a distinct event type; they correspond quite closely to the three types just discussed with respect to the notion of incremental theme. The first class includes the core incremental theme verbs. Consider eating an apple again. According to Tenny, the apple measures out the event, since "Some quantity of apple is consumed during each interval of eating, until the apple is entirely consumed" (1994: 15). The apple also delimits the event, since the eating event is over when the apple is entirely consumed. Here Tenny's measuring out perspective is very similar to the Krifka–Dowty perspective since both link the progress through the eating event to the quantity of apple consumed. A second, somewhat different type of example involves verbs that take what Tenny calls "path objects," as in *Sue walked the Appalachian trail* and *Jerry climbed the ladder*. Here the path – *the Appalachian Trail* or *the ladder* – measures out the event since the progress along the path determines the progress of the event, and its endpoint (i.e., the goal of motion) delimits the event. Tenny assimilates events like playing a sonata or translating a poem to events with path objects, since the sonata and the poem have the same aspectual role as the path, in that progress through the sonata or poem determines the progress through the event of playing the sonata or translating the poem. (On the Krifka–Dowty approach these events are simply treated as having regular incremental themes.) The third event type is represented by change-of-state verbs like *ripen* and *dry*. Tenny characterizes the patient as the measure, while recognizing that the event's temporal terminus "is achieved by progressing along measurable degrees of change in some property central to the verb's meaning" (1994: 17). Thus, she recognizes that, as already mentioned, it is not the actual extent of the direct object which is relevant to delimiting the event, but rather a scalar property of the object, such as its ripeness or dryness.[6] As we did above, Tenny (1994: 18) points out that these three types of verbs are all associated with a scale. Progress along the scale is correlated with progress through the event, and the end of the scale provides the point of delimitation of the event. Telicity is thus represented by the endpoint of a scale.[7] Although the notions of measure and incremental theme are quite similar and are often used interchangeably, we use the term "incremental theme" in what follows since it is more precisely defined; the exception is in discussions of Tenny's work, as it is explicitly couched in terms of the notion "measure."

These theories of telicity, then, offer an answer to the question posed above: the class of verbs whose direct objects (or PP complements) affect the telicity of the events being described are those which have an incremental theme or those associated with a scale or path which provides a way of determining the progress of the event. Two major questions require further resolution: the extent to which verbs lexically specify whether or not they are associated with such a scale, path, or incremental theme and what can serve this function. Thus, some researchers, most notably, Borer (1994, 1998), propose that telicity is never lexically specified, while Folli and Ramchand (to appear) and Rappaport Hovav and B. Levin (2002) propose that, in at least some instances, telicity must be lexically specified.

Although this point is not always appreciated (Dowty 1991: 568, 607; Tenny 1994: 15, 1995: 68, n. 20), telicity is independent of "incremental theme." A predicate can have an incremental theme, even if it is atelic (Filip 1999; Hay, Kennedy, and B. Levin 1999; Jackendoff 1996b; Krifka 1992; B. Levin and Rappaport Hovav 1995; Ramchand 1997). The independence of incremental theme and telicity is evident in sentences with the change-of-state verbs which Dowty (1979: 88–90) calls "degree achievements" – verbs such as *cool*, *lengthen*, and *widen* (Abusch 1986; Bertinetto and Squartini 1995; Hay, Kennedy, and B. Levin 1999). The scale associated with these verbs has no inherent bound (e.g., something can keep getting longer), unlike the scale associated with verbs such as *clean* and *empty*, which does have such a bound (e.g., once something is empty, it cannot get emptier). Yet, the change in the value of this property determines the progress of the event described by degree achievements, and, in this sense, sentences with these verbs always have an incremental theme. If the degree of change is unbounded, the predicate is atelic, while if it is bounded, the predicate is telic (Hay, Kennedy, and B. Levin 1999). Thus, in (14a), which contains an *in* time adverbial, the soup must have reached a specified temperature, conventionally room temperature, at the end of the twenty minutes, so that there is a specified degree of change, while in (14b), with a *for* time adverbial, the soup's temperature is lower than it was at the beginning of the three minutes, but the amount of change in the temperature is left unspecified and thus the predicate cannot be telic.

> (14) a. The soup cooled in twenty minutes.
>   b. The soup cooled for three minutes.

Similarly, when a verb such as *run* is used with a bounded path phrase, the predicate is telic, and when it is used with an unbounded path phrase the predicate is atelic, corresponding to specified and unspecified degrees of change along the path. More generally, when a predicate describes a specified degree of change on the associated scale, it is telic, and when it describes an unspecified degree of change, it is atelic (Kennedy and B. Levin 2001).

Furthermore, in some instances certain predicates may be telic, yet may lack an incremental theme. Examples discussed by Dowty (1991: 568) and Filip (1993) are punctual predicates like *recognize* and *touch the finish line*, which are telic, but have no incremental theme. Ackerman and Moore (1999, 2001) argue that direct objects in Estonian manifest an alternation between genitive (the Estonian counterpart of accusative) and partitive morphological case which signals an alternation between a telic and atelic interpretation of the predicate, though the telic interpretation may not involve an incremental theme. Thus, the Estonian counterpart of *The board waited for a decision* takes a direct object in the genitive case, if the sentence entails that a decision was made that brought the waiting to an end, and an object in the partitive case otherwise. The telic interpretation of the sentence with the genitive object comes from the entailment that the waiting comes to an end, though the event lacks any obvious incremental theme.

We now briefly review how the notion "incremental theme" is invoked in theories of argument realization.

4.2.2 Aspect and argument realization

The idea that aspectual properties influence argument realization dates back at least to Hopper and Thompson (1980), a study which includes telicity and punctuality among the factors determining transitivity. Since then researchers have tried to characterize more explicitly the ways in which notions such as telicity, measure, and incremental theme determine "components" of transitivity, such as whether a verb takes a direct object and, if it does, what morphosyntactic expression it should receive, as we describe in this section and the next. Nevertheless, in section 4.2.4 we show that these aspectual notions cannot handle all facets of argument realization.

Aspect was first implicated in analyses of argument realization within the generative framework, when phenomena purported to be sensitive to a notion of affectedness were reanalyzed in aspectual terms. One such phenomenon is the English middle construction, which is found with some, but not all, transitive verbs. For example, *cut* is found in this construction (e.g., *Freshly baked bread cuts easily*), while *abhor* is not (e.g., **Those kind of people abhor without any effort at all*). Delineating the relevant set of transitive verbs has been notoriously difficult, with some researchers invoking a notion of affectedness (Doron and Rappaport Hovav 1991: 81-82; Fiengo 1980: 37–38; Hale and Keyser 1987: 44; Jaeggli 1986: 607–08),[8] previously appealed to by M. Anderson (1978) in generalizations involving nominalizations. The proposal is that a middle requires a base verb taking an object that is an affected argument, which is defined as one that is "changed or moved" (M. Anderson 1979: 44; cited in Tenny 1994: 156). The verbs *cut* and *abhor* contrast in this respect. Subsequent work has argued for an aspectual characterization of verbs in the middle construction. Roberts (1987) proposes that middles may be found with accomplishments only, while Fagan (1992) proposes instead that middles may be found with activities and accomplishments. She cites *The car drives easily* and *This book reads easily* as examples of middles based on activity and accomplishment predicates, respectively (1992: 68, (12a), (13a)); she also notes that the *read* example is unexpected if middle formation requires base verbs with an affected object. Not surprisingly, Fellbaum (1987: 82–84) claims that the distribution of prenominal possessors in passive nominalizations, originally accounted for in terms of affectedness (M. Anderson 1979; Fiengo 1980; Rappaport 1983), receives a better account in aspectual terms: such nominalizations must be able to receive an accomplishment interpretation. Subsequent work continues to provide aspectual accounts of these and related phenomena, but appeals to more specific aspectual properties of predicates rather than to aspectual classes (Egerland 1998; Tenny 1987, 1992, 1994). For instance, Tenny proposes that measure is the relevant property and suggests that the notion of affectedness can be given more content if an "affected argument is one that measures out and imposes delimitedness on the event" (1994: 158); her motivation is the observation that the measure arguments of verbs of consumption and verbs of change of state are affected arguments. Although the notion of measure or incremental theme has been implicated in whether a predicate may have a middle, no one to our knowledge has provided an explanation of why this should be so; in contrast, there are various attempts at explaining why the notion of affectedness should play a part in this and other phenomena; see, for example, Ackema and Schoorlemmer (1994), Doron and Rappaport Hovav (1991), Egerland (1998), Giorgi and Longobardi (1991), Grimshaw (1993), Hale and Keyser (1987), Jaeggli (1986), and Zubizarreta (1987).

Tenny (1987, 1992, 1994) is the first to present a well-articulated aspectual approach to argument realization. Her starting point is the now quite widely accepted, though nevertheless controversial, Aspectual Interface Hypothesis.[9]

(15) Aspectual Interface Hypothesis:
     The universal principles of mapping between thematic structure and syntactic argument structure are governed by aspectual properties. Constraints on the aspectual properties associated with direct internal arguments, indirect internal arguments, and external arguments in syntactic structure constrain the kinds of event participants that can occupy these positions. Only the aspectual part of thematic structure is visible to the universal linking principles.

                                                          (Tenny 1994: 2)

Current aspectually driven theories of argument realization typically focus on the relation between choice and morphosyntactic expression of the direct object and notions such as telicity, measure, and incremental theme. Which notion is tied to direct object and exactly how this is accomplished varies from theory to theory. We start with Tenny's formulation of the relevant constraints on mapping, given in (16). (See Verkuyl [1993] for another implementation of the idea that there is a connection between objects and telicity.)

(16) Measuring-Out Constraint on Direct Internal Arguments:
     (i) The direct internal argument of a simple verb is constrained so that it undergoes no necessary internal motion or change, unless it is motion or change which 'measures out the event' over time (where 'measuring out' entails that the direct argument plays a particular role in delimiting the event).
     (ii) Direct internal arguments are the only overt arguments which can 'measure out the event'.
     (iii) There can be no more than one measuring-out for any event described by a verb.   (Tenny 1994: 11, (9))

(17) The Terminus Constraint on Indirect Internal Arguments:
     (i) An indirect internal argument can only participate in aspectual structure by providing a terminus for the event described by the verb. The terminus causes the event to be delimited.
     (ii) If the event has a terminus, it also has a path, either implicit or overt.
     (iii) An event as described by a verb can have only one terminus.
                                                          (Tenny 1994: 68, (128))

It follows from the conjunction of constraints (16)(i)–(ii) and (17)(i) that event delimitation takes place inside the VP. The direct object plays a crucial role, in that it is the only overt argument which can be a measure. Tenny explicitly allows for nonovert measures which are not direct objects, as in *push the cart to the wall*: here, the cart is *not* a measure, since *push the cart halfway to the wall* entails that half the path to the wall has been traversed, not that half the cart is at the wall. In this instance, the nonovert path argument is the measure, with the overt goal phrase representing the terminus of the path (Tenny 1994: 76). This example also shows that although only direct objects can be overt measures, a direct object is not necessarily a measure. *The cart* does not fall under (16)(i) in that it does not undergo any necessary internal motion or change, even though it does undergo a change of location.

A potential problem for Tenny's approach might be presented by the theme argument of causative change-of-location verbs – either inherently causative verbs, such as *move*, or verbs of imparting force, such as *push* or *pull*, which are used as causatives in the presence of a goal phrase: this argument is expressed as a direct object across languages, though it does not fall under any of her generalizations concerning the realization of arguments as direct objects, since it undergoes a change but is not a measure (see above). A way to rectify this problem is suggested by Kennedy and B. Levin (2001), who propose that the term "incremental theme" should be reserved for the scale which serves as the measure of an event and that the argument which gets mapped onto direct object is the argument which this incremental theme is predicated of. For verbs of change of state, such as *lengthen*, the incremental theme is the scalar property acquired by the theme – the argument whose state changes. For traditional incremental theme verbs, such as *eat* and *drink*, the incremental theme is the spatial extent of the theme argument. For verbs of motion, the incremental theme is the path traversed by the theme – that is, the argument whose position changes. It then becomes possible to formulate a single generalization identifying which argument of a verb with an incremental theme is expressed as its direct object: the direct object is the argument which the incremental theme is predicated of. We continue, however, to use the term "incremental theme" in traditional fashion, in order to avoid confusion. In summary, Tenny takes the notion of measure (or, alternatively, incremental theme) to be crucial to telicity, and, furthermore, she ties it to direct object, though not to any particular morphosyntactic expression of direct object, nor does she require every direct object to be a measure.

A slightly different approach is taken by a number of researchers, working primarily within the Minimalist Program (Chomsky 1995), including proponents of both the result state and incremental theme approaches to telicity. They propose that there is a special syntactic structure, usually a functional projection above the VP, dedicated to the encoding of telicity, often known as "AspP" (i.e., Aspect Phrase) (e.g., Arad 1998; Borer 1994, 1998; Kratzer 2004; McClure 1994, 1995, 1998; Pereltsvaig 1999; Ramchand 1997; Ritter and S. T. Rosen 1998, 2000; Sanz 1999, 2000; Schmitt 1995, 1996, 1999; Slabakova 1998, 2001; W. Snyder 1995; Travis 1991, 2000a, 2000b; van Hout 1996, 2000a, 2000b). Telic interpretations arise when a direct object moves into the specifier position of this functional projection and receives accusative case through specifier–head agreement. In order to allow for transitive structures that are not telic, direct objects can receive case even if they remain internal to the VP, though usually this is not accusative case (though see Pereltsvaig [1999, 2000] on Russian non-telicity-inducing accusative case). Objects receive telicity-inducing accusative case through movement into the special higher functional projection AspP. Along the same lines, van Hout (1996, 2000a, 2000b) and Ritter and S. T. Rosen (1998, 2000) suggest that the specifier positions associated with the heads AgrO (i.e., object agreement) and AgrS (i.e., subject agreement) are reserved for arguments whose function is to identify elements of event structure. For van Hout, telic event features must be checked in AgrOP. For Ritter and S. T. Rosen, the argument in the specifier position of this functional projection is the event delimiter. This work, thus, differs from Tenny's in two ways. First, it takes the notion of telicity, instead of the notion of measure or incremental theme, to mediate between event structure and syntax, and second, it assumes that there is a unique syntactic position which is responsible for the telic interpretation associated with the presence of certain types of arguments.

Several converging theoretical developments have led researchers to posit an AspP functional projection, though these are not always made explicit or even acknowledged in all work that adopts such a functional projection. These include the introduction of a special functional projection (AgrOP) for checking accusative case within the Minimalist Program (Chomsky 1991, 1995), Diesing's (1992) Mapping Hypothesis regarding the structural position of quantificational (or, roughly, specific) NPs, and the reinterpretation of certain alternations in the morphological case of objects, which had been described as quantificational in their import, as telicity alternations. These motivations are briefly summarized here; see Benua (2000) and Runner (1993, 1995) for more detailed discussion. Diesing's Mapping Hypothesis requires that quantificational NPs be external to the VP in syntax; in this way syntactic structure reflects the tripartite semantic structure assigned to sentences with quantificational NPs, which have such NPs outside the "nuclear scope" of the clause (Heim 1982). Runner (1993) brings Diesing's ideas together with the Minimalist Program's "checking" theory of NP licensing (Chomsky 1991, 1995); he suggests that the NPs that must move to the specifier of the AgrO projection to have their Case "checked" are precisely the quantificational NPs, rather than all NPs, as previously proposed; see also Mahajan (1991). The idea, then, is that quantificational NPs have their Case checked in a functional projection higher than the VP, while nonquantificational NPs remain in the VP. Alternations in the case of a direct object had independently been shown to be tied to the semantic interpretation attributed to object NPs in some languages – specifically, to a specific interpretation – and, de Hoop (1992) proposes that the accusative/partitive case alternation associated with certain NPs in Finnish and comparable alternations in other languages could be explained if partitive case were assigned within the VP and accusative case were assigned in a higher

functional projection. De Hoop's goal is to account for the fact that partitive
NPs act as if they have weak determiners (are nonspecific) and accusative NPs
strong determiners (are specific),[10] but as will be discussed in section 4.2.3,
others have noticed that the sentences with partitive NPs are atelic and those
with accusative NPs are telic (e.g., Filip 1993; Krifka 1986, 1989a, 1989b; also
Vainikka [1993] for Finnish). It is not a large step from there to reinterpreting
the extra functional projection as relevant to the calculation of telicity, even
if different researchers implement this idea in slightly different ways. In fact,
the presence of an AspP now seems to have become quite accepted in one
line of work on argument realization, in that it is now posited with little or no
discussion of its origins.

4.2.3   Evidence for aspectual theories of argument realization

Tenny's Aspectual Interface Hypothesis accounts quite well for the observation
that arguments which are direct objects of prototypical transitive verbs are
those which "measure out" an event. As noted in section 1.5, prototypical
transitive verbs are agent–patient verbs such as *destroy*, *cut*, or *open*; that
is, they denote an action in which an agent acts on and causes a change in
a patient. The direct objects of such verbs are typically incremental themes;
the verbs are canonical accomplishments in the Vendler–Dowty sense. Verbs
that deviate from this prototype are less likely to be transitive (i.e., to take a
subject and a direct object) crosslinguistically (see section 1.5), and they often
have objects which neither measure out, nor delimit, the event. For example,
statives, which, by definition, do not have arguments which measure out or
delimit an event, show a greater degree of variation in argument realization
crosslinguistically. Verbs of perception and verbs of psychological state each
include stative subclasses whose members show a range of argument realization
options across languages; see section 1.5 for references to argument realization
with verbs of psychological state and Croft (1993), and Tsunoda (1985), among
others, for discussion of verbs of perception.

   Much of the evidence for the theories outlined in section 4.2.2 comes from
various kinds of argument alternations. Van Hout (1996) makes the general
proposal that argument alternations represent event type-shifting. Three kinds of
argument alternations are relevant to this point: (i) the alternate realization of
an argument as a direct object or as an oblique; (ii) the alternate realization
of an argument as a direct object or as a subject; and (iii) alternations in
which of a verb's arguments is chosen as its direct object. The first two types
reflect alternations between telic and atelic uses of verbs. The third type reflects
alternate choices in the argument which determines the telicity of a sentence,
i.e., which serves as incremental theme. We illustrate each in turn.

   Van Hout (1996: 94–96) offers the Dutch data in (18) to illustrate the
alternate realization of an argument as a direct object or as an oblique (see also
Verkuyl [1972: 53]). In (18a) the Dutch verb *write* is intransitive, taking its

"effected" argument in an *aan* 'at' phrase, and the sentence is atelic, as indicated by the time adverbials which are compatible with it. When this argument is the object of the verb, as in (18b), the sentence is telic, again, as indicated by the compatible time adverbial.

> (18) a. Elena schreef jarenlang/ *binnen een jaar aan haar proefschrift.
>   Elena wrote   years-long/ within   a   year at her thesis
>   'Elena was writing (at) her thesis for years/*within a year.'
>
>   (van Hout 1996: 95, (17b))
>
>   b. Elena schreef haar proefschrift binnen een jaar/ *jarenlang.
>   Elena wrote   her thesis   within a   year/ *years-long
>   'Elena wrote her thesis within a year/*for years.'
>
>   (van Hout 1996: 95, (17c))

Direct object/oblique alternations can be found in other languages. German data comparable to the Dutch data in (18) is discussed in Kratzer (2004), though Filip (1989) argues that the German analogue of the oblique construction does not arise through event type-shifting. English shows similar examples, as Tenny (1994: 45) illustrates. When *eat* takes a quantized NP as a direct object, its sentence is telic, but when the same NP is expressed in an *at* complement, its sentence is atelic.

> (19) a. eat the apple in an hour
>   b. *eat at the apple in an hour   (Tenny 1994: 45, (78))

The accusative/oblique morphological case alternations attested in some languages are perhaps another instantiation of this phenomenon. One previously mentioned example is the accusative/partitive alternation in Finnish and Estonian, illustrated for Finnish in (20). What sets this alternation apart is that the NP showing the case alternation qualifies as the direct object independent of its morphological case (Kiparsky 1998: 275–76; Ackerman and Moore 2001: 90–91).

> (20) a. Ammu-i-n   karhu-a.
>   shoot-PAST-1SG bear-PART
>   'I shot at the (a) bear.'
>   b. Ammu-i-n   karhu-n.
>   shoot-PAST-1SG bear-ACC
>   'I shot the (a) bear.'   (Kiparsky 1998: 267, (1))

Ackerman and Moore (2001) develop an account for direct object/oblique alternations involving both changes in grammatical relations, as in the English and Dutch, and changes in case marking, as in Finnish and Estonian. Ritter and S. T. Rosen (2000) propose that the antipassive construction in West Greenlandic Eskimo, which expresses what is usually the direct object of a transitive verb using an oblique morphological case, is also accompanied by a corresponding change from a telic to an atelic predicate; see also Benua (2000) on the Central Yup'ik Eskimo antipassive. The Eskimo antipassive, then, is assimilated to the earlier examples involving Dutch, English, and Finnish; however, this parallel may turn out to be only apparent (Rappaport Hovav 2002: 700; Spreng 2001), and, at the very least, deserves further study.

Unaccusativity gives rise to a form of argument alternation via the phenomenon that B. Levin and Rappaport Hovav (1995) call VARIABLE BEHAVIOR VERBS – verbs that show dual characterizations as unaccusative or unergative. If unaccusativity is taken to be syntactically encoded, then the single argument of such verbs has two distinct realizations: subject when unergative and direct object when unaccusative. Manner-of-motion verbs, for example, have often been claimed to have such dual classifications. As evidence, researchers point to Dutch, German, and Italian, where such verbs can appear with the unaccusative auxiliary *be* or with the unergative auxiliary *have* (e.g., Centineo 1986, 1996; L. Levin 1986, 1987; Van Valin 1990; Zaenen 1993). These options are illustrated using the Italian examples in (21).

(21) a. Ugo ha   corso meglio ieri.
Ugo has run   better yesterday
'Ugo ran better yesterday.'   (C. Rosen 1984: 66, (86a))
b. Ugo è corso a casa.
Ugo is run   to home
'Ugo ran home.'   (C. Rosen 1984: 67, (86b))

Telicity has been implicated in the explanation of this type of multiple argument realization. Researchers propose that unergative uses are atelic and unaccusative uses are telic (e.g., Centineo 1986, 1996; Dowty 1991; Hoekstra 1992; L. Levin 1986, 1987; Van Valin 1990; Zaenen 1993). The Italian example in (21), for example, is consistent with this explanation. Given that unaccusative verbs have an underlying object, this correlation supports the proposed connection between objecthood and telicity. Furthermore, Borer (1998: 62) proposes that certain Hebrew intransitive verbs also show such dual classifications and that these classifications are associated with a subtle semantic distinction, which she characterizes in terms of telicity. For instance, when the Hebrew verb *naval* 'wilt' is found in the so-called "possessive" dative construction, which Borer and Grodzinsky (1986) argue is an unaccusative structure, the verb is interpreted as telic, e.g., as when flowers wilt to death. When the same verb is found in the so-called "reflexive" dative construction, which Borer and Grodzinsky argue is an unergative structure, the same verb is interpreted as atelic, e.g., as when flowers are simply in the process of wilting. This observation follows if telic predicates always have a direct object.

An example of the third type of argument alternation – alternate choices of direct object – is instantiated by the locative alternation. Dowty (1991) and Tenny (1994) point out that locative alternation verbs, such as *smear* or *cram*, necessarily describe events which inherently take two arguments that are potential measures or incremental themes: "the theme argument can be consumed in increments over time, and the goal is not a simple location, but something that can contain, or be filled up by, the material" (Tenny 1994: 51). The alternation is explained nicely by Tenny's theory, which requires a measure to be expressed as an object. (See Dowty [1991: 587–92] and Jackendoff [1996b] for clear evidence that in each variant the argument which is expressed as direct object serves as that variant's incremental theme, so that *the pencils* is the incremental theme in *Ariadne crammed the pencils into the jar*, but *the jar* is in *Ariadne crammed the jar with the pencils*.)

A property of the resultative construction in English and Dutch is also taken to support the connection between direct objecthood and telicity or incremental theme. The key observation is that when a result phrase is added to an activity verb, such as English *sing*, as in (22), thus delimiting the event it denotes and making it telic, a direct object is needed.

> (22) a. Pat sang for hours. (atelic)
>   b. Pat sang herself hoarse in two hours. (telic)
>   c. Pat sang the audience to their feet in twenty minutes. (telic)

Particularly striking is the reflexive pronoun in (22b), which is necessary even though it does not introduce an additional event participant, as the object does in (22c).[11] Similar examples are also found in Dutch (Hoekstra 1984, 1988).

We conclude this section by returning to the controversy over the scope of the generalization linking aspectual notions and direct objecthood, mentioned at the end of the previous section. There are two questions. One concerns whether the aspectual notion which mediates between event structure and the syntax of the VP is incremental theme or telicity. The second is whether the connection should be between these aspectual notions and direct objecthood or whether the appropriate generalization connects them to accusative case. With regard to the first question, B. Levin and Rappaport Hovav (1995) present evidence that degree achievement verbs, such as *cool* and *widen*, which can be either telic or atelic, are unaccusative both when telic and atelic. This observation suggests that the appropriate notion to tie to direct objecthood is incremental theme, assuming that a verb need not necessarily be telic in order to have an incremental theme (Filip 1999; Hay, Kennedy, and B. Levin 1999; Jackendoff 1996b; Krifka 1992; B. Levin and Rappaport Hovav 1995; Ramchand 1997), since, as already pointed out, the patients of these change-of-state verbs are incremental themes, even when they are used atelically. However, the link between incremental theme and direct object can only be implemented in a theory which distinguishes underlying from surface direct objects in order to reduce the numerous instances of incremental theme subjects, as in *The soup cooled*, to objects. Furthermore, as we discuss in the next section, some researchers claim that when incremental themes are realized as objects, this realization should be attributed not to the notion "incremental theme," but to other entailments associated with their verb, which happen to coincide with incremental themehood.

As for the second question, support for the association of accusative case and telicity or a closely related notion comes from the accusative/partitive case alternations of Finnish and Estonian, since, as already mentioned, Kiparsky and Ackerman and Moore argue that the NPs showing these alternations are direct objects independent of their morphological case. The association of telicity and accusative case also appears to receive support from the existence in some languages of durative temporal adverbials which take the form of accusative case NPs and which delimit an event, even though they are not arguments (Pereltsvaig 2000; Wechsler and Lee 1996), as in the Russian and Korean examples in (23) and (24), respectively.

(23) My rabotali nad etim projektom   celyj   god.
      we worked in   this.INST   project.INST whole.ACC year.ACC
      'We worked on this project for almost a whole year.'
                              (Pereltsvaig 2000, (1a); attributed to Jakobson (1962))

(24) Tom-um twu sikan-tongan-ul tali-ess-ta.
      Tom-TOP two hour-period-ACC run-PAST-DEC
      'Tom ran for two hours.'   (Wechsler and Lee 1996: 269, (1))

Pereltsvaig (2000) proposes that such adverbials occupy Spec of AspP. When they occur with a transitive verb, the verb's own object remains in VP, so that Spec of AspP is available for the adverbials. Her analysis, thus, makes a connection between telicity and accusative case, even in instances when the case-marked NP is not an argument of the verb.

Returning to the larger question, it appears that incremental themes are realized as direct objects, but in some languages they are only assigned accusative case in a sentence with a telic reading. In fact, the link between incremental theme and accusative case needs to be even weaker. As argued above, the single argument of an unaccusative verb is an incremental theme, but unaccusative verbs do not assign accusative case, so once again incremental theme cannot strictly be tied to accusative case.

4.2.4 Challenges to the aspectual approach

Aspectual approaches to argument realization fly in the face of the data which motivated Dowty's proto-role approach to argument realization, which, as we pointed out in chapter 3, embodies the claim that any one of a number of distinct entailments can suffice to determine whether an argument may be realized as direct object. Not only is no single Patient Proto-role entailment necessarily associated with direct objecthood, but only one of the entailments that Dowty suggests is aspectual in nature. It is not surprising, therefore, to find that the aspectual approach has not gone unchallenged, as we now review. We focus not on problems for particular instantiations of the approach, but rather challenges facing any attempt to describe the lexical semantics–syntax interface by making reference exclusively to aspectual notions.

Jackendoff (1996b) presents a comprehensive critical discussion of the notions "measuring out" and "incremental theme" and argues that they are not directly implicated in argument realization. He maintains that it is affectedness that is most basically implicated in the realization of an argument as direct object. He claims that an affected argument is not necessarily an incremental theme, pointing to verbs such as *chew, knead, jiggle*, and *spin*. Citing Jackendoff (1990b) and Lakoff (1970), he takes the ability of these verbs to be found in the *What X did to Y was …* construction as evidence for the affectedness of their objects: *What John did to the bread was chew/knead/jiggle/spin it.* (Jackendoff 1996b: 312, (12)). In fact, these verbs are problematic for Tenny's (1994: 11, (9)) proposal that "The direct internal argument of a simple verb is constrained so that it undergoes no necessary internal motion or change, unless it is motion or change which 'measures out the event' over time" (cited as (16)(i)), since they have direct objects which undergo necessary movement, but not movement along a path which can be measured.

Jackendoff, however, does not give a precise definition of affectedness that is independent of this diagnostic, and based on further scrutiny of this diagnostic, Rappaport Hovav and B. Levin (2001: 786–87) suggest that what Jackendoff calls "affected" arguments are better characterized as recipients of a transmitted force; see section 4.3. Moreover, crosslinguistic surveys are needed to verify whether the nonagent argument of these verbs is consistently expressed as a direct object in all languages or whether this is a property of English, which allows a very broad range of direct objects. As noted in section 1.5, there is some evidence that suggests that verbs of surface contact, whose nonagent arguments are semantically similar to those of *chew* and *jiggle*, allow these arguments to be expressed as obliques. If so, notwithstanding the English pattern, Tenny may be correct in not having her account determine the direct objects of these verbs; rather, she wants to account only for those arguments which are necessarily direct objects across languages. As mentioned in section 1.5, however, further investigations are necessary to achieve the appropriate understanding of the possible semantic ranges of verbs with direct objects in different languages.

Jackendoff presents a more serious challenge to the notion of incremental theme and its contribution to direct object selection. He acknowledges that when a verb has an incremental theme, it is most often the argument expressed as a direct object; however, he suggests that this generalization does not reflect a direct connection between incremental themehood and direct objecthood specified by the grammar. Rather, there are certain arguments whose associated entailments in the sense of Dowty (1991) naturally facilitate an incremental theme interpretation, and in most instances such arguments are expressed as direct objects for reasons independent of their potential incremental themehood. The most obvious of these entailments are the properties defining core incremental theme arguments, that is, changing state, being consumed, performed, or created. An additional entailment is what Jackendoff (1996b) calls the spatial distribution of a theme – the entailment associated with the argument that changes location with most locative alternation verbs, such as *spray* and *load*. Arguments with any of these entailments lend themselves to incremental interpretations since the changes they undergo are often associated with parts of individuals, with some property associated with these arguments changing in an incremental way over the parts of the individual. These entailments are usually associated with direct objects, since in many instances another argument is associated with the subject position by virtue of causing the change, being agentive or, at least, sentient.

Arguments associated with lexical entailments such as volition and sentience, which most often determine realization as subject, are incompatible with an incremental interpretation since these are entailments associated with individuals and not with parts of individuals. Moreover, the kinds of changes usually attributed to agents are not changes which are effected in an incremental manner: think of the kinds of changes which the agents of verbs like *eat* or *laugh* undergo. To support his position, Jackendoff points out that in the absence of a competing more agent-like argument, an argument associated with an incremental theme-type entailment can be expressed as subject, yielding an incremental theme subject. Jackendoff cites several examples of such subjects from Declerck (1979) and Dowty (1991) in support of this point; these are given in (25) and followed by some additional examples of Jackendoff's in (26); see also Filip (1996) and Verkuyl (1972: 101).[12]

(25) a. The endless procession walked by the church.

(Declerck 1979: 568, (19a))

b. John entered the icy water (very slowly).   (Dowty 1991: 570, (25a))

c. The crowd exited the auditorium (in 21 minutes).

(Dowty 1991: 570, (25b))

(26) a. Water gradually filled the boat.

b. Water descended the mountain for hours.

(Jackendoff 1996b: 314 (17a,b))

Confirming that the sentences in (26) have incremental theme subjects requires showing that analogous sentences whose subjects are quantized NPs are necessarily telic; sentences such as *The ten milliliters of solution filled the vial in fifteen seconds* suggest that this is so.

In support of his larger point, Jackendoff further claims that even arguments expressed as obliques can be incremental themes in the appropriate circumstances. For instance, the telicity of the locative alternation examples in (27) must be attributed to the obliques, as the corresponding sentences without them may be atelic, as shown in (28).

(27) a. Bill loaded the truck with three tons of dirt in/*for an hour.

b. Bill sprayed the wall with thirty gallons of water in/*for five minutes.

(Jackendoff 1996b: 347, (65))

(28) a. Bill loaded the truck for an hour.
      b. Bill sprayed the wall for five minutes.

The salient property of locative alternation verbs is that both arguments – the location and the theme of change of location – are associated with entailments which lend themselves to incremental theme interpretations (being filled/covered and distributed location, respectively). Typically, the argument expressed as direct object is interpreted as the incremental theme (perhaps due to pragmatic considerations), but to the extent that the sentences in (27) are grammatical, this interpretation is not absolutely required. Another clear example showing that a VP-internal argument other than a direct object may serve as an incremental theme is given in (29), suggested by Anita Mittwoch (p.c.).

(29) Sam distributed food to fifty senior citizens in three hours.

What makes this example striking is that the multiple recipients do not reflect an iteration over events since distribution inherently involves multiple recipients.

   What emerges is that in many examples when there is an incremental theme, it is a direct object or an intransitive subject, which, on some theories of syntax, can be analyzed as a direct object. The question remains whether there is really a direct connection between incremental themehood and the morphosyntactic realization of an argument or whether this general effect comes about in a less direct way. The aspectual approach to argument realization, however, makes a stronger point, in claiming that all aspects of morphosyntactic realization are mediated by aspectual properties. This is a position which Rappaport Hovav and B. Levin (2002) argue against. They point out that not all argument alternations can be understood in terms of event type-shifting or alternate choices of incremental theme, as has been claimed by many proponents of the aspectual approach. For instance, they show that the dative alternation is not aspectually motivated. Most dative verbs do not have incremental themes, since their theme is not affected incrementally: a giving event, for example, does not usually involve the incremental transfer of possession of the theme, nor is the associated path of transfer an incremental theme. The two alternative modes of argument realization exhibited by dative verbs are aspectually indistinguishable, and the alternate choice of direct object cannot be attributed to an alternate choice of incremental theme. Among the dative verbs are some like *read*, whose so-called theme argument is also an incremental theme. The telicity of sentences with one of these verbs is determined by this argument independent of its realization: it is the incremental theme whether it is the direct object in the *to*-variant of the alternation, as in (30), or the second object in the double object variant, as in (31).

(30) a. Dana read poetry to employees/her niece for an hour. (atelic)
      b. Dana read the story to employees/her niece in an hour. (telic)

(31) a. Dana read her niece poetry for an hour. (atelic)
b. Dana read her niece the story in an hour. (telic)

In the double object variant, the first object is usually taken to be the "true" object (see section 1.6), suggesting that in the dative alternation the choice of object is not aspectually determined. Still another argument alternation which does not appear to be aspectually motivated is illustrated by the pair *Cameron hit the fence with the stick* and *Cameron hit the stick against the fence*; here both variants are atelic, and neither has an obvious incremental theme.

Moving beyond traditional argument alternations, Rappaport Hovav and B. Levin (2002) also point out that when *out–* is prefixed to a verb, the verb's own direct object, even when an incremental theme, is replaced by a newly introduced direct object, which is never an incremental theme. In *Pat outate Chris*, the normal direct object of *eat*, which is an incremental theme, is not expressed, and, furthermore, *Chris*, the NP which is expressed as the object, is not an incremental theme since parts of Chris do not correspond to parts of the outeating event. Rather, the incremental theme seems to be the amount of eating that Pat did, and this notion is not expressed.

Furthermore, the insights that recent versions of the aspectual approach offer into argument realization are somewhat limited in scope. These approaches focus on a certain class of direct objects: those that represent arguments associated with the notions of incremental theme or telicity. The proposal is that such arguments are direct objects because they occupy the specifier position of a functional projection such as AspP, where they receive accusative case. However, many verbs, such as *jiggle* and *pound* may realize an argument as a direct object, yet this argument does not have a necessary aspectual contribution to make. It is not an incremental theme and, thus, does not move into the specifier position of a functional projection such as AspP. In this sense, Tenny's analysis is correct in being silent about whether such arguments may be direct objects, and, thus, not precluding this possibility, while allowing such verbs to express these arguments as obliques, as they do in some languages. However, aspectual approaches do not offer any insight into why these verbs should have objects. They need to be supplemented by a general theory of direct object selection, which would also encompass objects which do not necessarily receive accusative case, as in accusative/partitive case alternations, as well as "objects" which obligatorily receive oblique cases in some languages, such as the instrumental second arguments of Russian verbs of authority, ruling, and disposition, mentioned in section 1.5, which otherwise show direct object properties.

As stressed in chapter 1, a theory of argument realization needs to account for more than just the simple choices of subject and object. In this context, Rappaport Hovav and B. Levin (2002) make the more general point that verbs with similar aspectual characterizations do not share argument realization possibilities. For example, as already mentioned in section 4.2.1, certain theories give a unified analysis to traditional incremental theme verbs, such as *eat, memorize*, and *read*, and change-of-state verbs, such as *break, dim*, and *melt*. But change-of-state verbs have a more severely restricted range of argument realization options than the traditional incremental theme verbs. Thus, change-of-state verbs are obligatorily transitive, as shown by (32) and (33), and the theme of the change of state is the only argument which may appear as direct object, as shown by (34). In contrast, traditional incremental themes may or may not be expressed, as in (35), and need not be expressed as objects, as in (36); furthermore, other argument NPs or nonargument NPs may take their place as direct object, as illustrated in (37).

(32) *Pat broke/dimmed.

(33) a. Alex broke (*at) the vase.
     b. Sam dimmed (*at /from) the lights.

(34) a. *My kids broke me into the poorhouse.
     b. *The stagehand dimmed the scene dark.

(35) Dana ate/wrote.

(36) a. Chris ate the apple./Chris ate from/of the apple.
     b. I wrote my book./I wrote at my book.

(37) a. My kids ate me into the poorhouse.
     b. I wrote myself out of a job.

A theory of argument realization should be able to provide an appropriate characterization of semantic classes of verbs which show distinctive morphosyntactic behavior, and an aspectually based theory does not do this successfully to the extent that it cannot naturally distinguish between change-of-state verbs and traditional incremental theme verbs.

B. Levin and Rappaport Hovav (2004) point out crucial data involving the English resultative paradigm which does not follow from any of the current aspectual theories of argument realization. As is well known, in contrast to the data in (22), where an intransitive verb required the mediation of a direct object to be followed by a result XP, English allows certain intransitive verbs to be followed directly by a result XP, as in (38).

(38) a. The door rolled open.
     b. The gate swung shut.
     c. The cookies burned black.
     d. The coats steamed dry.

The contrasting behavior of a verb like *sing* in (22), repeated in (39), and verbs as in (38) has usually been attributed to a difference in unaccusativity: *sing* is unergative and the latter are unaccusative.

(39) a. Pat sang for hours. (intransitive; atelic)
     b. Pat sang herself hoarse in two hours. (transitive; telic)
     c. Pat sang the audience to their feet in twenty minutes. (transitive; telic)

If the result phrase must be predicated of a direct object (B. Levin and Rappaport Hovav's [1995: 34] Direct Object Restriction, following Simpson [1983]), the contrast receives an account. However, attempts to explain this contrast in terms of the notions of incremental theme and telicity are not successful. Neither an aspectual property of the verbs themselves, nor of the resultative constructions containing them explains why verbs such as *sing* require a "fake" reflexive object in a resultative, while verbs such as *roll* and *swing* do not. All these verbs are atelic in isolation, and all the resultatives are telic; however, only the subjects of verbs like *roll* and *swing* can be incremental themes without a fake reflexive, while the subjects of verbs such as *sing* cannot. B. Levin and Rappaport Hovav attribute the difference to another quasi-aspectual property, which they term "event complexity," discussed in the next section, and elaborated on in section 7.4.

As we have shown, most phenomena used to support the aspectual approach involve the choice and realization of the direct object of a verb. Tenny's Aspectual Interface Hypothesis has few implications for the argument selected as the subject, except that it requires that an argument realized as subject may not participate in the delimitation of the event denoted by the verb: "An external argument cannot participate in measuring out or delimiting the event described by a verb. An external argument cannot be a measure, a path, or a terminus" (Tenny 1994: 83, (165)). In contrast, Borer (1994, 1998), Ramchand (2002), Ritter and S. T. Rosen (1998, 2000), van Voorst (1988, 1993), and others also take subject selection to be aspectually determined. They consider the subject the "initiator" of an event, bounding the beginning of the event by providing its initial point. However, there are no well-articulated diagnostics for an initiator, and aspectual accounts have not provided much insight into the alternative semantic choices of subject, such as agent, instrument, or natural force, in the way that they have provided insight into alternative choices of object.

Finally, the aspectual approach has little to say about the distribution of prepositions in oblique phrases. The major distinction it makes is between goal phrases and all other obliques. Goal phrases are privileged elements in aspectual approaches since they participate in delimitation; see (17). In fact, the aspectual approach to argument realization forces oblique arguments which participate in event delimitation to be syntactically close to the verb, but it does not impose similar restrictions on other oblique arguments. Various diagnostics for VP-constituency such as *do so* substitution and VP-preposing suggest that goal phrases, which enter into event delimitation, are closer to the verb than certain other adjuncts, including locative adjuncts.

(40) a. *Terry pushed the cart into the barn, and Bill did so into the yard.
      b. Terry read the book in the barn, and Bill did so in the yard.

(41) a. *Terry said she would push the cart into the barn, and push the cart she did into the barn.
      b. Terry said she would read the book in the barn, and read the book she did in the barn.

To sum up, the notions of telicity, measure, and incremental theme appear to be implicated in certain facets of argument realization, especially in the choice and expression of direct objects. However, precisely how these notions are implicated in argument realization and how their contribution is best characterized remains to be fully worked out. Nevertheless, we have also shown that not all facets of argument realization can be reduced to these notions.

4.2.5   Event complexity

We now review another property, EVENT COMPLEXITY, which has also been implicated in argument realization. We discuss it in this section since some definitions of this property make reference to the internal temporal constituency of events, even if they do not make reference to telicity or the related notion of incremental theme, which aspectually based approaches usually take to be the properties which most directly affect argument realization.

In section 3.2 we pointed out that what makes event structures appealing as semantic representations is their ability to encode certain properties of events that cannot be represented with semantic role lists, including approaches that treat semantic roles as collections of lexical entailments associated with certain arguments of verbs, as Dowty (1991) does. For instance, event structures, by having a function–argument form, naturally define hierarchical relations between certain arguments. This property is desirable since, as we discuss in section 5.2.2, there are approaches to argument realization which make crucial reference to hierarchical relations among arguments in the mapping from semantics to syntax.

More generally, a lexical semantic representation formulated in terms of unordered sets of entailments associated with arguments cannot appeal to structural relations between arguments or any structural properties of events themselves. Event structures taking the form of a predicate decomposition usually include an additional type of structural information about an event: they represent what we called in section 3.2 its subeventual analysis, a notion we now elaborate on. A subeventual analysis indicates (i) the number and type of constituent subevents; (ii) the number and identity of the arguments participating in the particular subevent; and (iii) the nature of the temporal relations between the subevents. Event structures which include information of this kind have been developed by a number of researchers, including Engelberg (1994, 2000b), Grimshaw and Vikner (1993), B. Levin and Rappaport Hovav (1999), McClure (1994), Pustejovsky (1991b, 1995), Rappaport Hovav and B. Levin (1998a, 2000), van Hout (1996, 2000a, 2000b), Wunderlich (1997a, 1997b, 2000). Other theories of lexical semantic representation, including Role and Reference Grammar's logical structures (Van Valin and LaPolla 1997), can distinguish among events in terms of their subeventual analysis, but do not include any principles which make reference to such information.

Central to subeventual analysis is event complexity: whether an event is simple, consisting of a single subevent, or complex, consisting of more than one subevent, each of which can independently be a well-formed event. Although the simple/complex event distinction is crucial, these approaches may nevertheless recognize different types of simple events, which may themselves give rise to different types of complex events. The canonical complex event is a causative event, as in *Kerry opened the window*, composed of a causing event or process (Kerry doing something) and a second, caused event or result (the window opening); the caused event cannot be temporally prior to the causing event; see Pustejovsky (1995) for discussion. Single argument activity verbs represent prototypical simple events, though stative verbs also represent simple events.[13]

Various types of support have been adduced for positing a subeventual analysis for some events. The first type of evidence is familiar from the work of the generative semanticists, who argue for multiple sentential constituents underlying certain monoclausal sentences in order to account for observed ambiguities in the scope of a range of adverbials (McCawley 1968, 1971; Morgan 1969). These sentential constituents essentially represent distinct events, so that the arguments suggesting that certain apparently monoclausal sentences actually have multiclausal structure can be recast as arguments for attributing a complex event structure to an event, as in Pustejovsky (1991b, 1995) and von Stechow (1995, 1996; Rapp and von Stechow 1999). An example of this type of ambiguity that has received continuing attention is the availability of two readings for certain sentences with *again*, such as *The butler opened the door again* (McCawley 1971; Morgan 1969; Dowty 1979; von Stechow 1995, 1996). On the so-called repetitive reading, the butler once again opens a door he has opened before, while on the restitutive reading, the butler brings it about that the door is once again open (though he may not have opened it the first time). On the repetitive reading, *again* modifies the entire event, while on the restitutive reading, it modifies the state that results from the event. The availability of the restitutive reading suggests that the result state must be explicitly represented within the event structure.

Durative adverbials are used to make the same point. Certain durative adverbials are able not only to specify the duration of an event as a whole, but also to specify the duration of an event's result state, as in the celebrated sentence *The Sheriff of Nottingham jailed Robin Hood for 20 years* (Binnick 1969; McCawley 1971; Morgan 1969: 61). Here for pragmatic reasons, the durative phrase is most likely understood as describing the length of Robin Hood's jail term and not as describing the amount of time it took to jail him, though *for* phrases may specify the duration of an event (e.g., *Robin Hood hid for two weeks*). This sentence shows once again that it is possible to make reference to the result state of an event, and hence that this result state must be represented. Taking this idea further, Engelberg (1995, 2000b) shows that German uses different modifiers to indicate these two types of duration: *lang* phrases describe the duration of the event leading up to the result state, while *für* phrases describe the duration of a result state.

(42) a. Er joggte zwanzig Minuten lang.
'He jogged for twenty minutes.'
b. Er verließ das Haus für zwanzig Minuten.
'He left the house for twenty minutes.'   (Engelberg 2000b: 262, (11))

Engelberg uses German *für* phrases to make the additional point that event structures have to specify which participants are associated with which subevent. He points out that *für* phrases can indicate the duration of the result state, only if the agent is involved in maintaining this state. As support, he points to the contrasting acceptability of the sentences in (43); (43b) is unacceptable, according to him, since an agent cannot be involved in maintaining a state of loss.

(43) a. Sie blockierten die Straße für eine Stunde.
'They blocked the street for one hour.'
b. ?? Sie verlor den Schlüssel für einige Minuten.
'She lost the key for a few minutes.'(Engelberg 2000b: 262–63, (12a,c))

Engelberg suggests that the contrast in (43) shows that "event participants are linked to particular subevents for different verbs" (2000b: 263). In fact, event structures have to do more than specify which participants are linked to which subevent; they also have to specify which subevents are associated with the root. The need for this surfaced in our discussion in section 3.3 of the role the root plays in determining a verb's potential participation in the causative alternation. There we showed that the fact that the verb *smear* does not show the causative alternation (*We smeared mud on the wall/*Mud smeared on the wall*) can be attributed to the nature of its root, which is associated with both the causing subevent and the result subevent of a complex event structure.

Event complexity has been defined in two ways, either in terms of the result state definition of telicity or in terms of the temporal relations which hold between subevents. The first approach is taken by Pustejovsky (1991b, 1995) and van Hout (1996, 2000a, 2000b). They take any event that is aspectually telic to be a complex event. This approach receives its impetus from the proposal discussed in section 4.2.1 that a telic event involves a transition to a new state; the presence of such a transition is what makes the event complex. On this analysis, all telic events – whether achievements or accomplishments – are analyzed as transitions and, hence, as complex events. For instance, both causative and noncausative uses of change-of-state verbs would be considered complex events. However, we argue that even if such events could be considered complex, this type of event complexity does not matter for argument realization in the way that the type of event complexity defined by the second approach does.

B. Levin and Rappaport Hovav (1999) take a different approach to event complexity. They point out that if events are understood as sets of temporally anchored properties, then an event is defined by all those properties which are necessarily true of the same interval. However, a verb may be associated with properties which are not aligned temporally, and if so, the verb would be associated with more than one subevent, each with its own temporally aligned sets of properties. A complex event, then, has subevents which are not necessarily temporally aligned. By this criterion, a causative event, such as *Terry thawed the meat*, is a complex event. In this example, the causing event involving Terry need not extend the full length of the event of the meat thawing: Terry might simply have taken the meat out of the freezer and left it on the counter to thaw.

We now review B. Levin and Rappaport Hovav's arguments for taking this understanding of event complexity to be syntactically useful. Most researchers who appeal to event complexity in accounts of grammatical properties posit a principle which requires that each subevent in a complex event be given some form of syntactic realization (Grimshaw and Vikner 1993: 144; van Hout 1996: 201; Kaufmann and Wunderlich 1998: 25; B. Levin and Rappaport Hovav 1999: 202; Pustejovsky 1991b: 77; Rappaport Hovav and B. Levin 1998a: 112–13, 2001: 779). There are various formulations of this requirement; we cite Rappaport Hovav and B. Levin's (2001).

(44) THE ARGUMENT-PER-SUBEVENT CONDITION: There must be at least one argument XP in the syntax per subevent in the event structure.

> (Rappaport Hovav and B. Levin 2001: 779)

This requirement has the consequence that complex events must be expressed by dyadic predicates, and, in core instances, by transitive verbs. Rappaport Hovav and B. Levin (1998a) illustrate the effects of this requirement by contrasting the syntactic behavior of verbs which are basically noncausative activities and, thus, have a simple event structure with that of verbs which are basically causative and, thus, have a complex event structure.

(45) a. $[\text{x ACT}_{<MANNER>}]$
      b. $[[\text{x ACT}] \text{ CAUSE } [\text{BECOME } [\text{y } <STATE>]]]$

> (B. Levin and Rappaport Hovav 1998a: 108)

They take verbs of surface contact, such as *sweep* and *wipe*, which do not entail any result state, to represent the first type, and causative change-of-state verbs, such as *break* and *dry*, to represent the second. As already illustrated in section 4.2.4, change-of-state verbs have restricted argument realization options; in particular, the theme of the change of state must be expressed and must be expressed as a direct object. Rappaport Hovav and B. Levin (1998a) attribute these properties to their complex event structure, which requires their agent and theme to be expressed by the Argument-Per-Subevent Condition.

As they show, the very basic transitivity which follows from the complex event structure of verbs of change of state has a wide range of consequences. In particular, it accounts for the restricted range of argument alternations that these verbs appear in, a pattern which, as pointed out in section 4.2.4, is not explained by the aspectual approach to argument realization. (As we discuss in section 4.3, the causal approach is also unable to account for the constrained behavior of change-of-state verbs. Change-of-state verbs come out as the most "highly" transitive verb type on this approach, but there is no articulated explanation of the range of argument realization possibilities.)

Rappaport Hovav and B. Levin (2001) point out that the Argument-Per-Subevent Condition also explains the distribution of verbs across two forms of the English resultative construction, first mentioned in sections 4.2.3 and 4.2.4. Certain intransitive verbs can predicate a result phrase of their subjects directly, while others can only do so through the mediation of a "fake" reflexive pronoun; contrast (46a) and (46b).

> (46) a. The coats steamed dry.
> b. The diva was careful not to sing *(herself) hoarse.

As discussed in section 4.2.4, the distribution of verbs in these patterns is not entirely predicted by the aspectual approach; instead, B. Levin and Rappaport Hovav (1999) and Rappaport Hovav and B. Levin (2001) appeal to event complexity. They argue that although two subevents are potentially distinguishable in each pattern (steaming and drying in (46a); singing and becoming hoarse in (46b)), only the pattern with the fake reflexive qualifies as a complex event. Specifically, they show that what distinguishes the reflexive pattern from the other pattern is the temporal relation between their subevents. In the reflexive pattern, the two subevents need not necessarily unfold together: the hoarseness need not set in and develop simultaneously with the singing in (46b), but the steaming and the drying necessarily occur together in (46a). B. Levin and Rappaport Hovav (1999) argue that the necessary temporal dependence in (46a) is evidence that the events of steaming and drying should be viewed as a single event. If (46b) represents a complex event, then the presence of the reflexive follows from the Argument-Per-Subevent Condition, which requires one argument for each subevent; see Pustejovsky (1991b) for a similar analysis. In contrast, as a simple event, (46a) would not require the introduction of a reflexive.

Some accomplishment verbs, which have been considered causative verbs by those who equate accomplishments with causatives and, hence, are taken to have a complex event structure, are open to a different analysis on B. Levin and Rappaport Hovav's approach; see also Van Valin and LaPolla (1997: 111–13). These are verbs of consumption, such as *eat* and *drink*, verbs of creation, such as *write* and *build*, and other incremental theme verbs, such as *translate* and *study*. These verbs are analyzed as accomplishments since they involve an event with a duration and an endpoint: the endpoint is the ingestion of the food for *eat*, the creation of the complete written entity for *write*, and the translation of the entire text for *translate*. However, the activities of eating, writing, and translating are inherently coextensive with the processes of the food's disappearance and the written entity's or translation's coming into existence. In other words, the subevents constituting these events are necessarily temporally dependent. As a result, B. Levin and Rappaport Hovav (2004) predict that they have simple, rather than complex, event structures. The syntactic behavior of these verbs bears this prediction out. Unlike change-of-state verbs, the incremental theme argument of these verbs need not be expressed, as shown in (47); when it is expressed, it need not be expressed as the direct object, as shown in (48), though it is no longer an incremental theme when it receives this realization.

(47) a. Dana ate/drank.
     b. Drew wrote/carved.
     c. Kelly studied/translated.
(48) a. Dana ate (from/of) the apple.
     b. Drew wrote at her novel.
     c. Kelly studied from the textbook.

Thus, these verbs do not show the hallmarks of a complex event structure.

To summarize, the notion of event complexity – whether a verb has a simple or a complex event structure – appears to figure in the explanation of a range of argument realization phenomena. In fact, the simple/complex event structure distinction appears to work better than more often cited notions, such as telicity.

4.3   The causal approach

The third theory of event conceptualization takes causal notions to be central to determining argument realization. There are various instantiations of the causal approach, including those found in the work of Croft (1990, 1991, 1994, 1998), DeLancey (1984, 1985, 1990, 1991), Jackendoff (1990b), Langacker (1987, 1990, 1991, 1993), and van Voorst (1988, 1993, 1995); most are inspired by Talmy's work on causation (1976, 1988). For presentational purposes, we focus on Croft's formulation of this approach since it is particularly comprehensive and explicit, though we include references to other work where helpful. The most detailed analyses of causal notions and their grammatical consequences are found mainly in cognitive and functional frameworks, and, therefore, our explication of these notions is couched in the terms of those frameworks. It is unclear to us whether there is a conceptual affinity between the causal approach to event conceptualization and the theoretical underpinnings of these frameworks; we leave this question open.

The causal approach models events as CAUSAL CHAINS, consisting of a series of segments, each of which relates two participants in the event; a single participant may be involved in more than one segment. Verbs name segments of such a causal chain. The main features of an event conceptualized in causal chain terms, as set out by Croft (1991: 173), are listed below. (Croft adds additional assumptions later in the book [1991: 269], but the assumptions cited here are the central ones.)

> (49) a. a simple event [i.e. what is named by the verb] is a (not necessarily atomic) segment of the causal network;
> b. simple events are nonbranching causal chains;
> c. a simple event involves transmission of force;
> d. transmission of force is asymmetric, with distinct participants as initiator and endpoint . . .   (Croft 1991: 173)

According to Croft (1991: 173) "The prototypical event type that fits this model is unmediated volitional causation that brings about a change in the entity acted on (i.e., the manifestation of the transmission of force), that is, the prototypical transitive event . . . " (see also section 1.5). This model is schematized in (50). (Croft [1994: 37, n. 5] remarks on the notation: "a dot indicates a participant; an arrow indicates a relationship of transmission of force, which can be described by the capitalized label just below it; a line without an arrowhead indicates a noncausal (stative) relation; a parenthesized dot indicates that it is the same participant as in the preceding causal (or noncausal) segment.")

(50) Idealized Cognitive Model of a Simple Event (Croft 1994: 37):

Initiator		Endpoint		(Endpoint)		(Endpoint)
•	$\longrightarrow$	•	$\longrightarrow$	(•)	——	(•)
	CAUSE		CHANGE		STATE	

The causal chain representation of a particular event that fits this model is given in (51). The participants realized as subject, object, and oblique are indicated by SBJ, OBJ, and OBL respectively; we discuss the meaning of the hash signs below.

(51) Harry broke the vase. (Croft 1994: 38, (12))

Harry		(vase)		(vase)		(vase)
•	$\longrightarrow$	•	$\longrightarrow$	(•)	——	(•)
SBJ	CAUSE		CHANGE		STATE	OBJ
# # #			break			# # #

As the diagram shows, this sentence involves a three-part causal chain: (i) Harry acts on the vase, (ii) the vase changes state, and (iii) the vase is in a result state (i.e., broken). This causal chain conforms to (49). It is nonbranching; specifically, there is only a single result; furthermore, there is an asymmetric transmission of force from Harry to the vase, with distinct participants as the initiator (*Harry*) and the endpoint (*the vase*).

Central to most causal approaches is the notion of PROFILE (Croft 1998: 38–39, 42–47, 59–60; Langacker 1987: 118, 184, 214–22, 1991: 297–98).[14] Based on work by Fillmore (1982, 1985) and Langacker, Croft assumes that it is possible to distinguish in a particular use of a verb between what is presupposed and what is asserted. Presumably, the presupposed elements of meaning in a given sentence are always drawn from the root, i.e., that part of the meaning of the verb which remains constant across uses. This part of its meaning is sometimes also called the frame or base. What is asserted, or "profiled" in Croft's terms, can vary from use to use. In this way, the same causal chain can underlie more than one use of a particular verb, if each has a different portion of the chain "profiled." For example, as a representation of the transitive sentence *Harry broke the vase*, the whole causal chain in (51) is profiled, as indicated by the three hash signs at the beginning and end of the causal chain. To quote Croft (1994: 37, n. 5), the "three [hash] signs give the delimitation of the segment of the causal chain that is profiled by the verb, and the verb itself is placed between the delimiters." The same causal chain underlies the intransitive sentence *The vase broke*, but here only the last two segments of the chain are profiled; that is, the leftmost hash signs would be placed under the first occurrence of *vase*.

A causal chain perspective is implicit in many semantic role list approaches. By their very nature, semantic role lists force a representation of an event in terms of its participants and their interrelationships, and the roles agent, instrument, and patient, which invariably figure in a semantic role list, name important participants in a causal chain. However, Croft (1991, 1998) and Langacker (1987, 1990a, 1990b, 1991) point out that the causal chain approach is different from semantic role approaches in one very crucial way: it delineates an explicit model of event structure and organizes the relationships between individuals in an event in a way that semantic role-based accounts cannot. Specifically, with arguments represented as points in a causal chain, an organization is imposed on arguments according to their positions on the causal chain. The relationships between these positions are particularly important for the formulation of principles of argument realization. Some of the most commonly proposed semantic roles are given definitions in terms of configurations in causal chains, so that an agent is "the initiator of an act of volitional causation" (Croft 1991: 176) and an instrument is "an entity that is intermediate in a causal chain between the subject (initiator) and the object (final affected entity)" (Croft 1991: 176). The argument realization rules make reference to points on the causal chain: subject and object are the realization of the arguments at each end of the profiled segment of the causal chain lexicalized by a verb, with the subject being the argument that causally precedes the object.

A slightly different instantiation of the causal approach is developed by Jackendoff (1987, 1990b), based on work by Culicover and W. Wilkins (1984); see also sections 2.3.2 and 4.1. Jackendoff distinguishes between what he calls the thematic tier, dealing with notions of motion and location, and the action tier, dealing with what he calls actor–patient relations, which essentially encode force-dynamic relations between two participants in an event. The roles actor and patient are not given a specific definition; rather, they are identified primarily by distributional tests. Actors fill the NP slot in the frame *What NP did was ...* and patients fit into the NP slot in the frames *What happened to NP was ...* or *What Y did to NP was ....* The realization of arguments as subject or object in English is largely determined by the roles assigned to arguments on the action tier. The actor, if there is one, is always the subject, and any nonactor analyzed as a patient on the action tier is realized as a direct object (Jackendoff 1990b: 257–62). Since Jackendoff does not present a full picture of how all the participants in an event might be construed in terms of ordered positions in a causal chain, we do not make further reference to his work, beyond stressing that his work converges with the other work in taking the force-dynamic status of arguments to be essential to the determination of subject and object choice.

As Langacker (1990: 216, 1991: 296) and Croft (1998: 46) point out, the causal approach to subject and object choice explains the paradigm introduced by Fillmore (1968).

(52) a. The door opened.
      b. John opened the door.
      c. The wind opened the door.
      d. John opened the door with a chisel.   (Fillmore 1968: 27, (40)–(43))

Fillmore accounts for these data by positing a subject selection hierarchy, in which agents have precedence over instruments, which in turn have precedence over patients. The idea that the subject and object are the first and last elements in the profiled portion of the causal chain essentially explains why an instrument can be a subject only in the absence of an agent, and why the patient can be a subject only in the absence of both agent and instrument. Any other configuration would violate the ordering inherent in the causal chain representation of the event.

One of the most striking arguments in favor of the causal approach is that it allows an interesting distinction to be drawn among the semantic roles of arguments realized as obliques, a distinction which appears to be utilized crosslinguistically. These arguments can be classified according to their position on the causal chain, the major distinction being where they are located with respect to the endpoint of the segment of the causal chain lexicalized by a verb, i.e, the object. From this perspective their semantic roles fall naturally into two classes, which Croft terms the antecedent and subsequent roles, according to whether they are positioned before or after the argument in the causal chain realized as direct object. The antecedent roles include instrument, manner, means, comitative, and cause, while the subsequent roles include benefactive, recipient, and result. (A similar distinction is made by Langacker [1990: 238, 1991: 327] under the rubrics "source domain," including the agent and instrument, and "target domain," including theme, experiencer, and recipient.)

Croft shows that this subclassification is manifested in languages, as the two types of semantic roles have different realizations. Although there are case syncretisms involving the antecedent roles and case syncretisms involving the subsequent roles, there are no syncretisms that involve roles of both types, unless they involve all roles. For example in English, *with* marks three of Croft's antecedent roles, instrument, manner, and comitative, while *to* marks two of his subsequent roles, recipient and result.[15] Thus, the causal approach imposes a partial ordering on participants relevant to argument realization. Croft (1998: 40) also points out that as they acquire language, children often substitute one antecedent preposition for another (Clark and Carpenter 1989: 19). It is not clear whether the aspectual approach can make a comparable distinction, since it does not provide a full analysis of the entire causal chain. The most obvious distinction that the aspectual approach can make is between those roles that figure in event delimitation and those that do not, and in fact, two of Croft's three subsequent roles – recipient (i.e., goal) and result – do delimit events. We leave further exploration of this question for future research.

Further support for the antecedent/subsequent distinction is found in Marantz's (1993) discussion of properties of double object constructions, particularly those involving applicative verbs in various Bantu languages. He presents evidence in favor of treating benefactives – which are subsequent roles – differently from instruments – which are antecedent roles. Marantz explains the difference in behavior between benefactives and instruments in terms of the order of composition of the verb with its arguments.

(53) Affected object benefactives are compositionally outside the event constructed by the verb and theme/patient; affected object instruments and affected place locatives are affected inside this event and thus may be compositionally inside or outside the combination of verb and theme/patient.

(Marantz 1993: 123–24, (11))

Although Marantz's explanation, unlike Croft's, is couched in terms of order of composition of arguments, the two accounts agree that benefactives and instruments are integrated into event structure in different ways. It remains to be seen which approach has the best account for this.

There are many verbs that do not denote the asymmetric transfer of force associated with Croft's prototypical transitive event, and these verbs appear to present a problem for the causal approach. Croft (1991) proposes that the events denoted by such verbs are "coerced" into the mold of the prototypical event by being conceptualized as if they involve such an asymmetry, much in the ways events which are not events of motion and location are coerced into such a mold on the localist approach. For example, verbs of location such as intransitive *lean, sit,* or *stand,* are central to the localist approach, but describe events where there is no transfer of force. According to Croft, events of spatial location are conceptualized as if the theme antecedes the location in a causal chain and therefore with such verbs the theme – and not the location – is realized as subject. As support for this analysis, Croft points to causative verbs of change of location such as *put*, where the theme is moved to the location.

The prototypical transitive event in which one "participant acts on and causes a change of state in a second participant" instantiates the so-called "billiard ball" model of causation (Michotte 1963; see also Langacker 1991: 13–14, 283, 1993: 485), where the most important relation between participants in the underlying causal chain involves the asymmetric transmission of force from one participant to a second. Asymmetric transmission of force is only the most common of a larger set of force-dynamic relations identified by Talmy (1988),[16] and some of the other force-dynamic relations are also relevant to understanding argument realization. Croft (1998: 29, (8)) illustrates this with (54), where a location is expressed as the subject.

    (54) The table is supporting the vase.

This pattern does not conform to the spatial location coercion just described; rather, Croft suggests that it represents a force-dynamic relation that involves the extended causation of rest. In this relation, an antagonist resists the inherent tendency of an agonist to move; thus, the location is really force-dynamically acting on – and hence causally antecedent to – the theme, explaining why the location is realized as subject. This analysis accords with the intuitive understanding of what the verb *support* means, and explains why (54) feels pragmatically rather odd. A more natural sentence with this verb is *The large base supports the bridge*, where the fact that the base is exerting a force against gravity on the bridge is important for understanding why the bridge is structurally sound.

This approach to subject and object selection does not single out a particular semantic property associated with either subject or object, but rather takes order in the causal chain to be the most important factor in determining subject and object choice. It therefore accords with the observation that there is no single unifying lexical entailment which holds of all subjects or all objects. It allows for subjects which are not agents and objects of transitive verbs which are not patients, as long as the argument chosen as object is subsequent in the causal chain to the argument chosen as subject. It also accounts for the observation mentioned in section 3.1.1.2, that the lexical entailment of causally affecting another participant overrides other lexical entailments in subject choice. On this approach, perhaps no more needs to be said universally about subject and object selection, as languages differ widely in terms of the semantic notions they allow to be associated with subject and direct object; see section 1.5.

However, as we have discussed, verbs taking agent and patient arguments are indeed singled out crosslinguistically in that they are universally transitive, with the agent as subject and the patient as object; in addition, they show the least marked morphosyntactic expression available to two-argument verbs. On the causal approach, agents and patients turn out to be the prototypical subjects and objects respectively because of the special role played by subjects and objects. The arguments chosen to be subjects and objects are those that serve to individuate the event named by the verb from the larger set of happenings in the world, and, according to Croft (1991, 1994, 1998), by their very nature, events with a volitional agent and an affected patient are maximally individuated. Although it is often difficult to identify the ultimate cause of an event, when an event has a volitionally acting participant, i.e., an agent, "there is no antecedent transmission of force to a free agent, and hence the event is naturally delimited as to its initiator" (Croft 1994: 38–39). Likewise, when the action results in a change of state with a clearly identifiable result in a participant, i.e., a patient, the event is also delimited at its endpoint since "states in general do not cause other events to take place" (Croft 1994: 39). Perhaps for this reason volitional agents and affected patients constitute the core of the prototypical transitive event (cf. the idealized cognitive model of an event). This type of event serves as the mold for the prototypical event, and the analysis of other event types is understood in terms of extending this conceptual archetype, as Langacker (1990: 298–304, 1993: 472) calls it, to other domains.

Croft (1993) attributes the pervasive variability in the argument realization options of the experiencer argument of both types of psych-verbs, discussed in chapter 1, and verbs of perception to the availability of two types of force-dynamic relations in mental events: one type involves the experiencer directing attention to the stimulus (in which case the experiencer is force-dynamically prior) and the other involves a stimulus causing a mental state in the experiencer (in which case the stimulus is force-dynamically prior). Indeed, verbs such as *look at, listen to, watch* and *think about*, which lexicalize that the experiencer has control over directing attention towards a theme, consistently realize the experiencer as subject, while those which lexicalize a change of state in the experiencer, such as *surprise, frighten, shock* and *anger*, consistently realize the experiencer as object. Stative experiencer verbs such as *fear* and *hate* do not have any inherent causal directionality, and, therefore, crosslinguistically, as mentioned in section 1.5, stative verbs are found with either experiencer or stimulus subjects. Under this analysis, the notion of experiencer is only indirectly relevant to argument realization: the choice of subject and object is determined by force-dynamic relations among participants, but there still remains the generalization that in events involving experiencers, two force-dynamic relationships are possible. In contrast, the aspectual approach has less to say about experiencer verbs than the causal approach. Both approaches predict more than one argument realization option for stative verbs, since these verbs are not covered by the core principles of subject and object choice, but there are experiencer subject verbs and stimulus subject verbs which are aspectually the same. For example, *The clown amused the children for two hours* and *Bob looked at the painting for two hours* are both activities, but the linking of the stimulus to subject in the first and experiencer to the subject in the second is explained only by the causal approach.

Just as proponents of the aspectual approach use properties of argument alternations as evidence for their approach, so do proponents of the causal approach. In the aspectual approach, alternate choices of direct object are taken to represent alternate choices of incremental theme, while direct object/oblique alternations correspond to an argument being or not being an incremental theme (see section 4.2.3). Croft (1998) does not deny that this description of the semantic change which accompanies these alternations is often appropriate; however, he attributes the change to a process which he takes to be more basic than an alternate choice of incremental theme. According to Croft, argument alternations, such as the locative alternation, arise from differences in the profile associated with the verb in each variant, and the familiar semantic differences between variants are taken to follow from these differences. We defer a fuller discussion of these issues to chapter 7, but illustrate the basics of the approach here with the locative alternation.

(55) a. Pat sprayed paint on the wall.
      b. Pat sprayed the wall with paint.

The idea is that in (55a) the verb profiles the part of the causal chain that involves the force transmission to the material, but not the path of the material to the surface. As the endpoint of the causal chain, the material *the paint*, then, is the object. In (55b), on the other hand, the verb profiles not only the force transmission to the material, but also the path of the material to the surface. Now, the surface *the wall* is the endpoint of the causal chain, and, thus, is the object, with *the paint* expressed using *with*, the English preposition used for antecedent roles.

Croft argues that the verbal profile ideally should represent an event which can be conceptualized as self-contained. Therefore, those arguments which can best contribute to the individuatedness of the event are chosen as subject and object. In essence, subjects and objects delimit the causal chain on either end. Volitional agents and affected patients are the best "individuators," as they represent clear causal boundaries. The affectedness of the surface argument in (55b) is attributed to the fact that in this variant, the location argument is at the end of the causal chain and the affected interpretation contributes to its ability to clearly individuate the event (Croft 1998: 44). In this context, Croft also mentions the wide range of direct object/oblique alternations which "have to do with lowering the degree or totality of the effect of the action on the relevant participant" (1998: 45); these are essentially the same direct object/oblique alternations cited by proponents of the aspectual approach in support of the connection between direct objecthood and event delimitation; see section 4.2.3. Croft accounts for the semantic effect of the alternations in terms of whether or not the argument showing the alternate realization is included in a verb's profile: the affected – or delimited – interpretation arises naturally when this argument is included in the verb's profile because then the argument delimits the event and the prototypical event delimiter is an affected patient.

Croft provides comparable explanations of subject/oblique alternations. These also reflect differences as to the portion of a causal chain that is part of a verb's profile, but in this instance, the differences are with respect to the point in the causal chain that is taken to define the initiation of the event. Again, the profiled part of the causal chain must be defined as an event that can be conceptualized as self-contained. Such an event must have a clearly identifiable initiator, and this depends, in turn, on the type of causation and the degree of control the initiator has over this causation. For this reason, as Croft (1998: 45) notes, "subject–oblique alternations ... are sensitive to the directness of causation, or the degree of control of causation." DeLancey (1984, 1985, 1990, 1991) is particularly explicit about the initial segments in the causal chain – the segments involving the participants involved in bringing about an event – and, concomitantly, carefully distinguishes prototypical from nonprototypical types of event causation; he shows that the prototypical agent is one which is identified as both the ultimate and proximate cause (DeLancey 1984: 184). The expression of certain causes as obliques indicates a deviation from this prototype, as in *He died from pneumonia*, which has what DeLancey calls an "inactive cause."

4.4 The aspectual and causal approaches compared

In the previous chapter, we reviewed the entailments which Dowty (1991) suggested were relevant for subject and object selection in English. Among the questions raised there were where these entailments come from and why the entailments defining each proto-role belong together. By invoking an Agent Proto-role and a Patient Proto-role, Dowty pointed in the direction of an answer: these entailments are those typically associated with agents and with patients. The aspectual and causal approaches can in some sense be viewed as presenting more elaborated theories intended to answer these questions. The causal approach suggests that agents and patients are prototypical causes and effects, while the aspectual approach suggests that agents and patients are prototypical initiators and endpoints of events. Both approaches, for example, agree that sentience and volition are not the primary ingredients which determine subjecthood. We showed that this is indeed so in section 3.1.1.2: volition and sentience are prototypically associated with animate causes, but it is an argument's role as cause, not its volition or sentience, which determines its subjecthood. This point emerges clearly when sentience is attributed to one argument and causation to a second, as with *frighten* psych-verbs, which have experiencer objects, and periphrastic causatives such as *The joke made me laugh*, which in many languages can be lexicalized by a single verb. The primacy of the notion "cause" is also evident when its interaction with motion entailments is examined. As Dowty (1991: 573) points out, motion is an Agent Proto-role entailment, only if the movement is not caused, as in *The bullet overtook the arrow* or *The rolling tumbleweed passed the rock* (1991: 573, (29d)). In such instances, the subject's involvement is also temporally prior to the object's, since the bullet moves before it overtakes the arrow, as does the tumbleweed before it passes the rock. This last point invites a more general discussion of the parallelism between the aspectual and causal approaches.

As mentioned in section 4.2.2, some more recent instantiations of the aspectual approach distinguish an "aspectual" role of "originator" (Borer 1994) or "initiator" (Ritter and S. T. Rosen 1998). These authors provide the role with an aspectual – or temporal – analysis, in taking the initiator to be the participant which, temporally speaking, initiates an event. Since transfer of force between participants and the temporal order in which participants take part in an event can both be given a representation in terms of a notion of precedence, and the source of the transfer of force is often involved in the event before the recipient of the force, in the final analysis the two approaches end up using quite similar representations, which overlap considerably for most verbs. Thus, both approaches agree that the representation of events must impose a precedence order on the participants in the event. Temporal precedence often corresponds to precedence in the causal chain. Although there are exceptions, they probably can also be made to preserve this general correspondence. For example, in the events described by verbs of surface contact such as *rub*, *sweep*, and *wipe*, the agent and the surface are, strictly speaking, involved at the same time, even though there is an asymmetric transfer of force. However, it is possible that the agent typically begins the action before contact is made with the surface in the sense that an act of volition precedes the contact, and, if this is the case more generally, causal ordering and temporal ordering should almost always coincide.

We are not aware of any versions of the aspectual approach that fully work out the details of how the temporal order of involvement of participants fits into argument realization. The instantiations of this approach say little more than that the subject is associated with an initiator; they do not analyze this concept. Moreover, they take incremental theme and telicity to be central notions, but have little to say about the realization of arguments which are not associated with these aspectual notions. And as we have shown, it appears that telicity seems to be associated more often with the surface realization of grammatical relations, as in the distribution of morphological case, than with the determination of the grammatical relations themselves (see section 4.2.3).

Finally, we return to the notion of sentience. This notion figures among Dowty's Agent Proto-role entailments (see section 3.1.1), but does not fit neatly into either the causal or aspectual approaches, even though it or a related notion is clearly relevant to argument realization. As Dowty (1991: 572) notes, it is the only criterion that determines that the experiencer of noncausative, stative verbs of perception, cognition, or psychological state, such as *fear, love, see,* and *want*, is realized as subject. Sentience is more than animacy; Croft's characterization of a "mental-level entity" as "not just any role that may be occupied by a human being but one exercising his mental abilities in the action in question" (1991: 168) captures what is often intended. A somewhat different notion of sentience emerges from Wechsler's (1995: 31–40) characterization of the subjects of verbs such as *fear, love, want*, and *expect*. Drawing on Crimmins and Perry (1989), Wechsler suggests that the subject of such a verb has a "notion" of the individual denoted by its object; that is, a notion or idea of its object plays a role in the beliefs or mental states of its subject. Although, as just mentioned, sentience must be the determinant of subject choice for certain noncausative, stative verbs, neither the causal nor the aspectual approach can accommodate this, unless sentience is integrated into a more elaborated theory of initiators.

Sentience must be distinguished from volitionality. Under either characterization of sentience, volition entails sentience, but not vice versa: compare *murder* and *fear*. Even noncausative verbs differ as to whether their arguments are simply sentient or might also be interpreted as volitional, and this difference is reflected in their argument realization options in a way that suggests further refinements will be needed. Certain active perception and cognition verbs (e.g., *listen, think, watch*) take a volitional, sentient argument, and this argument patterns like a cause in terms of argument realization, perhaps because a volitional argument can be regarded as setting up a force-dynamic asymmetry (see Croft 1991: 166–69). It is realized as a subject and shows the morphological case of a prototypical agent: the nominative or ergative. In contrast, in many languages, verbs such as *fear, love, see* and *want*, whose sentient argument cannot be interpreted as volitional, realize this argument as a nonprototypical subject in that its morphological case is usually dative or locative and it might not show all the behavioral properties of subjects (see section 1.6). So although sentience is a determinant of subject choice, more needs to be said in a fully articulated theory of subject selection.

Finally, sentience should probably be distinguished from animacy, a notion dealt with in more detail in chapter 6. Animacy seems to be particularly important to determining the surface expression of arguments bearing particular grammatical relations, that is, their coding, rather than behavioral, properties. Phenomena which are sensitive to animacy include differential object marking (Aissen 2003; Bossong 1991, 1998), the choice of morphological case for certain goals (Aristar 1996, 1997), and the presence of pronominal object marking (Evans 1997; Morolong and Hyman 1977).

4.5   Conclusion

In this chapter we reviewed three approaches to event conceptualization – the localist, causal, and aspectual approaches. Each takes a different cognitively salient facet of events as relevant to determining argument realization. The first approach – at least, as presented by Gruber and Jackendoff – does not have a significant contribution to make to the understanding of argument realization, though it may be important for understanding extended meanings and polysemy. The other two incorporate notions that appear to be relevant to argument realization. We have shown that there is a certain affinity between the causal and aspectual approaches, and more generally it appears that both causal and aspectual notions are relevant to argument realization, though there are some phenomena neither approach covers. We have pointed out that causal notions take precedence over sentience in subject and object selection. However, sentience is still implicated in various argument realization phenomena, though the exact range and nature of these phenomena needs further investigation. We also showed that sentience is sometimes implicated in argument realization because of the way in which volitionality, which entails sentience, determines certain forms of causation. However, not all instances of sentience implicated in argument realization can be subsumed under causal notions.

What emerges from this chapter is that four broad types of semantic factors play a part in argument realization: causal notions, aspectual notions (e.g., telicity, incremental theme), event complexity, and notions such as sentience, animacy, and volitionality. In principle, it should be possible to delineate the realms of morphosyntactic realization for which each is relevant. For example, causal notions seem to determine to a large extent the choice of subject and object. Sentience is also implicated, a point we elaborate in chapter 6. Telicity is most likely implicated in the distribution of accusative case, and event complexity is implicated in the obligatory appearance of certain arguments. Animacy seems particularly relevant to determining the surface expression of arguments bearing particular grammatical relations, such as their morphological case. We leave it to future research to make the more principled link between these semantic factors and the various facets of morphosyntactic expression.

Notes

1   Jackendoff (1990b: 88–89) does discuss a set of verbs that he describes as "verbs of manner of motion and configuration" such as *dance*, *wave*, and *wiggle*. Although these verbs are a subset of activity verbs, Jackendoff does not discuss them in that context, but rather in the context of a discussion of verbs of motion, noting that they are used to "describe only the internal motion of the subject, with no implications with respect to their location, change of location, or configuration with respect to any other object" (1990b: 88). Jackendoff (1990: 90) proposes that *laugh* and *sneeze* may belong to the same class since they describe characteristic actions. Yet, it is not clear that these verbs should be singled out from other activity verbs, as they pattern together in many respects. For discussion of activity verbs, see B. Levin (1999). In any event, such manner-of-motion verbs do not have a natural localist analysis, since they cannot be based on Jackendoff's motion primitive GO, which necessarily takes a path argument.

2   Jackendoff does not formulate rules of argument realization in his early work. The closest he comes to this is in using semantic roles to account for certain purportedly unacceptable instances of passivization such as **Five dollars are cost by the book* (1972: 44, (2.70)). He proposes such sentences are ruled out because the subject of the passive sentence is higher in a hierarchy of semantic roles than the object of *by*. However, this use of a thematic hierarchy has been questioned by Bresnan and

Kanerva (1992), Comrie (1975), Freidin (1975), Gee (1974), and Hust and Brame (1976). For more discussion of thematic hierarchies see chapter 6.

3 Dowty (1991: 572, (27)) does include "movement (relative to the position of another participant)" among his Agent Proto-role entailments, but what he has in mind is broader than the type of motion along a path that is central to the characterization of theme in localist approaches. Dowty sees motion along a path as often being subsumed under the change-of-state entailment he associates with the Patient Proto-Role (1991: 574), rather than under the just-mentioned Agent Proto-role entailment.

4 In this book we concentrate on what is called "lexical aspect," which is intimately tied to the lexical semantic properties of verbs. For the most part, we ignore "viewpoint aspect," i.e., the temporal perspective from which a particular situation is presented (Sasse 2002; Smith 1991), which implicates the lexical semantics of verbs to a lesser degree. Furthermore, we continue to use the term "event" as we defined it in section 1.4: to refer to a happening whose properties get linguistically encoded. We reserve the term "event description" for the linguistic expressions used to describe these events, so that aspectual classes are classes of "event descriptions." We thus depart from the usage of "event" which reserves this term for either dynamic or telic event descriptions (Bach 1986).

5 The scope of the term "telicity" is a matter of debate. A sentence like *Sylvia ate apples for three minutes* is telic only under some definitions of telicity, such as those we discuss appealing to part structure in the nominal and verbal domains, since an event of eating apples for three minutes does not have a proper subpart which is also an event of eating apples for three minutes. In contrast, Declerck (1979) and Depraetere (1995) argue for a narrower definition, which takes telicity to be a lexical property of a predicate; concomitantly, they distinguish between "boundedness" and "telicity." Under such a definition, a sentence with a *for* adverbial would be bounded, but not necessarily telic. It appears that only telicity which is calculated in terms of some kind of lexically specified or lexically implicated scale (see section 4.2.2) affects the morphosyntactic expression of arguments, so any other kind is not of concern here.

6 It is possible to understand the physical extent of the denotation of the direct object as measuring out the event denoted by a change-of-state verb in some instances. In *Carrie melted the ice cream*, the event can be understood to be completed when all of the ice cream has melted. But even in these instances it is not clear that the characterization in terms of physical extent is the most appropriate one since all the ice cream could be softening as it slowly melts.

7 Jackendoff suggests that whether or not an argument of a verb is a measure (or incremental theme) is in fact pragmatically determined and depends on the nature of the entity denoted by that argument and the way the action denoted can be carried out on it. If you eat an apple, the apple is a measure since you eat the apple in a series of bites, but if you eat a grape, the grape is not a measure since you eat it in a single bite (1996b: 312). If you draw a circle with a pencil, then the circle is a measure, but if a computer printer sprays the entire circle onto the page at once, it is not a measure (1996b: 312–13). However, as M. Olsen (p.c.) points out, these facts show that the time taken by an event need not be an interval; see also Tenny (1994: 16–17). If an event is punctual, so is the measure of that event on the temporal scale, but the direct object is still the measure. In fact, Jackendoff (1996b: 312) acknowledges this: "the measuring-out property of *eat* is evidently connected

in part to the nature of the objects in question and the pragmatics of how the action can be carried out on them." Yet, on the basis of comparable arguments, Krifka (1996: 445) argues that it is premature to conclude, as Verkuyl (1993) does, that the accomplishment/achievement distinction is purely pragmatic and that "the length of the event does not seem to be a linguistic matter" (Verkuyl 1993: 49); see also Mittwoch (1991: 75).

8   Another use of the term "affectedness" is found in S. R. Anderson's (1977) discussion of the notion "theme." He uses "affectedness" in the narrow sense of total affectedness, which is intended to subsume the interpretation associated with the location argument of a locative alternation verb when it is expressed as the object (e.g., *spray the wall with paint*); see section 7.2.3.2 for discussion. In recent years, the phenomena Anderson discusses, including the locative alternation, have been reinterpreted as reflecting aspectual shifts. See section 4.2.5 for discussion.

9   Direct internal arguments are roughly underlying objects, indirect internal arguments are other VP-internal arguments, and external arguments are underlying subjects; see Rappaport and B. Levin (1988).

10   Although de Hoop takes Finnish partitive case as the paradigm example in making her point, Kiparsky (1998: 273–76) argues that there are serious problems with this assumption; Schmitt (1999: 388–89) also presents a critique. Nevertheless, what matters here is the role of de Hoop's work in the development of a functional projection associated with aspect.

11   A question arises as to why there is no unaccusative counterpart of (22c), i.e., *Pat sang hoarse*, since, if unaccusative, this example would also involve a direct object. See Rappaport Hovav and B. Levin (2001) for discussion.

12   Some have questioned the validity of such examples, suggesting that they involve covert unaccusative verbs, whose subject is really an underlying object. If so, they would lend further support to an incremental theme/direct object connection. See Dowty (1991: 571, n. 15), who argues such an analysis is not viable, and Mateu (2002), who argues in favor of such an analysis.

13   In some approaches to event structure such as Pustejovsky's (1991b, 1995), activity verbs are represented as being constituted of an iteration of subevents. However, this kind of internal structure is meant to represent the dynamism of such events, contrasting with the lack of dynamism of states. No principles of argument realization access such internal structure.

14   In earlier work, Croft (1991) refers to the "profile" as the "verbal segment." Croft's notion of profile differs somewhat from Langacker's. His use of the term also departs from Goldberg's (1995: 45–46); see Croft (1998: 40–41) for discussion. A similar notion, though not extensively developed, appears in van Hout's (1996: 118–22) discussion of alternations which arises from variation in "event foci."

15   Using a much broader crosslinguistic survey, Stolz (1996) shows that instrument/comitative syncretisms are not as widespread across languages as Croft's own survey suggests; rather, they are primarily attested in "European" languages. However, it is their existence that matters for Croft's claim.

16   See Wolff (2003) and Wolff, Song, and Driscoll (2002) for some efforts to identify English verbs with the major classes of predicates that emerge from the features that are essential to this force-dynamic model, thus supporting Talmy's (1988) model of force-dynamic relations.

5

The mapping from lexical
semantics to syntax

In this chapter we consider two hypotheses concerning the nature of the mapping from lexical semantics to syntax. These hypotheses are meant to impose constraints on the mapping, and their formulation depends on the nature of both the lexical semantic representation and syntactic representation assumed.

All the work reviewed in this book so far is predicated on the assumption that there is a relationship of general predictability between the lexical semantic representation of a verb and the syntactic realization of its arguments. This assumption is elevated to a linguistic hypothesis by Perlmutter (1978; Perlmutter and Postal 1984):

(1) Universal Alignment Hypothesis:
There exist principles of UG which predict the initial [grammatical] relation borne by each nominal in a given clause from the meaning of the clause. (Perlmutter and Postal 1984: 97)

The Universal Alignment Hypothesis is built on the widely accepted assumption that there are general principles which govern argument realization and that these principles are not tailored to individual verbs. As we have shown, there are semantically coherent classes of verbs whose members show similar behavior, and there are semantically defined classes of arguments that pattern together in terms of argument realization. However, the Universal Alignment Hypothesis is extremely general and does not take a position as to the nature of the mapping itself. The additional hypotheses considered in this chapter are more specific in this respect.

Most of the substantive hypotheses constraining the mapping process assume that certain facets of the lexical semantic representation are preserved in the syntax. There are two broad classes of hypotheses concerning the facet of the lexical semantic representation assumed to be preserved: (i) the equivalence classes of arguments that the representation defines or (ii) the prominence relations the representation – if appropriate – defines among arguments. As part of the discussion of these two classes of hypotheses, we show that each class is naturally correlated with a particular type of mapping process. In section 5.1 we discuss each class of hypotheses, and in section 5.2 we turn to the two types of mapping processes.

5.1 Equivalence class preservation constraints

In chapter 2 we showed that certain classes of arguments can be viewed as equivalence classes in that the mapping from lexical semantics to syntax treats the members of the classes alike. Similarly, certain classes of verbs also constitute equivalence classes for the lexical semantics-to-syntax mapping in that their arguments share the same syntactic realizations. The strongest hypothesis is that this mapping is one-to-one. In practice, this hypothesis has been taken to mean that either each distinct semantic class of arguments is associated with a distinct syntactic realization or that each distinct semantic class of verbs is associated with a distinct syntactic configuration. As mentioned in section 2.2, this hypothesis is incorporated into many semantic role list approaches, dating back to Fillmore's Case Grammar. Equivalence classes of arguments are trivially defined in representations that take the form of semantic role lists: each set of arguments bearing a particular semantic role constitutes an equivalence class. Given this, the feasibility of adopting an EQUIVALENCE CLASS PRESERVATION CONSTRAINT on the mapping has primarily been considered with respect to semantic role-based approaches to lexical semantic representation. As we discuss, the basic idea behind equivalence class preservation has also made its way into approaches which take lexical semantic representation to have the form of predicate decompositions. This extension is not surprising given that some researchers see predicate decompositions as giving rise to semantic roles; see section 3.2.

The major potential advantage of imposing an equivalence class preservation constraint on the mapping process is the retention of transparency in the mapping from lexical semantics to syntax. However, on the surface, at least, equivalence class preservation does not hold in the lexical semantics-to-syntax mapping since this mapping is apparently many-to-many. Consider just one illustration: arguments bearing the patient/theme role turn up as subjects, as objects, and arguably even as obliques, as in (2), while there are objects that qualify as patients, themes, goals, sources, experiencers, and locations, as in (3).

(2) a. *Water* splashed on my clothes. (subject)
    b. The children splashed *water* on my clothes. (object)
    c. The children splashed my clothes with *water*. (oblique)

(3) a. The construction crew widened *the road*. (patient)
    b. The boy pushed *the cart* into the barn. (theme)

c. Pat wrote *me* a letter. (goal)
d. The workers cleared *the road* of debris. (source)
e. The thunder terrified *the children*. (experiencer)
f. My cousins hiked *the Rockies*. (location)

A single semantic role can have multiple syntactic realizations, and more than one semantic role can have the same realization. More generally, the number of semantic roles usually posited as relevant to the mapping is greater than the number of syntactic distinctions they are to be mapped onto. Typically, no more than three core grammatical relations are identified: subject, direct object, and indirect object.

Equivalence class preservation, then, seems difficult to maintain. Two strategies have been adopted to reduce the discrepancy between the number of semantic and syntactic distinctions. The first uses abstract syntactic representations as a way of increasing the number of syntactically encoded distinctions. The second uses either coarser-grained definitions of semantic roles or generalized semantic roles (see section 3.1) as a way of reducing the number of semantic distinctions. Another option is to weaken equivalence class preservation, allowing the lexical semantics-to-syntax mapping to be many-to-one, rather than one-to-one; each semantic equivalence class, then, must have a specific syntactic realization, though it need not be a unique realization. Finally, sometimes several of these strategies are combined.

The use of abstract syntactic representations to preserve equivalence classes dates back at least to Case Grammar. Fillmore (1968) represents a verb and its arguments via a multibranching syntactic tree which serves as a "d-structure," in which each NP is associated with a particular preposition determined by its semantic role ("case" in Fillmore's terms). For example, the preposition associated with agents is *by*, with goals is *to*, and with instruments is *with*. Thus, this "d-structure" maintains a one-to-one mapping of semantic roles to syntactic positions. When an NP bearing a particular semantic role is made the subject or object via rules of "subjectivization" or "objectivization," its preposition is deleted. As Jackendoff (1990b: 246) puts it, "any of these 'rigid' theories entails various amounts of syntactic movement and deletion or insertion of prepositions in order to account for surface syntactic distribution." It is only at the surface that the relationship between lexical semantic and syntactic categories is ultimately many-to-many.

Fillmore's abstract syntactic representations allow a direct representation in the syntax of semantic role lists; in the Principles and Parameters framework and its descendants such representations tend to mirror predicate decompositions. The use of VP-SHELLS – verbal projections with empty heads, first introduced by Larson (1988) – helps achieve a one-to-one mapping. Each additional verbal projection provides a position for an NP as the specifier of that projection, allowing for an increase in the number of NP positions over those available in a single verbal projection; the goal is to allow enough distinct syntactic positions for arguments to parallel the range of lexical semantic distinctions. Through the use of movement rules, NPs are moved from their underlying syntactic positions to a select few positions, which correspond to surface grammatical relations. This is the source of the observed discrepancy between the number of semantic roles and the number of grammatical relations. The overall "geometry" of proposed VP-shell representations is reminiscent of previously proposed predicate decompositions and is justified by making reference to independently motivated semantic classes of verbs and their arguments. In this sense, proponents of VP-shells replicate complex semantic structures in the syntax, just as the generative semanticists did before them (Lakoff 1968, 1970; McCawley 1968, 1971). As Jackendoff (1990a: 453–54), Travis (2000a: 147–48), and Wunderlich (1997b: 39), point out, VP-shells effectively reintroduce predicate decomposition into the syntax.

Perhaps the best-developed example of how VP-shells can be used to preserve equivalence classes is found in the work of Hale and Keyser (1992, 1993, 1997a, 1997b, 1998, 1999, 2002; Hale 1996). They identify a small number of major semantic classes of verbs and assume that the verbs in each class are lexically associated with a particular syntactic structure that configurationally encodes the semantic relations between a verb of that type and its arguments; they call these "lexical syntactic structures." Thus, each lexical syntactic structure preserves an equivalence class of verbs and equivalence classes of arguments. For example, the verb *clear*, a verb of change of state, receives the lexical syntactic representation in (4), as do other deadjectival verbs of change of state, while the verb *saddle*, which is what Clark and Clark (1979) call a denominal "locatum" verb, receives the one in (5), as do other denominal locatum verbs.[1]

(4) Deadjectival verb   (Hale and Keyser 1997a: 211, (15))

(5) Denominal locatum verb   (Hale and Keyser 1997a: 213, (21))

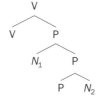

Both the structures in (4) and (5) involve the now familiar notion "root" (see section 3.2). In (4) the adjectival root is inserted in the *A* position, while in (5)

a nominal root is inserted in the N_2 position. Verbs are derived by "successive incorporation into immediately governing heads" (1997a: 205) of the root. In the representation in (4), an adjectival root, say *clear*, incorporates via movement into the lowest empty verbal head; for an intransitive deadjectival verb the root remains in this position, but for a transitive deadjectival verb it moves up to the higher empty verbal head. (The higher head and its projection are parenthesized in (4) to indicate that they are not always instantiated.) In (5), a nominal root, say *saddle*, first incorporates into the empty preposition; it incorporates next into the empty verbal head. Hale and Keyser (1997a, 1997b, 1998) argue that the incorporation of the root into an empty head is subject to the Head Movement Constraint (Baker 1988; Travis 1984) and use this constraint to explain why certain verb meanings are unattested: they involve incorporations that would violate this constraint. In fact, one of their reasons for positing lexical syntactic structures is a desire to harness independently needed syntactic principles to explain possible verb meanings (1992, 1993, 1997).

On Hale and Keyser's approach, simple transitive verbs do not all have the same lexical syntactic structure, as illustrated by *clear* and *saddle*. The object of *clear*, which is the entity that assumes the state named by the verb, originates as the specifier of a verbal projection in (4), while the object of *saddle*, which names the place that will be provided with the thing named by the verb, originates in the specifier of a prepositional projection in (5). The surface syntax, then, obscures both the underlying equivalence classes of verbs and of arguments.

Hale and Keyser's lexical syntactic structures are largely inspired by the meanings of the different types of verbs. Evidence for these structures includes the morphosyntactic shape of each verb type – a common form of evidence for representations of meaning (Dowty 1979; Foley and Van Valin 1984; Lakoff 1968, 1970; Van Valin and LaPolla 1997). Hale and Keyser also justify their lexical syntactic structures by pointing to syntactic differences among different types of verbs. For example, verbs like *clear* show the causative alternation, while denominal verbs like *saddle* and *shelve* do not.

(6)   a. We cleared the screen./The screen cleared.
      b. We shelved the books./*The books shelved.

                           (Hale and Keyser 1997b: 52, (38)–(39))

Hale and Keyser consider two explanations of this difference (1993 vs. 1997a, 1997b). Most recently, they attribute it to the nature of adjectival vs. prepositional heads in the lexical syntactic structures (Hale and Keyser 1997a: 214–16, 1997b: 57–60): adjectives are predicates, while prepositions form predicates, and prepositions thus require the additional subject argument.

Another widely accepted approach to the preservation of equivalence classes of verbs takes the equivalence classes to be aspectually defined: a specific syntactic configuration is associated with verbs in each aspectual class. This idea is first found in the work of Hoekstra (1992); see also Hoekstra (1988,

2000), Hoekstra and Mulder (1990), Mulder (1992), and Sybesma (1992). Hoekstra assumes that any predication relation, including the relation between an NP that changes state and its result state, must be explicitly encoded in a small clause. Thus, Hoekstra (1992) proposes that accomplishment verbs, as verbs of change of state, are found in the configuration in (7).

(7) V_{+dyn} [$_{sc}$ NP PRED]   (Hoekstra 1992: 163, (55))

This structure contrasts with the representation of comparable verbs given by Hale and Keyser in (4), where the result state and the NP it is predicated of do not form a constituent, but rather are the complement and specifier of a single head. (See Hoekstra [2000: 69–73] for discussion of this difference.)

Hoekstra does not present a syntactic representation for two-argument activity verbs, such as *push* in *He pushes the cart*, but Mulder (1992), who develops Hoekstra's ideas further, discusses such verbs, suggesting that they also should receive a small-clause analysis. He takes as his starting point the observation that *He pushes the cart* has a near paraphrase with a light verb, *He gives the cart a push*, and proposes (1992: 59) that *He pushes the cart* should be analyzed as in (8), where ϕ is an empty light verb. The predicate of the small clause then incorporates into the empty light verb.

(8) he ϕ [the cart push]   (Mulder 1992: 59, (18a))

Mulder (1992: 201–02) proposes that *He pushes the cart* is atelic because 'push,' the predicate of the small clause in (8), is a mass noun, contrasting with the result state in (7). This analysis of activities means that certain distinctions between aspectual classes are not reflected directly in their syntactic representations; rather, they arise from the nature of the predicate in a small clause. (See Hoekstra [2000] for some refinements on the representations given here and Vanden Wyngaerd [2001] for some discussion of issues raised by applying this approach to specific verbs.) Hoekstra's work contrasts with Hale and Keyser's in not making extensive use of VP-shells, though VP-shells have been used by some researchers who share with Hoekstra the assumption that aspectual classes of verbs should be maintained in the lexical semantics-to-syntax mapping (Erteschik-Shir and Rapoport 1996, 2004; McClure 1994, 1998; Slabakova 1998, 2000; Travis 1991, 2000a, 2000b).

A second approach to equivalence class preservation aims to bring the number of semantic distinctions more in line with the small number of surface syntactic distinctions, roughly, subject, direct object, indirect object, and oblique (or their configurational equivalents). This approach eschews abstract syntactic structures in favor of a monostratal – or, at least, not overly abstract – theory of syntax. The paucity of syntactic distinctions is taken to be a reflection of a comparable dearth of grammatically relevant semantic distinctions and the semantic role inventory is reduced accordingly.[2]

Some researchers adopt a coarse-grained analysis of semantic roles. By expanding the definitions of a few semantic roles so each encompasses what are more often considered distinct roles, the size of the role inventory is reduced. The notion of immediate cause, introduced in B. Levin and Rappaport Hovav (1995) and discussed in sections 2.2.1 and 3.2, represents a broadening of the notion "agent" to include natural forces, certain instruments, and the inanimate subjects of a variety of verbs, including *creak*, *shine*, and *quiver*. However, as discussed in chapters 2 and 3, broad, general semantic role definitions are usually considered undesirable, as they weaken the overall theory of lexical semantic representation. Instead, other researchers keep the number of semantic roles small by adopting generalized semantic roles, such as Role and Reference Grammar's macroroles, Schlesinger's (1995) A-case, or what we referred to in section 3.1.1 as the "reified" form of Dowty's (1991) proto-roles. (Dowty's own algorithm for mapping from semantic notions to grammatical relation is not equivalence class preserving as it involves counting proto-role entailments, rather than directly associating entailments with syntactic realizations.) Each generalized semantic role subsumes a range of semantic roles, just as a coarse-grained role does, but, as discussed in section 3.2, it is defined as a cluster or prototype concept. Since most researchers posit two generalized semantic roles, there is generally a simple association between these roles and the grammatical relations subject and object. (An exception is Primus [1999], who posits a third Recipient Proto-role, but even with three proto-roles, the association with grammatical relations is fairly simple.) But to the extent that generalized semantic roles do not represent semantic classes of arguments with a single, unified definition, some might argue that they are not truly faithful to the spirit of equivalence class preservation, even if they enable equivalence class preservation literally interpreted.

Some researchers reject the strongest form of equivalence class preservation, in favor of a weaker form in which the mapping from lexical semantics to syntax is many-to-one rather than one-to-one. By allowing several semantic roles to have the same syntactic expression, there is no need to posit an abstract syntactic structure intended to equalize the number of semantic and syntactic distinctions, nor is there any longer a need to use generalized semantic roles to reduce the number of semantic distinctions. B. Levin and Rappaport Hovav (1995) adopt this weaker approach, when they formulate two rules which map distinct semantic classes of arguments to direct object: one applies to the theme of change-of-state or change-of-location verbs and the other to the argument that comes into existence with verbs of appearance or whose existence is asserted with verbs of existence. In contrast, Kural (1996, 2002), who, like B. Levin and Rappaport Hovav (1995), does not want to collapse these semantic notions under a single semantic role, proposes that the two semantic notions are defined over distinct abstract syntactic structures, which give rise to the same surface realization of arguments.

The many-to-one approach is also embodied in some implementations of Baker's (1988) Uniformity of Theta Assignment Hypothesis.

(9) The Uniformity of Theta Assignment Hypothesis:
   Identical thematic relationships between items are represented by identical
   structural relationships between those items at the level of d-structure.

                                                    (Baker 1988: 46, (30))

Baker (p.c.) intends this hypothesis to allow for a many-to-one mapping from
semantics to syntax. All members of a semantic equivalence class must map
onto the same syntactic position, but there need not be a unique semantic equivalence class of arguments associated with each syntactic position. For instance,
the syntactic notion of subject need not be associated with a unified semantic
characterization. This approach allows certain essential semantic properties to
be preserved, without requiring that all semantic distinctions be reflected in
syntax. (See Baker [1997] for extended discussion of this hypothesis and a
comparison with similar hypotheses.)

A many-to-one mapping fails to explain why a particular disjunction of
semantic concepts underlies a particular syntactic realization. Perhaps as a
consequence, most proponents of equivalence class preservation constraints
strive to maintain such constraints in their strongest form through the use of
either abstract representations or coarse-grained semantic roles; however, both
these options have associated costs, even if they avoid disjunctions. As already
mentioned, generalized semantic roles can also be used to facilitate equivalence class preservation, although this might not be considered an improvement
over a many-to-one mapping since the algorithms for assigning generalized
semantic roles involve disjunctions. However, as discussed in section 3.1, the
disjunctions behind generalized semantic roles might really arise because certain components of meaning have priority over others with respect to argument
realization. If so, these disjunctions are not symptomatic of missed semantic
generalizations, but rather reflect properties of the lexical semantics-to-syntax
mapping that cannot be captured via equivalence class preservation constraints.
In fact, in the next section we discuss a second type of constraint on this mapping which allows for such differential priorities; we continue this discussion
further in the next chapter.

Finally, we review Baker's (1996a, 1997) attempt to maintain a strict
one-to-one mapping from semantic roles to syntactic positions. Baker accomplishes this by making both the theoretical moves we have discussed: he posits
fairly coarse-grained semantic roles and an abstract underlying syntactic representation. Baker recognizes three broad semantic roles: agent, theme, and
goal/path/location. His agent role, for example, encompasses all types of immediate causes (e.g., volitional and nonvolitional agents, natural forces, certain
instruments, and experiencers). The claim is that for the purposes of mapping
to "deep" subject, object, and oblique grammatical relations, only these three
semantic roles are necessary, although other generalizations may need to refer
to finer semantic distinctions, as discussed in section 2.2.1. In addition, Baker
adopts an abstract syntactic representation, which permits distinctions to be
made among surface subjects and direct objects: some are subjects and objects

only on the surface but not in the underlying syntactic structure and others are both "deep" and surface subjects and objects. Baker assumes that the basic structure of the clause for a three-argument verb is one in which, following Larson (1988) and Hale and Keyser (1997a, 1997b, 2002), there is a lower VP, with the lexical content of the verb, and a higher VP, with an empty verbal head. He takes the configurational positions for arguments to be specifier of the higher VP, specifier of the lower VP, and complement of the lower verb. He then proposes the rules in (10) which map the semantic roles agent, theme, and goal/path/location onto these three configurationally defined positions, roughly as in (11).

(10)   a. An agent is the specifier of the higher VP of a Larsonian structure.

   b. A theme is the specifier of the lower VP.

   c. A goal, path or location is the complement of the lower VP.

                                                    (Baker 1997: 120–21, (76))

(11)   Syntactic configuration assumed by Baker (1997)

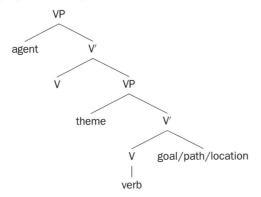

Baker allows for operations on the abstract syntactic structure in (11) in order to explain why on the surface there do not appear to be one-to-one correspondences between semantic and syntactic categories, and specifically, why objects can bear a range of semantic roles to the verb. Not every NP which is traditionally considered a direct object originates in the specifier position of the lower VP, and so not all surface direct objects will necessarily correspond to the theme argument of the verb. As support for this analysis, Baker (1997) develops several syntactic tests to determine when an NP that is a "surface" object actually originates in the specifier position of the lower VP. By applying these diagnostics, Baker concludes that the first object in a double object construction headed by a dative verb like *give* or *send* (i.e., a recipient/benefactive) does *not* originate as the "deep" object.

   We conclude this section by noting that in addition to syntactic realizations being associated with more than one semantic role, some semantic roles have more than one syntactic realization. For instance, the patient argument of many change-of-state verbs can be either a subject or an object, depending on the presence of an agent, as in the causative alternation. The locative and dative alternations can also be viewed as instances of multiple argument realization. Multiple syntactic realizations of a semantic role are often handled outside of the mapping process. Within the Principles and Parameters framework, syntactic movement rules are used to give rise to the multiple syntactic realizations of patient/theme arguments, which are always associated with the same d-structure position. Thus, the subject of a passive sentence and the object of the corresponding active sentence would originate in the same underlying syntactic position. Within Lexical-Functional Grammar's Lexical Mapping Theory (Bresnan and Kanerva 1989), semantic roles are associated with underspecified grammatical functions, allowing for a single lexical semantics-to-syntax mapping, but more than one syntactic realization, while maintaining a monostratal syntax. Grammatical functions are defined in terms of two features [r] and [o]. A patient/theme is associated with the feature [−r], which allows it to be realized as either a subject or an object, depending on the value of the yet unspecified feature [o] – a value determined by the larger context. What these two approaches have in common is the identification of an abstract syntactic "common denominator" that puts certain syntactic realizations into an equivalence class; this strategy allows equivalence class preservation in the face of multiple syntactic realizations. We return to a more serious form of the problem posed by arguments with multiple syntactic realizations in chapter 7, where we discuss verbs with multiple argument realizations.

5.2   Prominence preservation constraints

A second type of constraint on the lexical semantics-to-syntax mapping is designed to ensure that prominence relations encoded in the lexical semantic representation are preserved in the syntax. In such a mapping, to quote Jackendoff, "the syntactic prominence of an argument is determined (or largely determined) by its thematic prominence" (1992: 22). In this section we consider what is to be gained from having a prominence-preserving mapping.

Such a mapping presupposes lexical semantic and syntactic representations over which prominence relations among arguments can be defined, as well as an understanding of what prominence means with respect to each representation. Giving an independent interpretation of prominence is nontrivial, and often prominence relations – particularly semantic ones – are posited not on the basis of independent considerations, but because they facilitate the statement of generalizations.

In a configurational syntactic representation, prominence is defined using c-command or a comparable notion, so that a more prominent argument c-commands a less prominent one. C-command and its relatives have played a central role in syntactic generalizations, including those involving asymmetries between NPs of the type characteristic of binding and quantifier scope relations.

The postulation of prominence relations over a lexical semantic representation is probably inspired in part by their successful use in syntax, especially as the semantics has assumed a greater burden in the explanation of a variety of linguistic phenomena, including those whose syntactic explanation makes reference to prominence relations. By their very nature, phenomena like binding involve asymmetries that suggest semantic prominence relations, and one of the first explicit uses of lexical semantic prominence relations was in the explanation of certain binding facts (Jackendoff 1972: 148), and binding phenomena are now often given at least partially semantic accounts (e.g., Giorgi 1983–84; Jackendoff 1992; Van Valin and LaPolla 1997). Jackendoff, in fact, suggests that syntactic prominence relations have been appealed to in the absence of a worked-out theory of lexical semantic representation because "their effects are so similar to parallel conceptual structure conditions which are in fact the correct choice" (1992: 22). An additional incentive for defining a notion of semantic prominence is the tendency to view syntax as a projection of the properties of lexical items.

If relations of semantic prominence exist, they must be calculated over a more structured lexical semantic representation than simple semantic role lists or proto-role entailment lists provide. Such relations can be defined over a predicate decomposition or event structure, taking advantage of the articulated internal hierarchical structure. The dependency relations that Primus (1998: 439–31, 1999: 52) identifies as holding between the paired Agent and Patient Proto-role entailments (see section 3.1.1) could also be used as a basis for identifying the Agent Proto-role as more prominent than the Patient Proto-role; in fact, this ranking has independently been adopted by some linguists working in Optimal Typology (Aissen 1999; Asudeh 2001; H. Lee 2003). However, most often semantic prominence relations are stated in terms of a ranking of traditional semantic roles, that is, a THEMATIC HIERARCHY; this ranking is considered to reflect independent semantically defined prominence relations. We devote chapter 6 to a deeper understanding of the thematic hierarchy.

To ensure that prominence is preserved in the lexical semantics-to-syntax mapping, a notion of prominence must also be definable over the syntactic representation. Here too, prominence can be calculated over a configurational syntactic representation, or it can be explicitly defined via a hierarchy of syntactic relations. Such hierarchies take one of two forms: a hierarchy of grammatical relations or a hierarchy of morphological cases. The grammatical relations hierarchy was initially posited to account for crosslinguistic patterns of relativization under the label "NP-Accessibility Hierarchy" (Keenan and Comrie 1977), but it has been appealed to in accounts of other phenomena, such as case marking, agreement, word order, pronominal coreference, causativization, and other grammatical relation-changing rules. Discussion of this hierarchy and its coverage may be found in Blake (2001: 86–89), Comrie (1976b), Croft (2003b: 142–55), Gary and Keenan (1977: 83–87), Johnson (1979), Trithart (1975); see also Ross (1974) for a similar idea presented as "The Primacy Constraint." This hierarchy usually takes the form in (12), which, with its ranking of subject over object, is consistent with the typical configurational representation of these notions.

(12) subject > object > indirect object > oblique

This approach is congenial to those who argue grammatical relations are primitive rather than configurationally defined notions (Bresnan 1982c: 283–88; Perlmutter 1983a: ix–xii; Perlmutter and Postal 1983a; see Baker [2001] for a recent take on this debate). Hierarchies of morphological case have also been posited, again because they enter into the statement of generalizations, including generalizations about morphological case arrays, word order, reflexivization, and relative clause formation; see Ackerman and Moore (2001), Blake (2001: 89–90, 155–60), Ostler (1979: 150), Primus (1993: 692–93, 1998: 436–37, 1999: 154–55), Tsunoda (1981), Wunderlich (1997b: 48) for some discussion. For nominative–accusative languages, this hierarchy often takes the form in (13).

(13) nominative > accusative > dative > oblique cases

A range of prominence preservation hypotheses are offered. Perhaps the most general is Bouchard's Homomorphic Mapping Principle, "In a mapping from SR [= semantic representation] to SS [= syntactic structure], dominance relations are preserved" (1995: 96, (38)); Wechsler's (1995: 4) Isomorphy Condition represents a slightly different instantiation of the same idea. Most of these hypotheses, however, are proposed by researchers who presuppose the existence of a thematic hierarchy (Belletti and Rizzi 1988: 344; Jackendoff 1990b: 246; Larson 1990: 601; Ura 2000: 29), and, thus, a prominence preservation hypothesis reduces to a statement that the relations of semantic prominence among arguments as encoded in a thematic hierarchy should be maintained in the syntax; a representative example is (14).

(14) ... syntactic configurations projected from a given θ-grid should reflect the hierarchy, so that for every pair of θ-roles in the grid, the higher role in the hierarchy is projected to a higher structural position ...

(Belletti and Rizzi 1988: 344, n.36)

Larson (1990: 601) calls such a statement a "Relativized Uniformity of Theta Assignment Hypothesis," presenting it as a modification of Baker's original hypothesis, even though it is a prominence rather than an equivalence class preservation hypothesis; see Baker (1997: 108–17) for reactions.

Wechsler (1995: 4) points out that there is no reason, in principle, why a language couldn't map patients to subjects and agents to objects, yet no such language – or even verb within a language – exists (again, putting "true" ergative language aside; see chapter 1, note 4). The absence of such "reversals" in the expression of core arguments is ensured if the mapping from lexical semantics to syntax observes prominence relations. A mapping approach that adopts equivalence class preservation, in contrast, cannot account for this property.

Prominence preservation is sometimes assumed along with equivalence class preservation, as in Baker's (1997) study, discussed in section 5.2.1. Baker (1997: 123–26) assumes that the semantic notions he posits are in a prominence relation to each other, reflecting relevant predicate decompositions, and that his mapping to syntax maintains these relations. Thus, he makes the strongest possible claim, that there is a mapping between a structured lexical semantic representation and an identically structured underlying syntactic structure. However, prominence preservation and equivalence class preservation could, in principle, be independent. A one-to-one equivalence class-preserving mapping, for example, need not preserve prominence relations (though, as just mentioned, actual mappings do not seem to violate prominence relations). Furthermore, prominence preservation does not require equivalence class preservation, since it merely constrains the relative hierarchical relationships between the syntactic expressions of pairs of arguments, but does not force an argument to have a unique syntactic expression. We now illustrate this point since it is one reason that prominence preservation is appealing.

Belletti and Rizzi (1988) give an account for the alternate realizations of the arguments of Italian psych-verbs which exploits the possibility that a mapping can preserve prominence without requiring each semantic role to have a single realization. In Italian, the experiencer appears as a (preverbal) nominative NP with a psych-verb like *temere* 'fear' or as a (postverbal) accusative NP with a psych-verb like *preoccupare* 'worry,' while the theme appears as a nominative NP with *preoccupare* 'worry' and an accusative NP with *temere* 'fear.'

(15) a. Gianni teme questo.
         Gianni fears this   (Belletti and Rizzi 1988: 291, (1))
      b. Questo preoccupa Gianni.
         this   worries   Gianni   (Belletti and Rizzi 1988: 291, (2))

Belletti and Rizzi (1988: 344) assume the hypothesis in (14). Assuming that experiencers are semantically more prominent than themes, a verb's experiencer argument must be configurationally realized in a position that is higher than that of its theme argument. This requirement may be met in more than one way, explaining why there are two types of psych-verbs. Verbs like *preoccupare* 'worry' meet the requirement that the experiencer occupy a position higher than the theme, while expressing both within the VP, as schematized in (16).

(16) Syntactic representation of the VP for a *preoccupare*-type verb
                                         (Belletti and Rizzi 1988: 320, (76c))

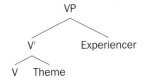

In contrast, *temere*-type verbs satisfy the requirement that the experiencer be higher than the theme with the experiencer VP-external and the theme VP-internal, as shown in (17).

(17) Syntactic representation for a *temere*-type verb

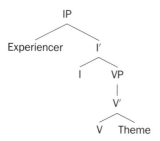

On this analysis, the theme is always the underlying object of the verb; with *temere*-type verbs, it remains the object, but *preoccupare*-type verbs have an unaccusative analysis and the theme moves to subject position. (The experiencer argument then gets accusative case-marking through a special process, making it appear to be the object.) Belletti and Rizzi present evidence in support of their general analysis, but many have critiqued it, including Arad (1998), Baker (1997: 24–25), Bouchard (1995: chapter 4), Grimshaw (1990: 31), and Pesetsky (1995: 19–53).

This analysis demonstrates that prominence preservation, like equivalence class preservation, is sometimes achieved through the use of abstract syntactic representations, with certain syntactic distinctions being neutralized on the surface. The surface objects of *temere* 'fear' and *preoccupare* 'worry' have very different sources. However, since disparities between the number of semantic and syntactic distinctions are not inherently problematic for prominence preservation approaches, their abstract syntactic representations are not used to maintain equivalent numbers of semantic and syntactic notions, as in equivalence class preservation approaches. Even if the lexical semantic representation distinguishes a fair number of semantic roles, since any given verb will typically have one to three arguments, the mapping simply needs to retain prominence relations between two or three arguments, whatever their semantic roles, and this requires at most three syntactic distinctions – the number of distinctions recognized for arguments in most syntactic theories. Thus, prominence preservation approaches are compatible with lexical semantic and syntactic representations that make different numbers of core distinctions.

Since prominence preservation approaches do not require that an argument bearing a particular semantic role have a unique syntactic realization, they can handle what we call the CONTEXT DEPENDENCE of argument realization in chapter 6: an argument whose realization depends on whether its semantic role is more or less prominent than the semantic role of any coarguments. For instance, a theme, *the cat*, is the object when it has an agent coargument, as in *Shannon moved the cat*, but the subject when it has a goal coargument in

The cat entered the room. Context dependence can be explained in terms of prominence preservation: a theme is less prominent than an agent, but more prominent than a goal, so it will be expressed as subject – the most prominent grammatical relation – only when it cooccurs with a goal, but not when it cooccurs with an agent. Context dependence is not so easily accommodated in an equivalence class preservation approach, where a particular argument has a single, constant realization. This phenomenon, then, suggests that a prominence preservation approach is to be preferred over an equivalence class preservation approach. (See chapter 6 for further discussion of context dependence as part of a larger discussion of the notion of prominence.)

Equivalence class preservation constraints take the relationship of individual arguments to their verb as most important in lexical semantic representation, while prominence preservation constraints take the overall hierarchical structure of this representation to be critical. This emphasis dovetails with a recurring conjecture about the relationship between the semantic and syntactic representations of a verb and its arguments, namely, that the compositional structure of the semantic representation is preserved in the syntactic representation.[3] This view is succinctly articulated by Marantz (1993: 143, (51)): "Constituent structure at D-structure represents (the) semantic compositionality (of events)"; similar ideas are presented by Baker (1989, 1997: 123–26, 2001: 43–49), Grimshaw (1990), Kiparsky (1985: 30, 1997), Wunderlich (1996, 1997a, 1997b, 2000), among others. Given the nature of compositionality, an argument realization process that preserves prominence relations would preserve compositionality in the syntax. (The hypothesis that syntactic compositionality reflects semantic compositionality has implications for the treatment of unaccusativity since, as unaccusative and unergative verbs have a single argument, it is not clear how they would be differentiated; see Baker [1997], Grimshaw [1990], and Kaufmann [1995a] for treatments of unaccusativity within the context of this hypothesis.)

There are a few suggestions in the literature concerning the rationale for prominence preservation. Bouchard (1995: 95) suggests that it is the strongest feasible constraint on the lexical semantics-to-syntax mapping. Williams (2003) confronts this question more broadly, arguing that mappings between linguistic representations should minimize "shape distortion" (2003: 1). A lexical semantics-to-syntax mapping that preserves prominence fulfills this criterion, though Williams does not discuss this mapping. He (2003: 7, 15) goes on to propose that shape preservation constraints can be viewed as economy principles.

5.3 Types of mapping algorithms

The two types of constraints on the lexical semantics-to-syntax mapping dovetail naturally with two kinds of mapping algorithms. We distinguish mapping algorithms that make direct reference to specific semantic notions defined on the lexical semantic representation, which we refer to as ABSOLUTE MAPPING algorithms, from those we characterize as RELATIVE MAPPING algorithms, which allow researchers to avoid direct reference to specific semantic notions, for instance, through the use of a thematic hierarchy. As we discuss, the first type of algorithm embodies equivalence class preservation and the second type prominence preservation.

5.3.1 Absolute mapping approaches

The simplest approaches to mapping utilize what we refer to as ABSOLUTE MAP-PING RULES – statements that explicitly specify the morphosyntactic realization of an argument of a verb bearing a particular semantic description. By their very nature, absolute mapping rules preserve equivalence classes and are not sensitive to prominence relations, whether semantic or syntactic, and so they are associated with theories that assume equivalence class preservation.

Absolute mapping rules can take various forms. The syntactic realization of an argument can be described in a number of ways, including in terms of grammatical relations (e.g., S. R. Anderson 1977), configurationally defined positions in a syntactic representation (e.g., Baker 1996a, 1997), or argument structure positions (e.g., B. Levin and Rappaport Hovav 1995). The semantic descriptions used in absolute mapping rules also vary. Most often they are stated in terms of semantic roles (e.g., S. R. Anderson 1977; Baker 1996a, 1997), generalized semantic roles (e.g., Aissen 1999; Asudeh 2001; H. Lee 2003; Primus 1998, 1999; Van Valin and LaPolla 1997), or positions in a predicate decomposition (e.g., Jackendoff 1990b). Although absolute mapping rules often make reference to traditional semantic roles, they can use coarser-grained notions, as in B. Levin and Rappaport Hovav's (1995) Immediate Cause Linking Rule in (18a), or finer-grained notions, as in their Directed Change and Existence Linking Rules in (18b) and (18c), whose content was mentioned in section 5.1.

(18) a. Immediate Cause Linking Rule:
          The argument of a verb that denotes the immediate cause of the eventu-
          ality described by that verb is its external argument.
                                        (Levin and Rappaport Hovav 1995: 135, (1))
      b. Directed Change Linking Rule:
          The argument of a verb that corresponds to the entity undergoing the
          directed change described by that verb is its direct internal argument.
                                       (Levin and Rappaport Hovav 1995: 146, (24))
      c. Existence Linking Rule:
          The argument of a verb whose existence is asserted is its direct internal
          argument.   (Levin and Rappaport Hovav 1995: 153, (47))

A disadvantage of theories of absolute mapping is that they impose few con-straints on the set of possible mapping rules. Furthermore, the absolute mapping approach faces the problem of context dependence in argument realization, introduced in section 5.2. As mentioned, many theories of syntax maintain that the theme always maps onto the underlying object and either treat themes realized as subjects as instances of syntactic movement, as in the multistratal Principles and Parameters framework, or as the filling out of underspecified feature matrices, as in monostratal Lexical-Functional Grammar's Lexical Mapping Theory. However, some instances of argument realization that demonstrate context dependence cannot be handled by syntactic movement or the filling in of underspecified feature matrices. For example, as pointed out in section 2.1, instruments can be realized as subjects, but only in the absence of an agent. No theory postdating Fillmore's (1968) Case Grammar has, for example, postulated a syntactic rule "moving" an instrument from a prepositional phrase to subject position. Therefore, an absolute mapping approach would require a disjunctive rule to deal with the alternate realization of instruments. An alternative strategy is to argue that the instruments realized as subjects are conceptually different from those realized as obliques; discussions of the concept of agency in Baker (1997), DeLancey (1985), and Van Valin and D. Wilkins (1996) suggest that there is merit to this approach.

The main drawback of absolute mapping approaches is that they do not explain why any particular set of absolute mapping rules is possible. Why, for example, should an agent be realized as a subject and a patient/theme as a direct object ("true" ergative languages aside)? The question here is similar to the questions that have been raised about the syntactic transformations of the 1960s or about explicit grammatical relation-changing rules: why are such rules formulated in the way they are and not in some other way? For instance, why is there a rule such as passive that "promotes" a direct object to subject, but no rule that "demotes" a subject to direct object? One exception is Baker's (1997) proposal regarding the lexical semantics-to-syntax mapping, which, as reviewed in section 5.2.1, involves absolute mapping fortified by prominence preservation. According to Baker (1997: 123) prominence preservation would explain why his absolute mapping rules are formulated as they are. In the next section, we turn to a second approach to argument realization, the relative mapping approach, which can be viewed as an effort to confront questions about why mapping algorithms take the form they do.

5.3.2   Relative mapping approaches

Absolute mapping rules can be contrasted with what we call RELATIVE MAPPING RULES. Such rules do not make explicit reference to specific elements in a lexical semantic representation, such as semantic roles or particular primitive predicates. Instead, they take advantage of additional organization inherent in or imposed on this representation to identify the arguments that receive a particular syntactic realization. One of the earliest examples of relative mapping proposed by Carter (1988a [1976]) uses rules that identify arguments in terms of the general structure of a predicate decomposition and not in terms of specific primitive predicates. This property contributes toward explaining why particular semantic roles are realized as they are. As we also discuss, relative mapping approaches are usually employed by theories which assume prominence preservation; as discussed in section 5.2.2, such theories are concerned with mappings that maintain relative relations among arguments, rather than with realizations of particular semantic classes of arguments.

We devote this section to the most prevalent form of relative mapping approaches: those making crucial use of a thematic hierarchy; chapter 6 is devoted to an understanding of the hierarchy itself. By defining prominence relations among arguments, a thematic hierarchy allows arguments to be referred to in terms of their ranking, without appeal to specific semantic role labels, as in "the argument that bears the most highly ranked semantic role" or "the argument that bears the lowest ranked role" or perhaps even "an argument that bears neither the highest nor the lowest ranked role," as in Joppen and Wunderlich (1995). Arguments identified in these ways are then associated with particular grammatical realizations. For instance, a commonly proposed subject selection rule, which has its antecedents in an idea in Fillmore (1968: 33), essentially chooses the argument bearing the highest ranked semantic role as subject (e.g., Bresnan and Kanerva 1989: 27). Given this subject selection rule, the generalization that the agent, if there is one, is subject can be captured by placing it at one end of the thematic hierarchy, which by convention is the top. Other semantic roles that are candidates for association with subject are then appropriately ranked below agent, so that subject selection can proceed down the hierarchy if a verb lacks an agent. Mapping algorithms differ, however, in the way they formulate the object selection rule with respect to the subject selection rule. There are two broad classes of algorithms, which we refer to as HIERARCHY-ALIGNING ALGORITHMS and BIDIRECTIONAL ALGORITHMS. We now discuss each type of algorithm.

Since most mapping algorithms which identify arguments in relative terms assume a prominence preservation mapping, they also identify the syntactic realization of these arguments in relative terms. The targets of the mapping rules must be organized according to a relation of syntactic prominence (see section 5.2). The most (or, alternatively, least) prominent argument semantically is matched with the most (least) prominent syntactic realization and the next most (less) prominent semantically with the next most (less) prominent syntactic realization, and so on, until all the arguments of a verb are exhausted. In this way, the mapping algorithm becomes a hierarchy-aligning algorithm, and the mapping is prominence preserving. In some sense, such algorithms are reminiscent of the notion of harmonic alignment in Optimality Theory (Aissen 1999: 679–85; McCarthy 2002; A. Prince and Smolensky 1993: 136).

Hierarchy-aligning algorithms differ according to whether their targets, which vary from theory to theory, are explicitly organized into hierarchies of grammatical relations or morphological cases, or implicitly organized into

hierarchies by being defined over positions in a configurational syntactic structure. The idea of arranging morphological cases into a universal hierarchy for
the purposes of mapping is, to our knowledge, first proposed by Ostler (1979);
a representative example of its use is found in Carrier-Duncan (1985: 7).

(19) Hierarchical Linking Rule:
Order a verb's unlinked θ-roles according to the Thematic Hierarchy.
Link θ-roles to case-markers in order of precedence on their respective
hierarchies.   (Carrier-Duncan 1985: 7, (12))

More often the mapping uses a hierarchy of grammatical relations or configurationally defined syntactic positions, as in Larson's (1988, 1990) algorithm in
(20).

(20) If a verb α determines theta-roles $\theta_1, \theta_2, \ldots, \theta_n$, then the lowest role on
the Thematic Hierarchy is assigned to the lowest argument in constituent
structure, the next lowest role to the next lowest argument, and so on.
                                                    (Larson 1988: 382)

Hierarchy-aligning algorithms also differ as to whether the matching-up of
semantic roles with grammatical realizations proceeds top-down, i.e., from most
to least prominent, as in the Carrier-Duncan algorithm in (19), or bottom-up,
i.e., from least to most prominent, as in Larson's in (20). The upshot of both
algorithms is that the NP with the highest semantic role in the sentence gets
the highest syntactic realization and the one with the lowest semantic role the
lowest realization.

The hallmark of a top-down algorithm is that the most prominent syntactic realization is associated with the most prominent semantic role in the
thematic hierarchy, the next most prominent syntactic realization is associated
with the next most prominent role, and so on. Such algorithms seem particularly attractive to those who adopt what we call the natural prominence
scale conception of the thematic hierarchy in section 6.4.2: semantic roles are
ranked in decreasing order of some notion of cognitive salience. Proponents
of such algorithms sometimes see grammatical relations as directly encoding the information structure notion of topic (Givón 1984b: 134), so that the
hierarchy-aligning algorithm matches semantically more salient arguments with
the grammatically more topical realizations.

In contrast, bottom-up algorithms are used predominantly in conjunction
with approaches which assume a configurationally represented syntactic structure, as in the Principle and Parameters framework and its descendants. The
mapping, then, is between semantic roles and positions in a configurational
syntactic structure, as in the algorithm proposed by Larson (1988), cited in
(20). Given the assumption often made in this work that syntactic structure is
binary-branching, a bottom-up algorithm associates the lowest ranked semantic
role with the "lowest" configurationally defined position, which is typically

the syntactic position closest to the verb, and as the mapping proceeds up the thematic hierarchy, semantic roles are associated with syntactic positions increasingly removed from the verb. Consequently, the bottom-up algorithm meshes naturally with the conjecture mentioned in section 5.2 that syntactic structure preserves semantic compositional structure. Order of semantic composition, then, will be reflected in syntactic depth of embedding: the argument the verb composes with first will be the most deeply embedded in the syntactic representation (see section 6.4.1).

Some researchers opt for an algorithm that combines a subject selection rule that applies from the top of the hierarchy downwards with an object selection rule that applies from the bottom of the hierarchy upwards, giving a BIDIREC-TIONAL ALGORITHM. This algorithm is implicit in Stockwell, Schachter, and Partee's (1973: 52–56, 59–63) elaboration of the mapping rules in Fillmore's "Case for Case" (1968), though they do not formulate an explicit thematic hierarchy. A bidirectional algorithm is also found in the work of Van Valin and his colleagues (Foley and Van Valin 1984; Van Valin 1993b): the macroroles Actor and Undergoer, which figure prominently in the RRG mapping rules, are assigned by moving respectively down and up the thematic hierarchy (or the hierarchy of positions defined over fragments of predicate decompositions that replace it in Van Valin and LaPolla [1997]; see section 3.1.2). Even if macroroles are considered semantic notions by Van Valin (see section 3.1.2), the part they play in the lexical semantics-to-syntax mapping is comparable to that of syntactic notions in other theories.

Since most bidirectional algorithms deal with subject and object selection only, they essentially reduce to hierarchy-aligning algorithms, though conceptually they are quite different. Bidirectional algorithms are not intended to be prominence preserving. Instead, they treat the notion of object as in some sense "opposed" to that of subject, rather than as the second most prominent notion. Consequently, these two types of algorithm might require a different ranking of semantic roles. A hierarchy-aligning algorithm favors a ranking of semantic roles that emphasizes the similarities between semantic correlates of subjecthood and objecthood, while a bidirectional algorithm favors a ranking that emphasizes dissimilarities. The emphasis on dissimilarities makes a bidirectional algorithm reminiscent of Dowty's (1991) subject and object selection rules, which make reference to the number of Agent and Patient Proto-role entailments, respectively. As discussed in section 3.1.1.2, many of the Agent and Patient Proto-role entailments can be paired in that they refer to entailments that identify "opposing" participants in semantic relations, and, thus, they emphasize dissimilarities among arguments. In fact, Dowty (1991: 578) explicitly proposes that the thematic hierarchy is simply a reflection of the rankings of semantic roles in terms of their similarity to the prototypical agent and patient.

More generally, relative mapping algorithms need not be prominence preserving, as illustrated by the algorithm proposed by Wunderlich (1997b: 48;

Joppen and Wunderlich 1995: 125), based on ideas of Kiparsky's (1985, 1993, 2001). This algorithm, like a bidirectional algorithm, makes reference to both highest and lowest ranked roles, though the mapping from these roles to grammatical relations is done differently. Wunderlich introduces two binary features, [+/−hr] "there is a/no higher role" and [+/−lr] "there is a/no lower role" to classify arguments, with the result that arguments of a verb are specified as to whether they have the highest role, the lowest role, or an intermediate role. Wunderlich's mapping rules make reference to one or both of the features and are applied in order of decreasing specificity. Dative case is assigned to an intermediate argument (i.e., [+hr, +lr]), if there is one. Next, accusative case is assigned to an argument if there is another more highly ranked argument. Nominative case is assigned otherwise. The result is that nominative case is assigned to the highest ranked argument as in other algorithms, though through a default rule, in contrast to the other algorithms reviewed.

It might seem surprising that mapping algorithms incorporating the thematic hierarchy take several forms since after all they are based on what is taken to be a single theoretical construct (though, as we discuss in chapter 6, there is good reason to reject this assumption). As we have shown, there are sometimes independent reasons to prefer one mapping algorithm over another.

As is implicit in our discussion, the choice of mapping algorithm and the ranking of particular semantic roles in a thematic hierarchy are mutually interdependent, and thus some disagreements about the statement of the hierarchy may be traced to a failure to recognize this interdependence. Although subject and object selection are often formulated with reference to the same thematic hierarchy, they can make different demands of this hierarchy. Across algorithms, semantic roles that can be associated with subjects have to be ranked higher on the hierarchy than those that cannot, while roles that are likely to be associated with objects need to be placed lower on the hierarchy; however, precisely how low the roles associated with objects need to be put depends on the mapping algorithm being used.

Consider the ranking of semantic roles needed to determine the object of the verb *put*, which takes agent, theme, and location arguments. To ensure the realization of the theme as object, a top-down hierarchy-aligning algorithm has to be coupled with a hierarchy which places the theme higher than the location, while a bottom-up hierarchy-aligning algorithm or a bidirectional algorithm will require that the location be ranked above the theme. In fact, Foley and Van Valin (1984) and Van Valin and LaPolla (1997) place the location above the theme in their hierarchy mainly because object selection is done bottom-up. The majority of researchers, however, choose the opposite ranking, but they also use a top-down algorithm for object selection. The point is that these two rankings lead to the same result when combined with the appropriate mapping algorithm: the theme is realized as an object. However, when the domain of data is expanded there may be empirical consequences. When a bidirectional algorithm is used the ranking needed for agent–theme–location verbs is at odds with that needed for theme–location verbs. The majority of theme–location verbs, such as *enter, remain, sit*, and *stay* have a theme as subject and a location as either object or oblique, suggesting a theme-over-location ranking, yet the argument realization of agent–theme–location verbs suggests the opposite ranking.

The formulation of the mapping algorithm also depends on the syntactic theory assumed. Whether or not themes and patients even compete with other arguments for subjecthood depends to a large extent on the theory of syntax that is being adopted. In a theory that differentiates between surface and underlying grammatical relations or syntactic positions such as Relational Grammar or the Principles and Parameters framework, a theme or patient argument of an agentless verb can be a surface subject and still be an underlying object. This analysis is one implementation of the Unaccusative Hypothesis (Burzio 1986; Perlmutter 1978). Thus, if the mapping rules simply determine underlying grammatical relations, there is never a need for a rule that realizes themes or patients directly as subjects. They would fall under the object selection rule and would become subjects only through a syntactic movement rule; as a consequence, there would be less interaction between subject and object selection. However, if unaccusativity is not syntactically represented, there might be a potential disparity between the ranking that a theme or patient argument needs to ensure it can become a subject and the ranking it needs to become an object. The different formulations of the object selection rule reviewed in section 5.3.1 have significant implications for the placement of the theme or patient in the hierarchy: if the rule is stated in terms of the second highest role, then the theme or patient will have to be placed higher on the hierarchy than if the rule involves the lowest role. This interdependence seems to be the motivation for placing the theme above location in the works of Dik (1978, 1980, 1997a) and Givón (1984b, 1990, 2001).

5.4   Conclusion

Perhaps the most important observation that emerges from this overview of treatments of the mapping from lexical semantics to syntax is the assiduous-ness with which equivalence class and prominence preservation constraints, as well as mapping algorithms compatible with these constraints, are pur-sued. Researchers find it desirable to see the syntax as maintaining certain semantic distinctions. Researchers who adopt prominence preservation take this idea particularly seriously, as expressed by Bouchard: "I assume that the very form of semantic representations has meaning and, crucially, that this meaning affects the syntax adopted" (1995: 16). Nevertheless, prominence preservation approaches are often based on what many view as a problematic theoretical construct, the thematic hierarchy, which is a statement of semantic prominence relations among arguments. In the next chapter, we scrutinize this construct to determine whether it can indeed be used to buttress this general view of the lexical semantics–syntax relation.

Notes

1 The analysis in (5) suggests that the predicate decomposition for *saddle* is something along the lines of 'provide x with a saddle' rather than the more often suggested 'put a saddle on x' (e.g., Carter 1976; Clark and Clark 1979; Jackendoff 1990b: 170–71). The alternative analysis, also adopted by Kiparsky (1997: 483–85), allows a decomposition similar to that suggested for the semantically related location verbs, such as *bottle*, as in 'put x into a bottle.' Hale and Keyser's analysis changes the parallel from the predicates in the decomposition to the position in the decomposition that the constant fills (1992: 130–32).
2 Hale and Keyser (1997b: 30) take the opposite tack. According to them, the small number of semantic roles is a reflection of the small number of positions available to arguments in the syntax, given the constraints imposed by a general theory of phrase structure. This proposal may reflect a guiding assumption in Hale and Keyser's work: it is desirable to syntacticize the semantics since the semantics can then be constrained by independently motivated syntactic principles, leading to a more parsimonious theory of grammar.
3 A similar, though not exactly equivalent, hypothesis is that there is a relation of iconicity between the representation of the event denoted by a verb and the syntactic realization of this event, as suggested by Haiman (1985) in discussions of causative events and subordinate clauses.

6

Thematic hierarchies in argument realization

The discussion of the semantic determinants of argument realization in previous chapters centered on individual arguments of a verb, but interactions between arguments that affect argument realization cannot be ignored. These interactions suggest that there are precedence – or prominence – relations among arguments statable in terms of their semantic roles. This chapter examines the possible sources of these relations through an in-depth examination of the construct known as the thematic hierarchy – a ranking of semantic roles chosen because it figures in the statement of linguistic generalizations.[1] Although this construct has been widely implicated in linguistic phenomena, particularly those involving argument realization, many conflicting formulations have emerged, leading some researchers to voice skepticism concerning its validity. It is for this reason that we devote an entire chapter to the thematic hierarchy. Three major questions are the focus of this chapter: which notion of prominence underlies the ranking that defines a particular formulation of the thematic hierarchy, which linguistic phenomena is it supposed to account for, and can its effects be derived from more basic components of a lexical semantic representation?

We show that two major conceptions of prominence find their way into analyses of linguistic phenomena that appeal to a thematic hierarchy. On the first, the ranking of semantic roles is determined by structural properties of a lexical semantic representation – properties defined over a predicate decomposition or event structure. On the second, the ranking is determined by entailments associated with arguments. Our examination of these two conceptualizations supports the conclusions of earlier chapters that the mapping from lexical semantics to syntax needs to make reference to arguments in both ways. We show that the two notions of prominence are sometimes used to account for distinct phenomena, though the hierarchy as defined by either notion is a derived, rather than primitive construct. We assume that at least some of the controversies over the correct formulation of the thematic hierarchy reflect differences in the understanding of the notion of prominence and its relevance to argument realization. Therefore, untangling the sources of these various formulations should help shed light on the nature of prominence itself.

Distinct formulations of the thematic hierarchy can be compared only if the ranking among the roles is given the same interpretation and the ranking is intended to explain the same range of phenomena. As we show, proposed hierarchies differ from each other significantly in both respects. The thematic hierarchy is sometimes used in the algorithm which maps from lexical semantics to syntax (see section 5.3.2), but, as we discuss in this chapter, thematic hierarchies are put to other uses. Furthermore, even when different instantiations of the thematic hierarchy are designed for use in a mapping algorithm, the rankings of semantic roles defining each instantiation can be compared only if they are posited in the context of similar assumptions about the nature of syntax and its relation to a lexical semantic representation.

As we also discuss, in some instances a thematic hierarchy is simply used to provide a shorthand for capturing a local empirical generalization underlying a specific linguistic phenomenon; such a hierarchy cannot be taken to represent a universal construct. We show that sometimes such phenomena are accounted for in terms of semantic properties other than semantic roles and the thematic hierarchy effects are only apparent, arising because the relevant semantic properties distribute across traditional semantic roles in a systematic way. In other instances, the ranking of roles captures a valid empirical generalization which is the result of a complex interaction of factors. We conclude that in general a thematic hierarchy is a notational device that is given various interpretations and is put to a variety of uses, and, hence, there is no single universal ranking of arguments which will capture all valid generalizations expressing regularities in the association of semantic roles with morphosyntactic realizations.

6.1   Thematic hierarchies: appealing, but problematic

Thematic hierarchies have proved appealing because they allow an argument of a verb to be referred to in terms of its relative position on the thematic hierarchy, instead of in terms of its semantic role. The advantage of this way of referring to arguments is illustrated throughout this section and the next.

In previous chapters, we showed that a range of semantic roles can be associated with both subject and direct object and that even for a given verb arguments bearing various semantic roles can be realized as subject and object. Since there is so much variability, formulating general algorithms which determine which of a verb's arguments is its subject or direct object presents a real challenge. Fillmore's subject selection rule in (1) represents a well-known early attempt to confront this challenge.

(1)   If there is an A [=Agent], it becomes the subject; otherwise, if there is an I
      [=Instrument], it becomes the subject; otherwise, the subject is the O
      [=Objective, i.e., Patient/Theme]. (Fillmore 1968: 33)

This rule implicitly establishes precedence relations among the semantic roles mentioned and could be simplified to (2), if used in conjunction with the hierarchy of roles in (3) (Bresnan and Kanerva 1989; Givón 1984b, 2001; Kiparsky 1985; Grimshaw 1990).

(2) The argument of a verb bearing the highest-ranked semantic role is its subject.

(3) Agent > Instrument > Patient/Theme

Consistent with Fillmore's algorithm, (2) has the effect of realizing a verb's agent, if there is one, as its subject; in the absence of an agent, it allows an argument bearing another semantic role to be the subject. The generality of (2) – for instance, its lack of reference to specific semantic roles – makes mapping algorithms that appeal to a thematic hierarchy attractive.

Besides subject and object selection, accounts of a range of other phenomena involving argument realization have also appealed to thematic hierarchies, including passivization (Bresnan and Kanerva 1989; Givón 1990; Grimshaw 1990; Jackendoff 1972; Trithart 1979), causativization (Carrier-Duncan 1985; Dik 1980; Foley and Van Valin 1984; Polinsky and Kozinsky 1992) and other morphosyntactic processes (Alsina 1994, 1999; Alsina and Mchombo 1993; Bresnan and Kanerva 1992; Carrier-Duncan 1985; Hawkinson and Hyman 1974; Morolong and Hyman 1977), serial verbs (Baker 1989; Carstens 2002), compounding (Foley and Van Valin 1984; Grimshaw 1990; Y. Li 1990; Potter 1991), and light verbs (Grimshaw and Mester 1988). For instance, Bresnan and Kanerva (1989: 27, (64)) propose that passivization involves the suppression of the argument of a verb that bears the highest semantic role, an idea which receives similar, though not identical, expression in Grimshaw (1990), while Carrier-Duncan (1985: 14, (38)) proposes that the rule of reciprocal verb formation in Tagalog is "assign a reciprocal interpretation to the lowest thematic role and bind it to the next higher one."

Researchers have also proposed that the thematic hierarchy figures in the statement of typological implicational generalizations about the range of semantic roles that can be realized as subject or object in a given language, as well as in the statement of generalizations concerning which subject or object choices are most likely to receive a "marked" expression (Asudeh 2001; Dik 1978, 1980, 1997a; Givón 1984a, 1984b, 2001). In this connection, thematic hierarchies have figured, often in combination with person and animacy hierarchies, in generalizations concerning the surface manifestations of argument realization – what Keenan (1976) calls "coding" properties, including unmarked word order (K. P. Mohanan and T. Mohanan 1994; Siewierska 1988, 1993; Uszkoreit 1987), agreement (Duranti 1979; Evans 1997; Hawkinson and Hyman 1974; Morolong and Hyman 1977; Trithart 1979), inverse marking (Aissen 1999) and case marking (Aissen 1999; Joppen and Wunderlich 1995). As this list suggests, thematic hierarchies are invoked in the analysis of phenomena from a wide range of languages, including Albanian (Sells 1988), Chinese (Y. Li 1990), Dutch (Dik 1980), English, German (Uszkoreit 1987), Greek

(Everaert and Anagnostopoulou 1997), Hindi (K. P. Mohanan and T. Mohanan 1994), Japanese (Grimshaw and Mester 1988), Tagalog (Carrier-Duncan 1985), Kwa languages (Baker 1989), and Bantu languages (Alsina 1994, 1999; Alsina and Mchombo 1993; Bresnan and Kanerva 1989, 1992; Bresnan and Moshi 1990; Duranti 1979; Hawkinson and Hyman 1974; Morolong and Hyman 1977; Polinsky and Kozinsky 1992; Trithart 1979).

Thematic hierarchies also figure in the accounts of a range of other linguistic phenomena, including anaphoric relations (Everaert and Anagnostopoulou 1997; Kuno 1987; Jackendoff 1972; Schwartz 1986; Sells 1988; Van Valin and LaPolla 1997; W. Wilkins 1988) and control (Chierchia 1983; Nishigauchi 1984). We do not, however, discuss these other uses. Following the methodology set out by Dowty (1991), we restrict our attention to the hierarchy as it is used in argument realization, on the assumption that this focus is most likely to uncover a unified conceptual characterization of the hierarchy as it pertains to one particular domain (though, as we show, even in this restricted domain there is no unified notion of a thematic hierarchy). Furthermore, as far as we are aware, most attempts to appeal to a thematic hierarchy in other domains have been unsuccessful in that the generalizations have been shown either to follow from other factors or to be spurious. For instance, Nishigauchi (1984) argues that the thematic hierarchy helps determine the controller of a PRO subject of an infinitival complement; however, Ladusaw and Dowty (1988) reexamine the data and argue that "the verb's entailments and facts about human actions always determine the controller" (1988: 68).

The apparent relevance of the thematic hierarchy to the characterization of numerous phenomena in diverse languages has made it an attractive theoretical construct. It has been adopted by proponents of a range of theoretical frameworks, including Functional Grammar, Lexical-Functional Grammar, the Principles and Parameters framework, and Role and Reference Grammar. But the attitude towards the thematic hierarchy largely parallels the attitude towards the semantic roles which comprise it. It is convenient to posit a thematic hierarchy when it seems to be implicated in robust linguistic generalizations, but acknowledgment of its usefulness is tempered by an uneasiness concerning its status. This uneasiness has two sources. First, if, as discussed in chapters 2 and 3, semantic roles are derived constructs, then any hierarchy defined in terms of them should also be a derived construct. The question then arises as to what the ranking of the arguments is derived from. Second, and more problematic, is the lack of agreement over the appropriate formulation of the thematic hierarchy, in terms of both the roles constituting it and the ranking of these roles. These considerable disagreements have led some critics to reject the notion outright (Newmeyer 2002: 65).

In this chapter we review the primary uses of the thematic hierarchy, while bearing in mind these two important problems. In section 6.2, we illustrate what we consider its major motivation, namely, context dependence in argument realization. We point out that thematic hierarchies have been used to account for very different kinds of generalizations over a variety of domains, although they all involve context dependence in an abstract sense. In section 6.3 we review a sample of the thematic hierarchies proposed in the literature, highlighting the major contrasts among them. In section 6.4 we consider hypotheses concerning what these thematic hierarchies are meant to represent, what phenomena hierarchies are meant to account for, and how they have been considered to be derived from more basic components of lexical semantic representations. In section 6.5, we review possible sources for the various formulations of the thematic hierarchy. First, we set aside the generalizations which appear to implicate a thematic hierarchy but are more likely attributable to other semantic factors. Then, we show that the thematic hierarchy is put to use in several ways, giving rise to various formulations; specifically, in a given instantiation, the set of semantic roles and their relative rankings is determined by the interpretation given to the hierarchy and by the types of generalizations being captured.

Since the thematic hierarchy has played a key part in the explanation of numerous complex linguistic phenomena, we cannot survey all its instantiations, let alone identify the interactions between it and various other linguistic notions that have been implicated in the explanations of these phenomena. We hope that the exposition of the various conceptions of the thematic hierarchy and the discussion of factors that can complicate the comparison of particular hierarchies will assist future researchers in making progress in the analysis of specific phenomena.

6.2   The primary motivation for hierarchies: context dependence

As already mentioned, thematic hierarchies allow arguments to be referred to in terms of their relative ranking. As Baker (1997: 109) and Speas (1990: 73) note, this property makes them a particularly useful device for dealing with what we called the "context dependence" pervasive in argument realization: the options for the syntactic realization of a particular argument are often not determined solely by its semantic role, but also by the semantic roles borne by its coarguments. In this section we present several argument realization generalizations which illustrate context dependence. In the following sections we demonstrate that these generalizations are not all of the same kind, leading us to propose that there is no single universal ranking of semantic roles.

Consider first the subject selection paradigm in (4), which was the motivation for Fillmore's subject selection rule (1), together with the further examples that fill out this paradigm in (5).

(4) a. The door opened.
     b. John opened the door.
     c. The wind opened the door.
     d. John opened the door with a chisel.   (Fillmore 1968: 27, (40)–(43))

(5) a. *The door opened with the wind.
    b. *The door opened by John.
    c. *The chisel opened the door by John.

No single semantic role is consistently associated with the grammatical relation subject, and, conversely, no semantic role consistently shows a particular
syntactic realization. Yet, whether an argument bearing a particular semantic
role can be realized as subject depends on the semantic roles of the other
arguments in the sentence, as the contrast between (4) and (5) makes clear. For
instance, a patient cannot be a subject in the presence of an agent, instrument,
or natural force. This pattern follows from the subject selection rule (2), in
conjunction with an appropriate thematic hierarchy, which ranks patient below
agent, instrument, or natural force. The syntactic expression of the patient
depends on this role's position in the hierarchy relative to the roles of other
arguments in the same clause. The patient can only be the subject when it is
the sole argument of the verb (see (5)) or when any other arguments bear roles
lower in the hierarchy, such as location, as in *The cat sat on the windowsill.*
This account extends to instruments, which also show context dependence: they
can only be subjects in the absence of an agent. Similarly, Speas (1990: 73)
points out that a recipient – the animate goal in an event of physical or abstract
transfer of possession – may be a subject, but only in the absence of an agent,
citing (6).

(6) a. John received a package from Baraboo.
    b. Mary sent a package to John from Baraboo.   (Speas 1990: 73, (102))

This asymmetry follows if agent is higher than recipient in the thematic hierarchy, and the argument bearing the highest role is selected as subject. It is
usually assumed that the precise statement of the thematic hierarchy will emerge
from an examination of the interrelations in the realization of all semantic
roles.
   Context dependence is also found in the realization of arguments bearing
the experiencer role. As discussed in sections 1.2 and 1.5, experiencers can
be expressed as subjects of psych-verbs such as *fear* (e.g., *The toddler feared
the lion*) or objects of psych-verbs such as *frighten* (e.g., *The lion frightened
the toddler*). The realization of the experiencer depends on the semantic role
of the nonexperiencer argument of the verb, which, as argued in section 1.2,
differs for the two types of verbs. With *frighten* verbs, the semantic role of
the nonexperiencer argument could be characterized as an agent, instigator,
effector, or cause (Grimshaw 1990; Pesetsky 1995). In formulations of the
hierarchy that include an experiencer (Belletti and Rizzi 1988; Bresnan and
Kanerva 1989; Grimshaw 1990; Speas 1990), the agent-like roles such as agent,
instigator, effector, or cause are ranked the highest and thus have priority over
the experiencer for expression as subject. In contrast, with the *fear* verbs, the
nonexperiencer argument cannot be analyzed as bearing an agent-like role, but

is better analyzed as bearing the stimulus (or theme) role. If experiencer is ranked above stimulus in the hierarchy (Belletti and Rizzi 1988; Grimshaw 1990; Van Valin 1990), *fear* verbs will have an experiencer subject.[2]

A somewhat different instantiation of context dependence is reflected in Polinsky and Kozinsky's (1992) appeal to a thematic hierarchy in the analysis of the applicative construction in the Bantu language, Kinyarwanda. In this construction, an NP, normally expressed as an oblique, is expressed as an object, and the verb also has an "applicative" morpheme affixed to it; this morpheme often identifies the semantic role of the added object. Kinyarwanda allows NPs bearing a wide range of semantic roles to be introduced as objects by the applicative morpheme; these include recipients, benefactives, possessors, instruments, and comitatives. When a sentence has NPs bearing more than one of these roles, which of these NPs can be expressed as an object, rather than as an oblique, is dependent on the semantic roles of the other NPs within the sentence. For instance, when a benefactive and an instrument cooccur, only the benefactive – and not the instrument – can be expressed as an object. Polinsky and Kozinsky point out that the asymmetries can be captured using a thematic hierarchy. The just-described asymmetry would follow if benefactives are ranked above instruments, and if accessibility to objecthood is determined by a thematic hierarchy, with the NP in the pair having the higher-ranked role being the object.

The thematic hierarchy is also used to explain properties of the applicative construction in another Bantu language, Chicheŵa. In Chicheŵa the choice of added semantic role is apparently constrained by the roles of the original arguments of the base verb (Alsina 1999: 26–27; Bresnan and Kanerva 1992: 117–18). A verb whose only argument bears the patient/theme role cannot be found with a benefactive introduced by the applicative morpheme, while a verb whose only argument bears the agent role can be, as can a verb that takes both agent and patient/theme arguments. Alsina (1999: 26) and Bresnan and Kanerva (1992: 117) propose that the applicative morpheme can only introduce an argument whose semantic role is lower on the thematic hierarchy than that of one of the verb's original arguments. The distribution of applicative objects can then be captured with a thematic hierarchy in which benefactive is lower than agent, but higher than patient/theme. Furthermore, Alsina (1999: 26–27) and Bresnan and Kanerva (1992: 118) place location lower than patient/theme based in part on the fact that a verb whose only argument bears the patient/theme role can be found with a location applicative object.

Context dependence also motivates reference to the thematic hierarchy in the statement of crosslinguistic generalizations about argument realization.[3] This use is most explicitly and thoroughly explored by Dik (1978, 1980, 1997a, 1997b) within Functional Grammar, but a comparable use is found in Givón's work (1984a, 1984b, 1990, 2001). "Deep" ergative languages aside, all languages allow a verb's agent argument to be expressed as subject, but differ as to whether they allow arguments bearing other semantic roles to be expressed as subject in the absence of an agent argument (see section 1.6). Although the set of semantic roles expressible as subject varies from language to language, Dik (1978) proposes that the range of variation is constrained and takes a form that can best be described through reference to a thematic hierarchy; see Givón (1984b) for a similar proposal. Languages choose the semantic roles that can be realized as subject or object from a continuous portion of the hierarchy starting with the agent for the subject and with the second-highest role for the object and working downwards, as stated in Dik's Continuity Hypothesis in (7).

(7) For any language, if Subj or Obj function can be assigned to some semantic function S_j, then Subj or Obj can be assigned to any semantic function S_i, such that S_i precedes S_j in SFH [=Semantic Function Hierarchy, i.e., the thematic hierarchy] (for Obj assignment, $S_i \neq Ag$).   (Dik 1978: 76)

Crosslinguistic differences are restricted to choice of cut-off points for subject-hood and objecthood on the hierarchy. The result is that, "we can specify the possibilities of Subj and Obj assignment for a language simply by giving the last semantic function in the SFH to which Subj and Obj can be assigned" (Dik 1978: 75). Assuming the thematic hierarchy in (8), all languages have agent subjects, some might have agent and patient subjects, others agent, patient and recipient subjects, and so on. None, however, would have patient, benefactive, and instrument subjects only.[4]

(8) Agt > Pat > Rec > Ben > Inst > Loc > Temp   (Dik 1978: 70, (3))

Dik presents evidence from a range of languages to illustrate that all the possible cut-off points are instantiated. This hypothesis, then, represents an implicational generalization of the type familiar from work on language universals. Furthermore, the same hierarchy, with the agent removed, figures in crosslinguistically valid implicational generalizations about object selection (Dik 1978: 76, 1997: 246, (41); Givón 1984a: 163) and passivization (Givón 1990: 566). For example, according to (8) a language would only allow benefactive objects, if it allowed patients and recipients also to be objects.

    These typological generalizations involve a somewhat different instantiation of context dependence than the examples discussed earlier. The other instances involve priorities among the coarguments of a verb with respect to their potential realization as subject; that is, they involve priorities relevant to the mapping algorithm. In contrast, Dik's and Givón's generalizations apply across verb types and across languages. They define a set of possible languages with respect to the options for the realization of different semantic roles as subject and object. For example, while Dik's generalization states that a language will only allow recipients as subjects, if it also allows agents and patients as subjects, the other type of generalization involves whether a recipient may be realized as the subject of a particular verb in a language which allows such subjects; this possibility is determined in the context of the coarguments of that verb. The ranking of semantic roles used in the statement of typological generalizations, then, may turn out not to be the same as the one that might be used by a mapping algorithm. In sections 6.4 and 6.5, we show that recognizing that different kinds of generalizations capture context dependence over different domains is critical for understanding why not all proposed thematic hierarchies are alike. First, we review the various formulations of the thematic hierarchy, as a prelude to trying to uncover their sources.

6.3   Formulations of the thematic hierarchy

In this section, we lay out representative formulations of the thematic hierarchy; additional hierarchies are listed in Newmeyer (2002: 65–67, (25)). This comparative presentation, which is inspired by those in Baker (1996a: 7–8, (2)) and Macfarland (1991: 105), is intended to highlight the most important differences among the hierarchies.[5] As noted by Baker and Macfarland, much of the controversy centers around the placement of the patient/theme role with respect to other roles, particularly the spatial roles such as goal and location. For this reason, the hierarchies have been grouped according to their treatment of the patient/theme role, which is italicized for ease of identification. In section 6.5 we discuss the sources of the controversy over the ranking of these roles. The following abbreviations are used in the hierarchies: Act – actor, Ag – agent, Be – benefactive, Da – dative, Eff – effector, Ex – experiencer, In – instrument, G – goal, L – location, P – path, Pa – patient, Re – recipient, S – source, Th – theme. Certain oblique roles have been omitted from the bottom of Dik's, Fillmore's (1971a), Givón's, Larson's, and Speas' hierarchies; Dik's "goal" role (see note 4) and Fillmore's "objective" role have been relabelled "patient" to conform to more common usage; Bresnan and Kanerva's hierarchy uses the label "recipient," which can be understood as a type of goal and is treated as such in the comparative presentation; see below for further discussion. Some hierarchies do not rank all roles with respect to each other; roles that are ranked together – and, thus, are unranked with respect to each other – are separated by a slash.[6]

No mention of goal and location:

Belletti & Rizzi 1988:	Ag >		Ex >	*Th*
Fillmore 1968:	Ag >	In>		*Pa*

Goal and location ranked above patient/theme:

Grimshaw 1990:	Ag >		Ex >	G/S/L >	*Th*
Jackendoff 1972:	Ag >			G/S/L >	*Th*
Van Valin 1990:	Ag >	Eff > Ex >		L >	*Th > Pa*

Goal and location ranked below patient/theme:

Baker 1989:	Ag >	In>	*Th/Pa* > G/L
Baker 1997:	Ag >		*Th/Pa* > G/S/L
Carrier-Duncan 1985:	Ag >		*Th* > G/S/L
Dik 1978:	Ag >		*Pa* > Re > Be > In
Fillmore 1971a:	Ag > Ex > In>		*Pa* > G/S/L
Jackendoff 1990b:	Act >	*Pa*/Be > *Th* >	G/S/L
Larson 1988:	Ag >		*Th* > G
Speas 1990:	Ag > Ex >		*Th* > G/S/L

Goal ranked above and location below patient/theme:

Bresnan & Kanerva 1989:	Ag > Be > Re/Ex > In> *Th/Pa* > L
Kiparsky 1985:	Ag > S > G > In> *Th/Pa* > L
Givón 1984b:	Ag > Da/Be > *Pa* > L > In

Besides the varying rankings of the goal, source, and location roles with respect to the patient/theme role, a few other differences are worth noting. First, some hierarchies include semantic roles associated only with arguments, but others include semantic roles more likely to be associated with adjuncts. Second, hierarchies differ in the roles which are ranked. A particular hierarchy may contain a small number of roles, simply reflecting the set of roles relevant to the analysis of a particular phenomenon, as in Belletti and Rizzi's (1988) hierarchy, which is motivated by a study of psych-verbs. Differences in roles ranked may sometimes be linked to the granularity of the analysis: some hierarchies are based on a rather fine-grained semantic analysis which leads to the inclusion of a number of roles, while other hierarchies contain fewer roles, often reflecting a coarser-grained semantic analysis. For example, Bresnan and Kanerva (1989) distinguish a recipient role from a purely spatial goal role, and lump all the spatial locative roles, including the spatial goal, under a location role; others consider the recipient role simply to be a subtype of goal and do not single it out, while still others distinguish between the spatial goal role and other spatial roles. Van Valin (1990) makes a distinction between an agent role, in the sense of an animate, volitional instigator, and an effector role – the role of a participant that brings something about (Van Valin and LaPolla 1997: 118; Van Valin and D. Wilkins 1996), ranking the former higher than the latter, while still others do not make this distinction. Van Valin (1990; Van Valin and LaPolla 1997: 126–27) also posits distinct theme and patient roles, ranking theme above patient. Others do not make this distinction; they either include only one of these two roles or rank them together. Some hierarchies specifically do not rank noncooccurring argument types, while others do.

The proliferation of thematic hierarchies has provoked two reactions. Newmeyer takes the multiple formulations as evidence that the construct is simply not useful: "There is reason for strong doubt that there exists a Thematic Hierarchy provided by UG. That seems to be the best explanation for the fact that after over three decades of investigation, nobody has proposed a hierarchy of theta-roles that comes close to working" (2002: 65). Other linguists apparently assume that there is a universal ranking of semantic roles and that it should be possible to resolve the conflicting role rankings reflected in the various statements of the hierarchy in favor of a single ranking once the supporting data is more carefully scrutinized (e.g., the debate between Bresnan and Kanerva [1989, 1992] and Schachter [1992]).

Deciding whether it is possible to identify a thematic hierarchy that "comes close to working" requires determining which generalizations a thematic hierarchy should capture. It does not make sense to choose between two hierarchies which are meant to account for different sets of phenomena. As already reviewed, a heterogeneous collection of generalizations can be validly captured using a ranking of semantic roles, and there is no reason to expect to find a single ranking of roles which works for all of them. Distinct facets of argument realization are sensitive to different types of semantic notions, which may be defined at various levels of granularity. In order to understand why different hierarchies rank roles differently, it is necessary to realize that thematic hierarchies introduced to capture particular generalizations are derivative constructs: they are convenient devices that allow valid linguistic generalizations to be captured, but ultimately they derive from the more basic components of the lexical semantics of verbs and the properties of the NPs which serve as their arguments. A lack of consensus about "the" thematic hierarchy is not, on its own, a reason to reject any particular hierarchy; rather, it is a reason to probe the basis for any given ranking of semantic roles. There is much to be gained, then, from an attempt to understand the various rankings of semantic roles, as they often do express valid generalizations.

6.4   The grounding of the thematic hierarchy

Since semantic roles are now largely viewed as derivative constructs defined over the more basic components of the lexical semantic representations of verbs, the semantic roles constituting the thematic hierarchy and their rankings should also derive from these components. In chapter 3 we reviewed two ways of defining semantic roles: in terms of positions in an elaborated lexical semantic representation and in terms of clusters of lexical entailments associated with arguments. As we show, each way of defining semantic roles is naturally associated with a distinct conception of the thematic hierarchy. On either conception the hierarchy is derivative.

The two interpretations of the thematic hierarchy are characterized by distinct interpretations of "prominence," as hinted by Bresnan and Kanerva (1989: 23–24). On the first, prominence is defined "structurally" over the lexical semantic representation of a verb (Baker 1997; Croft 1998; Jackendoff 1990b; Kiparsky 1985). This conception fits well with the view of semantic roles as labels for positions in an articulated lexical semantic representation, such as a predicate decomposition or an event structure. The thematic hierarchy is viewed as a statement of a generalization, but not as an independent construct (Baker 1996a, 1997; Croft 1991: 186, 1998; Kiparsky 1985; Wunderlich 1997a, 1997b). On the second interpretation, prominence is taken to be akin to cognitive salience, and the thematic hierarchy is taken to be one of a number of "natural prominence scales," such as the person, animacy, number, and definiteness hierarchies. The other scales, however, each provide a ranking of the possible values of a particular attribute of an argument, while the thematic hierarchy does not rank an argument according to the values of a single attribute. A range of semantic properties determine the salience of an argument, so that the thematic hierarchy is better viewed as "the cumulative result of a number of interacting relative prominence relations between semantic entities," to quote T. Mohanan (1994: 28). There is, then, a natural affinity between a thematic hierarchy incorporating this interpretation of prominence and the conception of semantic roles as clusters of properties of arguments. Although some of the properties which determine the salience of an argument involve its semantic role, many, in fact, are properties of the NPs which typically fill this semantic role. They should not, strictly speaking, be considered defining properties of the semantic role; however, since the properties of the role fillers may align in particular ways with the associated semantic roles, they may also give rise to what appear to be thematic hierarchy effects.

6.4.1 Structurally based thematic hierarchies

For a thematic hierarchy derived from a structured representation of verb meaning, prominence is defined over this representation. When one semantic role is ranked higher than a second, the first is assumed to be structurally more prominent than the second. Some researchers pair structural prominence with the interpretation of semantic roles as labels for positions in a more elaborated lexical semantic representation, such as an event structure. Prominence, then, is defined in terms of the geometry of the representation, as discussed in section 4.2.5. Other researchers take structural prominence to be defined by the order of composition of arguments with their verb. This order presumably reflects a verb's lexical semantic representation, though proponents of this viewpoint usually do not posit an explicit lexical semantic representation to undergird the posited orders.

When prominence is defined over an event structure, it is taken to be inversely correlated with depth of embedding in the event structure, or, as Kiparsky (1997: 484) puts it, "the order of Th-roles is a reflection of their semantic depth," an idea that he attributes to Bierwisch and that is further refined in related work by Wunderlich (1997a: 102, 1997b: 44). Prominence relations defined in this way can as a matter of convenience be expressed by a thematic hierarchy.

The second structural interpretation of prominence takes the thematic hierarchy to be a reflection of the order in which a verb composes with its arguments: the argument that composes first is lowest in the hierarchy, the argument that composes next is the next lowest, and so on. This view is adopted by Kiparsky (1985, 1997) and shared by Larson (1988: 382–83). Kiparsky (1997) and Wunderlich (1997a, 1997b) bring these two positions together: they take semantic roles to represent positions in an event structure and they propose that order of composition of arguments can be determined from the structure of this representation. Order of composition, then, reduces roughly to depth of embedding in a semantic representation. In fact, there is much to recommend this move. As Kratzer (1996: 115–16) argues, from a formal semantic viewpoint, differences in the order of composition of the arguments of a multiargument verb (or predicate) have no semantic consequences; order of argument composition is semantically meaningful only if the relevant arguments are arguments of distinct predicates in an event structure. Therefore, order of composition can provide independent motivation for the statement of the thematic hierarchy, only if order of composition is equated with depth of embedding in a semantic representation.

The structural conception of the hierarchy is usually coupled with a prominence preservation approach to mapping (see section 5.2). Such a mapping ensures that the semantic prominence relations among arguments whether defined by depth of embedding in an event structure or by order of composition are preserved in the corresponding syntactic structure. For example, in Principle and Parameters terms, if one position in an event structure is more prominent than another, then the argument in the syntactic d-structure associated with the first position asymmetrically c-commands the argument in the syntax associated with the second.

The geometry of the lexical semantic representation is claimed to be at the root of certain generalizations regarding argument realization. For example, in languages with noun incorporation, dative verbs – verbs with agent, theme, and recipient arguments – can incorporate the theme, but not the recipient (Baker 1988: 453–54, n. 13, 1996b: 292–93). Kiparsky (1997: 484) argues that this asymmetry reflects the structure of the lexical semantic representation: the theme is closer to the verb than the recipient in this representation, and, therefore, the verb composes with it first. He captures this generalization by appealing to a thematic hierarchy and proposing that the argument of a verb whose semantic role is lowest on the hierarchy has precedence for noun incorporation. This explanation is extended to asymmetries in the structure of idioms. English dative verbs are found in a multitude of idioms with fixed themes and variable recipients (e.g., *lend x an ear, promise x the moon, read x the riot act, show x the ropes*), but not in idioms with fixed recipients and variable themes. Explanations of this and other idiom asymmetries take as their starting point the assumption that verbs form idioms with items they compose with first, a property that would be reflected in these items bearing the lowest-ranked of the semantic roles associated with the verb (Kiparsky 1985; Larson 1988). If this assumption is correct, the idiom data provide evidence that recipients are ranked above themes. Idiom asymmetries have figured prominently in discussions of the hierarchy, particularly with respect to the ranking of recipients and themes, and we consider this type of evidence and its validity further in section 6.5.3 in the context of a more detailed examination of the ranking of these two roles.

Although a structurally based hierarchy is defined with respect to a verb and its arguments, it can be broadened to include semantic roles of what are typically considered syntactic adjuncts, if these "adjunct" roles can be defined over an "augmented" event structure associated, say, with an applicative verb. Marantz (1993: 143–44), for example, gives applicative verbs complex event structures, distinguishing an "inner" – or embedded event – and an "outer" event, with instruments included in the inner and benefactives in the outer event. The idea is that the verb composes first with the arguments belonging to the inner event and only then with those belonging to the outer event, giving rise to thematic hierarchy effects involving adjuncts, as we discuss further below.

On the structural conception, the thematic hierarchy is epiphenomenal, algorithmically derived from an articulated lexical semantic representation or, alternatively, from whatever determines order of composition of arguments with their verb. There is no single independently formulated thematic hierarchy which exhaustively ranks all semantic roles. Rather, each event type gives rise to its own structurally defined hierarchy composed of the semantic roles associated with that event type; a hierarchy, then, cannot rank noncooccurring arguments, such as agent and effector or experiencer and recipient. The semantic role which is most prominent for a given event type shares with the most prominent semantic roles for other event types only the property of representing the argument that is structurally highest among the coarguments. Constraints on the possible realizations of arguments bearing particular semantic roles derive from the depth of embedding of the positions in the event structures which define the relevant roles; the possible realizations are derived from the pool of possible event structures.

On this understanding of the structurally based thematic hierarchy all con- straints on a verb's argument realization options should arise from differences in the relative depth of embedding of its arguments in its event structure. However, some constraints on a verb's argument realization options cannot be explained in this way since depth of embedding does not always impose an exhaustive ranking on all arguments of a verb. Often, particular predicates in an event structure have more than one argument. For example, two-argument stative verbs, such as *have, love, see,* or *want,* have a single predicate in their event structure, with two arguments associated with it; the same holds of two- argument activity verbs, such as *rub, wipe, push,* and *study* (e.g., B. Levin 1999; Rappaport Hovav and B. Levin 1998a; Van Valin and LaPolla 1997). (There are "technical" ways around this limitation; for instance, extra predicates could be introduced, but their introduction and the ranking they impose on arguments can be hard to justify.) As mentioned, Kratzer (1996) points out that the order of composition of arguments of a single predicate cannot be independently established, except through their grammatical realization, which is what order of composition is supposed to explain to begin with. Consequently, depth of embedding does not prevent a verb like *want* from expressing its experiencer as object or a verb like *push* from expressing its theme as subject; however, such mappings are unattested. Although the thematic hierarchy is supposed to preclude them, it is unable to do so, if it is determined by the depth of embedding of arguments. Thus, such two-argument verbs are problematic.

In order to impose a ranking on the arguments of all verbs, proponents of structurally based thematic hierarchies sometimes postulate event embedding within a verb's predicate decomposition, even where it is not clearly justified. Baker (1997: 123–24, 2003: 79–83), for example, postulates event embedding in the form of a causative event structure for all transitive verbs to explain observed prominence relations common to the arguments of such verbs. Yet, this assumption has never been seriously entertained by lexical semanticists, and it is explicitly argued against in B. Levin (1999) and Van Valin and LaPolla (1997: 101–02).

One way of distinguishing among arguments in an event structure is to take advantage of a distinction among event structure participants introduced in Rappaport Hovav and B. Levin (1998a) and elaborated in B. Levin (1999), building on an idea in Grimshaw (1993). These papers propose that roots (see section 3.2) are associated with some number of participants and that when roots are integrated into event structures, some or all of these participants are associated with argument positions in the event structures. With change-of-state verbs, the root is associated with a cause and an entity that changes state, and in the event structure the first of these participants is associated with the argument of the causing subevent and the second with the argument of the result subevent, respectively. The roots associated with two-argument activity or stative verbs are also associated with two participants, but only one of these root participants is associated with an argument position in event structure. For instance, the surface-contact verb *wipe* has a root associated with an agent and a surface, but its activity event structure only specifies an agent. Its other root participant is only licensed by the root itself. The result is an asymmetry in the status of two arguments within the same level of event structure embedding, which might be reflected in prominence relations in the syntactic realization of the arguments. This approach to ranking, however, is only viable if "pure" root participants can be identified in a principled way, but this remains to be worked out.

Croft (1991: 186, 1998) offers an alternative account of how the thematic hierarchy derives from the internal structure of events, which provides an independent criterion for ranking all the arguments of a verb. For him, the internal structure of an event is defined by the causal chain that makes explicit force-dynamic relationships among the event participants (see section 4.3). The position of arguments in the causal chain serves to impose a ranking on the arguments, in which prominence is defined by force-dynamic antecedence and is the source of thematic hierarchy effects. For Croft, then, only force-dynamic antecedence, and not depth of embedding, is the relevant structural notion, and, furthermore, there is an independently defined notion of antecedence for coarguments of single predicates. Langacker (1990: 238) also proposes that "energy flow," as he calls the force-dynamic relationships along a causal chain, gives rise to a thematic hierarchy. In a similar vein, Siewierska (1991) considers the thematic hierarchy as grounded in what DeLancey (1981) calls "natural attention flow," which she writes "refers to the actual development of events in the real world, the basis for the perception of naturalness being temporal order" (1991: 105). These views may be related to Primus' proposal (1999: 48–51) that the asymmetries among event participants embodied by the paired entailments in Dowty's lists of proto-role properties (see section 3.1.1) are instantiations of a general notion of control. This notion could be interpreted as a generalization over various force-dynamic relations and might provide a way to impose ordering where depth of event embedding fails. In what follows, we make reference primarily to causal order, leaving open whether it subsumes these other notions.

Since causal order only defines relations of precedence, and not hierarchical relations, approaches which refer to causal order are typically accompanied by approaches to argument realization which also do not appeal to hierarchical structure. This correlation is not necessary. Marantz (1993: 144–45) also shares this general view of the origins of the thematic hierarchy, though he instantiates the idea in terms of event embedding. He suggests that the instrument and the patient/theme belong to an event embedded inside another event, which includes the benefactive. As the instrument figures among Croft's antecedent roles, while the benefactive is one of Croft's subsequent roles (see section 4.3), the hierarchical relations imposed by event embedding mirror causal order.

The question, then, is whether these two ways of understanding structural prominence – in terms of depth of embedding or order of composition and in terms of causal order – are related. Prominence relations among arguments established by depth of embedding in event structure are indeed preserved in the syntax, and it appears that they take precedence over other semantic properties implicated in argument realization. For instance, as shown in section 3.1.1, the inanimate cause arguments of morphological causatives are always realized as subjects, even in the context of animate causees. The causees are presumably arguments of an event embedded under the causing event that includes the cause and, thus, will have a less prominent realization than the cause. But embedding relations often reduce to causal order, since in a causative event the least embedded argument, the cause, also force-dynamically antecedes the other arguments. Can causal order, then, replace embedding relations as the criterion used to rank arguments?

Causal order sometimes does impose a ranking where depth of embedding fails. For example, the activity event structure of the surface-contact verb *wipe* contains a single predicate, and its arguments, as coarguments of this predicate, are not distinguished by depth of embedding. Its agent, however, force-dynamically antecedes the argument representing the surface, consistent with its realization as subject. But even causal order has apparent limitations. As noted in section 3.1.1, two-argument verbs with one necessarily sentient argument, such as *fear*, *love*, *see*, and *want*, express this argument as subject, suggesting it is more highly ranked than the nonsentient argument; however, it can be difficult to independently motivate a particular causal order for the arguments of all such verbs (see section 4.3). Neither causal order, nor depth of embedding, then, is adequate for ranking all arguments of a verb for subject or object selection. Yet, as shown in chapter 3, a mere counting of entailments as in Dowty's (1991) proto-role approach does not give the right results either, since the causation entailment overrides all other entailments in determining subject choice. Perhaps depth of embedding is always respected in the mapping to syntax, as expected on the prominence preservation approach to mapping. When depth of embedding does not impose an exhaustive ranking on a verb's arguments, causal order is appealed to, if applicable. When causal order also fails to impose a complete ranking, other semantic properties of the verb's arguments may determine their relative ranking. A thematic hierarchy built around entailments associated with semantic roles and their fillers is the topic of the next section.

6.4.2   The thematic hierarchy as a natural prominence scale

As Bresnan and Kanerva (1989: 23–24) point out, some researchers interpret the thematic hierarchy as a topicality hierarchy; arguments bearing semantic roles higher on the hierarchy are said to be more likely to be topics than those bearing roles lower on the hierarchy (Fillmore 1977b; Givón 1984b; Hawkinson and Hyman 1974; Trithart 1979). On this conception, the thematic hierarchy is one of a family of "natural prominence scales." Such scales rank the possible values of some attribute of a particular linguistic unit – semantic, conceptual, pragmatic, or morphological – according to an intuitive notion of prominence, perhaps, characterizable as cognitive salience. As McCarthy writes, "Natural language is replete with natural scales, with one end more prominent, in the abstract sense, than the other" (2002: 21). Other natural prominence scales include the animacy hierarchy, the person hierarchy, and the definiteness hierarchy; some also include the grammatical relations hierarchy and the morphological case hierarchy among them, though these seem different in nature. The ranking represented by each scale essentially prioritizes the possible values of an attribute for a range of linguistic phenomena, including facets of argument realization. For this reason, Dik (1997a: 36) calls them "priority hierarchies."

A given NP in a sentence usually has various attributes and, thus, is associated with values drawn from several natural prominence scales. The values
of the various attributes associated with a given NP tend to be chosen from
the same ends of the relevant scales. So the agent role is ranked high on the
thematic hierarchy, and agents tend to be human, a value high on the animacy
hierarchy; the agent role is also usually associated with subject, which is high
on the grammatical relations hierarchy, and with nominative case, which is
high on the morphological case hierarchy. Consequently, certain clusters of values are considered unmarked combinations, and, therefore, natural prominence
scales are central to discussions of markedness. As discussed in section 1.5,
agent–patient verbs are considered the prototypical transitive verbs crosslinguistically, expressing their agent and patient arguments as subject and object,
respectively. Divergences from this pairing of semantic roles with grammatical relations typically involve explicit morphosyntactic marking. For instance,
when the patient argument of an agent–patient verb is realized as a subject,
passive morphology is found on the verb in many languages; the marked subject choice is reflected in the morphologically marked passive verb form. These
effects can be derived using a thematic hierarchy along with the assumptions
that agent is ranked highest on a thematic hierarchy, subject is ranked highest
on a grammatical relations hierarchy, and the mapping from semantic roles to
grammatical relations preserves prominence relations, that is, it shows what
is called harmonic alignment in Optimality Theory (Aissen 1999; McCarthy
2002; A. Prince and Smolensky 1993: 136; see also section 5.3.2).

Languages vary, however, as to how tight an alignment they demand. Some
allow only the very highest values in the various natural prominence scales to
be aligned, while others allow the highest value on one scale to be aligned with
a range of values on a second scale. Each language, then, defines cut-off points
for the purposes of aligning values on the prominence scales, which results in
the implicational generalizations discussed in section 6.2 concerning the range
of semantic roles with access to subjecthood and objecthood in a particular language. Dik (1978: 76–78, 1997a: 265–69) provides a comprehensive discussion
of the various types of argument realization generalizations that follow from
such uses of the thematic hierarchy both within and across languages (see also
Givón 1984a: 163). Surveying a number of languages, Dik illustrates that languages prefer NPs bearing the semantic roles higher in the hierarchy to be
encoded as subject or else object. Usually when a lower-ranked role is chosen
as subject or object, the choice is accompanied by special verb morphology,
such as passive affixes or the applicative affixes of Bantu languages that appear
when benefactive, instrument, or locative NPs are objects. As Dik (1997a: 266)
writes, "as we proceed through the SFH [=Semantic Function Hierarchy, i.e.,
the thematic hierarchy] ... Subj and Obj assignment become more and more
'difficult', and the resulting constructions become more and more 'marked'."

Although all languages align the more highly ranked semantic roles with
subject, they encode grammatical relations in various ways, most commonly

via word order, morphological case, and verb agreement, but also via specialized voice morphology (e.g., active vs. passive voice, direct vs. inverse marking, applicative morphemes; see section 1.6). Other natural prominence scales, such as the animacy and definiteness hierarchies, are implicated in this surface expression of arguments; Aissen (1999: 677), K. Allen (1987: 51), Artstein (1998: 1), Croft (2003b: 128–32), Dik (1997a: 37), and Siewierska (1988: 29–103, 1993: 831) present fairly comprehensive, though nonidentical, lists. Languages vary as to which scales, if any, the surface expression of arguments is sensitive to. For example, many languages show "differential object marking" (Aissen 2003; Bossong 1991, 1998): an animate object receives a distinct morphosyntactic expression from an inanimate object, and, typically, one that is more morphosyntactically marked. This observation is interpreted in terms of the markedness of the alignment of values on different scales: an animate patient is a marked choice for direct object of an agent–patient verb since the prototypical patient is inanimate. As Aissen (2003) shows, the relevant generalization is best restated in terms of a natural prominence scale because animacy is not a binary-valued attribute; rather, there are multiple values for animacy that can be arranged in an animacy hierarchy, ranging from most to least "animate" (K. Allen 1987; Comrie 1989: 185; Corbett 2000: 55–66; Croft 2003b: 128–32; Silverstein 1976: 116–22; Van Valin and D. Wilkins 1997: 313–17), and languages with differential object marking can choose larger or smaller segments of the animacy hierarchy as the domain of differential object marking.

Often, a marked expression with respect to the thematic hierarchy allows a less marked expression with respect to another prominence scale. For example, some languages such as Lummi (Jelinek and Demers 1983, 1994) require that the NP bearing the patient role be the subject of a passive verb if its referent is higher on the person hierarchy than the referent of the agent NP; this requirement allows a preference for first- and second-person subjects to be met at the expense of a marked association of patient with subject. Thus, a more marked expression with respect to one attribute allows a less marked expression with respect to another (Artstein 1998: 1; Evans 1997: 420–21), a situation which suggests, in turn, that there is a precedence ranking among the natural prominence scales. Recently, these ideas have been pursued within Optimality Theory, which includes mechanisms for stating the relevant generalizations and for delineating the range of crosslinguistic variation in the surface coding of arguments (Aissen 1999, 2003; Artstein 1998; Asudeh 2001; Lee 2003; Legendre, Raymond, and Smolensky 1993).

What property of semantic roles organizes them into a natural prominence scale? And, if there is such a property, is it involved in organizing other natural prominence scales? As already mentioned, an intuitive notion of cognitive salience has been said to underlie all these scales. For the scales relevant to argument realization, Newmeyer writes, "Human NPs are more central to the human experience than inanimates; agents are more central than instruments;

subjects are more central than objects of prepositions; and so on" (2002: 50). More generally, the ranking of the various values of the attributes which define each natural prominence scale is said to reflect the contribution of the attribute to the topicality of the argument bearing this attribute (Artstein 1998; Hawkinson and Hyman 1974; Jelinek and Carnie 2003; Trithart 1979). This perspective is reminiscent of Givón's (1984b: 134) proposal that the thematic hierarchy ranks semantic roles based on their topicality. Inherent topicality, however, is not a property of a semantic role, even if it might be indirectly associated with a role due to the potential topicality of the NPs that prototypically fill that role, as we discuss shortly.

Siewierska (1993: 834–36) identifies two criteria that might determine the ranking of arguments in a natural prominence scale. First, the notion of natural flow of events, reviewed in the previous section and equated with causal order, provides a basis for imposing a ranking on semantic roles. However, the causal ordering of arguments does not constitute a natural prominence scale – a ranking of arguments according to values of an attribute. Siewierska's second criterion ranks roles in relation to the personal hierarchy – or extended animacy hierarchy, to use Croft's (2003b: 130) term – which conflates traditional animacy and person hierarchies; this hierarchy is often viewed as reflecting the inherent topicality of NPs, with animates, for instance, assumed to be more topical than inanimates (e.g., Hawkinson and Hyman 1974: 161; Trithart 1979: 25). Although animacy is often not taken to be criterial in definitions of semantic roles (Fillmore 1971a: 42), the two are interconnected in that verbs often presuppose that the prototypical filler of each semantic role "has a specifiable value on the person/animacy hierarchy," to quote Evans (1997: 420), defining what he calls "person/animacy referential prototypes." For example, the prototypical agent is animate and the prototypical patient inanimate. This interdependence is implicitly acknowledged in the prototype or cluster concept view of semantic roles (see section 3.2), as also noted by Evans. For instance, Givón (1984b: 107) includes animacy in his cluster concept definition of agency, while Dowty (1991: 572) includes sentience, which presupposes animacy, in his list of Agent Proto-role entailments. Tomlin (1986: 103–09) sees the thematic hierarchy and the animacy hierarchy as defining different facets of "animatedness," a property he considers crucial to whether one NP precedes a second in a sentence.

There are two drawbacks in using the personal hierarchy as a basis for ranking semantic roles. First, properties such as person and definiteness (or, perhaps, assumed familiarity), which are often taken to be components of the extended animacy hierarchy, are properties of the fillers of roles and are not event-based properties – that is, they are not derived from entailments which a verb imposes on its arguments by virtue of the parts they play in the event it describes. This can be true of animacy as well, if a verb does not entail the animacy of any of its arguments. These properties, then, should not be relevant to a hierarchy of event-based roles. Second, even when animacy is taken to be event-based, it imposes a rather coarse-grained ranking, since NPs bearing the agent, experiencer, benefactive, and recipient roles, for instance, are all typically animate. Animacy, then, does not impose an exhaustive ranking on all the semantic roles associated with a particular verb, let alone on all roles across verbs. This observation reflects a more general point: the thematic hierarchy is unlike most natural prominence scales because it ranks arguments on a fundamentally different basis from them. Other scales rank arguments according to the values of a "simple" attribute, such as animacy or definiteness – an attribute whose values fall along a single dimension. Although a semantic role may be considered a value of an attribute of arguments, it is not a "simple" attribute. At best, a semantic role can be viewed as defined by a cluster of properties, such as Dowty's proto-role entailments (see section 3.1.1), with each property representing a value of a simple attribute. Furthermore, if the lexical entailments that make up Dowty's proto-roles are representative, then most of these properties divide the set of semantic roles in two: those which are associated with the entailment and those which are not. No single attribute imposes a ranking on all semantic roles; rather, each role can only be characterized in terms of the value of several attributes.

It is perhaps not surprising, then, that some researchers have replaced a thematic hierarchy with a set of more basic statements, each identifying priorities among arguments based on associated semantic properties. Fillmore (1977b: 102), for example, adopts a series of preference statements for subject selection. T. Mohanan (1994: 28, (13)) also proposes a set of statements intended to establish prominence relations among arguments for purposes of argument realization. Fillmore includes some statements based on properties of the fillers of semantic roles (e.g., "A 'definite' element outranks an 'indefinite' element" and "A complete or individuated element outranks a part of an element" (1977b: 102)), as well as other event-based properties; Mohanan only provides the second type of statement. Both Fillmore and Mohanan single out causers as more prominent than noncausers, experiencers or sentient entities as more prominent than other entities, and changed/moved entities as more prominent than unchanged/stationary entities. These properties all overlap with Dowty's proto-role entailments and are also singled out in work sympathetic to Dowty's approach (Davis and Koenig 2000; Primus 1999; Wechsler 1995). The result, as Mohanan writes, is that "the traditional notion of the Thematic Hierarchy is the cumulative result of a number of interacting relative prominence relations between semantic entities" (1994: 28). It is noteworthy that most of these statements impose priorities among arguments precisely where depth of embedding is inadequate.[7]

Building on the conclusions of the previous section, we suggest that in the mapping to syntax the geometry of event structure is respected in general, ensuring that depth of embedding is also respected. When depth of embedding does not determine a ranking between two arguments of a predicate in event structure, certain entailments relating to the establishment of salience among the arguments will determine their ranking. These assumptions will handle verbs such as *wipe* and *want*, whose arguments are not differentiated by depth of embedding. As mentioned, some of the properties Fillmore identifies (e.g., definiteness, individuation, and, perhaps, animacy) hold for the NPs filling the semantic roles – precisely, the types of properties defining often cited natural prominence scales. As we discuss in the next section, properties of the NPs filling a semantic role are not usually implicated in the choice of grammatical relation that realizes these NPs, but rather are more often implicated in the morphosyntactic realization of that grammatical relation, as in differential object marking.

The prominence scale conception of the thematic hierarchy differs from the structural conception in several respects. Since semantic roles are not viewed as discrete entities, but rather as defined by a set of properties, semantic roles of finer or coarser grain-size can be ranked. It is possible to rank the roles associated with a verb's own arguments, but it is also possible to rank roles across verbs. Indeed, some generalizations require one type of ranking and others the other. In contrast to the structural conception, the prominence scale conception is relevant to determining not only structural relations in the syntax between cooccurring arguments, but also crosslinguistic generalizations concerning the possible realization of arguments bearing particular roles. Of course, the set of roles ranked for a particular type of generalization depends on the nature of the generalization and the language involved. However, when the prominence scale conception is implicated in an account of some phenomenon, it is most likely because more basic semantic properties relevant to argument realization distribute across semantic roles in systematic ways, as manifested, for instance, in person/animacy referential prototypes. The result is apparent thematic hierarchy effects. We argue that certain local empirical generalizations stated in terms of the thematic hierarchy, as in Polinsky and Kozinsky's (1992) analysis of applicatives, actually have such an explanation. Statements of crosslinguistically valid implicational generalizations about subject and object choice such as those mentioned in section 6.2 might also turn out not to implicate the thematic hierarchy.

With this investigation of potential groundings for the thematic hierarchy as a foundation, we now examine the sources of different formulations of the thematic hierarchy.

6.5 Towards an understanding of differences between thematic hierarchies

Before trying to explain differences among various formulations of the thematic hierarchy, we must ensure that they indeed have empirical consequences. In this context, we reiterate a point made in section 5.3.2. There, we examined how the thematic hierarchy is incorporated into mapping algorithms, and we demonstrated interactions between the choice of algorithm and the ranking of roles in a thematic hierarchy. Due to these interactions, certain distinct role rankings do not have any empirical consequences and can be used to capture the same range of generalizations about argument realization.

It is also important to recognize that when a particular semantic role appears in different instantiations of the thematic hierarchy, it may not actually have the same extension. This point was made in section 2.4 with respect to patient/theme, but a more pertinent example here is goal. Some researchers reserve the term "goal" for purely spatial goals. Others use it for "abstract" goals, a category which includes recipients and perhaps also experiencers. For still others, the notion is very broad, encompassing both spatial and abstract goals. Proponents of the Localist Hypothesis may even subsume the final state in a change-of-state event under the notion "goal" (see section 4.2). Finally, some researchers may simply dispense with an independent goal role, subsuming the various types of goals under a broadly defined location role, as in Foley and Van Valin (1984: 53). As this suggests, similar issues arise for the semantic role "location," which for Foley and Van Valin includes sources and goals, as well as more traditional locations. Dik (1997a: 272–74) suggests that "inner" or "selected" locations should be distinguished from other, more adjunct-like locations, with only the former figuring in his thematic hierarchy. A comparison and evaluation of the relative ranking of semantic roles will only yield meaningful results if the notions being compared are truly comparable. Thus, a prerequisite for this exercise is establishing what semantic notions are actually hiding behind role labels.

6.5.1 Thematic hierarchies as statements of local empirical generalizations

As already mentioned, some thematic hierarchies simply allow the formulation of empirical generalizations of greater or lesser generality; they are not meant to represent a universal primitive linguistic construct. Evaluating such a hierarchy requires figuring out what is behind the empirical generalization that the hierarchy expresses. Take the hierarchy used to account for Fillmore's well-known subject selection paradigm: "Agent > Instrument > Patient" (see section 6.1). It has perhaps been taken to be a universal primitive construct, but closer scrutiny reveals that such an understanding is incorrect. This hierarchy cannot be given a "structural" interpretation in that it does not capture the syntactic c-command relations among the NPs bearing the roles it includes. There is no sentence with a morphologically basic verb and an agent, an instrument, and a patient in which the instrument is structurally more prominent than the patient. Yet, this hierarchy does not seem to be a natural prominence scale either, since instruments are almost always ranked low in terms of their "cognitive salience." It appears that Fillmore's hierarchy conflates two distinct semantic criteria. The verb *break*, which is used to exemplify Fillmore's subject selection paradigm, is a change-of-state verb, taking cause and patient arguments. The cause argument can be "filled" by agents, instrument, or natural forces. Fillmore's ranking of agent over instrument indicates that the choice of instrument as the cause argument precludes the expression of an agent, while the choice of agent as the cause argument does not preclude the expression of an instrument (see section 6.2 on context dependence). The ranking of agent and instrument above patient can be given a structural prominence interpretation, by stipulating that causes are always structurally more prominent than patients. In sum, Fillmore's hierarchy aptly captures the generalizations behind the paradigm he introduces, though it is not a primitive linguistic construct.

The thematic hierarchy is also used to provide a convenient statement of a local generalization by Polinsky and Kozinsky (1992). As discussed in section 6.2, they introduce the hierarchy in (9) to identify the first object of an applicative verb in Kinyarwanda; as it is also intended for use with morphological causative verbs, it includes a causee role.

(9) recipient > benefactive > possessor > causee > instrument > comitative
　　　　　　　　　　　　　　(Polinsky and Kozinsky 1992: 440, (40))

Polinsky and Kozinsky explicitly recognize the nonprimitive status of this hierarchy, writing that it "is simply a generalization of the empirical regularities" (1990: 440). They stress that it emerges from more basic semantic properties of the ranked semantic roles, specifically, animacy and what they call "semantic immediacy." Semantic roles associated with animate participants, they propose, are ranked higher than those that are not, and within each of these two groups, roles are ranked by "semantic immediacy." This property is roughly equivalent to semantic obligatoriness, so that benefactives, which are sometimes selected by a verb, are ranked higher than possessors, which are never selected, but lower than recipients, which are more often selected. We do not assess why these semantic properties are relevant; rather, we underscore two points. First, Polinsky and Kozinsky's hierarchy is not a primitive construct. It expresses a surface generalization which stems from the interaction of more basic semantic notions with the processes of applicativization and causativization. Second, the form of the hierarchy is determined by the nature of the relevant generalization. Since this generalization involves first objects in applicative and causative constructions, the associated hierarchy includes a range of semantic roles typically associated with adjuncts, rather than patient/theme – the role most often associated with basic direct objects. Moreover, since the concern is Kinyarwanda, which allows NPs bearing a wide range of semantic roles as applicative objects, the hierarchy includes a relatively large set of roles; if a language allows NPs bearing a smaller range of roles as applicative objects, the comparable hierarchy would rank fewer roles.

The real generalization may sometimes be one which does not directly involve semantic roles. As discussed in section 6.2, Alsina (1999: 26) and Bresnan and Kanerva (1992: 117) propose that the applicative morpheme must introduce an argument whose semantic role is lower on the thematic hierarchy than that of one of the verb's original arguments. This proposal is supposed to account for why benefactive applicative objects are impossible with verbs like *fall*, whose only argument is a theme (Bresnan and Kanerva 1992: 118, (19)). Yet, in a further study, Alsina and Mchombo cite precisely such an example: the Chicheŵa counterpart of "Jesus died for all people" (1993: 36, (36)). It is presumably this data which leads them to the weaker proposal that the applicative morpheme simply accompanies the addition of another argument (1993: 28). However, the verb *die* involves an argument that can receive an agent-like reading in the context of religious martyrdom; specifically, the theme in some sense assumes control over the event (Van Valin and D. Wilkins 1996: 312–13). This suggests an alternative generalization: benefactives can only be introduced if they will have a coargument with control over the event. Typically, the relevant coargument is the agent, which is taken to bear the highest semantic role. Presumably, this property underlies Bresnan and Kanerva's thematic hierarchy-based generalization, which requires benefactives to be introduced in the context of a higher-ranked argument. Since in the *die* example, control is associated with a theme, the thematic hierarchy-based generalization is violated, but the deeper generalization that benefactives must have a coargument with control over the event is not. This example illustrates how phenomena may be governed by a semantic property which does not on its own define a semantic role, although such semantic properties usually distribute across semantic roles in a systematic way.

6.5.2   Thematic hierarchies in crosslinguistic implicational generalizations

Since the ranking of semantic roles depends on the interpretation given to the thematic hierarchy and the generalizations it is meant to account for, role rankings must be examined relative to a particular interpretation and use. In this section we consider this question in the context of crosslinguistic implicational generalizations. Such generalizations are often expressed by making reference to some type of hierarchy (Comrie 1989; Croft 2003b: 122–28). When the generalization being captured involves semantic roles borne by arguments, the relevant hierarchy will look like a thematic hierarchy. However, any hierarchy used in formulating such a generalization, including a thematic hierarchy, simply provides a way of stating the relevant generalization and is not taken to be primitive linguistic construct. Furthermore, varying instantiations of the thematic hierarchy can figure in such generalizations since the insight being captured determines the set of semantic roles to be ranked, including the appropriate grain-size for these roles.

As an illustration, consider the placement of recipient and benefactive. Hierarchies differ as to whether or not benefactives and recipients are ranked relative to each other, as well as in their relative ranking with respect to patient/theme. As we now show, several rankings can express valid generalizations, which are the result of interacting factors. These generalizations cannot all be captured with a single thematic hierarchy, and none of the relevant hierarchies is in any way primitive.

First, we compare the alternate ranking of the patient/theme and benefactive in two hierarchies: Dik (1978: 76, 1980: 14, 1997a: 265) ranks benefactive lower than patient/theme, while Givón (1984) ranks the benefactive higher than patient/theme.[8] This difference can be traced to the phenomena of interest. Dik aims to capture the range of semantic roles normally associated with subject and object. Crosslinguistically, it is much more common to have patient/theme subjects or objects than benefactive subjects or objects, hence the ranking of patient/theme over benefactive. Moreover, since Dik wants to capture the generalizations about both subject and object with a single hierarchy, he must place the patient/theme higher than the recipient and benefactive. This placement may also be meant to capture the observation that recipients and benefactives, unlike patient/themes, do not appear as subjects of intransitive verbs (cf. Baker's [1996a, 1997] observation that there is no unaccusative counterpart of the dative alternation). In contrast, Givón (1984) ranks recipient and benefactive above patient/theme. Many languages allow not only recipients, but also benefactives to be expressed using some core grammatical relation, for example, as the first object in the double object construction in English or as a dative NP in German (see section 1.6). In English double object constructions, the recipient and the benefactive often usurp some object properties from the patient/theme, including adjacency to the verb, control of object agreement, and the ability to become the subject of the corresponding passive verb (cf. *Dale was given the book, Jan was baked a cake, *The book was given Dale, *A cake was baked Jan*). Since Givón takes these properties to be indicators of topicality, and prominence in his hierarchy is taken to be a reflection of degree of topicality, the recipient and the benefactive must be ranked higher than the patient/theme.

Next, we compare hierarchies that rank recipient and benefactive together with those which rank them with respect to each other. Since Givón's hierarchy captures generalizations about recipients and benefactives in double object constructions, where they cannot cooccur (*I wrote my brother my mother a letter*), a statement about the ranking of these roles relative to, say, the patient/theme, does not have to distinguish between them. Therefore, it is not surprising that Givón ranks recipient and benefactive together. Other generalizations, however, require them to be ranked with respect to each other. Thus, Polinsky and Kozinsky (1992) rank recipient above benefactive because recipient takes precedence over benefactive with respect to access to expression as first object in applicatives (see section 6.2).

6.5.3 Conflicting rankings of theme and recipient

We now turn to thematic hierarchies intended to govern the realization of a verb's own arguments, probing the sources of disagreement in the ways they are formulated. We focus on the major point of contention, which was mentioned in section 6.3: the appropriate placement of the patient/theme role, particularly with respect to the goal and location roles. As also noted, the notion of goal is not understood in the same way by all researchers, and the real controversy involves the relative ranking of "goal as recipient" and theme. (We use "theme" rather than "patient/theme" in this discussion since the relevant argument fits the narrow localist definition of theme; see section 4.1.) All hierarchies which rank goal above theme take goal to mean recipient, while some hierarchies still place recipient below theme. No existing thematic hierarchy places spatial goal above theme;[9] proponents of those hierarchies listed in section 6.3 which rank goal above and location below theme restrict the notion "goal" to recipients, subsuming spatial goals under "location." We focus our attention, then, on the relative ranking of recipients and themes.

As Baker (1997) points out, conflicting rankings arise because in English and certain other languages, dative verbs have two argument realization options, each suggesting a different relative ranking of theme and recipient, as manifested in the dative alternation. When the theme is expressed as a direct object and the recipient as an oblique, as in the *to* variant *Alex sent the package to Sam*, the theme shows evidence of being more prominent than the recipient. When the recipient is realized as the first of two objects in English and some other languages, as in the double object variant *Alex sent Sam the package*, or as a dative NP in others (e.g., Albanian; Massey 1992; Marantz 1993: 118), its behavior with respect to various linguistic phenomena (binding of pronouns by quantifiers and *wh*-words, ability to antecede reflexives and reciprocals) suggests that it is syntactically more prominent than the theme (Baker 1997; Barss and Lasnik 1986; Polinsky 1996, 2001). Of course, as we have stressed throughout this chapter, we can only evaluate proposed rankings of roles once we make explicit what the ranking is meant to account for. As suggested in previous sections, it appears that event structure prominence – the basis for the structural interpretation of the thematic hierarchy – and, thus, order of composition, determines the basic grammatical relations. Priorities among arguments in terms of various event-based properties determine salience when structural prominence does not. Finally, non-event-based properties of NPs typically filling these arguments influence the surface morphosyntactic realization of the grammatical relations. These considerations are pertinent to an evaluation of the evidence for particular rankings of theme and recipient.

A further complication relates to whether or not a dative verb such as *give* is associated with two meanings and, hence, two event structures – a question we discuss at length in the next chapter. If dative verbs are associated with two event structures, these event structures might give rise to distinct argument rankings, which, in turn, lead to two distinct morphosyntactic realizations. This idea is implemented in Harley's recent analysis of dative verbs (1995, 1997, 2003). She suggests that dative verbs are polysemous, associated with two distinct event structures, corresponding roughly to "[x CAUSE [y HAVE z]]" and "[x CAUSE [y GO [TO z]]]" (see section 7.2.3.1). Given the assumptions laid out in section 6.4.1, the relative prominence relations among the arguments in the event structure are preserved in their syntactic realization. As a result, the recipient c-commands the theme in one argument realization – the one that corresponds to the double object construction – and the theme c-commands the goal in the other – the *to* construction. However, in section 7.2.3.1 we review the evidence adduced to support the polysemy of dative verbs and conclude that the evidence does not, in fact, support this position.

If there is, then, only one event structure underlying both argument realizations available to a dative verb, there should be a single event-based ranking of arguments independent of their morphosyntactic realization. Establishing the appropriate ranking requires identifying a diagnostic for underlying grammatical relations. As mentioned above, binding facts are sometimes used to motivate a relative ranking of recipient and theme. However, since any reordering of arguments in the dative alternation involves A-movement, which alters the c-command relations relevant to binding, such phenomena do not necessarily reflect the "underlying" syntactic position of theme and recipient and do not bear on their relative ranking.[10]

As discussed in section 6.4.1, certain linguistic phenomena can be viewed as direct reflections of order of composition and can then be used to diagnose the ranking of arguments in the syntactic structure which is the output of the mapping algorithm. In particular, dative verbs can incorporate the theme, but not the recipient in languages with noun incorporation, and this pattern is said to reflect the fact that the theme composes with the verb before the recipient. Similar asymmetries are evidenced by English compounding, where the theme, but not the recipient, can be the nonhead of a compound based on a dative verb (*story-telling to children*, but **children-telling of stories*). The same order of composition is also said to explain asymmetries in the structure of idioms, and we focus on these data since they have been most extensively explored. Specifically, English has idioms based on dative verbs with fixed themes and variable recipients (e.g., *lend x an ear, promise x the moon, read x the riot act, show x the ropes*), but no idioms with fixed recipients and variable themes.

Strikingly, this asymmetry in the distribution of fixed parts of idioms holds for dative verbs regardless of how they realize their arguments (e.g., *show x the ropes, show the ropes to x*).[11] We take this as strong evidence that the two variants are not associated with distinct event structures and that the ranking of semantic roles associated with both variants is "agent > recipient > theme," a ranking compatible with the causative change-of-possession event structure "[x CAUSE [y HAVE z]]." Consistent with this ranking, idioms with fixed recipients always have a fixed theme, as in *sell one's soul to the devil*.

Furthermore, there are some idioms with dative verbs which appear only in the *to* variant. It is noteworthy that the fixed part of these idioms is the NP in the *to* phrase. These idioms, however, are not problematic for the proposed ranking of recipient above theme, because the fixed NP is invariably interpreted as a spatial goal rather than a recipient (O'Grady 1998). This pattern is explained if these idioms describe events of causative change of location, rather than events of causative change of possession. If so, they would be associated with an event structure of the form "[x CAUSE [y GO [TO z]]]," so that their verb would compose first with the goal. Such idioms would not be expected to alternate, given the assumption that the first object in the double object construction represents a recipient, while the object of *to* represents an abstract goal, whether a spatial goal or a recipient (Goldsmith 1980; Pinker 1989).

The use of idiom data to argue for order of composition and, hence, role ranking, faces some challenges. Nunberg, Sag, and Wasow (1994: 525–31) propose that animacy considerations may go a long way towards explaining some asymmetries in the distribution of the fixed parts of idioms. They point out that NPs with animate referents generally are not found as fixed parts of idioms. The reason, they suggest, is that such NPs are not good inputs to metaphors. Since recipients are generally animate, they would be unlikely to be the fixed part of idioms involving dative verbs. The question that requires further investigation, then, is whether there is nevertheless a residue of idiom data that does bear on order of composition and role ranking, as suggested in O'Grady (1998: 305–09). We do not pursue this question further here because the relevant patterns of data are quite intricate, as Nunberg, Sag, and Wasow's discussion makes clear.[12]

Contrary to our claim, Baker (1997) argues that in all languages the appropriate ranking is "agent > theme > recipient," no matter how the arguments are realized. The distributional properties that lead him to this ranking include the same compounding and incorporation facts that we have taken to support the alternative ranking; however, Baker interprets them differently. According to him, the failure of recipients to incorporate in a language with noun incorporation and their inability to be the nonhead of a deverbal compound shows that recipients, although first objects in the double object construction, do not show direct object properties. Baker (1997: 94, 100) explains these facts by assuming that the recipient is governed at d-structure by a null preposition which blocks government of the recipient by the verb and prevents the recipient from compounding or incorporating. This preposition is a reflection in the syntax of the ranking of the recipient below the theme in the event structure. However, these empirical generalizations can be captured equally well under our assumptions that the recipient is ranked above the theme and that both noun incorporation and compounding operate on the lowest argument (cf. Kiparsky 1997: 484).

The surface morphosyntactic realization of themes and recipients varies greatly from language to language. Notions such as animacy, as noted in chapter 4, seem not to be implicated in the grammatical relation associated with a particular semantic role, but rather in the morphosyntactic realization of that grammatical relation. In double object type structures, the recipient often usurps from the theme certain of the morphosyntactic properties normally associated with a theme realized as a direct object, such as adjacency to the verb and control of pronominal agreement markers. These morphosyntactic properties, however, may not be sensitive to semantic roles per se, but rather to semantic properties of the NPs filling the roles, such as animacy, definiteness, and even person (Comrie 1989; Evans 1997; Haspelmath 2002). Furthermore, in some languages, whether or not these morphosyntactic properties are associated with the recipient depends on the animacy, person, or definiteness of both the recipient and theme. For example, according to Evans (1997: 421), in Mayali the recipient controls object pronominal marking only if the theme is not animate. As discussed in section 6.4.2, the semantic properties implicated in the morphosyntactic realizations of the recipient and theme are precisely those which form the various natural prominence scales, with the prototypical recipient associated with values that are above those of the prototypical theme. Again, phenomena which appear to implicate the thematic hierarchy actually more deeply implicate these other scales. Once more, the reason is that semantic roles typically align themselves in particular ways with the properties figuring in the natural prominence scales.

6.6   Conclusion

In this chapter, we have shown that it is impossible to formulate a thematic hierarchy which will capture all generalizations involving the realization of arguments in terms of their semantic roles. Broadly speaking, there are two ways of understanding the thematic hierarchy, which correspond to two ways of understanding semantic roles. These uses of the thematic hierarchy further confirm these two understandings of semantic roles and add weight to our earlier suggestions that both understandings of semantic roles are relevant to the calculation of argument realization. We argue that some thematic hierarchy effects arise because embedding relations among arguments in an event structure are always respected in argument realization, with more embedded arguments receiving less prominent syntactic realizations. When two arguments are not ranked with respect to each other by depth of embedding, other semantic properties, such as sentience and causal order, become relevant to their realization. Since these also classify arguments, they too can give rise to apparent thematic hierarchy effects. Properties of the NPs that typically fill certain semantic roles, which are often confused with properties of the semantic roles themselves, may affect the most surface realization of these NPs, but this surface realization most probably does not reflect true thematic hierarchy effects. Finally, many thematic hierarchies are meant to be a technical shorthand for capturing a local empirical generalization and should not be considered a universal construct.

Notes

1   Jackendoff (1972), following Gruber (1965), calls his set of semantic roles "thematic relations" because the role "theme" is central (see section 4.2). He then calls the hierarchy built on these notions a "thematic hierarchy," and following now established usage we adopt this term rather than "semantic role hierarchy."

2   This account works for English, but not necessarily for other languages. As mentioned in section 1.5, there is crosslinguistic variability in the realization of arguments of noncausative psych-verbs, although, in a broad sense, context dependence in the expression of the experiencer argument still holds even in languages that show other argument realization options. Nevertheless, it remains an open question how a thematic hierarchy can be used to account for such variability in argument realization.

3   Comparable generalizations are also stated in terms of a grammatical relations hierarchy (see section 5.2) rather than a thematic hierarchy. Such hierarchies take the form "subject > object > indirect object > oblique," mirroring the order "agent > patient > recipient > location." We do not choose between these two approaches to the generalizations; our interest is simply in illustrating a use of the thematic hierarchy.

4   Dik's own label for the "patient" in (7) is "goal"; however, since his "goal" corresponds to what is more traditionally called the patient role, it has been relabelled "patient" throughout this chapter to conform to more established usage and to avoid confusion with the more common understandings of "goal" as the destination of a moving entity or as a recipient.

5   A thematic hierarchy that adds a "possessor" role to the top of a more familiar hierarchy is used to capture restrictions on extraction out of NPs, particularly in Romance languages (Dimitrova-Vulchanova and Giusti 1999; Godard 1992; Moritz and Valois 1994; Pollock 1989: 158–59). We do not discuss such uses further, but see Kolliakou (1999) for arguments against them.

6   Since our goal is comparative, we include Van Valin's (1990) early formulation of the thematic hierarchy in terms of semantic roles, even though he (Van Valin and LaPolla 1997) later replaces this hierarchy with a ranking of arguments identified by the substructures in predicate decompositions which underlie the roles (see section 3.1.2).

7   T. Mohanan (1994: 28) brings the two views of the thematic hierarchy together by including among her statements of relative ranking one that ranks arguments that are more deeply embedded below those that are less deeply embedded.

8   Alsina (1999) and Bresnan and Kanerva (1992), following Bresnan and Kanerva's (1989) lead, rank benefactive higher as well. As discussed in section 6.5.1, Alsina (1999) and Bresnan and Kanerva (1992) are concerned with conditions on the well-formedness of applicative constructions, which involve a verb and its arguments, not with typological implicational generalizations. As we have shown, the relevant generalization is likely to be sensitive to a participant's potential to control the unfolding of an event and, thus, indirectly to its animacy or sentience. From this perspective, benefactive is ranked higher than patient/theme.

9   The exception is Grimshaw's (1990) hierarchy, which places spatial goal and location above patient/theme. However, we disregard this ranking as it is motivated by a narrow range of data, whose connection to the thematic hierarchy is unclear. Van Valin and LaPolla (1997) rank location above patient/theme, but this ranking

reflects their argument realization algorithm; the reverse ranking would be possible with a slightly different algorithm, generally without empirical consequences.

10 Binding phenomena may, nevertheless, be relevant to a thematic hierarchy intended to rank arguments in terms of prominence.

11 Contrary to what Harley (1995, 1997, 2003), Richards (2001) and others suggest, the fixed part of an idiom based on a dative verb is not inherently connected to the dative alternation variant the idiom appears in. For instance, Harley assumes that idioms with fixed themes and variable recipients (e.g., *lend x an ear*) appear in the double object variant; however, such idioms are actually attested in either variant (Bresnan and Nikitina 2003; B. Levin and Rappaport Hovav 2002). As we discuss in section 7.3, the *to* variant is dispreferred with fixed theme idioms due to information-structure considerations, and, when these are overcome, the *to* variant may be found.

12 Similarly, animacy considerations might be implicated in the theme–recipient asymmetry observed in noun incorporation. Mithun (1984: 863) points out that animates, which tend to be topical, might not be expected to be incorporated since noun incorporation is a backgrounding device. The noun incorporation evidence has yet to receive as much attention as the idiom evidence; it needs to be scrutinized further to choose between possible explanations.

7

Multiple argument realization

As discussed in chapter 1, generative grammar traditionally assumed the realization of a verb's arguments to be determined by information registered in a structured lexical entry for that verb. In early versions of generative grammar, the syntactic expression of a verb's arguments is directly encoded in its lexical entry in the form of a subcategorization frame. Later, semantically based representations of argument-taking properties replace subcategorization frames (Bresnan 1982b; Marantz 1984; Pesetsky 1982; Rappaport and B. Levin 1988; Stowell 1981; Williams 1981), and the realization of a verb's arguments is calculated from these "argument structures" via mapping algorithms in ways illustrated in chapter 5. In Rappaport Hovav and B. Levin (1996, 1998a), we call such theories PROJECTIONIST. There are a variety of projectionist theories which all share the fundamental assumption that a verb's lexical entry registers some kind of semantically anchored argument structure, which in turn determines the morphosyntactic expression – or projection – of its arguments.

In this chapter we consider a set of phenomena involving argument realization which pose a challenge to projectionist theories, the phenomena falling under the label MULTIPLE ARGUMENT REALIZATION. Perhaps its most intensively studied manifestation is what we called ARGUMENT ALTERNATIONS. This form of multiple argument realization is typified by pairs of sentences with the same verb, related by paraphrase or subsumption. The dative and locative alternations are illustrated in (1) and (2). A third alternation is illustrated in (3); as it lacks a conventionally accepted name, we refer to it as the *with/against* alternation (B. Levin 1993).

(1) a. Terry gave the newspaper to Kim. (*to* variant)
    b. Terry gave Kim the newspaper. (double object variant)

(2) a. Devon smeared butter on the toast. (locative variant)
    b. Devon smeared the toast with butter. (*with* variant)

(3) a. Kerry hit the stick against the fence.
    b. Kerry hit the fence with the stick.

Argument alternations are usually manifested by sets of semantically related verbs (see section 1.3). Thus, the pair of alternate argument realization options shown by *give* is characteristic of the class of verbs in (4a), and the pairs shown by *smear* and *hit* are characteristic of the verbs in (4b) and (4c), respectively.

(4) a. bring, hand, loan, read, sell, send, take, teach, write, ...
    b. cram, pack, pile, spray, splash, spread, sprinkle, stuff, ...
    c. beat, knock, pound, rap, slap, tap, thump, ...

The dative, locative, and *with/against* alternations are OBJECT ALTERNATIONS, involving alternate realization of the V'-internal arguments of three-argument verbs, with one argument always being realized as the object.

Two-argument verbs also show alternate modes of argument realization, as illustrated in (5)–(7).

(5) a. Bees are swarming in the garden.
    b. The garden is swarming with bees.

(6) a. Pat hit the door.
    b. Pat hit at the door.

(7) a. Water leaked from the tank.
    b. The tank leaked water.

The alternation in (5) is sometimes analyzed as an intransitive version of the locative alternation (B. Levin 1993; Salkoff 1983), but Dowty (2000) convincingly argues against this analysis. The alternation in (6), known as the CONATIVE ALTERNATION (Guerssel et al. 1985; B. Levin 1993; van der Leek 1996), is characterized by the alternate realization of an argument as an object or oblique and is reminiscent of the direct object/oblique alternations mentioned in section 4.2.3.[1] The alternation exemplified by the pair in (7) is defined by the alternate realization of a source argument as an oblique in (7a) or as a subject in (7b). Perhaps one of the best-known alternations is the causative alternation, introduced in chapter 1 and illustrated in (8).

(8) a. The clumsy waiter broke a whole tray of glasses.
    b. A whole tray of glasses broke.

Researchers have investigated not only the range and distribution of argument alternations, but also the scope of multiple argument realization more generally. These investigations revealed that multiple argument realization is pervasive, as illustrated by the examples below, which involve verbs drawn from three distinct semantic classes: verbs of surface contact, verbs of sound emission, and verbs of manner of motion.

(9) a. Terry swept.
  b. Terry swept the floor.
  c. Terry swept the leaves into the corner.
  d. Terry swept the leaves off the sidewalk.
  e. Terry swept the floor clean.
  f. Terry swept the leaves into a pile.
                        (Rappaport Hovav and B. Levin 1998a: 97–8, (1))

(10) a. Kim whistled.
  b. Kim whistled at the dog.
  c. Kim whistled a tune.
  d. Kim whistled a warning.
  e. Kim whistled me a warning.
  f. Kim whistled her appreciation.
  g. Kim whistled to the dog to come.
  h. The bullet whistled through the air.
  i. The air whistled with bullets.
                        (Rappaport Hovav and B. Levin 1998a: 98, (2))

(11) a. Pat ran.
  b. Pat ran to the beach.
  c. Pat ran herself ragged.
  d. Pat ran her shoes to shreds.
  e. Pat ran clear of the falling rocks.
  f. The coach ran the athletes around the track.
                        (Rappaport Hovav and B. Levin 1998a: 98, (3))

These sentences show that not all instances of multiple argument realization take the form of alternate realizations of a single set of arguments. Sentences (9c) and (9d) are not related by paraphrase, as in (2), or subsumption, as in (8); rather, the first describes a putting event and the second a removing event. Yet, both still seem to involve the same verb *sweep* since both describe events involving the conventional use of a broom.

More important, many of the examples in (9)–(11) involve the addition of one or two elements not selected by the verb: an NP, a predicate, or both. Consider, for example, (11). (11a) invokes an event of running, which involves a single participant, the runner. In (11c) and (11d) reference is made not only to an event of running, but also to an event of the runner becoming "ragged" in (11c) and an event of the shoes falling to shreds in (11d). The material after the verb in these two sentences is nonsubcategorized (e.g., *Pat ran herself* and *Pat ran her shoes*). In terms of event structure, *run* is associated with a simple event structure in (11a), while the addition of the predicates *ragged* and *to shreds* gives rise to a complex event structure (Carrier and Randall

1993; Goldberg and Jackendoff 2004; Jackendoff 1990b; Rappaport Hovav and B. Levin 2002; Wunderlich 1997a, 1997b). Consider also (10h): here the directional PP appears to represent an introduced event of directed motion, not lexically associated with *whistle*. More generally, complex events typically appear to be derived through the introduction of an additional argument-taking predicate, an additional argument, or both (see section 7.4). We refer to multiple argument realization which involves the addition of nonadjunct nonlexically entailed complements as EVENT COMPOSITION, although this term is not strictly accurate. If events are happenings in the world, and verbs are predicates of events, what is derived is a complex event description, rather than a complex event. We choose the term "event composition" since it provides an informal semantic characterization of the phenomenon that should hold independent of its actual linguistic analysis. We avoid the term "complex predicate formation," since this term is often applied more generally, for instance, to refer to light verb constructions (e.g., *give a kick*, *take a bath*).

To summarize, some instances of multiple argument realization can be construed as "alternations," involving an alternate realization of a single set of arguments; others involve event composition, with an added argument-taking predicate and, possibly, additional arguments. We discuss these two forms of multiple argument realization separately because they raise distinct questions. Certain types of multiple argument realization, however, do not clearly fall under one label or the other and have received both classifications.

In section 7.1 we review a major theoretical question which arises in the context of multiple argument realization. Section 7.2 surveys analyses of argument alternations, while section 7.3 examines the role of information packaging and other factors in choosing among the variants constituting an alternation. Section 7.4 turns to analyses of event composition. Finally, section 7.5 reviews efforts to explain why verbs differ in their options for multiple argument realization.

7.1 Projectionist and constructional perspectives

Multiple argument realization did not seem to pose a challenge to projectionist approaches as long as the phenomenon seemed to be restricted to a few delimited classes of verbs and the inventory of alternations seemed rather small. On the assumption that the complement structure of a verb is determined by its semantics, argument alternations could be seen as a by-product of verbal polysemy: a verb with multiple meanings would be expected to have multiple argument realizations. The existence of a well-delimited and fairly small set of polysemous verbs seemed reasonable. However, it soon became clear that multiple argument realization is widespread, at least in English. The preponderance of verbs appear in a range of syntactic contexts, as shown by the examples in (9)–(11) and as reinforced by the examples in (12) based on a nonce denominal verb.

(12) a. The factory horns sirened throughout the raid.
      b. The factory horns sirened midday and everyone broke for lunch.
      c. The police car sirened the Porsche to a stop.
      d. The police car sirened up to the accident site.
      e. The police car sirened the daylight [sic] out of me.

(Borer 2003a: 40, (13), citing Clark and Clark 1979)

Furthermore, the phenomena we classified as involving event composition do not lend themselves as naturally to a polysemy analysis. As Goldberg (1995) notes, the meaning encoded in sentences like (11d) does not seem to be natural as a word meaning. In fact, not all instances of multiple argument realization are even associated with a well-established name. While (9c) and (9d) are instances of what Goldberg (1995) calls the "caused motion" construction and (9e) is an instance of the resultative construction, there is no conventionally accepted name for (9f) or for the "alternations" illustrated in (12). If such variation is the rule, then the lexicon must contain a vast number of verbs with multiple lexical entries. With instances of the resultative construction or other forms of event composition, the whole construction must then be derived "in the lexicon." This wholesale polysemy seems counterintuitive, since almost all the instances of multiple argument realization illustrated in (9)–(11) involve a "single" verb. There is no difference in the running in (11d) and (11f): both involve people moving their limbs repeatedly in a particular pattern. The same holds for the verb *siren* in (12), as Borer points out. Even all the uses in (10) involve a core invariant meaning of *whistle* – the emission of a high-pitched sustained sound, usually produced by forcing air through a narrow aperture.

The pervasiveness of multiple argument realization has brought into question the main tenet of the projectionist approach: that a verb has a structured lexical entry which alone determines the projection of its arguments. Since, in many instances, each distinct option for argument realization is accompanied by a distinct meaning, theories have been developed in which it is the syntactic expression of the arguments which determines major facets of meaning, rather than differences in meaning which determine different argument realizations. In these theories, which we call CONSTRUCTIONAL in Rappaport Hovav and B. Levin (1996, 1998a), the lexical entry of the verb registers only its core meaning – or "root" (see section 3.2) – and this core meaning combines with the event-based meanings which are represented by syntactic constructions themselves or are associated with particular syntactic positions or substructures. This eliminates wholesale polysemy and multiple lexical entries for verbs which appear in multiple syntactic contexts. It also allows a natural solution to a problem raised by the *run* examples in (11): only some material in their VPs can be said to be licensed by the basic meaning of *run*, so there must be an alternate source for these complements. In constructional theories, the verb is integrated into the construction, rather than determining the construction, and the construction itself licenses some of the complement structure.

There are various instantiations of the constructional approach, which fall into two broad classes of approaches: the "traditional" constructional approach, represented by Goldberg (1995, 1997, 1998), Jackendoff (1997), Kay (2000, 2002), and Michaelis and Ruppenhofer (2000, 2001), and a "neoconstructionist" approach, represented by Arad (1998), Borer (1994, 1998, 1999, 2003a, 2003b, in press a, in press b), Erteschik-Shir and Rapoport (1996, 2004), Ghomeshi and Massam (1995), Hoekstra (1992), Hoekstra and Mulder (1990), and Ritter and S. T. Rosen (1998).

The earliest comprehensive constructional approach to multiple argument realization is presented by Goldberg (1995); it represents the traditional approach. She argues for the existence of ARGUMENT STRUCTURE CONSTRUC-TIONS: pairings of meanings with syntactic frames.

(13) a. Ditransitive:
          Example: *Pat faxed Bill the letter.*
          Form: Subj V Obj Obj2
          Meaning: X causes Y to receive Z
      b. Caused-motion:
          Example: *Pat sneezed the foam off the cappuccino.*
          Form: Subj V Obj Obl
          Meaning: X causes Y to move Z
      c. Resultative: Example: *She kissed him unconscious.*
          Form: Subj V Obj XCOMP
          Meaning: X causes Y to become Z
                              (excerpted from Goldberg 1998: 206, Table 1)

A verb is treated as comparable to what we called a "root" in section 3.2: it comes with its own minimal meaning and associated arguments. This minimal meaning is integrated with the meaning of an argument structure construction; the integration includes a process in which the verb's arguments are fused with positions in the construction. Argument alternations arise when verbs are compatible with more than one construction. In the dative alternation, for example, the double object variant is an instance of the ditransitive construction (Goldberg 1995: 49–50), while the *to* variant is a subtype of the rather general caused-motion construction (Goldberg 1995: 152–53; see section 7.2.3.1). Instances of event composition are also analyzed as constructions; the caused-motion and resultative constructions are illustrated in (13b) and (13c).

Constructions are conventionalized associations of pieces of meaning with pieces of structure, much in the way words are. Support for the constructional approach is adduced from apparent idiosyncrasies in form–meaning associa-tions. According to Goldberg (1995), individual constructions show a range of related meanings, which must be "recorded," just as multiple meanings for words must be. In fact, the constructionists stress that there is no sharp divi-sion between the lexicon and the syntax, since "lexical (i.e. stored) items are of heterogeneous sizes, from affixes to idioms and more abstract structures" (Jackendoff 2002: xv).[2]

Certain more recent constructional approaches – or NEOCONSTRUCTION-IST approaches (Borer 2003b) – use more elaborated syntactic representations that are associated with specific semantic interpretations (see section 5.1). Constructions, then, are not stipulated as form–meaning pairs, as in the traditional constructional approaches. Rather, constructional meaning is encoded directly in the syntax, and the meaning of the construction is compositionally derived from the meaning of the verb together with the meaning encoded in the syntactic structure. The neoconstructionists use elaborated syntactic structures and tend to reduce the properties attributed to lexical items to a minimum. Typically, the lexical entry of a verb contains just its root, without any associated arguments; arguments are contributed by the construction into which the root is inserted. (Borer assumes that a root even lacks a lexical category, acquiring one by virtue of the position it fills in the syntactic structure.) A verb root may enter freely into various syntactic contexts, constrained only by a requirement that the verb's core meaning and the meaning of the syntactic construction be compatible. Constructions with shared syntactic substructures share facets of meaning.

The traditional constructionists and the neoconstructionists, then, both assume that certain facets of meaning are not attributable to verbs themselves, and that clause structure is not determined by the verb; they differ, however, in how they treat constructions. The traditional constructionists take constructions to be stored linguistic units, while the neoconstructionists view the meaning encoded in syntactic structures as compositionally derived. Traditional constructionist studies pay more careful attention to fine-grained semantic distinctions, while the neoconstructionists tend to stress generalizations which cut across constructions.

Although both forms of the constructional approach represent a departure from the traditional conception of the relationship between the lexicon and the syntax, current versions of all approaches – projectionist, constructional, and neoconstructionist – share certain features. It is noteworthy that the semantic notions that figure in constructional approaches are essentially those characterized as being grammatically relevant in nonconstructional approaches to similar phenomena. Furthermore, as discussed in section 4.1, all theories of event structure distinguish between the verb root and the structural aspect of meaning or event structure. A basic insight emerging from recent research is that at least some instances of multiple argument realization with a single verb involve a single core element of meaning associated with different event types chosen from the ontology of event types relevant to argument realization (Croft 1998; Goldberg 1995; van Hout 1996, 2000a, 2000b; Michaelis and Ruppenhofer 2000, 2001). All approaches must assume some mechanism which makes the various event structures, whether encoded syntactically or not, available for combination with the root in a productive and compositional way. All approaches agree that to a certain degree argument projection is determined compositionally, as stressed by Butt and Geuder (1998a: 2).

Moreover, there are important challenges confronting all approaches. The first is determining the nature of each alternation. Some researchers have suggested that not all alternations accompanied by a change in meaning arise from a shift in event structure. Some arise from a shift in what Croft calls the "verbal profile" – the part of an event described by a verb (see section 4.3) – with a concomitant shift in argument realization (see section 7.2.3.4). Second, some alternations may not involve a change in meaning. For example, there is a lively debate as to whether certain differences between the variants of the dative alternation should be ascribed to a meaning difference or to distinct modes of "information packaging" – the way in which the information conveyed in each variant is encoded as given or new within the discourse context (see section 7.3). Finally, at least some alternations appear to be "pure" alternations in morphosyntactic expression, in that they involve alternate morphosyntactic expressions of arguments without any clear associated semantic effect. One proposal is that a tendency to put heavier material later in a sentence may cause one variant to be favored over the other. Thus, it is necessary to determine for each alternation whether it involves a change in semantics or not, and if there is a semantic change, how best to characterize this change. If any "pure" argument alternations exist, the conditions giving rise to them must be identified too.

A second challenge concerns the distribution of verbs across syntactic contexts. As stressed by Rappaport Hovav and B. Levin (1998a) and Erteschik-Shir and Rapoport (2004) and as illustrated vividly using the resultative construction by Boas (2000, 2003), not every verb can appear in all syntactic contexts. The neoconstructionists sometimes speak of "free" projection of verbs into the syntax, with the options constrained only by some kind of "compatibility." For example, Ghomeshi and Massam introduce the "Compatibility Constraint": "Meaning contributed from a given source must be compatible with meaning contributed from all other sources" (1995: 199, (5)). But articulating what constitutes compatibility between a root and an event type is not trivial. Preliminary research suggests that there are constraints on this integration process. As we discuss in section 7.5, the range of contexts available to a given verb seems to be determined largely by the nature of the root. So, although neoconstructionists sometimes propose that the syntax alone determines the meaning (Borer 1994, 1998, 2003a, 2003b, in press a, in press b), this proposal is not completely accurate. Research into the nature of the root and the articulation of general principles which govern the integration of the idiosyncratic and event-based facets of meaning is of the utmost importance.

The discussion in the following sections abstracts away as much as possible from the projectionist/constructional debate. This is not because resolution of the debate is unimportant, but because our aim is to investigate the syntactic, semantic, and pragmatic factors which drive multiple argument realization, and, as these are largely common to the approaches, they can be studied without resolving the controversies between the projectionists, constructionists, and neoconstructionists.

7.2   Alternations involving a "single" set of arguments

In this section we examine the types of analyses offered for argument alternations. Our focus is on what "drives" these alternations; therefore, our presentation ignores many facets of these alternations, particularly their syntactic properties, such as extractability and scope freezing as it affects the VP-internal arguments, though these have received considerable attention (e.g., Aoun and Li 1989; Basilico 1998; Bruening 2001; Erteschik-Shir 1979; Fillmore 1965; Kayne 1984; Larson 1990; Oehrle 1983; Whitney 1983; Ziv and Sheintuch 1979). We begin with a brief overview of the major proposed sources for argument alternations, before discussing each in more detail.

7.2.1   What drives argument alternations?

Argument alternations raise three broad interrelated questions. First, do the variants, despite their obvious relatedness, differ in meaning? Second, what mechanism gives rise to the variants? And, finally, what determines which variant is chosen in a given context? The answer to the first question partially determines the answer to the other two. If a verb in an argument alternation has two meanings, then the two variants are most likely a direct reflection of the multiple meanings and arise from general mapping algorithms. The choice of variant in a given context is to a large degree determined by which meaning is appropriate in that context. However, if alternating verbs have a single meaning, then the mechanism giving rise to the two variants depends heavily on the assumptions of the overall theory. Most transformational theories incorporate some version of Baker's (1988) Uniformity of Theta Assignment Hypothesis (see sections 1.1 and 5.1), so that mapping algorithms are assumed to associate each semantic role with a unique syntactic expression. If so, the algorithms cannot give rise to alternations; instead, such theories generally relate the variants by means of syntactic transformations. In contrast, monostratal syntactic theories, which do not have recourse to transformations, may use algorithms which allow for a single meaning to give rise to two distinct argument realization options, contra Baker's hypothesis, for example, as in Dowty's proto-role approach (1991) and in Lexical-Functional Grammar (Butt, Dalrymple, and Frank 1997). If the two variants do not differ in meaning, then the choice between the variants in an alternation can be determined by other factors, including information structure and heaviness considerations.

The move from semantic role lists to event-based lexical semantic representations allows for a more finely textured and better-articulated notion of verb meaning (see sections 3.2). In particular, with the distinction between root and event structure, the question of what is common across variants and what differs can receive a more sophisticated answer than was possible solely making reference to semantic roles. (See also Jackendoff [1987] and Rappaport and B. Levin [1988] on the limitations of semantic role list approaches.) We discuss two answers to this question in section 7.5.

Nevertheless, there is no reason to assume that all argument alternations have the same analysis. Most researchers recognize that only some alternations are a reflection of differences in meaning. The locative alternation is now generally assumed to involve two distinct but related meanings, while locative inversion, illustrated in (14), is not.

(14) a. A well-dressed smiling child emerged from the house.
      b. From the house emerged a well-dressed smiling child.

A locative inversion sentence such as (14b) is taken to share the same truth-conditional meaning as its noninverted counterpart, just as an active sentence does with its passive counterpart. Presumably, there are simply two options for realizing a particular set of arguments, making (14) a "pure" argument alternation. The same label might be applied to other alternations whose variants can be characterized as lacking any obvious difference in meaning. These include the *with/against* alternation, the possessor–attribute factoring alternation, as in *Tony admired them for their integrity* and *Tony admired the integrity in them*, and pairs such as *Water leaked from the tank* and *The tank leaked water* or *The tank filled with water* and *Water filled the tank*. As we discuss, there is real controversy as to whether the variants of still other alternations, such as the dative alternation, differ in meaning.

Whatever the source of the two realizations of arguments defining an alternation, the question of what determines the choice among them in a given context needs to be answered. Where there is a clear difference in meaning between the variants, only one variant may be applicable in a given context; however, the meanings are often close enough that both variants might be applicable in certain contexts, and in these instances, other factors enter into the choice. One suggestion is that the choice is attributable to "information-packaging" considerations. For instance, the locative inversion construction, as in (14b), is said either to signal presentational focus or to mark the postverbal NP as relatively unfamiliar (e.g., Birner 1992, 1994; Birner and Ward 1998; Bolinger 1977; Bresnan and Kanerva 1989; Guéron 1980; Penhallurick 1984; Rochemont 1986); however, there has been considerably less discussion of what determines the choice of variant for other alternations in the absence of an apparent difference in meaning between the variants.

In section 7.3 we turn to the factors which determine a choice among variants in a particular context, focusing on information structure considerations. First, in this section we review the types of analyses offered for argument alternations. These analyses center around alternations already mentioned in this chapter: the dative and locative alternations. These, however, are only two of the numerous alternations found in English, according to B. Levin (1993), and, ultimately, any analysis must be assessed against this larger range of alternations, many of which have received little systematic attention.

7.2.2 Structure-driven analyses of argument alternations

The first type of analysis starts from the assumption that argument alternations are just that: alternate modes of realizing a single set of arguments. The focus is on delineating formal mechanisms that allow for these multiple argument realizations. The rules relating the two variants are typically stated over structured syntactic representations, either constituent structures or sets of grammatical relations.

7.2.2.1 *Traditional transformational analyses*

A textbook argument for the distinction between "deep" and "surface" structures related by transformations comes from an alternation in the syntactic expression of arguments of a verb: the relation between an active sentence and its passive counterpart (Akmajian and Heny 1975; Keyser and Postal 1976; Soames and Perlmutter 1979; among others). The preponderance of transitive verbs in English allows their arguments to be expressed in either an active or a passive sentence, as in (15).

> (15) a. The mouse ate the cheese.
> b. The cheese was eaten by the mouse.

Chomsky (1957, 1965) suggests capturing the relatedness between these sentence pairs by having the active and passive forms of a verb inserted into the same underlying syntactic structure. A single lexical entry is assumed for both forms of a verb, accounting for the identical selectional restrictions on the subject of the passive form of the verb and the object of the active form and for the fact that the subcategorization frame of the passive form of the verb is entirely predictable from the subcategorization frame of the active form. Both the active and passive verb forms share a subcategorization frame and, hence, are found in the same underlying syntactic structure, but their sentences have different syntactic derivations. In the active, the surface structure is a direct projection of the underlying one, while a transformation applies to give rise to the surface structure of the passive.

Transformational accounts have been extended to the dative and locative alternations: an alternating verb has a single projection of arguments onto the syntax, with a second realization of arguments being transformationally derived from the first. In the dative alternation, the *to* variant is taken as basic by Hall (1965: 58), with the double object variant derived from it – a position maintained in many subsequent accounts (e.g., Emonds 1972), though Fillmore (1965) argues for a more complex account in which both variants are derived. Following Hall (1965: 87), accounts of the locative alternation typically take the locative variant as basic, deriving the *with* variant from it.

Structural accounts of alternations are also given in Relational Grammar, which posits rules that relate one variant to a second in terms of changes in grammatical relation assignments, rather than "transformations" of syntactic structures. This approach reflects the central assumption of Relational Grammar that many linguistic generalizations are best stated in terms of grammatical relations, which are taken to be primitives. Generalizations stated over grammatical relations are assumed to be more valid crosslinguistically because languages vary in the surface instantiations of grammatical relations, but not in the grammatical relations themselves. Passivization is described as "2-to-1 advancement," where a "1" is a subject and a "2" an object (Perlmutter and Postal 1983b). Similarly, the dative alternation is stated as a rule of "3-to-2 advancement," where "3" is the grammatical relation of an indirect object or *to* phrase (Chung 1976). The locative alternation is analyzed in comparable terms by Channon (1980).

It soon became apparent, however, that some argument alternations differ from the active–passive alternation in just those properties which motivate a structurally based grammatical relation-changing account. The locative alternation is such an alternation. First, its pattern of selectional restrictions diverges from that shown by active–passive pairs. In the locative alternation, the range of NPs found as the direct object of the locative variant is not the same as can appear as the object of *with* in the *with* variant. Thus, Fraser (1971) points out triples as in (16) and (17).

(16) a. They loaded a box onto the truck.
      b. *They loaded the truck with a box.
      c. They loaded the truck with (?the) boxes.   (Fraser 1971: 606, (4))

(17) a. The girl planted a tree in the garden.
      b. *The girl planted the garden with a tree.
      c. The girl planted the garden with (?the) trees.   (Fraser 1971: 606, (4))

Furthermore, while the sentences in an active–passive pair are taken to be truth-conditionally equivalent – quantifier scope considerations aside (see Chomsky [1957: 100–01] and Katz and Postal [1964: 72–73] for different viewpoints on this issue) – certain meaning differences are detectable between the variants of other alternations. Again, the locative alternation demonstrates such differences, as discussed in section 4.2.3, where they were characterized in aspectual terms (see also section 7.2.3.3).

Such data led many researchers to conclude that the relatedness between the variants in argument alternations should not be captured by transformational or grammatical relation-changing rules. This conclusion is partly informed by the hypothesis that transformations do not change meanings (Katz and Postal 1964). Even in later "interpretive" transformational accounts (Jackendoff 1972), the changes in meaning effected by transformations are different in nature: they involve not the lexical content of a verb but facets of sentence-level meaning, such as quantifier scope and focus assignment. The notion of lexical redundancy rules, to be discussed in section 7.2.3, is introduced as an alternative way of relating various uses of words which do not lend themselves well to a transformational account, though transformational accounts have yet to be completely abandoned, as we now discuss.

7.2.2.2 Neotransformational analyses

A weakness of the earliest transformational approaches to grammatical relation-changing rules is a lack of constraints on the changes that transformations could effect. In reaction, "neotransformational" theories were designed that appealed to independently motivated constraints on movement rules in order to restrict the range of changes in grammatical relations which transformations could effect and, thus, to explain the range of attested argument alternations. Arguments for the neotransformational analysis are reminiscent of Hale and Keyser's arguments that a syntactically instantiated lexical semantic represen-tation allows the set of possible verb meanings to be explained in terms of independent syntactic constraints (see section 5.1).

The neotransformational approach is first developed by Baker (1985, 1988), who takes as his starting point the assumption that the variants in the alter-nations he treats – the dative alternation and comparable alternations in other languages – are "thematic paraphrases," i.e., have the same meaning. This prop-erty is reflected in the assignment of identical underlying syntactic structures (d-structures) to the variants, following his Uniformity of Theta Assignment Hypothesis, discussed in sections 1.1 and 5.1 and repeated in (18).

> (18) The Uniformity of Theta Assignment Hypothesis:
>   Identical thematic relationships between items are represented by identical structural relationships between those items at the level of d-structure.
>
>   (Baker 1988: 46, (30))

Morphology also plays a crucial role in Baker's analysis. He takes his inspi-ration from the applicative construction of certain languages (see section 1.6). In this construction, the verb has an "applicative" morpheme affixed to it, which licenses an extra argument, typically, a goal or a benefactive, expressed as an object. Since in Chicheŵa and some other languages with applicative construc-tions, goals and benefactives can also be expressed as obliques, these languages show the equivalent of the English dative alternation. Compare the Chicheŵa applicative construction in (19a) to its prepositional counterpart in (19b).

> (19) a. Mbidzi zi-na-perek-*er*-a   nkhandwe msampha.
>   zebras SP-PAST-hand-*to*-ASP fox   trap
>   'The zebras handed the fox the trap.'   (Baker 1988: 229, (3a))
>   b. Mbidzi zi-na-perek-a   msampha *kwa* nkhandwe.
>   zebras SP-PAST-hand-ASP trap   *to*   fox
>   'The zebras handed the trap to the fox.'   (Baker 1988: 229, (2a))

Baker suggests that the Chicheŵa applicative affix *–ir* (with allomorph *–er*) in (19a) fulfills the same semantic function as the preposition *kwa* in (19b).

Consistent with the Uniformity of Theta Assignment Hypothesis, both sentences in (19) have the d-structure in (20), as they are thematic paraphrases.

(20) d-structure for (19a) and (19b)   (Baker 1988: 230, (4))

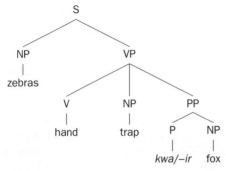

The effects of a grammatical relation-changing rule are achieved through the "incorporation" of the applicative affix into the verb, which forces a change in the syntactic expression of certain arguments. Affixes cannot stand alone as words (Baker's "Stray Affix Filter" (1988: 140)), so the applicative affix must attach to a verbal head. This "incorporation" of the affix into the verb means that the recipient, as the argument (i.e., sister) of the applicative affix, is now governed by the verb and, thus, is now expressed as an object. The s-structure for the applicative sentence (19a) is schematized in (21).

(21) s-structure for applicative sentence (19a)   (Baker 1988: 231, (5))

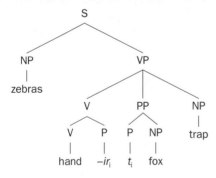

Furthermore, Baker (1988) explains certain differences between benefactive and instrumental applicatives by assigning them distinct d-structures: the verb governs the benefactive NP, but not the instrument NP. The difference in government relations results in distinct movement possibilities for benefactives and instruments, and, thus, distinct "changes" in grammatical relations. In this way, distinctive properties of the two types of applicatives are reduced to independently motivated properties of movement.

Baker's "incorporation" analysis can be extended to the English dative alternation, on the assumption that both variants share a single underlying syntactic – and hence semantic – structure, with the double object variant involving the covert "incorporation" of a preposition; see den Dikken (1995: 132) and Pesetsky (1995) for such analyses. Preposition incorporation accounts have also been offered for other alternations. Brinkmann (1997) and Wunderlich (1987) argue for such an account of the German and Dutch locative alternation, which is characterized by the affix *be–* on the verb in the *with* variant; however, they propose that the preposition incorporation is accomplished via a lexical rule (see section 7.2.2.3), rather than a syntactic movement (Brinkmann 1997: 87–89).

Another widely adopted neotransformational analysis of the dative alternation is presented by Larson (1988, 1990). Moving beyond Baker's concerns, Larson makes much of apparent differences in the c-command relations between the VP-internal arguments in the two variants. Data such as (22) and (23), whose implications are first discussed by Barss and Lasnik (1986), show that in the double object variant the recipient appears to c-command the theme, while in the *to* variant the c-command relation is reversed.

(22) a. I showed Mary herself.
     b. *I showed herself Mary.   (Larson 1988: 336, (3a))

(23) a. I presented/showed Mary to herself.
     b. *I presented/showed herself to Mary.   (Larson 1988: 338, (5a))

To handle these c-command relations, Larson assumes a uniformly right-branching structure for all English verbs and their complements, including dative verbs. Larson motivates this analysis on purely syntactic grounds, with no semantic support; see Jackendoff (1990a) for extensive discussion of this assumption and Larson (1990) for a response. Like Baker, he derives the two variants of the dative alternation from a single underlying structure, given in (24).

(24) send a letter to Mary/send Mary a letter   (Larson 1988: 342, (13b))

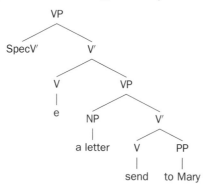

The change in c-command relations – and, hence, the alternation – arises from a passive-like operation on the lower VP in (24), which results in the recipient occupying its specifier position and the theme expressed as an "adjunct" position in the double object variant. By occupying the specifier position of the lower VP, the recipient in the double object variant is in some sense a subject, under the VP-internal subject hypothesis (Fukui and Speas 1986; Koopman and Sportiche 1991; Kuroda 1988; Sportiche 1988). In this way, this analysis captures an insight that emerges from other work that the recipient in the double object variant shares many subject-like properties with the agent – properties other analyses attribute to the discourse-prominence of both recipients and agents (Thompson 1990: 241, 1995: 158) (see sections 6.5.3 and 7.3).

An important question is left open in Baker's impressive study and inherited by the work that builds on it: what qualifies as a thematic paraphrase? If the Uniformity of Theta Assignment Hypothesis is to serve as the motivation for a particular analysis of an alternation, it must be possible to determine when two sentences instantiate identical semantic relationships between a verb and its arguments. The variants in the locative alternation, for example, are generally assumed to differ in meaning, so that a neotransformational analysis cannot be extended to this alternation. Many researchers even believe there is good reason to reject Baker's and Larson's starting assumption that the variants in the dative alternation are thematic paraphrases (Harley 1995, 1997, 2003; Pesetsky 1995; Richards 2001; Speas 1990). Instead, they retain Larson's solution to the c-command problem by assuming a right-branching structure for both variants, but posit a distinct underlying right-branching structure for each variant: in one, the recipient c-commands the theme and in the second the theme c-commands the recipient. The two structures are motivated by tying each to a unique lexical semantic representation. We discuss this approach in section 7.2.3 in the context of a broader consideration of meaning-driven approaches to argument alternations. (See Basilico [1998] for an extension of this approach to a wider range of alternations.)

7.2.2.3   Lexical Rule Analyses
In response to the problems mentioned in section 7.2.2.1, Jackendoff (1975) and Oehrle (1976), building on ideas introduced in Chomsky (1970), develop a theory of lexical redundancy rules, which offers a technical alternative to transformations for capturing relatedness among lexical items. These rules express generalizations holding across words in the lexicon, specifying how certain well-defined classes of words are systematically related to each other phonologically, syntactically, and semantically. This notion is introduced by Chomsky (1970) to express the relation between a verb and its nominalization (e.g., *decide/decision*); this treatment is intended to replace the transformational derivation of such nominals proposed in Lees (1966).

Proponents of lexical rules stress that despite perceptions of relatedness among certain lexical items, such as verbs and their nominalizations, there is unpredictability in both the morphological and semantic dimensions of this relatedness. For instance, though *arrive* has *arrival* as its nominalization, the nominalization of *derive* is *derivation*. Some derived nominals show additional meanings that are not semantically transparent, as in the use of *transmission* to refer to a part of a car. Such properties are said to distinguish lexical from syntactic phenomena.

Subsequently, lexical rule analyses were extended to various argument alternations, a trend which received a boost from Wasow (1977), which clearly delineated the criteria that distinguish phenomena that should receive lexical accounts from those that should receive transformational accounts. By these criteria, the dative alternation should receive a lexical analysis. One motivation for such an analysis is the apparent unpredictability of the verbs which show the alternation, as illustrated by the following minimal pairs, which suggest that not every verb found in the *to* variant can be found in the double object variant.

(25) a. Steve told Irv the secret.
     b. Steve told the secret to Irv.

(26) a. *Steve reported Irv the secret.
     b. Steve reported the secret to Irv.

(27) a. *Steve revealed Irv the secret.
     b. Steve revealed the secret to Irv.

Another motivation for lexical analyses is that such analyses are "structure preserving": the output of the relevant lexical rule is a syntactic structure that needs to be base-generated for nonalternating verbs. In fact, structure preservation is posited as a hallmark of lexical rules, with Wasow (1980: 286), for example, suggesting that there are no structure-preserving transformations. Bresnan (1980, 1982b) makes a case for handling a range of argument alternations via lexical rules, including the passive and the dative alternation. She proposes a grammatical relation-based lexical rule for the dative alternation, which derives the double object variant from the *to* variant, as in (28).

(28) (OBJ) $\mapsto$ (OBJ2)
     (TO OBJ) $\mapsto$ (OBJ)   (Bresnan 1982b: 25, (42))

As this example illustrates, these lexical rule analyses, like the transformational analyses, assume a single lexical semantic representation, with two morphosyntactic realizations. The lexical rule approach has been widely adopted; Dowty (1978), for example, proposes a lexical rule approach to the dative alternation and other argument alternations within Montague and categorial grammar.

Rappaport and B. Levin (1988) and Rappaport Hovav and B. Levin (1998b) suggest that if a lexical entry specifies a lexical semantic representation along with the assignment of a syntactically based argument structure, it should be possible, in principle, to distinguish two kinds of lexical rules: rules which relate lexical items with the same lexical semantic representation, but with different syntactic realizations – the kind of rules discussed in this and the next section – and rules which relate lexical items with distinct, but systematically related, lexical semantic representations; see also Ackerman (1992) and Ackerman and Moore (2001). This second idea leads to meaning-driven analyses of alternations, discussed in section 7.2.3.

7.2.2.4 One representation but two mappings to the syntax

Transformational, grammatical relation-changing rule, and lexical rule analyses preserve the idea that mapping algorithms deterministically give rise to argument realization options and that there is a type of rule which operates on the output of the mapping algorithms to give rise to an alternate argument realization. However, analyses have been proposed which deny that mapping algorithms necessarily produce a single output for a given verb meaning, even though they often do. These analyses include mapping algorithms which allow a single meaning to give rise to more than one surface pattern of argument realization and, hence, an argument alternation.

Dowty's (1991) proto-role approach, reviewed in section 3.1.1, has this property. According to Dowty, the choice of subject and object in English is determined by a counting algorithm which compares the number of Agent or Patient Proto-role entailments across a verb's arguments; the argument with the most Agent Proto-role entailments is chosen as subject, while the argument with the most Patient Proto-role entailments is chosen as object. Crucially, when this algorithm does not unambiguously identify a particular argument as subject or object, variation in argument realization is allowed. The *with/against* alternation arises just for this reason: neither of the nonsubject arguments has more Patient Proto-role entailments than the other, so both are possible objects. Specifically, both are causally affected by another participant, and both lack the incremental theme and change-of-state entailments.

Although most forms of Lexical-Functional Grammar's Lexical Mapping Theory (Bresnan 2001: 302–17; Bresnan and Kanerva 1989) allow a particular set of semantic roles to give rise to one realization of arguments, some forms allow a single set of semantic roles to give rise to more than one argument realization option. As discussed in section 5.1 in Lexical Mapping Theory, arguments are associated with underspecified grammatical relations according to their semantic roles by what is known as "intrinsic role classification." Lexical rules (e.g., passive) may then augment these underspecified grammatical relation assignments. Finally, any remaining underspecified grammatical relations are filled out by "default role classifications," yielding the actual grammatical relations assigned to a given set of semantic roles. Because lexical rules may intervene between the intrinsic role classification and the default role classification, a particular underspecified grammatical relation assignment can give rise to more than one option for argument realization, as in active and passive pairs (Bresnan and Kanerva 1989). However, Butt, Dalrymple, and Frank (1997) assume that the set of intrinsic and default classifications do not uniquely determine the grammatical relations realizing a specific set of semantic roles, but give rise to a set of grammatical relation assignments, whose members are then ranked by preference constraints. They further allow for multiple optimal mappings, which are ranked equally by the preference constraints. In these instances other factors, such as pragmatic considerations, can determine the choice of argument realization. They propose such an account for both locative inversion and the dative alternation.

Jackendoff (1990b) also allows a single lexical semantic representation to give rise to two different syntactic realizations. This happens when a particular position in a lexical semantic representation can be realized by an argument or an adjunct. He provides such an analysis of the alternation in (29) displayed by *fill* in its noncausative sense. (Although Jackendoff does not discuss the *leak* alternation in (7), this alternation could be handled similarly.)

(29) a. Water filled the tank.
     b. The tank filled with water.

Jackendoff (1990b: 159–63) proposes that both variants have a lexical semantic representation corresponding to the paraphrase 'Water came to be in the tank.' He focuses on the two options for the realization of the material – *water* in (29). For Jackendoff, these options arise because the position in the lexical semantic representation corresponding to the material can be marked for realization as an argument, giving (29a), where it is the subject, or as an adjunct, giving rise to (29b), where it is expressed in a *with* phrase (1990b: 251–54). The same mapping rules apply to the two variants, but the expression of the material as subject is precluded when it is marked as an adjunct; instead, it is expressed using the relevant preposition. Jackendoff uses a slight twist on this idea to derive the dative alternation (1990b: 266–67). Thus, for Jackendoff some argument alternations arise because certain positions in a lexical semantic representation are only optionally marked for realization by arguments.

Lexical Mapping Theory takes advantage of the same idea in its treatment of the double object construction (Bresnan 2001: 314–17). Typically, a verb like *cook* is taken to have two arguments, an agent and a theme, optionally allowing a benefactive adjunct. As the most patient-like argument, the theme is realized as an object, and the benefactive as an adjunct is realized as an oblique. This verb can also take the benefactive as an argument. As an argument, the benefactive is considered more patient-like than *cook*'s own theme, and thus, has precedence over it for realization as an object (Bresnan and Moshi 1990: 168). The theme is then realized as a second object, giving rise to the double object construction. If categorization as both an "argument" and an "adjunct" is the key to certain argument alternations, then the factors that sometimes make this option available need to be understood; this, in turn, will require a clearer understanding of the ill-understood argument–adjunct distinction.

7.2.2.5 Summary

The structural approaches to argument alternations share two important properties. First, they assume that alternating verbs have a single meaning underlying both variants. Second, alternations arise from rules which map the arguments onto two different morphosyntactic realizations; often one realization is taken as basic and the second is derived from the first. Such accounts tend to ignore the fine-grained differences in meaning between the variants which often accompany these alternations, as well as differences in their information structure. However, though there do appear to be some "pure" argument alternations, the variants in at least some alternations clearly differ in meaning. If so, the distinct meanings might be the source of the distinct argument realizations. This insight is the starting point for meaning-driven approaches.

7.2.3 Meaning-driven analyses of argument alternations

In analyses of argument alternations that take differences in meaning between the variants to give rise to differences in the realization of arguments, the locus of explanation becomes the representations of meaning and the mapping algorithms. The elements of meaning implicated in argument alternations are the same as those singled out in the approaches to event conceptualization reviewed in chapter 4. Meaning-driven analyses must identify precisely how the variants differ in meaning, and at the same time they must explain the near-paraphrase relation between them. Most analyses take advantage of highly articulated event structures to make explicit how the meanings of the variants are related and how they differ. Analyses differ with respect to what they identify as the critical elements of meaning and the sources of the systematic meaning differences taken to define alternations.

Differences in meaning between variants are also cited in accounts of why certain verbs alternate, while others are only found in one variant. For instance, Dowty (2000, 2001) hypothesizes that each alternation is manifested by a characteristic set of verbs because one variant in an alternation has a more specific meaning than the other, and the more specific meaning acts as a filter on the verbs undergoing the alternation. It is perhaps not surprising, then, that descriptions of the actual distribution of verbs across alternations make reference to rather fine-grained semantic classes (e.g., Green 1974; B. Levin 1993; Pinker 1989). In contrast, the semantic notions that figure in the theories of mapping to the syntax that give rise to the alternate realization of certain arguments are quite general, subdividing the verb lexicon into broad semantic classes. In this section we focus on semantic determinants of argument realization as they apply to argument alternations; we turn to the facets of meaning relevant to the distribution of verbs across alternations in section 7.5.

7.2.3.1 The basics of meaning-driven analyses

To illustrate the fundamentals of meaning-driven accounts, we present Rappaport and B. Levin's (1988) analysis of the locative alternation, as it is one of the earliest attempts at clearly articulating the relevant lexical semantic representations. They point out that if systematic variations in meaning between the variants are a reflection of different lexical semantic representations, then well-established mapping algorithms can apply to these representations to give rise to just the right pattern of argument realization. The lexical semantic representations which they propose are given in (30); (a) is for the locative variant and (b) is for the *with* variant.

(30) a. *load:* [x CAUSE [y TO COME TO BE AT z] /LOAD]

    b. *load:* [[x CAUSE [z TO COME TO BE IN STATE]]

        BY MEANS OF [x CAUSE [y TO COME TO BE AT z]] /LOAD]

(Rappaport and B. Levin 1988: 26, (25))

The overall structure of these representations is motivated by the observation that the *with* variant entails the locative variant, but not vice versa. This insight is captured by subsuming the lexical semantic representation of the locative variant in that of the *with* variant, as shown by a comparison of (30a) and (30b). This overlap captures the intuition that the variants are near paraphrases. Furthermore, since in the representation (30b) the location (z) is now the first argument of a change (i.e., TO COME TO BE), it qualifies for mapping to the direct object position in the *with* variant, just as the material (y) does in the locative variant. The analysis is also motivated by the existence of two related classes of verbs, which support the postulation of the two lexical semantic representations. Specifically, English has a class of nonalternating verbs of putting which have the same syntax and semantics as the locative variant (e.g., *drip, pour, put*), and a class of nonalternating verbs of filling and covering which have the syntax and semantics of the *with* variant (e.g., *cover, fill*). An open question, however, is why some verbs are found in both variants and others are not.

    Pinker (1989) extends this analysis to the dative and causative alternations. He suggests that for both alternations the two variants have a distinct lexical semantic representation and that the difference in syntactic expression of arguments is a by-product of this difference, effected by independently established mapping rules. The causative alternation appears to be a natural candidate for a meaning-driven account, given that the transitive variant adds a notion of cause to the intransitive variant. The dative alternation, in contrast, is a less obvious candidate, particularly since it has figured prominently in structure-driven accounts. Pinker, however, is not alone in proposing that its variants have distinct lexical semantic representations (Arad 1998; Bowers 1993; Harley 1997, 2002; Krifka 1999, 2001; Pesetsky 1995; Speas 1990). The motivation for these accounts is discussed in section 7.2.3.2; here we sketch their properties. These accounts are couched in a range of formalisms and incorporate different assumptions about the relation between lexical semantics and syntax, but they all assume that the *to* variant expresses a change in the location of the theme, while the double object variant expresses a change in the possessor of the theme, as schematized in the representations proposed by Speas (1990) in (31).

(31)   a.   *to* VARIANT: x cause [y to come to be at (possession) z]
      b.   DOUBLE OBJECT VARIANT: x cause [z to come to be in STATE (of possession)]
         by means of [x cause [y to come to be at (poss) z]]
                             (Speas 1990: 88, (134); 89, (136))

As with the locative alternation, the distinct meanings underlying the variants result in different arguments satisfying the conditions for realization as a direct object. In both variants the first argument of the TO COME TO BE embedded under CAUSE is realized as the direct object, but in the *to* variant it is the theme and in the double object variant the recipient.

As in Rappaport and B. Levin's lexical semantic representations for the locative alternation, the semantic relation between the variants is captured by subsuming the lexical semantic representation of the *to* variant in that of the double object variant. More often, though, the proposed lexical semantic relation of the double object variant does not embed the *to* variant's representation, so that the double object variant is simply given a representation roughly along the lines of 'x CAUSE z TO HAVE y,' contrasting with the *to* variant's 'x CAUSE y TO BE AT z.' Researchers who pursue this analysis often do not spell out how the near-paraphrase relation between the variants arises. Krifka (2001), however, confronts this question directly. He proposes that the paraphrase relation follows because many verbs have similar truth conditions in both variants. For instance, since transfer of possession typically entails an abstract movement in the possessional field in the Localist Hypothesis sense (see section 4.1), if a verb's meaning is typically appropriate for the double object variant, then it is appropriate for the *to* variant. As support for this proposal, Krifka points to certain double object variants lacking *to* variant counterparts, as in (32).

(32)   a.   Ann's behavior gave Beth this idea.
      b.   *Ann's behavior gave this idea to Beth.   (Krifka 2001: 6, (62))

Unlike a typical change-of-possession event, this one involves the theme – here, an idea – coming into existence. There is no source and, hence, no literal or metaphorical transfer of possession. As Krifka (1999), Larson (1988: 376), and Pinker (1989: 212–13) discuss, the intended meaning, then, is compatible with the semantic representation for the double object variant which simply describes the causation of possession and does not involve a path from a source to a goal. The intended meaning is incompatible, however, with the *to* variant; this variant, which describes a change of location, must include a path.

More recently, constructional versions of this approach are proposed by Goldberg (1995) and others (e.g., Inoue 2001; Iwata 1998; Kay 2000; Michaelis and Ruppenhofer 2000, 2001; Nemoto 1998). The same semantic notions figure in the constructional approaches as in projectionist approaches, but the line dividing what is lexical and nonlexical shifts. According to Goldberg (1995: 49–50), the double object variant of the dative alternation represents a construction which pairs the change-of-possession meaning 'X CAUSE Y to RECEIVE Z' with the grammatical relations subject, first object, and second object. The *to* variant is a subtype of the more general caused-motion construction, which pairs the change of location meaning 'X CAUSES Y to MOVE Z' (Goldberg 1995: 152) with the grammatical relations subject, object, and oblique (Goldberg 1992: 68–69). The possessive meaning associated with the *to* variant arises via a metaphor of "transfer of ownership as physical transfer" that allows the caused-motion construction to encode transfer of possession (Goldberg 1995: 90), along the lines suggested by proponents of the Localist Hypothesis. As a consequence, the caused-motion construction ends up being synonymous with the double object construction, which basically encodes transfer of possession (1995: 91).

The following sections review attempts to provide a unified meaning-driven treatment of argument alternations. Some suggest a common semantic source for all alternations. Others suggest a single mechanism for deriving the two variants across alternations.

7.2.3.2 *Affectedness*

Object alternations pose a challenge because two arguments typically described as bearing distinct semantic roles can both be realized as objects. This phenomenon appears to fly in the face of attempts to identify a single semantic determinant of objecthood. The meaning-driven treatments of object alternations just reviewed overcome this challenge by attributing distinct meanings to the variants, so that in one variant one argument meets the semantic determinant of objecthood and in the other variant the other argument does. The first unified meaning-driven treatments of alternations propose that the same semantic characterization of objecthood extends across a range of alternations. This approach begins with S. R. Anderson (1977), who suggests a common source for the locative alternation and certain direct object/oblique alternations, proposing they are sensitive to the semantic notion "affectedness," first mentioned in section 4.2.2. The same notion is then implicated in the dative alternation (Arad 1998: 89; Larson 1988: 376–77; Shopen 1986: 152–53; Wierzbicka 1986: 123). Although this notion is most often associated with themes or patients, arguments of verbs that are not typically considered to be affected, such as locations or recipients, are taken to be so interpreted with certain verbs, and in such instances, they can be expressed as objects. The consequence is that the relevant verbs show object alternations. Subsequent meaning-driven approaches try to retain the original intuition, while giving it additional substance through more sophisticated lexical semantic representations. We turn now to the evidence behind the insight itself.

The existence of a meaning difference between variants is particularly striking in the locative alternation. One of the earliest characterizations of this difference is in terms of what S. R. Anderson (1971) calls a "holistic/partitive" effect. (See also S. R. Anderson 1977; Dowty 1991; Gropen et al. 1991; Jackendoff 1987, 1996b; Jeffries and Willis 1984; Laffut 1997, 1998, 1999; Pinker 1989; Rappaport and B. Levin 1988; Schwartz-Norman 1976; Tenny 1987, 1994; among others for further discussion of the best characterization of this effect.) Anderson notes that the argument expressed as the object of each variant is understood to be wholly involved in the action denoted by the verb. For example, the location argument is understood as completely covered with butter – that is, as totally affected – when it is expressed as direct object, as in (33b), though it is not necessarily understood as totally affected when it is expressed in a prepositional phrase, as in (33a).

(33) a. Devon smeared butter on the toast. (locative variant)
     b. Devon smeared the toast with butter. (*with* variant)

Similarly, if someone loads a truck with hay, then the truck is understood to be full, but if someone loads hay onto a truck, that may or may not be so. Anderson chooses the label "holistic/partitive" effect to capture this difference because "the property with which we are dealing seems to be a matter of whether the whole of something is affected by the action described by the sentence, or just a part of it is affected" (1971: 389). Consistent with this characterization, Anderson points out that (34a) is fine, but (34b) is contradictory.

(34) a. John smeared paint on the wall, but most of the wall didn't get any paint on it.
     b. John smeared the wall with paint, but most of the wall didn't get any paint on it.   (S. R. Anderson 1971: 389, (7))

Since a location argument is necessarily associated with a holistic interpretation when expressed as an object, certain scenes might be describable using one variant only. For this reason, the triples from Fraser (1971), cited in (16)-(17), show acceptability differences. Thus, the holistic/partitive effect is taken to be a consequence of the affected interpretation associated with direct objects.

The applicability of affectedness extends beyond the locative alternation. Anderson (1977) cites direct object/oblique alternations as in (35) and (36).

(35) a. The farmer plowed the field.
     b. The farmer plowed in the field.   (S. R. Anderson 1977: 369, (4a))

(36) a. John painted my picture this morning.
     b. John painted on my picture this morning.
                                  (S. R. Anderson 1977: 369, (4b))

As he points out, in the (a) examples, the field is understood to be completely plowed and the picture completely painted, but in the (b) examples this need not be so. Thus, these pairs also show the holistic/partitive effect. Again, an argument, which is expressible as an object or oblique necessarily receives an affected interpretation only when expressed as an object.

Affectedness is also implicated in accounts of other phenomena, specifically passive nominals (M. Anderson 1978; Fellbaum 1987; Fiengo 1980; Jaeggli 1986) and middles (Hale and Keyser 1987; Roberts 1987; Zubizarreta 1987); see also Jackendoff (1987, 1990b). Hopper and Thompson (1980) include this notion among the ingredients figuring in their prototype characterization of transitivity. These independent uses further buttress the potential importance of affectedness in explaining alternations. However, as noted in section 4.2.2, the notion "affectedness" has proved difficult to pin down, and later researchers have tried to subsume it under the aspectual notions of telicity and incremental theme. Nevertheless, as discussed in sections 4.2.3 and 4.2.4, the best semantic characterization of linguistic phenomena that have been considered under the label "affectedness" is still an open question.

Subsequent researchers have proposed that the recipient of dative verbs necessarily receives an affected interpretation when expressed as the first object (i.e., in the double object variant), but not when expressed in a *to* phrase. This proposal is motivated by apparent differences in the entailments or implicatures associated with the variants of the dative alternation, which have been interpreted in terms of affectedness of the recipient. These differences are first discussed by Green (1974: 156–67) in the context of the pair in (37), which has been repeatedly cited in subsequent work.

(37) a. Mary taught John linguistics.
      b. Mary taught linguistics to John.   (Green 1974: 157, (2))

As Green (1974: 157) writes, "Sentence (2a) [=(37a)] implies or entails that John learned linguistics, while (2b) [=(37b)] merely states that he was a student of linguistics, and is neutral as to whether his teacher Mary had any success in her efforts." Based on this and other data, Oehrle (1976: 70–77) suggests that the double object variant is associated with an entailment of successful transfer. Due to this entailment, the recipient could be characterized as affected when expressed as a first object. Also suggestive of the relevance of affectedness are certain double object variants that lack *to* variant counterparts (Green 1974; Oehrle 1976; Pesetsky 1995; Pinker 1989). For instance, the sentence *The constant chatter gave me a headache* (Oehrle 1976: 60, (58)) lacks a *to* variant counterpart (**The constant chatter gave a headache to me*); the reason given is that a headache necessarily affects someone.

However, the idea that the double object variant necessarily has different entailments than the *to* variant has been challenged. As the following examples show, double object sentences do not necessarily involve the just-proposed entailment of successful change of possession – a point made by Baker (1997: 89), Davidse (1998: 302), and Oehrle (1977: 206).

(38) a. I taught them English for a year, but they don't seem to have learned a thing.

      b. I threw John the ball, but it didn't reach him because of the strong wind.

                                      (Baker 1997: 89, (20b))

      c. I throw you a lifeline and you giggle.

                      (Leuven Drama Corpus; Davidse 1996: 313, (79))

      d. I read him the figures, but when I looked up, he was gone.

                                    (Oehrle 1977: 206, (4))

      e. When I took him his mail, I found that he had disappeared.

                                    (Oehrle 1977: 206, (4))

If the success of the transfer is merely an inference,[3] it should not be encoded in the semantic representation of the double object variant. Further, in section 7.3 we suggest that contrasts such as (32) have another explanation and cannot be used to buttress a meaning-driven approach.

Setting aside the question of whether a meaning-driven approach to the dative alternation is viable, we briefly discuss two approaches to representing differences in meaning between variants. Jackendoff incorporates the insight that differences in affectedness underlie many argument alternations into his theory of lexical semantic representation. As mentioned in sections 2.3.2 and 4.1, he (1987, 1990b) adopts a two-tier representation, and a major function of his action tier is indicating which argument, if any, is affected. The central meaning of a verb is represented in the thematic tier, which is localist in inspiration. An argument in the thematic tier may be singled out as affected – a property indicated in the action tier. Some verbs allow two distinct action tiers to be associated with a single thematic tier, with each identifying a distinct thematic tier argument as affected. Locative alternation verbs have this property (Jackendoff 1987: 397–98, 1990b: 130). Since affected arguments have priority for realization as objects, when a verb allows more than one argument to be affected, each can be expressed as object. The result is an object alternation. Since alternating verbs maintain the same thematic tier, the near-paraphrase relation between variants can be attributed to this tier, while the meaning differences can be tied to the action tier. As mentioned in section 7.2.2.4, Jackendoff also uses the two tiers in his account of the dative alternation. This alternation arises because some verbs allow their recipient to be marked as affected only in one variant; thus, it is realized as the object when affected and as an oblique otherwise.

Van Valin's (2002: 11) Role and Reference Grammar account of the English dative alternation is similar. He assigns *give* and other English causative transfer of possession verbs a single lexical semantic representation, but proposes that either the theme or recipient qualifies for identification as the Undergoer macrorole. As discussed in section 3.1.2, this assignment allows either to be expressed as an object, giving rise to an object alternation.

7.2.3.3 Event type-shifting

The notion of affectedness, while suggestive, is not easily formalizable, and, as discussed in section 4.2.2, it has been aspectually reinterpreted. Many current meaning-driven approaches view argument alternations as arising from "shifts" in the event type that a root can be associated with, as most explicitly argued for in van Hout (1996) (see section 4.2.3). Alternate realizations of an argument as direct object or oblique as in the conative alternation reflect shifts between telic and atelic uses of verbs. Alternate choices of object for a single verb as in the locative alternation reflect alternate choices in the argument which determines the telicity of its sentence, i.e., which serves as incremental theme.

In fact, as discussed in section 4.2.3, argument alternations are cited to support the claim that the semantic determinants of argument realization are aspectual. Dowty (1991) and Tenny (1994) propose that the locative alternation arises because the alternating verbs can impose an incremental theme entailment on either of their two VP-internal arguments, and this entailment gives an argument priority in object selection. Both van Hout (1996) and Tenny analyze various argument alternations in this way, and Arad (1998) extends such analyses to an even broader range of multiple argument realization phenomena.

As also discussed in section 4.2.3, aspectual approaches to argument realization have received support from the multiple argument realizations demonstrated in many languages by verbs which pattern as both unaccusatives and unergatives. When a verb has a dual classification, its single argument alternates between subject and underlying object realizations, so these alternate realizations could be viewed as yet another form of argument alternation. Many researchers (Centineo 1986; Hoekstra 1984; L. Levin 1986, 1987; B. Levin and Rappaport Hovav 1989, 1995; van Hout 1996; Van Valin 1990) point out that verbs of manner of motion such as *run* and *fly* behave as unergative verbs when atelic, but as unaccusative verbs in the presence of a goal phrase, that is, when telic. Borer (1998: 61–62) discusses Hebrew verbs like *hitporer* 'crumble' and *naval* 'wilt,' which alternately show unaccusative and unergative behavior, and suggests that sentences with these verbs are telic when their verb shows unaccusative behavior and atelic otherwise. Given the link to telicity, such phenomena could be viewed as further supporting meaning-driven approaches and, specifically, the proposal that alternations involve shifts in event type.

The event type-shifting analysis has a major advantage. It attributes argument alternations to notions that are independently considered to be important to argument realization. Furthermore, the alternations essentially reflect natural classes of relations between event types, for instance, the relations between telic and atelic predicates. As discussed in chapter 4, however, there are limitations to the aspectual approach to argument realization, and these carry over to the event type-shifting analyses of argument alternations. Essentially, the importance of aspectual notions in the analysis of argument realization phenomena has been overstated; the open question, then, is whether such notions do have a place in a theory of argument realization.

7.2.3.4 *Approaches based on verbal profile*

Whereas many analyses consider argument alternations to arise from a single verb root associated with two event types, Croft (1998) argues that the variants in many argument alternations involve a single verb root and a single event type, but two distinct verbal "profiles." As discussed in section 4.3, the verbal profile is that part of a verb's meaning that is asserted, rather than presupposed, in a given use. Croft proposes that the portion of a verb's event structure that is profiled can vary from one use to another, and the difference in profiles yields an argument alternation. Croft's approach contrasts with aspectually driven analyses which take argument alternations to reflect a shift in event structure. Croft, however, cannot analyze argument alternations in terms of distinct event structures since he takes event structure to encode force-dynamic relations between participants (see section 4.3), and the variants in argument alternations, such as the locative alternation, do not differ in force-dynamic relations. Rather, what varies, according to Croft, is the part of the causal chain defined by the event that is profiled. The difference is illustrated in (39) and (40): the locative variant profiles the first two segments of the causal chain, while the *with* variant profiles the whole chain.[4]

(39) Jane sprayed paint on the wall.   (Croft 1991: 200, (16))

Jane		paint		wall
•	$\longrightarrow$	•	$\longrightarrow$	•
SBJ		OBJ		OBL
###	spray	###		

(40) Jane sprayed the wall with paint.   (Croft 1991: 200, (17))

Jane		paint		wall
•	$\longrightarrow$	•	$\longrightarrow$	•
SBJ		OBL		OBJ
###		spray		###

The locative relation between the "figure" (located element) and "ground" (location) does not establish a causal order between these elements. Rather, locative relations are construed as if the figure causally precedes the ground. This construal is legitimized because the figure is acted on by the initiator of the event (Croft 1991: 198–206) and, thus, must directly follow the initiator (see section 4.3).

Croft (1998: 39) argues that a universal principle of argument realization determines that the verbal profile is delimited by the subject and the object of the clause. Thus, variation in the verbal profile necessarily involves a change in choice of subject or object. In the locative alternation, the location is the object in the *with* variant precisely because the verbal profile ends with it, while the material is expressed in the *with* phrase, which is used to express arguments that are intermediate in the causal chain between the subject and object. In contrast, in the locative variant the location is an oblique because the verbal profile ends with the material argument and the location is outside of the causal chain. Another alternation which involves a change in the verbal profile is the causative alternation. An alternating verb such as *break* has the entire causal chain in its profile when used transitively, whereas its intransitive use has just the change of state profiled; see also Langacker (1990: 216–17, 1991: 331–33) for a similar approach.

Croft proposes there are constraints on what can be profiled: "a possible verb must have a continuous segment of the causal chain in the event ICM [= idealized cognitive model] as its profile and as its base; it appears that for underived verb forms, profile and base must in addition coincide" (Croft 1998: 48). He briefly explores predictions that follow from this constraint (48–50). The verbal profile itself must, however, be semantically motivated, so as not to qualify as a diacritic which merely stipulates what the subject and object are. The verbal profile is meant to individuate the event named by the verb, and so it "represents a high degree of self-containedness of the event" (Croft 1998: 46). The most highly individuated type of event is one which describes volitional direct causation of a definite change of state. The volition of the agent represents the ultimate cause which marks the initiation of the event and the definite change of state marks the unambiguous termination of the event.

To a large extent, what is lexicalized in the verb determines what its profiling options are. A verb which lexicalizes both a volitional action and a definite change of state, being inherently delimited on both ends of the event, obligatorily has the entire causal structure profiled. And indeed, verbs such as *murder*, which denote necessarily volitional changes of state, do not have an intransitive use, since this would involve "deprofiling" a portion of the causal chain – the initial portion – which is inherently profiled. Other change-of-state verbs, like *break*, lexicalize a definite change of state, but nothing specific about the cause of this change; thus, they are only inherently delimited at the end of the causal chain. Therefore, they allow an intransitive use in which the causing subevent is not profiled, as well as a transitive use where it is profiled, giving rise to the causative alternation.

Returning to the locative alternation, Croft (1998: 43–45) takes the subsumption relation between the meanings of the two variants noted in section 7.2.3.1 as evidence that the verbal profile for one variant is larger than for the other. In the *with* variant, it is delimited by the location – the wall in (40). In the locative variant, it is delimited by the material – the paint in (39). By taking a different argument be the delimiter in each variant, he relates the difference in affectedness to the shift in profile: the delimiter is the affected argument. To the extent that a verb describes an event where more than one participant can be construed as a delimiter, as with locative alternation verbs, there may be more than one profile compatible with the root. A single language may show variation in argument realization (as in the locative alternation); furthermore, there may also be variation across languages as to whether the less prototypical delimiters of the event can be construed in the same way that the more prototypical delimiters are in a particular language. This variation, according to Croft (1998: 47), is the source of crosslinguistic variation in the range of verbs showing any given argument alternation.

Direct object/oblique alternations, such as the conative alternation, are characterized by shifts in affectedness or aspectual classification comparable to those observed in the locative alternation (S. R. Anderson 1971, 1977; Tenny 1987, 1992, 1994). Given this similarity, Croft (1998: 45) has proposed that they too can be analyzed in terms of shifts in verbal profile. (Interestingly, Croft [1991: 208] treats the dative alternation differently: it involves changes in the verbal profile accompanied by changes in the causal chain.) Shifts in verbal profile can also involve the beginning of a causal chain, as described in section 4.3: the presence of instrument subjects represents such a shift. Once again, such shifts are only available if the concomitant shift in delimiter identifies an appropriate delimiter for the causal chain. So, for instance, verbs that require – and, hence, lexicalize – a volitional agent do not show such shifts, since they cannot "deprofile" the agent and must express it as their subject. In summary, the examples in this section show how shifts in verbal profile allow for a unified account of a range of argument alternations, while maintaining a single lexical semantic representation for alternating verbs.

7.2.3.5 *Summary*

All the meaning-driven accounts reviewed share a fundamental property. They focus on object alternations and strive to maintain a single unified semantic basis for objecthood. Despite this, they allow for argument alternations by proposing some mechanism that allows some verbs to optionally construe one "argument" (in the conative alternation) or more than one "argument" (in the locative and dative alternations) as satisfying the semantic determinant of objecthood. These mechanisms range from the use of different lexical semantic representations which allow different associations of a semantic notion such as affectedness with a verb's arguments to shifts in a verb's event type or a verb's choice of incremental theme to shifts in verbal profile.

Not all researchers agree, however, that there is a single semantic determinant for all object alternations. Dowty (1991) introduces his proto-role approach precisely because he believes there is no single determinant of objecthood (or subjecthood). His discussion of argument alternations supports this contention. For him, the locative alternation arises because either the material or location argument of the alternating verbs may have an incremental theme entailment; the argument with this entailment has one more Patient Proto-role entailment than the other and, thus, is realized as the object. In contrast, the *with/against* alternation arises because there is no Patient Proto-role entailment that favors one VP-internal argument over the other, allowing either to be chosen as object.

Nevertheless, since argument realizations are determined by proto-role entailments, Dowty's approach still qualifies as a meaning-driven approach broadly speaking.

7.3   Information-packaging considerations and more

So far we have focused on how the variants defining an alternation may arise; in this section we investigate how a speaker chooses which variant to use in a particular context when a verb allows alternate realizations of its arguments. If some alternations are truly meaning-driven, then only the meaning associated with one variant may be appropriate in a given context, forcing a choice. This situation is likely to arise with the conative alternation, since a sentence such as *Philomena swatted the fly* entails that Philomena made contact with the fly and, thus, this sentence, unlike *Philomena swatted at the fly*, cannot describe a situation where she did not succeed in doing so. However, we have suggested that some alternations, such as the *with/against* and locative inversion alternations, are not meaning-driven. Furthermore, for some choices of arguments both variants of apparently meaning-driven alternations may appropriately describe the same event. In both circumstances, meaning does not offer an explanation for any observed preference for one variant over the other. An alternative explanation is that the variants differ in how they "package" the information they convey, making one variant preferable to another in a certain discourse context. Additionally, other considerations, such as the "weight" or "heaviness" of postverbal constituents, are claimed to play a part in the choice between variants. We examine such factors in this section to round out the picture of argument alternations.

The study of information structure is concerned with "the system of options which grammars offer speakers for expressing given propositional contents in different grammatical forms under varying discourse circumstances" (Lambrecht 1994: xiii). If a discourse is to be coherent, a speaker must properly relate one sentence in a discourse to the next. Within each sentence, a speaker usually accomplishes this goal by introducing novel information in the context of information known from the preceding discourse. Thus, one of the speaker's concerns is indicating what information in a sentence can be assumed to be "given" and what "new."[5] Languages provide several devices for conveying information status, including the use of prosody or special grammatical forms and the ordering of sentence constituents (Vallduví and Engdahl 1996).

Information-structure considerations are relevant to argument alternations due to the well-known general tendency for given material to precede new material in a sentence (Firbas 1966; Quirk et al. 1985: 1361).[6] This tendency has been claimed to influence the choice between variants in certain alternations because the variants offer alternative orderings of the same arguments. Such considerations have been implicated, for example, in the choice between a locative inversion sentence and its noninverted counterpart. As noted in section 7.2.1, such pairs of sentences are truth-conditionally equivalent, so any observed preferences for one sentence over the other cannot be traced to meaning differences. In fact, drawing on an extensive corpus study, Birner (1992, 1994) and Birner and Ward (1998) find that a locative inversion sentence is favored over its noninverted counterpart when it meets the general preference for placing given material before new material in a sentence. Specifically, "the preposed constituent in an inversion must not represent less familiar information in the discourse than does the postposed constituent" (Birner and Ward 1998: 165).

Information-structure considerations are also potentially applicable to object alternations. In fact, the dative alternation has received significant attention in the information-structure literature (Arnold et al. 2000; Davidse 1996; Erteschik-Shir 1979; Givón 1984a; Halliday 1970; Polinsky 1996; Ransom 1979; Smyth, Prideaux, and Hogan 1979; K. M. Snyder 2003; Thompson 1990, 1995; Wasow 1997, 2002). The basic proposal is that the choice between the double object and *to* variants is determined by the relative information status of the recipient and theme. Following the principle that given material precedes new material, the double object construction is expected when the recipient is no newer than the theme and the *to* variant when the theme is no newer than the recipient. More generally, studies of texts confirm that the distribution of the variants is indeed largely governed by information-structure considerations (e.g., Arnold et al. 2000; Davidse 1996; Givón 1984a; K. M. Snyder 2003; Thompson 1990, 1995; Wasow 1997, 2002).

One consequence is that for certain choices of theme and recipient, only one variant may be felicitous. Since recipients are typically human and, therefore, more likely to be the topic of conversation than themes, which are typically inanimate, they are more likely to be given and thus should linearly precede themes. The result should be an overall preference for the double object variant over the *to* variant – a preference which is indeed observed (Bresnan and Nikitina 2003). Certain previously noted asymmetries in the dative alternation, such as the much-discussed pair in (41), may also have their source in information-structure considerations. In this pair, *the book* represents the idea that embodies the storyline of the book rather than the book as a physical object (Cruse 1992/93: 91–92; 2000: 34, 39–41; Postal 1966: 88, n. 16; Pustejovsky 1991a: 427–30), making it analogous to the pair cited earlier as (32).

(41) a. Interviewing Richard Nixon gave Norman Mailer a book.

                                                     (Oehrle 1976: 44, (2))

    b. *Interviewing Nixon gave a book to Norman Mailer.

Most likely, in (41) the recipient, *Mailer*, is the topic of conversation and thus given, while the theme, *a book*, is new information, so the double object variant is preferred. Supporting this proposal, if the notion of a book idea is given, perhaps as in the scenario in (42), the *to* variant is fine and may even be preferred.

(42) A: It is very difficult to get book ideas simply from interviews.
     B: Well, interviewing Nixon gave an idea for a book to Mailer.

Thus, once the effects of information structure are understood and controlled for, both variants can be shown to be available. This observation has larger ramifications since contrasts in acceptability as in (41) have been used to support meaning-driven accounts of the dative alternation. The fact that these contrasts are to be attributed to information-structure considerations raises further questions about the meaning-driven approach, whose viability was already questioned in section 7.2.3.2.

Information-structure considerations may not figure as centrally in variant choice in all object alternations. Laffut (1997) confronts this question with respect to the locative alternation and shows that the choice between variants cannot be attributed solely to information-packaging considerations. This finding is consistent with the proposal that the variants truly differ in meaning since differences in meaning might be expected to overwhelm information-structure considerations when they are at odds with them. In the literature on this alternation, discussions of the factors influencing variant choice have revolved almost entirely around differences in truth-conditional meaning, and Laffut himself argues that "holism" – roughly, "affectedness" – is the critical factor. The precise nature of the interactions between information-structure considerations and semantic determinants of argument realization require further investigation through a systematic examination of how both play out across a range of alternations. It is likely that both have a part to play in many alternations, though properties of individual alternations may give one prominence over the other.

Other nonsemantic considerations are also implicated in argument alternations. Studies of a range of constructions reveal that in ordering two postverbal constituents, there is a preference for placing "heavy" – or grammatically more complex – material at the end of a sentence, an observation originally attributed to Behagel (1909/10).[7] The effects of the relative "weight" of postverbal constituents is perhaps best known from its manifestation in "heavy NP-shift" (Hawkins 1994); however, it also affects variant choice in the dative alternation, as confirmed by corpus and experimental studies reported in Arnold et al. (2000) and Wasow (1997, 2002). This finding is not surprising given that the variants offer alternate options for ordering the recipient and theme. As a result, the heavier-last preference can result in one variant being preferred. In fact, the *Mailer* paradigm cited in (41) also illustrates the dative alternation's sensitivity to heaviness. As K. M. Snyder (2003) shows, the *to* variant in this paradigm becomes possible when the recipient is a heavy NP, as in (43).

(43) a. Nixon's behavior gave Mailer an idea for a book.
     b. #Nixon's behavior gave an idea for a book to Mailer.
     c. Nixon's behavior gave an idea for a book to every journalist living in
         New York City in the 1970s.   (K. M. Snyder 2003: 35, (47a,b), (48))

The effect of heaviness on acceptability suggests again that the unacceptability of (41b) should not receive a semantic explanation, as this categorically disallows the *to* variant. Again, it appears that meaning-driven approaches to the dative alternation are built on data that should fall outside their purview.

Heaviness considerations would be expected to interact with information-structure considerations in variant choice. With the dative alternation both typically favor the double object construction since recipients, as animates, are more likely to be given than themes, and given material tends to be expressed via shorter constituents, often pronouns. K. M. Snyder (2003: 28) suggests that information-structure considerations take precedence over heaviness considerations, while Arnold et al. (2000) argue that both influence constituent order. More generally, the discussion of corpus and experimental evidence in Wasow (2002: 71–72, 81–82) suggests that achieving a full understanding of the interactions between these considerations will not be easy.

To conclude, information-structure and heaviness considerations contribute to variant choice in argument alternations, even if they do not themselves determine argument realization options. When meaning differences between variants are slight, argument alternations present alternative argument orders, which can be used for information-packaging and heaviness purposes, as illustrated with the dative alternation. We conclude by pointing out that argument alternations, however, are not alone in this respect. Clefting, extraposition, topicalization, and left-dislocation also give rise to alternate constituent orders without affecting truth-conditional meaning, and, although quite different from argument alternations, they too are exploited for information-packaging purposes (Birner and Ward 1998; Lambrecht 1994; E. Prince 1979, 1985; Ward and Birner 2004).

7.4 Multiple argument realization involving event composition

We turn next to instances of multiple argument realization characterizable as involving event composition. In these instances, a verb's complement structure contains, in addition to its own arguments, either an added argument, an added argument-taking element, or both. Perhaps the best-known example of event composition is presented by the resultative construction, which was used to introduce this notion at the outset of this chapter.

(44) a. The athletes ran the pavement thin.
b. The blacksmith hammered the metal flat.
c. Sheila yelled herself hoarse.
d. Dana cried her eyes out.

In this construction, the main verb is found with a complement, the result phrase, which describes a change of state which comes about as a result of the action denoted by the verb, even though this state is not lexically entailed by the verb itself. The event described by the verb and the additional event evoked by the result phrase are construed as a single event. Evidence for a single event construal comes from the nonadjunct status of the result phrase, which is as closely bound to the verb as a normal subcategorized complement (B. Levin and Rappaport Hovav 1995; Roberts 1988; Tenny 1994). All analyses take the resultative construction to have an event structure different from that associated with the verb heading the construction. The verbs in (44) are basically activity verbs, licensing a simple event structure, yet the sentences in (44) are commonly given a causative event structure, following an intuition first made explicit in generative semantic analyses (Green 1972, 1973; McCawley 1971). This complex event structure consists of a causing event encoded by the base verb and a result subevent encoded by the result phrase. Basically, it captures the observation that (44c), for example, means roughly 'Sheila's yelling caused her to become hoarse.' The derivation of a resultative construction, then, is taken to involve event composition. The question is whether event composition always gives rise to a complex, causative event structure, and, if not, what other types of event structure are possible?

These are only two of a range of questions concerning the analysis of event composition. Other issues that need to be resolved include: the range of argument realization options that qualify as instances of event composition, the licensing of the extended event structure, the principles that determine the morphosyntactic expression of the arguments of a composed event, and the compatibility of particular verbs or semantic classes of verbs with particular types of event composition. We deal with each, leaving the last for the next section, since it arises for all forms of multiple argument realization.

Beginning with the first question, analyses of phenomena falling under the label "event composition" typically distinguish between two types of compositionally derived event structures: those that are still simple in that they consist of a single subevent and those that are complex in that they have two subevents, typically causally related. This distinction reflects a recognition that a causative event structure is not appropriate for all instances of event composition. A case in point is the use of verbs of manner of motion with directional complements, illustrated in (45a). These uses are analyzed as involving event composition, since the path described by the directional phrase is not lexically entailed by the verb. A manner-of-motion verb need not lexically entail that its theme move along some path; if it did, (45b) would be expected to be a contradiction, contrary to fact.

(45) a. Dana jumped/ran/danced/whirled onto the table.
     b. Dana jumped/ran/danced/whirled in place.

Some researchers (Croft 1991: 160; Kenny 1963: 177; Pustejovsky 1991b: 63; Van Valin 1990: 224) have proposed a causative and, hence, complex event structure for such examples; however, B. Levin and Rappaport Hovav (1999) and Van Valin and LaPolla (1997: 101) argue against such an analysis.[8] In fact, Jackendoff (1990b) proposes a derived simple event structure, roughly along the lines of the paraphrase in (47) for (46).

(46) Willy wiggled/danced/spun/bounced/jumped into Harriet's arms.
(Jackendoff 1990b: 223, (29))

(47) Willy went/got into Harriet's arms (by) wiggling/dancing/spinning/bouncing/jumping.
(Jackendoff 1990b: 223, (30))

Having established that some instances of event composition give rise to complex event structures, while others give rise to simple event structures, the question is what conditions determine whether a derived event structure will be complex or simple. A closer scrutiny of a range of resultative types can lead to a possible answer. Sentences with verbs of manner of motion plus directional phrases, such as those in (46), have been analyzed as instances of the resultative construction, since they predicate a "result" location of the subject of the verb. A question that has received considerable attention is why in such sentences and some others with intransitive verbs result phrases are directly predicated of the subject, while in others a "fake" reflexive pronoun is necessary for the result phrase to be predicated of the subject (Simpson 1983). Thus, (48a), (49a), and (50a) all involve the formation of a composed event structure; yet, (48a) requires the fake reflexive, but (49a) and (50a) do not allow one.

(48) a. Sheila yelled herself hoarse.
    b. *Sheila yelled hoarse.
(49) a. Jasper ran to the store.
    b. *Jasper ran himself to the store.
(50) a. The door rumbled open.
    b. *The door rumbled itself open.

One answer identifies an event structure difference between resultative constructions in which the result phrase is predicated directly of the subject and those in which it is predicated of an object; the fake reflexive resultatives are included among the latter (Jackendoff 1990b; Kaufmann and Wunderlich 1998; Rappaport Hovav and B. Levin 2001; Van Valin 1990; Wechsler 2001; Wunderlich 2000). Such analyses draw on the observation that the intransitive verbs found with fake reflexives qualify as unergatives, while those without qualify as unaccusatives (see section 4.2.5). According to these analyses, fake reflexives only appear with unergative verbs, because unergative and unaccusative verbs are associated with distinct event structures when combined with result phrases. As already mentioned, resultatives such as (49a) and (50a) are taken to have a simple, though derived, event structure, while resultatives such as (48a) are given a derived, though complex, event structure. Since there are verbs, such as *break*, *open*, and other causative change-of-state verbs, that are lexically associated with a complex event structure (e.g., Dowty 1979; McCawley 1971; Parsons 1990; Pustejovsky 1991b, 1995), whatever principles account for the realization of the arguments of nonderived complex events should be invoked in the realization of arguments of compositionally derived complex events. Since lexical causatives have obligatory direct objects, these analyses implicitly or explicitly assume that the appearance of the reflexive pronoun is a reflex of this complex event structure. For example, as discussed in section 4.2.5, Rappaport Hovav and B. Levin (2001) attribute the obligatory presence of the reflexive to the requirement that a syntactic argument is required for each subevent in a complex event. Kaufmann and Wunderlich (1998) also assume that the presence of the reflexive is due to the rules realizing the arguments of complex events.[9]

When does the addition of a nonlexically entailed result give rise to a complex event structure and when to a simple event structure? The crucial factor seems to be the semantic relation between the two subevents, but there is some controversy as to its precise characterization. B. Levin and Rappaport Hovav (1999) suggest that when the introduced event and the event denoted by the verb are temporally dependent, they are represented as a derived simple event in event structure terms (see section 4.2.5). Similarly, Wechsler (2001) suggests that the simple event structure arises when there is an argument-to-event homomorphism. Along related lines, Kaufmann and Wunderlich (1998), drawing on Washio (1997), distinguish between "weak" and "strong" resultatives. Weak resultatives include a result phrase which further specifies the nature of a change already implied by the verb, as in *The thugs smashed the window to smithereens* and *The cook melted the chocolate soft*. The "addition" of this result phrase, then, does not involve the introduction of a new subevent. In contrast, strong resultatives describe derived complex events, in which the result phrase introduces a second nonlexically entailed subevent, which combines with the event described by the verb. So, for Kaufmann and Wunderlich, the criterion for whether or not a resultative construction involves a complex event structure depends on whether or not the change introduced by the result phrase is implied by the verb.[10] Similar approaches are adopted by Pustejovsky (1991b, 1995) and Rothstein (2000).

In addition to explicating the nature of the derived event structure, a full analysis of event composition must delineate how the participants of the two subevents come together in the composed event and how a mapping algorithm operates on the composed event structure. For instance, in *Sheila yelled herself hoarse*, the yelling and becoming hoarse events each have one argument, though these arguments have the same referent, a fact brought out by expressing one with a reflexive pronoun. In contrast, in *Kay pushed the door open*, *the door* is understood as an argument of two events, yet it is only syntactically represented once. In *The cows ate the field bare*, however, one of the arguments of *eat* – the food eaten, presumably the grass or crops in the field – is simply not expressed at all. The reason, most likely, is that there are only a limited number of NP positions in the syntax, precluding the expression of both the object of *eat* and the subject of the result phrase. In general, composed events have more arguments than the verbs they are built on, so some kind of accommodation needs to be made. Here we simply acknowledge this issue, but do not delve into it; for discussion see Carrier and Randall (1992, 1993), Goldberg (1995), Jackendoff (1990b), and Wunderlich (1997b). This issue has received considerable attention with respect to related phenomena such as causatives, compound verbs, and serial verbs, where the restrictions are more complex and more diverse (Alsina and Joshi 1991; Baker 1989; Butt 1995; Li 1990; Matsumoto 1996).

We now turn to the remaining questions posed above concerning event composition. One is what other modes of argument realization are to be analyzed as involving event composition. The discussion so far suggests that a verb accompanied by a nonsubcategorized postverbal NP and an additional predicate is a clear candidate. If so, one or both variants in some argument alternations might also be viewed as instances of event composition. Although the pair in (51) is usually presented as variants of the removing subtype of the locative alternation, the verb *sweep* is a surface-contact verb and does not strictly entail the existence of any arguments besides the surface and the entity making contact with that surface – the arguments expressed in (51a). Specifically, it does not entail the "material" argument that is the object in (51b); therefore, it seems appropriate to analyze (51b) as an instance of event composition.

(51) a. Terry swept the sidewalk.
      b. Terry swept the leaves off the sidewalk.

This analysis is reinforced by the existence of other sentences with *sweep* that also do not express the surface as the object (if at all), yet each includes a distinct "nonsubcategorized" result phrase instead.

(52) a. Kelly swept the leaves onto the rug.
      b. Kelly swept the leaves into the corner.
      c. Kelly swept the leaves into a pile.

Event composition can be found outside of recognized argument alternations. For instance, *throw* describes the exertion of a force on an entity, setting it in motion, but does not entail that it reaches a particular goal. Yet, that goal may be expressed, as in *Brett threw the ball into the field*. The verbs *push* and *tug* do not even entail that the entity the force is directed at moves (*Fred tugged/pushed the carton, but it didn't budge*), but they too can be found with a goal, as in *Fred tugged/pushed the carton into the garage*. Furthermore, as B. Levin and Rapoport (1988) show, English has a wide range of nonsubcategorized objects that are not entailed by a verb, which might be analyzed as involving event composition. Particularly striking are examples such as *Kim whistled her appreciation* or *The guard glared his disapproval*. These sentences lack any argument-taking predicate in addition to the verb, yet they have paraphrases suggesting event composition: Kim expressed her appreciation by whistling and the guard expressed his disapproval by glaring. Clearly, a theory is needed which will predict the range of possible interpretations in instances such as these.

Wunderlich (2000) argues that whenever a verb appears with a nonsubcategorized NP, there is event composition, since it is possible to augment the event structure of a verb with an additional argument only through the introduction of a new event. (Wunderlich's proposal resonates with the Minimalist Program assumption that there be a verbal predicate for each argument [Hale and Keyser 1993; Larson 1998].) Wunderlich accordingly analyzes German sentences with nonsubcategorized dative NPs as involving event composition. These NPs, which receive an "ethical" dative, possessive, or benefactive interpretation, are accompanied by the introduction of a new subevent, headed by the predicate POSS, to the verb's event structure.

(53) Er wusch mir   das Hemd.
     He wash me-DAT the shirt
     'He washed my shirt.'   (Wunderlich 2000: 263, (37a))

Finally, we turn to the licensing of the extended event structure. Since, by definition, in the examples we considered in this section the verb does not license the extended event structure, what gives rise to it? Carrier and Randall (1993) and Kaufmann and Wunderlich (1997a, 1998) derive resultatives using a lexical rule, while Jackendoff (1990b) proposes that resultatives can be derived by what he calls an "extralexical" rule; alternatively, Jackendoff proposes that resultatives can be analyzed as "constructional idioms," which he describes as "a specialized syntactic form with an idiomatic meaning" (1990b: 221). Others propose that the resultative construction is a construction in the Construction Grammar sense, with certain verbs being compatible with this construction (Boas 2000, 2003; Goldberg 1995; Kay 2000; Verspoor 1997). Finally, neo-constructionists assume that the complex event structure is directly encoded in the syntax, and that verbs may be inserted into the relevant syntactic structure (Hoekstra 1992; Ritter and S. T. Rosen 1998).

What distinguishes among these approaches is the extent to which the meaning of the resultative construction is taken to be compositionally derived. Ascertaining the degree of compositionality is a complicated issue (Boas 2000, 2003; Jackendoff 1997, 2002), and we do not address it since it is largely orthogonal to the issue that concerns us: identifying the semantic determinants of argument realization. However, the question we address in the next section impinges on the debate over these different approaches: to what extent are the verbs which enter into each resultative pattern predictable? If the sets of verbs need to be stipulated, this argues against the neoconstructionist approach, where such stipulations are unexpected.

7.5   The distribution of verb classes in multiple argument realization

Argument alternations and event composition are both manifested by limited and apparently semantically coherent classes of verbs. A challenge, then, is predicting the distribution of verbs in particular instances of multiple argument realization. There are two facets to the question of distribution: a data-oriented question – properly delineating the extent of the alternations and other multiple argument realization phenomena – and a theoretical question – explaining why these phenomena should be restricted in the attested ways. Participation in a particular argument alternation is not determined in strictly structural terms; what appears to be a degree of idiosyncrasy in alternating verbs is one motivation for moving away from transformational analyses of many alternations. However, it is not easy to determine the range of verbs which enter into particular instances of multiple argument realization, and this difficulty is reflected in debates over which verbs show alternations in the first place. We use the dative alternation to illustrate the complexities of this issue, but the same question arises with respect to the whole range of multiple argument realization. The theoretical explanation offered for the differential participation of verbs in multiple argument realization phenomena has to be compatible with whatever turns out to be the most accurate picture of linguistic reality in verb distribution.

Many nonalternating verbs are similar to alternating verbs in meaning, which poses a challenge for any account. Researchers have often made this point about the dative alternation (e.g., Goldberg 1992, 1995; Green 1974; Krifka 1999, 2001; B. Levin 1993; Oehrle 1976; Pinker 1989; Wierzbicka 1986). Many studies cite verbs of continuous imparting of force (Krifka 1999; Pinker 1989: 110–11) and verbs of manner of speaking (Green 1974: 89; Krifka 1999; Pinker 1989: 112) as found in the *to* variant of the dative alternation, but not in the double object variant, yet compare the meanings of nonalternating *carry*, a verb of imparting force, and alternating *take,* or the meanings of nonalternating *scream*, a verb of manner of speaking, and alternating *tell*.[11]

(54) a. Pat carried the rabbit to the vet.
      b. *Pat carried the vet the rabbit.

(55) a. Pat took the rabbit to the vet.
      b. Pat took the vet the rabbit.

(56) a. The first player screamed the score to the second.
      b. *The first player screamed the second the score.

(57) a. The first player told the score to the second.
      b. The first player told the second the score.

A small set of verbs are apparently only found in the double object variant, and some of these are not obviously different from alternating verbs; compare nonalternating *ask* and alternating *tell*.

(58) a. The teacher asked the student a question.
     b. *The teacher asked a question to the student.

Simply treating the ability to alternate as an idiosyncratic, lexically listed property of certain verbs is not the answer. As Goldberg (1992, 1995), Marantz (1984: 177), and Pinker (1989), among others, point out, the dative alternation, like other alternations, shows limited productivity: it may be extended to certain new verbs. The denominal verb *fax* now numbers among the dative verbs. Similarly, Marantz (1984: 177) notes that if a new verb *shin* meaning 'to kick with the shin' were coined, it could be used in the dative alternation.

(59) a. The ticket agent faxed my receipt to me.
     b. The ticket agent faxed me my receipt.
(60) a. Tracy shinned the ball to Sam.
     b. Tracy shinned Sam the ball.

The dative alternation is also found sporadically with verbs that are generally considered not to alternate. That is, there are what Pinker (1989: 317) calls "one-shot innovations," as in his example *The bank credited my account $100* (cf. *The bank credited $100 to my account*) (1989: 157, (4.542f)) or in an example Bresnan and Nikitina (2003) cite from the *American Heritage Dictionary*'s definition of *abnegate: To deny (something) to oneself.* An account of the dative alternation must allow for this restricted productivity in adult speech, as well as comparable uses in child speech (Pinker 1989: 21–22).

The same questions arise with respect to instances of multiple argument realization attributable to event composition. As shown in Rappaport Hovav and B. Levin (1998a), some verbs cannot be the basis of composed events, as in the following examples with *break*, each of which is parallel to an attested composed event built on another verb.

(61) a. *The naughty child broke the cupboard bare.
           (: The child broke the dishes so that the cupboard ended up bare.)
     b. The naughty child ate the cupboard bare.
(62) a. *Kelly broke the dishes off the table.
           (meaning: Kelly removed the dishes from the table by breaking the table.)
     b. Kelly wiped the crumbs off the table.
(63) a. *Kelly broke the dishes off the table.
           (meaning: Kelly broke the dishes and as a result they went off the table.)
     b. Kelly pushed the dishes off the table.

As with the dative alternation, there are also minimal pairs, with verbs that apparently belong to the same semantic class differing with respect to the result phrases they can combine with (Boas 2000, 2003; Goldberg 1995: 136–37; Verspoor 1997; Wechsler 2001).

(64) a. The bandit shot/*battered the sheriff dead.
      b. The bandit shot/battered the sheriff to death.

As in the case of argument alternations, the question is what verbs allow what kind of "augmented" event structures. Also an issue is the simultaneous restrictiveness on the one hand and productivity on the other. Although some verbs are not found in resultative constructions, certain newly coined verbs can be, as in (65) and (66), and children also use the construction in ways that sound odd to adult ears (Bowerman 1982: 330–31).

(65) Clea eggbeatered the covers into a knot ... (I. Marcuse, *The Death of an Amiable Child*, Walker, New York, 2000, p. 124)

(66) ... patrol cars pincering the big machine to a halt ... (L. M. Roberts, *Almost Human*, Ballantine, New York, 1998, p. 217)

In section 7.4, we proposed that sentences such as *Terry swept the leaves off the sidewalk* could be analyzed as describing complex events built on verbs of surface contact. Such sentences have analogues with verbs outside this semantic class, as in Goldberg's (1997: 384) example, *Elena sneezed the foam off the cappuccino* or the nonce example in (67).

(67) "Oh, baby" she whispered, kissing the sweat from his scrawny little neck ...
                    (J. Graham, *Sarah's Window*, Putnam, New York, 2001, p. 78)

However, as Boas (2000, 2003), Kay (2000: 16; 2002), and Verspoor (1997) point out, not all verbs can be found in comparable sentences, as the examples in (68) illustrate, with even semantically similar verbs evoking different judgments, as in (69).

(68) a. They laughed him off the stage.
      b. *They coughed him off the stage.
      c. *He bragged her out of the room.
      d. *She screamed him under the bed.   (Kay 2002: 13, (21); 14, (26))

(69) a. They laughed John out of the room.
      b. *They tittered John out of the room.   (Verspoor 1997: 119, (4.43ei,ii))

Pinker devotes the bulk of his book *Learnability and Cognition* (1989) to the question of productivity. He takes a meaning-driven lexical rule approach to multiple argument realization and posits the existence of both broad-range rules, which determine whether an alternation is in principle available with particular semantic classes of verbs, and narrow-range rules, which determine whether the alternation is actually found with specific subclasses of these classes.[12] On Pinker's approach, then, it is not strict compatibility which determines the pairing of an idiosyncratic or root-based meaning and a structural or event-based meaning. To some extent, this pairing involves conventionalization and is ultimately stipulated by individual grammars, though there is a general logic, or what Pinker calls "motivation" (1989: 109) to the pairing of verb roots with particular narrow-range rules. As an example, consider Pinker's discussion of verbs of continuous imparting of force like *push* or *pull*, which, as already mentioned, do not show the dative alternation, and verbs of instantaneous imparting of force like *throw*, which do. Pinker suggests that since the "thematic core" – or central meaning – of the double object structure involves an agent causing a recipient to possess something, a verb like *throw* could be found in the double object construction since throwing typically involves aiming in a particular direction, and so an event of throwing might involve a recipient. An event of pulling, in contrast, "can be initiated without having the receiver in mind" (1989: 118), and so it is less likely than *throw* to inherently involve a recipient. Such motivations cannot be deduced from any universal principles, but can be posited post hoc.

As a consequence, Pinker (1989: 109) suggests that languages might differ with respect to the range of application of the dative and comparable alternations. That is, if English allows the dative alternation with *fax* and other verbs of instrument of communication, but not with *scream* and other verbs of manner of speaking, then some other language should allow the alternation with verbs like *scream*, but not verbs like *fax*. Extensive crosslinguistic study of this matter is lacking and would clearly help resolve some of these issues. An exploratory study by Croft et al. (2001) suggests that there is more systematicity than Pinker's proposal suggests. Their study uncovers the "ditransitivity hierarchy" in (70): a language only shows the double object construction with a verb at a given point on the hierarchy if it allows it for verbs to its left.

(70) 'give' < 'send' < 'throw'   (Croft et al. 2001: 2)

If Croft et al. are right, then narrow-range rules may be less arbitrary than Pinker's work suggests. The motivation for such a hierarchy is likely to be nonlinguistic, related to how the relevant happenings in the world are construed. As Croft et al. note, this hierarchy "can be accounted for in terms of the nature of the events in terms of transfer of possession ↔ change of location" (2001: 14): that is, giving events necessarily involve transfer of possession, with change of location being incidental; in contrast, throwing is about change of location, which might incidentally be a transfer of possession; sending is both a change-of-possession and change-of-location event. Therefore, all languages allow verbs of giving to be expressed as change-of-possession verbs, but only some languages allow a verb like *throw* to be used as a transfer-of-possession verb. Although the ditransitivity hierarchy is derived from properties of the happenings in the world each verb can describe, a given language will choose its own cut-off point with respect to expression in the double object construction. Haspelmath (1993) suggests that crosslinguistic differences in verbs showing the causative alternation can also be described in this way. For example, some verbs consistently participate in the causative alternation both within and across languages, while others participate in the alternation only sporadically within and across languages (B. Levin and Rappaport Hovav 1995; Haspelmath 1993). Haspelmath proposes a hierarchy which ranks verbs in terms of the inherent likelihood that the event they denote can occur spontaneously. Verbs that are least likely to denote such events are the ones that are most likely to be lexicalized as transitive causatives, with their intransitive uses showing an "anticausative" morpheme. Verbs that are most likely to denote such events are most likely to be lexicalized as intransitive verbs. Again, languages vary as to where on the hierarchy they make the cut-off between verbs lexicalized as transitives or intransitives. Both studies suggest that there is still a degree of conventionalization, as in Pinker's analysis, but the range of possibilities is more restricted than he suggests.

The idea that the pairing of root meaning with event-based meaning is partly conventionalized plays a central role in the analysis of multiple argument realization in constructional approaches. Goldberg (1992, 1995) and Michaelis and Ruppenhofer (2000, 2001) stress that argument structure constructions are very much like words, being form–meaning pairings which must be recorded in the grammar. Like words, argument structure constructions may show poly-semy: a single construction can be associated with various senses, though one sense is typically recognized as the central sense, with the others being related to it (or sometimes another sense). Goldberg proposes that "the central senses of argument structure constructions designate scenes which are semantically privileged in being basic to human experience" (1995: 40), such as causing a change in location or a change in state. "Polysemy links" specify the "nature of the semantic relations between a particular sense of a construction and any extensions from this sense" (Goldberg 1995: 75); these links provide the moti-vation for the meaning extensions, though they cannot be predicted a priori. There is a reconciliation procedure, as Michaelis and Ruppenhofer (2000, 2001) put it, by which the meaning of a verb is integrated into an individual sense of a construction. The verbs that participate in a particular variant of an alternation are determined to a very large degree by their compatibility with the individual senses of the construction.

Constructions, then, are associated with a family of related senses. For instance, the central meaning of the double object construction is 'X CAUSES Y TO RECEIVE Z,' as with *give*, but it can also mean 'X INTENDS TO CAUSE Y TO RECEIVE Z,' as with *leave* or *grant*, 'X ENABLES Y TO RECEIVE Z,' as with *permit*, or 'X CAUSES Y NOT TO RECEIVE Z,' as with *deny* or *refuse* (Goldberg 1995: 38, 75). Goldberg (1995: 76) also supports this approach by showing other constructions display some of the same types of polysemy. Thus, the caused-motion construction, whose central sense is 'X CAUSES Y TO MOVE Z,' as in *Pat pushed the piano into the room*, also has a sense 'X ENABLES Y TO MOVE Z,' as in *Pat allowed Chris into the room*. However, constructions may not exhibit precisely the same patterns of polysemy; for instance, the double object construction has no sense that is analogous to the caused-motion construction's sense 'X HELPS Y TO MOVE Z' found in *Pat assisted Chris into the room* (Goldberg 1995: 76).

A hallmark of the constructional approach is the recognition of a central sense for a construction, which according to Goldberg (1992, 1995), is essential for dealing with the productivity of a construction. This point comes out clearly when the constructional approach is contrasted with an "abstractionist" approach. An abstractionist approach subsumes all instances of a construction under a single semantic representation, which tends of necessity to be quite abstract. Yet, linguistic reality does not conform to the predictions of the abstractionist approach. A close look at previously proposed lists of verbs participating in the dative alternation reveals some disagreements among them. Take verbs of continuous imparting of force, such as *push* and *carry*: Green (1974: 80, 85) includes them among the alternating verbs, while Pinker (1989: 111) lists them as nonalternating. These disagreements correlate with differential judgments about the acceptability of these verbs in the double object construction (Bresnan and Nikitina 2003). Abstractionist approaches to the double object construction (Shibatani 1996; Wierzbicka 1986) are unable to deal with disagreements about status and with the differential acceptability of certain instances of the construction, since any instance should either fit the proposed semantic representation or not. On the constructional approach, such examples are limited extensions of the central sense and do not need to be treated on a par with other examples (Goldberg 1995: 36).

An abstractionist approach has been proposed for the German applicative construction with the prefix *be* – (e.g., Brinkmann 1997). In this construction, arguments which normally appear as obliques, appear as direct objects of verbs with this prefix. This prefix is used with many verbs which participate in the English locative alternation, such as *schmieren* 'smear,' as in (71), to produce a counterpart of the English *with* variant; however, the prefix is also used with verbs outside the set of locative alternation verbs, as in (72).

(71) Sie beschmierte die Leinwand mit Farbe.
      'She smeared the canvas with paint.'
                              (Michaelis and Ruppenhofer 2000: 336)

(72) Nun hatte ich wohl die Ostsee befahren und die Nordsee geschmeckt [...]
      'True, I had sailed around the Baltic Sea and I had had a taste of the North Sea.'
                              (NK1/NHE.00000, Heuss, *Erinnerungen 1905–1933*;
                              Michaelis and Ruppenhofer 2000: 373, (41))

Recently, Michaelis and Ruppenhofer (2000, 2001) have argued that an abstractionist account of this construction should be rejected in favor of a constructional account. Instead of a single abstract meaning, they posit a central sense for the construction, which involves a theme covering the planar region of a location (or an agent causing such covering). This sense is exemplified in the most prototypical uses of the prefix, such as the two just illustrated. They propose that in some other senses of the construction, coverage is metaphorically rather than literally interpreted, as in (73).

(73) Später auf Deck äußerte Sabeth (ohne Drängen meinerseits) den Wunsch, einmal den Maschinenraum zu besichtigen, und zwar mit mir [...]
'Later on deck Sabeth expressed the wish (without me urging her) to tour (lit. sight) the engine-room, and to do so with me [...]'
(MK1/LFH.00000, Frisch, *Homo Faber*, Roman. Suhrkamp; Michaelis and Ruppenhofer 2000: 377, (51))

Here seeing is understood as coming into contact with a "percept," and thoroughly looking over a percept is taken to mean coverage of the percept (Michaelis and Ruppenhofer 2000: 377, 2001: 73–74). There is no way to predict a priori that a language will allow perception verbs to participate in such a construction via this metaphor, though there is clear motivation for their participation. Such an extended use of the construction would be problematic for an abstractionist account, but is easily accommodated in the constructional account, which distinguishes a central sense, but allows for additional senses to arise via metaphoric processes.

The different constructional senses of constructional approaches are comparable to Pinker's narrow-range classes of verbs. For example, Goldberg's constructional sense 'X INTENDS TO CAUSE Y TO RECEIVE Z' (1998: 37–39) for the double object construction corresponds to Pinker's narrow-range class, the verbs of future having (1989: 111), a class earlier recognized by Green (1974: 90–91). The constructional senses can be seen as stand-ins for verb classes, as highlighted in Croft's (2003a) and Kay's (2000) critiques of Goldberg's approach to the double object construction. Both argue that there is redundancy between several of the senses Goldberg posits for this construction and the meanings of the associated verbs. For example, Kay suggests that a 'X CAUSES Y NOT TO RECEIVE Z' sense is unnecessary since the negation, which sets this sense apart from the basic sense, is present in the meaning of the verbs *deny* or *refuse* (see also Koenig and Davis 2001: 80).[13] It appears, then, that some stipulation is necessary, though perhaps less than Goldberg suggests. Choosing the appropriate set of constructional senses, however, is not a trivial matter, nor is parceling out meaning appropriately between a construction and individual verbs.

So far our focus has been on fine-grained semantic distinctions which influence the distribution of verbs across constructions. Rappaport Hovav and B. Levin (1998a, 2002) suggest that the restricted distribution of change-of-state verbs across syntactic contexts can be attributed to principles that make reference to coarse-grained semantic distinctions between event structures. B. Levin and Rappaport Hovav (2003) elaborate on this earlier work. They confront the partial productivity of argument alternations by distinguishing necessary from sufficient conditions on alternations, as Pinker does with his broad- and

narrow-range rules, but they propose an event-based necessary condition on a
verb's ability to show object alternations: a verb must have a root that is basically associated with a simple event structure. The actual range of alternations
a verb is attested in depends on properties of its root; consequently, verbs with
roots of similar types exhibit similar alternations, giving rise to the perception
that alternations are shown by semantically coherent classes of verbs.

Rappaport Hovav and B. Levin (1998a) and B. Levin and Rappaport Hovav
(2003) point out that verbs which lexicalize a manner component of meaning,
such as *sweep, wipe,* or *sew,* show a greater range of argument realization
options, whether characterizable as argument alternations or as event composition, than verbs which lexicalize a result state component, such as *break,
open,* or *empty.*[14] The reason, they suggest, is that manner verbs are inherently
associated with simple event structures, which can be augmented under the
appropriate circumstances. Verbs with simple event structures may allow object
alternations, since the rules associating event structure and syntax require only
that the subject argument be realized; object alternations may arise when there
are two nonactor arguments associated with a simple event verb and two ways
of expressing both simultaneously. They argue that event simplicity, rather
than say the aspectual notion of "activity," which also characterizes many
manner verbs, is the crucial factor since stative verbs, which are also simple
event verbs, can show object alternations, as in (74). To do this, however,
a stative verb must have the right number of arguments, and there must be
prepositions which allow either nonsubject argument to be expressed as an
oblique.

(74) a. Tony admired them for their integrity.
     b. Tony admired the integrity in them.
     c. Tony admired them.
     d. Tony admired their integrity.

Verbs from certain semantic classes, including verbs of change of state,
consistently lack object alternations. These verbs are plausibly analyzed as
being inherently associated with a complex event structure – an event structure
which prevents them from participating in most argument alternations. As
discussed in sections 4.2.5 and 7.4, there must be one argument in the syntax
for each subevent in a complex event structure. Thus, the object of such verbs
must correspond to a participant in their basic event structure, so that alternative
object choices and, hence, object alternations, are disallowed.

(75) a. Lee broke the fence with the stick.
     b. Lee broke the stick against the fence.
        (cannot mean: Lee broke the fence)
(76) a. Corey shortened the dress.
     b. *Corey shortened an inch off the dress.

(77) a. Shannon put/*filled the groceries into the bag.
    b. Shannon filled/*put the bag with the groceries.

(78) a. Shawn obtained the rare metal from Transylvania.
    b. *Shawn obtained Transylvania of the rare metal.

Such verbs also cannot undergo event composition, which adds another subevent, since they already have a maximally articulated event structure, thus, the unacceptability of *The clumsy child broke his knuckles raw* and *The stage-hand dimmed the scene dark.*[15] Having a simple event structure is a necessary, but not sufficient, condition for both object alternations and event composition. Complex event structures consist of two parts, a causing subevent and a result subevent. Result subevents fall into different types, giving rise to different types of complex events, and variants in argument alternations can be distinguished by the associated type of result, such as being located or existing. When verbs with manner roots are found in a complex event structure, the type of result must be one that can be naturally obtained given the type of manner. Thus, only verbs with roots describing manners relevant to obtaining a range of result types can show multiple argument realization options. The verb *sew* has such a root, and, indeed, it is found in the locative alternation, as in (79), the material–product alternation, as in (80), and in an "attachment" alternation, as in (81).

(79) a. Kelly sewed bows on the costume.
    b. Kelly sewed the costume with bows.

(80) a. Kelly sewed the piece of silk into a ball gown.
    b. Kelly sewed a ball gown out of the piece of silk.

(81) a. Kelly sewed the lining to the skirt.
    b. Kelly sewed the lining and skirt together.

In contrast, a verb whose root describes a manner used to obtain a very specific result should not display a range of alternations. The verb *vacuum*, which takes its name from an instrument designed to remove stuff from surfaces, is only found in the removing form of the locative alternation.

(82) a. I vacuumed the rug.
    b. I vacuumed the crumbs off the rug.

(83) a. *I vacuumed the rug with crumbs.
    b. *I vacuumed the crumbs onto the rug.

(84) a. *I vacuumed the crumbs into a pile.
    b. *I vacuumed a pile out of the crumbs.

This approach accommodates the limited productivity of argument alternations, whether in the form of new verbs or one-shot innovations. If new verbs have roots of the appropriate type, they should show alternations. If an existing verb has a manner root associated with a real-world happening that might on some occasion be the manner of bringing about some result, then the verb can be used to describe the appropriate derived complex event, giving rise to a one-shot innovation.

To conclude, accounts of argument alternations must explain the distribution of verbs across alternations, including the limited productivity of these alternations. Accounts that include both necessary and sufficient conditions are most successful at meeting this challenge, particularly when the necessary conditions are stated in terms of event structure and the sufficient conditions in terms of the root. Such accounts emphasize once again how much can be gained from a better understanding of how roots and event structure are integrated, yet much remains to be done to fully understand how this integration happens.

Notes

1   The conative alternation should be distinguished from "differential object marking," where the morphosyntactic expression of the object of a transitive verb alternates, for instance, between accusative and either dative or genitive case. The choice of case depends on semantic properties such as the animacy or definiteness of the NP filling the object position, making differential object marking "filler"-driven in the sense of section 6.4.2. In contrast, the conative alternation depends on event-based properties of the object. Differential object marking is not accompanied by any change in meaning, again unlike the conative alternation.

2   The idea that semantic compositionality is not exclusively associated with phrases and idiosyncrasy is not solely associated with words is also adopted by researchers who are not proponents of the constructional approach. This idea, for example, underlies Di Sciullo and Williams' (1987) notion "listeme," which can be a word, a phrase, or a sentence. What sets the constructionists apart, however, is that they take it to be a nontrivial and challenging task to explicate the nature of what is listed and how it enters into combination with other listed elements; others tend to view this task as trivial and not of central concern.

3   The successful transfer inference itself needs an explanation. We believe that it arises from Gricean considerations working in conjunction with the information structure and heaviness considerations discussed in section 7.3.

4   We draw primarily on the discussion of the locative alternation in Croft (1998), as it is more extensive than that in Croft (1991). Nevertheless, we illustrate the relevant causal chains using the notation of Croft (1991) to maintain consistency with the discussion in section 4.3. Croft (1998) presents these causal chains in a slightly different notation, but the particulars of interest have not changed fundamentally. See Croft (1998: 58–59) for discussion of the motivation for revising the notation.

5   We use the labels "given" and "new," recognizing that this basic dichotomy has received a variety of "aliases," to cite E. Prince (1981: 225). Thus, alongside the discussions of "given" or "old" vs. "new," there are discussions of "theme" vs. "rheme," "topic" vs. "focus" or "comment," and "presupposition" vs. "assertion";

furthermore, E. Prince (1981) suggests additional refinements under the "given-new" heading. What matters is that something akin to the given vs. new dichotomy is central to all work on information structure. See Chafe (1976), Gundel (1978, 1985), Lambrecht (1994), Polinsky (1999), E. Prince (1981), Reinhart (1982), Vallduví (1992), among others, for discussion of foundational issues in this area.

6 Our assumption is that information structure may force a choice between alternative argument realization options in some circumstances, but that it is not itself the source of these alternate options, even though some researchers suggest that it is. Typically, these researchers view grammatical relations as grammaticalizations of discourse notions: a subject is a primary topic and a direct object is a secondary topic. The dative alternation arises because a three-argument verb such as *give* allows either its theme or recipient to be a secondary topic, and, hence, realizable as an object (Givón 1984a, 1984b). We do not pursue such approaches since grammatical relations are unlikely to be grammaticalizations of discourse notions in all languages and since variant choice does not correlate with information-packaging considerations in all argument alternations.

7 There are a range of understandings of heaviness or weight, which are reviewed and evaluated in Wasow (1997, 2002). We do not choose among them since we are simply concerned with establishing that such considerations can result in one variant in an alternation to be preferred to a second.

8 If the causative analysis of sentences with verbs of manner of motion in combination with directional phrases turned out to be valid, then the verbs found in such examples might show a causative morpheme in some languages, just as lexically causative verbs do (Haspelmath 1993). We have found no evidence of such morphological marking, and neither have Van Valin and LaPolla (1997: 101). Van Valin and LaPolla further point out that where causative forms of verbs of manner of motion do exist, they are understood to be the causatives of the simple, manner-of-motion sense (e.g., *The guards shuffled the unruly teenagers out of the room*). Thus, the morphologies of languages support a causative analysis for verbs of change of state like *break* or *dry*, but not for verbs of manner of motion in combination with directional phrases.

9 Earlier analyses were purely syntactic, attributing the distribution of the fake reflexive to a constraint that a result phrase only be predicated of a direct object (see sections 4.2.4 and 4.2.5). Since the sole argument of an unaccusative verb is an underlying object, (49a) and (50a) meet the "Direct Object Restriction" directly. In contrast, the sole argument of an unergative verb is an underlying subject, so a fake reflexive object allows a result phrase to be predicated of the subject in (48a), while meeting the direct object restriction (Bresnan and Zaenen 1990; B. Levin and Rappaport Hovav 1995; Rothstein 1992). However, a nonsyntactic account, such as the one offered here, may be preferable since the Direct Object Restriction faces empirical problems (Rappaport Hovav and B. Levin 2001; Verspoor 1997; Wechsler 1997), which cast doubt on the viability of a syntactic account. One problem is presented by result phrases predicated of the subject of a transitive verb, as in *The wise men followed the star out of Bethlehem* (Wechsler 1997: 313, (15a)). Also problematic are minimal pairs where a verb–result phrase combination occurs with or without a fake reflexive, as in *The hostage kicked (himself) free* (Rappaport Hovav and B. Levin 2001: 774). In these pairs there is no semantic difference that the presence or absence of the fake reflexive can be tied to, yet such a difference is critical to the

analysis of similar pairs such as *Jordan swam clear of the oncoming boat/Jordan swam himself sober*, which share a verb, but have distinct result phrases (B. Levin and Rappaport Hovav 1995).

10 Kaufmann and Wunderlich (1998) propose that resultatives based on unaccusative verbs are weak resultatives, whereas those based on unergative verbs are strong resultatives since the former but not the latter imply a change of state; however, Rappaport Hovav and B. Levin (2001) show that the dichotomy does not fall neatly along these lines and present data inconsistent with their analysis. Consider, for example, *The clothes steamed dry*: the result state is not lexically entailed by the verb, as in a strong resultative, yet the syntax is that of a weak resultative.

11 There is considerable agreement that there is a morphophonological or etymological explanation for why some verbs do not show the dative alternation (e.g., Green 1974; Oehrle 1976; Pinker 1989). The failure of certain verbs (e.g., *describe, donate, explain*) to alternate has been attributed to their Latinate origin (e.g., **The university donated the charity its old computers*), since they contrast with commonly cited alternating verbs in this respect (e.g., *give, sell, send, show*). Grimshaw (1989), however, suggests that the constraint is prosodic. Nevertheless, such factors cannot explain all the distributional facts since some verbs that fail to alternate, such as verbs of manner of speaking (e.g., *mumble, scream*), are not Latinate.

12 Pinker's (1989) work is motivated by learnability considerations, and researchers in first and second language acquisition have further explored and sometimes critiqued the broad- vs. narrow-range rule distinction itself (e.g., Bley-Vroman and Yoshinaga 1992; Bowerman 1996).

13 Kay's (2000) reduction of senses is effected by recognizing something akin to what Koenig and Davis (2001) call "sublexical modality," which is akin to what Croft (2003a: 62) calls "modulation": the modal, negation, or temporal operators that modify the "situational core" shared by certain verbs. For instance, *promise* and *give* share a situational core, but differ in sublexical modality: "a promise entails a transfer of possession in models in which the set of circumstances is restricted to those in which people honor their promises …With respect to these restricted models, the characteristic entailments of recipients go through; in those worlds, if you are promised something, you receive something" (Koenig and Davis 2001: 85). Sublexical modality, then, could be part of what we have called the verb root, while the situational core corresponds to an event structure.

14 For more on the division of the verb lexicon into manner and result verbs, see B. Levin and Rappaport Hovav (1991, 1995), who draw on ideas that go back to Talmy (1975, 1985) and on work on child language acquisition (Behrend 1990; Gentner 1978; Pinker 1989).

15 Change-of-state verbs are sometimes found with a result-like PP, as in *He broke the mirror into fragments*, but in these examples the PP further specifies the result encoded in the verb and, thus, does not introduce an added event. We hope to deal with more problematic examples, such as *Tory broke the eggs into the bowl*, in future work.

8

Postscript

Over thirty-five years have passed since the publication of Fillmore's "The Case for Case" (1968), the first substantive generative attempt to lay out a program of deriving the morphosyntactic realization of a verb's arguments from relevant semantic properties. In this book we have reviewed a considerable number of issues pertaining to this research program. In this postscript we step back from the myriad details and take stock of the overall picture which has emerged, asking how our understanding of this complex area has advanced since Fillmore's seminal paper. In the introduction we set out the issues which a comprehensive theory of argument realization must address. We now use these issues as a framework for summarizing the results presented in our survey of argument realization, reviewing what kind of consensus has emerged with respect to each. As we stressed at the outset, we do not present results meant to be embedded in any particular theory of grammar, and we have tried to abstract away from issues which divide linguists of different theoretical persuasions. We believe that a body of knowledge has accumulated about which there should be little dispute and which needs to be taken into consideration in developing a theory of argument realization regardless of the larger grammatical framework in which it is couched.

Which elements of meaning are relevant for the mapping from lexical semantics to morphosyntactic expression? As mentioned in the conclusion to chapter 4, broadly speaking these are aspectual notions, causal notions, and notions related to sentience or potential volitionality. These are all event-based notions – that is, notions derived from entailments which a verb imposes on its arguments by virtue of the parts they play in the event it describes. In chapters 4 and 6 we pointed out that the properties of the "fillers" of these roles – that is, the individuals referred to by the noun phrases corresponding to the arguments of the verbs – also contribute to argument realization, though apparently in a restricted way. Specifically, what is relevant is the salience of the fillers, as defined by notions such as animacy and definiteness. Furthermore, there might be relatively fine-grained semantic subregularities defining semantic subclasses of verbs that enter into the assignment of "semantic" cases or prepositions to some of their arguments. Such a subregularity might underlie the use of instrumental case to indicate the nonagent argument of Russian verbs of governing, authority, and disposition (see section 1.5). Such limited generalizations must find a place in a comprehensive theory of argument realization, even though we have ignored them.

What form should a lexical semantic representation take that encompasses the components of meaning which determine argument realization? As reviewed in chapter 2, semantic role lists prove inadequate. Rather, what is necessary is a lexical semantic representation that explicitly encodes properties of events, including their "subeventual" structure – a desideratum recognized by the now common use of the term "event structure" to refer to such representations. Event structures have a well-articulated internal structure, with most theories distinguishing between what we have characterized as the structural facets of meaning, which define the basic pool of event types relevant to argument realization, and the root, which represents idiosyncratic information, distinguishing among events of the same type. We have emphasized that not only is the structural facet of meaning relevant to argument realization generalizations, but so is the root, a point we return to below.

What is the nature of the mapping from lexical semantics to syntax? We showed, particularly in chapter 6, that it is not possible to derive all facets of argument realization from the "structure" of the event structure alone. Nevertheless, the realization of arguments seems to respect the geometry of event structure: structural prominence relations in the event structure are preserved in the syntax. It also appears that the complexity of event structure is reflected in argument realization. Certain event-based properties, such as sentience, which are not obviously derivable from the geometry of event structure, are also relevant to argument realization. In addition, as just mentioned, certain semantic characteristics of the fillers of the argument positions also influence argument realization. We suggest that event-based semantic notions determine the grammatical relations borne by arguments, while filler-based notions are determinants of the morphosyntactic realization of the grammatical relations. Therefore, any theory of the morphosyntactic expression of arguments has to make reference to an event structure enriched by some statement of properties of the arguments of the verb and of the fillers of these arguments, though these different facets must be kept distinct.

To what extent do nonsemantic factors such as information-packaging and heaviness interact with argument realization? As discussed in chapter 7, some argument alternations are the by-product of a verb being associated with more than one lexical semantic representation. In addition, there are "pure" argument alternations, such as locative inversion, involving no detectable semantic difference between the variants. In some accounts, it is the algorithm mapping from lexical semantics to syntax which allows more than one morphosyntactic realization for a given event structure; in others, some mechanism other than the mapping algorithm, such as a syntactic transformation, gives rise to alternative surface realizations. However, particularly where there is little or no truth-conditional difference between the variants, the variant chosen appears to be largely governed by factors such as the information-structure status and heaviness of the arguments. We suggest that even in these instances the semantics of the root is relevant, as we elaborate below.

To what extent are the semantic determinants of argument realization lexical and to what extent are they nonlexical? As reviewed, there is disagreement over whether or not the type of information encoded in an event structure should be considered lexical; it is this question which is at the heart of the constructional vs. projectionist debate. There is a widespread belief that the semantics of the root, which is indubitably lexical, is not relevant to argument realization and only the event structure associated with a verb, which in some theories is nonlexical, determines argument realization. In this spirit, Fillmore (1970) suggests that only the components of meaning encoded in his semantic role lists are linguistically relevant. As he puts it, the difference between *hit* and *break* is the concern of the linguist, while the difference between *break, shatter*, and *smash* on the one hand and *bump, hit, slam*, and *strike* on the other is the concern of the lexicographer. As should be evident from section 7.5, however, the meaning associated with the root is relevant to generalizations concerning argument realization. We now elaborate this point.

Throughout this book and in other work, we have stressed that object alternations are restricted to verbs which are lexically associated with a simple event structure and that this property follows from the nature of the mapping from event structure to morphosyntactic realization. As far as we know, this constraint is obeyed by all languages. This constraint, however, considerably underdetermines the range of object alternations possible in any language, as the discussion in section 7.5 illustrates. For example, many verbs like *hit* alternate in English (e.g., *Kim hit the fence with the stick/Kim hit the stick against the fence*), but they do not alternate in many other languages. Even in English, *bang, beat, bump, hit*, and *kick* alternate, while the semantically similar *clobber, club, punch*, and *spank* do not (e.g., *Kim punched the robber with her right fist/*Kim punched her right fist against the robber*) (Dowty 1991; Fillmore 1970; B. Levin 1993). The distribution of verbs across the alternating and nonalternating classes is not completely idiosyncratic, but is governed by fine-grained semantic properties of the events these verbs describe (Dowty 1991, 2000; Pinker 1989). There are several ways to deal with these differences: in languages in which these verbs do not alternate one argument may be lexically associated with a particular preposition or case or the inventory of case markers and prepositions may not allow more than one variant to surface. However these differences are handled, the fine-grained distinctions cannot be captured using traditional semantic roles, the primitive predicates most commonly employed in event structures, or proto-role entailments; rather, they reflect facets of the root. Speakers of English must be aware of these in order to know that certain verbs including *hit* alternate in English and others including *punch* do not, while neither type alternates in, say, Hebrew.

Every language must specify the ways in which roots can combine with basic event types and the ways it can sanction different kinds of event composition. The attested possibilities, in turn, govern its patterns of regular verbal polysemy. The regularities in the pairing of roots with event types is a rich, but neglected, research area. Here, too, the fine-grained semantics of the root, comes into play. For example, Rappaport Hovav and B. Levin (1998a) suggest that "manner" roots are basically associated with activity event structures. However, English allows manner roots to be associated with a wide range of other event types, as manifested in argument alternations and other forms of multiple argument realization. For this reason, English allows any manner-of-motion root to be associated with an event type expressing directed motion, as in *Avery ambled into the kitchen* or *Shelby danced off of the stage*. Many languages, however, do not allow word-for-word translations of these sentences. They differ from English in not allowing most verbs of manner of motion to take certain directional complements (Slobin 1987, 1991, 1996, 1997, 2000, 2003; Talmy 1975, 1985, 1991, 2000; Wienold 1995). Yet, even these languages allow a few basic manner-of-motion verbs, such as *run* and *fly*, to take these directional complements (Cummins 1996, 1998; Folli and Ramchand to appear; Martínez Vázquez 2001; Stringer 2003). More generally, we showed in section 7.5 that the distribution of verbs across argument alternations is both partially predictable and partially conventionalized. This combination of properties can be naturally captured in implicational hierarchies of the type mentioned in that section; the two mentioned there encode the likelihood that verbs of particular semantic types participate in the dative (Croft et al. 2001) and causative (Haspelmath 1993) alternations across languages. The classes figuring in these hierarchies also reflect fine-grained distinctions among the roots in much larger classes of verbs, reminiscent of the distinctions drawn by Pinker's (1989) narrow-range rules.

In addition, as Slobin's and Wienold's investigations of the expression of motion events across languages demonstrate, languages vary as to how many roots they have of a particular ontological type. Thus, English and other Germanic languages have a large number of manner-of-motion roots, as reflected in their rich inventory of manner-of-motion verbs (Snell-Hornby 1983), while the Romance languages have far fewer (Slobin 1997: 458–60). The size of the stock of a particular type of root in a given language may have far-reaching effects. For instance, it might partly determine how many verbs participate in each argument alternation. The locative alternation, for example, is attested in many languages, but these languages vary with respect to how many verbs show the alternation. English has about fifty alternating verbs (B. Levin 1993; Pinker 1989), while Hebrew and Italian have very few. This difference in the size of the alternating verb inventory might be traced to a general predisposition in English to lexicalize verbs with distinct manner roots. These would include verbs with roots specifying particular manners of placing, while restricting both the nature of the stuff and of the surface or container – the type of roots which characterize locative alternation verbs (Pinker 1989).

The fine-grained semantics of the root is relevant to another facet of argument realization. In B. Levin and Rappaport Hovav (1995: chapter 6), we demonstrate that locative inversion is not restricted to a particular semantic class of verbs, though verbs in some semantic classes are more likely to show locative inversion than those in other classes. The same holds of the dative alternation, as Bresnan and Nikitina's (2003) corpus study shows. Specifically, locative inversion is associated with a particular discourse function – roughly characterizable as presentational focus (Birner 1992, 1994) – and B. Levin and Rappaport Hovav (1995) show in great detail that verbs from some semantic classes are likely to be favored in locative inversion because their meaning naturally fits the discourse function of the construction (see also Birner 1995). It is only through a careful study of the semantics of the verbs that the distribution of verbs in this construction can be fully understood.

In chapter 1 we stressed the importance of isolating the "grammatically relevant" facets of verb meaning. Most linguists take this type of meaning to be what we characterized as the "structural" components of verb meaning. How does this convergence fit in with our repeated assertion that the semantics of the root is important to many facets of argument realization? We suggest that the basic mapping from event structure to syntax is indeed governed by a relatively small set of semantic notions: the grammatically relevant facets of meaning expressed in an event structure. However, the semantics of the root determines the range of event structures a particular verb is associated with, the distribution of semantic cases, and the compatibility of a verb with particular modes of information-packaging.

It is perhaps fitting to conclude this book with the observation that the lexical semantics of the root determines in many complex ways different facets of argument realization. This observation is worthy of note in light of a recent trend towards shifting the burden of explanation to extralexical factors. Although such factors are clearly present, the recognition that lexical semantic factors are still very relevant affirms research programs that pay close attention to the lexical semantics of verbs, despite the notoriously elusive nature of word meaning.

References

Abusch, D. (1986) "Verbs of Change, Causation, and Time," Report CSLI-86–50, Center for the Study of Language and Information, Stanford University, Stanford, CA.

Ackema, P. and M. Schoorlemmer (1994) "The Middle Construction and the Syntax-Semantics Interface," *Lingua* 93, 59–90.

Ackerman, F. (1992) "Complex Predicates and Morpholexical Relatedness: Locative Alternation in Hungarian," in I. A. Sag and A. Szabolcsi, eds. (1992), 55–83.

Ackerman, F. and J. Moore (1999) "'Telic Entity' as a Proto-property of Lexical Predicates," *Proceedings of the LFG99 Conference*, CSLI Publications, Center for the Study of Language and Information, Stanford University, Stanford, CA.

(2001) *Proto-properties and Grammatical Encoding: A Correspondence Theory of Argument Selection*, CSLI Publications, Center for the Study of Language and Information, Stanford University, Stanford, CA.

Aikhenvald, A. Y. (2000) "Transitivity in Tariana," in R. M. W. Dixon and A. Y. Aikhenvald, eds., *Changing Valency: Case Studies in Transitivity*, Cambridge University Press, Cambridge, 145–72.

Aissen, J. (1999) "Markedness and Subject Choice in Optimality Theory," *Natural Language and Linguistic Theory* 17, 673–711.

(2003) "Differential Object Marking: Iconicity vs. Economy," *Natural Language and Linguistic Theory* 21, 435–83.

Aitchison, J. (1994) *Words in the Mind*, Blackwell, Oxford. (Second edition.)

Akmajian, A. and F. Heny (1975) *An Introduction to the Principles of Transformational Syntax*, MIT Press, Cambridge, MA.

Alalou, A. and P. Farrell (1993) "Argument Structure and Causativization in Tamazight Berber," *Journal of African Languages and Linguistics* 14, 155–86.

Alexiadou, A., ed. (2002) *Theoretical Approaches to Universals*, John Benjamins, Amsterdam.

Allen, C. L. (1986) "Reconsidering the History of *Like*," *Journal of Linguistics* 22, 375–409.

(1995) *Case Marking and Reanalysis: Grammatical Relations from Old to Early Modern English*, Oxford University Press, Oxford.

Allen, K. (1987) "Hierarchies and the Choice of Left Conjuncts (with Particular Attention to English)," *Journal of Linguistics* 23, 51–77.

Alsina, A. (1994) "Bantu Multiple Objects: Analyses and Fallacies," *Linguistic Analysis* 24, 153–74.

(1996) *The Role of Argument Structure in Grammar*, CSLI Publications, Center for the Study of Language and Information, Stanford University, Stanford, CA.

(1999) "Where's the Mirror Principle?," *The Linguistic Review* 16, 1–42.

Alsina, A., J. Bresnan, and P. Sells, eds. (1997) *Complex Predicates*, CSLI Publications, Center for the Study of Language and Information, Stanford University, Stanford, CA.

Alsina, A. and S. Joshi (1991) "Parameters in Causative Constructions," *CLS 27, Part 1: Papers from the General Session*, Chicago Linguistic Society, Chicago, IL, 1–15.

Alsina, A. and S. A. Mchombo (1993) "Object Asymmetries and the Chicheŵa Applicative Construction," in S. A. Mchombo, ed. (1993), 1–46.

Amberber, M. (2002a) "Quirky Alternations of Transitivity: The Case of Ingestive Predicates", in M. Amberber and P. Collins, eds., *Language Universals and Variation*, Praeger, Westport, CT, 1–20.

(2002b) *Verb Classes and Transitivity in Amharic*, LINCOM Europa, Munich.

Anderson, J. M. (1971) *The Grammar of Case*, Cambridge University Press, Cambridge.

(1977) *On Case Grammar*, Humanities Press, Atlantic Highlands, NJ.

Anderson, M. (1978) "NP Preposing in Noun Phrases," *NELS 8*, Graduate Linguistics Student Association, University of Massachusetts, Amherst, MA, 12–21.

(1979) "Noun Phrase Structure," Doctoral dissertation, University of Connecticut, Storrs, CT.

(1983–4) "Prenominal Genitive NPs," *The Linguistic Review* 3, 1–24.

Anderson, S. R. (1971) "On the Role of Deep Structure in Semantic Interpretation," *Foundations of Language* 7, 387–96.

(1977) "Comments on the Paper by Wasow," in P. Culicover, T. Wasow, and A. Akmajian, eds. (1977), 361–77.

Andrews, A. D. (1985) "The Major Functions of the Noun Phrase," in T. Shopen, ed., *Language Typology and Syntactic Description I: Clause Structure*, Cambridge University Press, Cambridge, 62–154.

Aoun, J. and Y. A. Li (1989) "Scope and Constituency," *Linguistic Inquiry* 20, 141–72.

Arad, M. (1998) "VP-Structure and the Syntax-Lexicon Interface," Doctoral dissertation, University College London, London.

(1999) "What Counts as a Class? The Case of Psych-verbs," *Papers from the UPenn/MIT Roundtable on the Lexicon*, MIT Working Papers in Linguistics 35, Department of Linguistics and Philosophy, MIT, Cambridge, MA, 1–23.

(2002) "Universal Features and Language-Particular Morphemes," in A. Alexiadou, ed. (2002), 15–39.

Aranovich, R. (2000) "Split Intransitivity and Reflexives in Spanish," *Probus* 12, 165–86.

Aristar, A. R. (1996) "The Relationship between Dative and Locative: Kuryłowicz's Argument from a Typological Perspective," *Diachronica* 13, 207–24.

(1997) "Marking and Hierarchy Types and the Grammaticalization of Case-Markers," *Studies in Language* 21, 313–68.

Arnold, J. E., T. Wasow, A. Losongco, and R. Ginstrom (2000) "Heaviness vs. Newness: The Effects of Structural Complexity and Discourse Status on Constituent Ordering," *Language* 76, 28–55.

Artstein, R. (1998) "Hierarchies," unpublished ms., Rutgers University, New Brunswick, NJ.

Asudeh, A. (2001) "Linking, Optionality, and Ambiguity in Marathi," in P. Sells, ed., *Formal and Empirical Issues in Optimality Theoretic Syntax*, CSLI Publications, Center for the Study of Language and Information, Stanford University, Stanford, CA, 257–312.

Bach, E. (1981) "On Time, Tense, and Aspect: An Essay in English Metaphysics," in P. Cole, ed. (1981), 63–81.

(1986) "The Algebra of Events," *Linguistics and Philosophy* 9, 5–16.

Baker, M. C. (1985) "Incorporation: A Theory of Grammatical Function Changing," Doctoral dissertation, MIT, Cambridge, MA.

(1988) *Incorporation: A Theory of Grammatical Function Changing*, University of Chicago Press, Chicago, IL. (Revision of Baker 1985.)

(1989) "Object Sharing and Projection in Serial Verb Constructions," *Linguistic Inquiry* 20, 513–53.

(1996a) "On the Structural Positions of Themes and Goals," in J. Rooryck and L. Zaring, eds. (1996), 7–34.

(1996b) *The Polysynthesis Parameter*, Oxford University Press, New York.

(1997) "Thematic Roles and Syntactic Structure," in L. Haegeman, ed., *Elements of Grammar. Handbook of Generative Syntax*, Kluwer, Dordrecht, 73–137.

(2001) "Phrase Structure as a Representation of 'Primitive' Grammatical Relations," in W. D. Davies and S. Dubinsky, eds., *Objects and Other Subjects: Grammatical Functions, Functional Categories and Configurationality*, Kluwer, Dordrecht, 21–51.

(2003) *Lexical Categories: Verbs, Nouns, and Adjectives*, Cambridge University Press, Cambridge.

Barker, C. and D. Dowty (1993) "Non-verbal Thematic Proto-Roles," *NELS* 23, Graduate Linguistics Student Association, University of Massachusetts, Amherst, MA, 49–62.

Barss, A. and H. Lasnik (1986) "A Note on Anaphora and Double Objects," *Linguistic Inquiry* 17, 347–54.

Basilico, D. (1998) "Object Position and Predication Forms," *Natural Language and Linguistic Theory* 16, 541–95.

Behagel, O. (1909/10) "Beziehungen zwischen Umfang und Reihenfolge von Satzgliedern," *Indogermanische Forschungen* 25, 110–42.

Behrend, D. A. (1990) "The Development of Verb Concepts: Children's Use of Verbs to Label Familiar and Novel Events," *Child Development* 61, 681–96.

Belletti, A. and L. Rizzi (1988) "Psych-verbs and Θ-Theory," *Natural Language and Linguistic Theory* 6, 291–352.

Benua, L. (2000) "Yup'ik Antipassive and the AspP Hypothesis," *Indigenous Languages*, University of Massachusetts Occasional Papers in Linguistics 20, Graduate Linguistics Student Association, University of Massachusetts, Amherst, MA, 107–38.

Bertinetto, P. M. and M. Squartini (1995) "An Attempt at Defining the Class of 'Gradual Completion' Verbs," in P. M. Bertinetto, V. Bianchi, J. Higginbotham, and M. Squartini, eds., *Temporal Reference Aspect and Actionality, 1: Semantic and Syntactic Perspectives*, Rosenberg and Sellier, Turin, 11–26.

Binnick, R. (1969) "On the Nature of the 'Lexical Item,'" *CLS* 4, Chicago Linguistic Society, Chicago, IL, 1–13.

(1991) *Time and the Verb: A Guide to Tense and Aspect*, Oxford University Press, Oxford.

Birner, B. J. (1992) "The Discourse Function of Inversion in English," Doctoral dissertation, Northwestern University, Evanston, IL.

(1994) "Information Status and Word Order: An Analysis of English Inversion," *Language* 70, 233–59.

(1995) "Pragmatic Constraints on the Verb in English Inversion," *Lingua* 97, 233–56.

Birner, B. J. and G. Ward (1998) *Information Status and Noncanonical Word Order in English*, John Benjamins, Amsterdam.

Bittner, M. and K. Hale (1996) "The Structural Determination of Case and Agreement," *Linguistic Inquiry* 27, 1–68.

Blake, B. J. (1977) *Case Marking in Australian Languages*, Australian Institute of Aboriginal Studies, Canberra.

(2001) *Case*, Cambridge University Press, Cambridge. (Second edition.)

Bley-Vroman, R. and N. Yoshinaga (1992) "Broad and Narrow Constraints on the English Dative Alternation: Some Fundamental Differences between Native Speakers and Foreign Language Learners," *University of Hawaii Working Papers in ESL* 11, Department of ESL, University of Hawaii, Manoa, HI, 157–99.

Blume, K. (1998) "A Contrastive Analysis of Interaction Verbs with Dative Complements," *Linguistics* 36, 253–80.

Boas, H. C. (2000) "Resultative Constructions in English and German," Doctoral dissertation, University of North Carolina at Chapel Hill, Chapel Hill, NC.

(2003) *A Constructional Approach to Resultatives*, CSLI Publications, Center for the Study of Language and Information, Stanford University, Stanford, CA. (Revision of Boas 2000.)

Bobaljik, J. D. (1992) "Nominally Absolutive is not Absolutely Nominative," *WCCFL* 11, Stanford Linguistics Association, Stanford, CA, 44–60.

Bolinger, D. (1965) "The Atomization of Meaning," *Language* 41, 555–73.

(1977) *Form and Meaning*, Longman, London.

Borer, H. (1994) "The Projection of Arguments," *Functional Projections*, University of Massachusetts Occasional Papers 17, Graduate Linguistics Student Association, University of Massachusetts, Amherst, MA, 19–47.

(1998) "Passive without Theta Grids," in S. G. Lapointe, D. K. Brentari, and P. M. Farrell, eds., *Morphological Interfaces*, CSLI Publications, Center for the Study of Language and Information, Stanford University, Stanford, CA, 60–99.

(2003a) "Exo-skeletal vs. Endo-skeletal Explanations: Syntactic Projections and the Lexicon," in J. Moore and M. Polinsky, eds., *The Nature of Explanation in Linguistic Theory*, CSLI Publications, Center for the Study of Language and Information, Stanford, CA, 31–67.

(2003b) "The Grammar Machine," in A. Alexiadou, E. Anagnostopoulou, and M. Everaert, eds., *The Unaccusativity Puzzle*, Oxford University Press, Oxford, 288–331.

(in press a) *Structuring Sense 1: In Name Only*, Oxford University Press, Oxford.

(in press b) *Structuring Sense 2: The Normal Course of Events*, Oxford University Press, Oxford.

Borer, H. and Y. Grodzinsky (1986) "Syntactic Cliticization and Lexical Cliticization: The Case of Hebrew Dative Clitics," in H. Borer, ed., *Syntax and Semantics 19: The Syntax of Pronominal Clitics*, Academic Press, New York.

Bossong, G. (1991) "Differential Object Marking in Romance and Beyond," in D. Wanner and D. A. Kibbee, eds., *New Analyses in Romance Linguistics*, John Benjamins, Amsterdam, 143–70.

(1998) "Le marquage différentiel de l'objet dans les langues d'Europe," in J. Feuillet, ed., *Actance et Valence dans les Langues de l'Europe*, Mouton de Gruyter, Berlin, 193–258.

Bouchard, D. (1995) *The Semantics of Syntax: A Minimalist Approach to Grammar*, University of Chicago Press, Chicago, IL.

Bowerman, M. (1982) "Reorganizational Processes in Lexical and Syntactic Development," in E. Wanner and L. R. Gleitman, eds., *Language Acquisition: The State of the Art*, Cambridge University Press, Cambridge, 319–46.

(1996) "Argument Structure and Learnability: Is a Solution in Sight?," *BLS* 22, Berkeley Linguistics Society, Berkeley, CA, 454–68.

Bowers, J. (1993) "The Syntax of Predication," *Linguistic Inquiry* 24, 591–656.

Bresnan, J. (1980) "Polyadicity: Part I of a Theory of Lexical Rules and Representations," in T. Hoekstra, H. van der Hulst, and M. Moortgat, eds. (1980), 97–121. Also in J. Bresnan, ed. (1982a), 149–72.

ed. (1982a) *The Mental Representation of Grammatical Relations*, MIT Press, Cambridge, MA.

(1982b) "The Passive in Lexical Theory," in J. Bresnan, ed. (1982a), 3–86.

(1982c) "Control and Complementation," *Linguistic Inquiry* 13, 343–434. Also in J. Bresnan, ed. (1982a), 282–390.

(1994) "Linear Order vs. Syntactic Rank: Evidence from Weak Crossover," *CLS 30, Part 1: Papers from the Main Session*, Chicago Linguistic Society, Chicago, IL, 57–89.

(2001) *Lexical-Functional Syntax*, Blackwell, Oxford.

Bresnan, J. and J. Kanerva (1989) "Locative Inversion in Chicheŵa: A Case Study of Factorization in Grammar," *Linguistic Inquiry* 20, 1–50. Reprinted in T. Stowell and E. Wehrli, eds. (1992), 53–101.

(1992) "The Thematic Hierarchy and Locative Inversion in UG. A Reply to Paul Schachter's Comments," in T. Stowell and E. Wehrli, eds. (1992), 111–25.

Bresnan, J. and L. Moshi (1990) "Object Asymmetries in Comparative Bantu Syntax," *Linguistic Inquiry* 21, 147–85. Also published in S. A. Mchombo, ed. (1993), 47–92.

Bresnan, J. and T. Nikitina (2003) "Categoricity and Gradience in the Dative Alternation," unpublished ms., Stanford University, Stanford, CA.

Bresnan, J. and A. Zaenen (1990) "Deep Unaccusativity in LFG," in K. Dziwirek, P. Farrell and E. Mejías-Bikandi, eds., *Grammatical Relations: A Cross-Theoretical Perspective*, Center for the Study of Language and Information, Stanford University, Stanford, CA, 45–57.

Brinkmann, U. (1997) *The Locative Alternation in German*, John Benjamins, Amsterdam.

Brinton, L. J. (1988) *The Development of English Aspectual Systems: Aspectualizers and Post-Verbal Particles*, Cambridge University Press, Cambridge.

Bruening, B. (2001) "QR Obeys Superiority: Frozen Scope and ACD," *Linguistic Inquiry* 32, 233–73.

Burzio, L. (1986) *Italian Syntax: A Government-Binding Approach*, Reidel, Dordrecht.

Butt, M. (1995) *The Structure of Complex Predicates in Urdu*, CSLI Publications, Center for the Study of Language and Information, Stanford University, Stanford, CA.

Butt, M., M. Dalrymple, and A. Frank (1997) "An Architecture for Linking Theory in LFG," *Proceedings of the LFG97 Conference.* http://www-csli.stanford.edu/publications/

Butt, M. and W. Geuder (1998a) "Introduction," in M. Butt and W. Geuder, eds. (1998b), 1–20.

eds. (1998b) *The Projection of Arguments: Lexical and Syntactic Constraints*, CSLI Publications, Center for the Study of Language and Information, Stanford University, Stanford, CA.

Carrier-Duncan, J. (1985) "Linking of Thematic Roles in Derivational Word Formation," *Linguistic Inquiry* 16, 1–34.

Carrier, J. and J. H. Randall (1992) "The Argument Structure and Syntactic Structure of Resultatives," *Linguistic Inquiry* 23, 173–234.

(1993) "Lexical Mapping," in E. Reuland and W. Abraham, eds. (1993), 119–42.

Carstens, V. (2002) "Antisymmetry and Word Order in Serial Constructions," *Language* 78, 3–50.

Carter, R. J. (1976) "Some Constraints on Possible Words," *Semantikos* 1, 27–66.

  (1977) "Towards a Linking Grammar of English," *Recherches Linguistiques* 4, Université de Paris VIII, Vincennes, 13–31. Reprinted in B. Levin and C. Tenny, eds. (1988), 93–108.

  (1978) "Arguing for Semantic Representations," in *Recherches Linguistiques* 5–6, Université de Paris VIII, Vincennes, 61–92. Reprinted in B. Levin and C. Tenny, eds. (1988), 139–66.

  (1988) "Some Linking Regularities," in B. Levin and C. Tenny, eds. (1988), 1–92. (Written in 1976.)

Centineo, G. (1986) "A Lexical Theory of Auxiliary Selection in Italian," *Davis Working Papers in Linguistics 1*, Department of Linguistics, University of California, Davis, CA, 1–35.

  (1996) "A Lexical Theory of Auxiliary Selection in Italian," *Probus* 8, 223–71.

Chafe, W. (1976) "Givenness, Contrastiveness, Definiteness, Subjects, Topics and Point of View," in C. N. Li, ed. (1976), 25–56.

Channon, R. (1980) "On Place Advancements in English and Russian," in C. V. Chvany and R. D. Brecht, eds., *Morphosyntax in Slavic*, Slavica, Columbus, OH, 114–38.

Chierchia, G. (1983) "Outline of a Semantic Theory of (Obligatory) Control," *WCCFL* 2, Stanford Linguistics Association, Stanford, CA, 19–31.

Chomsky, N. (1957) *Syntactic Structures*, Mouton, The Hague.

  (1965) *Aspects of the Theory of Syntax*, MIT Press, Cambridge, MA.

  (1970) "Remarks on Nominalization," in R. A. Jacobs and P. S. Rosenbaum, eds. (1970), 184–221.

  (1981) *Lectures on Government and Binding*, Foris, Dordrecht.

  (1986) *Knowledge of Language: Its Nature, Origin and Use*, Praeger, New York.

  (1991) "Some Notes on Economy of Derivation and Representation," in R. Freidin, ed., *Principles and Parameters in Comparative Grammar*, MIT Press, Cambridge, MA.

  (1995) *The Minimalist Program*, MIT Press, Cambridge, MA.

Chung, S. (1976) "An Object-Creating Rule in Bahasa Indonesia," *Linguistic Inquiry* 7, 41–87.

Clark, E. V. (1978) "Discovering What Words Can Do," *Papers from the Parasession on the Lexicon*, Chicago Linguistic Society, Chicago, IL, 34–57.

Clark E. V. and K. L. Carpenter (1988) "On Children's Uses of *from, by* and *with* in Oblique Noun Phrases," *Journal of Child Language* 16, 349–64.

  (1989) "The Notion of Source in Language Acquisition," *Language* 65, 1–30.

Clark, E. V. and H. H. Clark (1979) "When Nouns Surface as Verbs," *Language* 55, 767–811.

Cole, P., ed. (1981) *Radical Pragmatics*, Academic Press, New York.

Cole, P. and J. M. Sadock, eds. (1977) *Syntax and Semantics 8: Grammatical Relations*, Academic Press, New York.

Comrie, B. (1975) "Review of R. S. Jackendoff: *Semantic Interpretation in Generative Grammar*," *Linguistics* 160, 71–85.

  (1976a) *Aspect*, Cambridge University Press, Cambridge.

  (1976b) "The Syntax of Causative Constructions: Cross-Language Similarities and Divergences," in M. Shibatani, ed. (1976), 261–312.

  (1989) *Language Universals and Linguistic Typology*, University of Chicago Press, Chicago, IL. (Second edition.)

Coopmans, P., M. Everaert, and J. Grimshaw, eds. (2000) *Lexical Specification and Insertion*, John Benjamins, Amsterdam.

Cook, W. A. (1989) *Case Grammar Theory*, Georgetown University Press, Washington, DC.

Corbett, G. G. (2000) *Number*, Cambridge University Press, Cambridge.

Craig, C. (1976) "Properties of Basic and Derived Subjects in Jacaltec," in C. N. Li, ed. (1976), 99–123.

Crimmins, M. and J. Perry (1989) "The Prince and the Phone Booth: Reporting Puzzling Beliefs," *The Journal of Philosophy* 86, 685–711.

Croft, W. (1986) "Surface Subject Choice of Mental Verbs," presented at the Annual Meeting of the Linguistic Society of America, New York.

(1990) "Possible Verbs and the Structure of Events," in S. L. Tsohatzidis, ed., *Meanings and Prototypes: Studies in Linguistic Categorization*, Routledge, London, 48–73.

(1991) *Syntactic Categories and Grammatical Relations*, University of Chicago Press, Chicago, IL.

(1993) "Case Marking and the Semantics of Mental Verbs," in J. Pustejovsky, ed. (1993), 55–72.

(1994) "The Semantics of Subjecthood," in M. Yaguello, ed., *Subjecthood and Subjectivity: The Status of the Subject in Linguistic Theory*, Ophrys, Paris, 29–75.

(1998) "Event Structure in Argument Linking", in M. Butt and W. Geuder, eds. (1998), 21–63.

(2003a) "Lexical Rules vs. Constructions: A False Dichotomy," in H. Cuyckens, T. Berg, R. Dirven, and K.-U. Panther, eds., *Motivation in Language: Studies in Honor of Günter Radden*, John Benjamins, Amsterdam, 49–68.

(2003b) *Typology and Universals*, Cambridge University Press, Cambridge. (Second edition.)

Croft, W., C. Taoka, and E. J. Wood (2001) "Argument Linking and the Commercial Transaction Frame in English, Russian and Japanese," *Language Sciences* 23, 579–602.

Croft, W., J. Barðdal, W. Hollmann, M. Nielsen, V. Sotirova, and C. Taoka (2001) "Discriminating Verb Meanings: The Case of Transfer Verbs," handout, LAGB Autumn Meeting, Reading.

Cruse, D. A. (1973) "Some Thoughts on Agentivity," *Journal of Linguistics* 9, 11–23.

(1992/93) "On Polylexy," *Dictionaries* 14, 88–96.

(2000) "Aspects of the Micro-structure of Word Meanings," in Y. Ravin and C. Leacock, eds. (2000), 30–51.

Culicover, P., T. Wasow, and A. Akmajian, eds. (1977) *Formal Syntax*, Academic Press, New York.

Culicover, P. and W. Wilkins (1984) *Locality in Linguistic Theory*, Academic Press, New York.

Cummins, S. (1996) "Movement and Direction in French and English," *Toronto Working Papers in Linguistics* 15, Department of Linguistics, University of Toronto, Toronto, Canada, 31–54.

(1998) "Le mouvement directionnel dans une perspective d'analyse monosémique," *Langues et Linguistiques* 24, 47–66.

Davidse, K. (1996) "Ditransitivity and Possession," in R. Hasan, C. Cloran, and D. Butt, eds., *Functional Descriptions: Theory in Practice*, John Benjamins, Amsterdam, 85–144.

(1998) "Agnates, Verb Classes and the Meaning of Construals: The Case of Ditransitivity in English," *Leuvense Bijdragen* 87, 281–313.

Davidson, D. and G. Harman, eds. (1972) *Semantics of Natural Language*, Reidel, Dordrecht.

Davis, A. R. (2001) *Linking by Types in the Hierarchical Lexicon*, CSLI Publications, Center for the Study of Language and Information, Stanford University, Stanford, CA.

Davis, A. R. and J.-P. Koenig (2000) "Linking as Constraints on Word Classes in a Hierarchical Lexicon," *Language* 76, 56–91.

Declerck, R. (1979) "Aspect and the Bounded/Unbounded (Telic/Atelic) Distinction," *Linguistics* 17, 761–94.

DeLancey, S. (1981) "An Interpretation of Split Ergativity and Related Patterns," *Language* 57, 626–57.

(1982) "Lhasa Tibetan: A Case Study in Ergative Typology," *Journal of Linguistic Research* 2:1, 21–31.

(1984) "Notes on Agentivity and Causation," *Studies in Language* 8, 181–213.

(1985) "Agentivity and Syntax," in *Papers from the Parasession on Causatives and Agentivity*, Chicago Linguistic Society, Chicago, IL, 1–12.

(1990) "Ergativity and the Cognitive Model of Event Structure in Lhasa Tibetan," *Cognitive Linguistics* 1, 289–321.

(1991) "Event Construal and Case Role Assignment," *BLS* 17, Berkeley Linguistics Society, Berkeley, CA, 338–53.

(1995) "Verbal Case Frames in English and Tibetan," unpublished ms., Department of Linguistics, University of Oregon, Eugene, OR.

Depraetere, I. (1995) "On the Necessity of Distinguishing between (Un)boundness and (A)telicity," *Linguistics and Philosophy* 18, 1–19.

Dezsö, L. (1982) *Studies in Syntactic Typology and Contrastive Grammar*, Mouton, The Hague.

Diesing, M. (1992) *Indefinites*, MIT Press, Cambridge, MA.

Dik, S. C. (1978) *Functional Grammar*, North-Holland, Amsterdam.

(1980) *Studies in Functional Grammar*, Academic Press, London.

(1997a) *The Theory of Functional Grammar. Part 1: The Structure of the Clause*, Mouton de Gruyter, Berlin. (Second, revised edition; edited by K. Hengeveld.)

(1997b) *The Theory of Functional Grammar. Part 2: Complex and Derived Constructions*, Mouton de Gruyter, Berlin. (Edited by K. Hengeveld.)

Dikken, M. den (1995) *Particles: On the Syntax of Verb-Particle, Triadic, and Causative Constructions*, Oxford University Press, Oxford.

Dimitrova-Vulchanova, M. (1998) "Incremental 'Walls,'" *Nordic Journal of Linguistics* 21, 1–16.

Dimitrova-Vulchanova, M. and G. Giusti (1999) "Possessors in the Bulgarian DP," in M. Dimitrova-Vulchanova and L. Hellan, eds., *Topics in South Slavic Syntax and Semantics*, John Benjamins, Amsterdam, 163–92.

Di Sciullo, A.-M. and E. Williams (1987) *The Definition of Word*, MIT Press, Cambridge, MA.

Dixon, R. M. W. (1972) *The Dyirbal Language of North Queensland*, Cambridge University Press, Cambridge.

(1979) "Ergativity," *Language* 55, 59–138.

(1994) *Ergativity*, Cambridge University Press, Cambridge.

Doron, E. and M. Rappaport Hovav (1991) "Affectedness and Externalization," *NELS* 21, Graduate Linguistics Student Association, University of Massachusetts, Amherst, MA, 81–94.

Dowty, D. R. (1978) "Lexically Governed Transformations as Lexical Rules in a Montague Grammar," *Linguistic Inquiry* 9, 393–426.

(1979) *Word Meaning and Montague Grammar*, Reidel, Dordrecht.

(1989) "On the Semantic Content of the Notion 'Thematic Role,'" in G. Chierchia, B. Partee, and R. Turner, eds., *Properties, Types and Meaning II*, Kluwer, Dordrecht, 69–129.

(1991) "Thematic Proto-Roles and Argument Selection," *Language* 67, 547–619.

(2000) "'The Garden Swarms with Bees' and the Fallacy of 'Argument Alternation,'" in Y. Ravin and C. Leacock, eds. (2000), 111–28.

(2001) "The Semantic Asymmetry of 'Argument Alternations' (and Why It Matters)," *Groninger Arbeiten zur germanistischen Linguistik* 44, Center for Language and Cognition, Groningen.

Duranti, A. (1979) "Object Clitic Pronouns in Bantu and the Topicality Hierarchy," *Studies in African Linguistics* 10, 31–45.

Dziwirek, K. (1994) *Polish Subjects*, Garland, New York.

Egerland, V. (1998) "The Affectedness Constraint and AspP," *Studia Linguistica* 52, 19–47.

Egli, U., P. E. Pause, C. Schwarze, A. von Stechow, and G. Wienold, eds. (1995) *Lexical Knowledge in the Organization of Language*, John Benjamins, Amsterdam.

Emonds, J. (1972) "Evidence that Indirect-Object Movement is a Structure-Preserving Rule," *Foundations of Language* 8, 546–61.

Engelberg, S. (1994) "Valency and Aspectuality," in D. W. Halwachs and I. Stütz, eds., *Sprache, Sprechen, Handeln I*, Niemeyer, Tübingen, 53–59.

—— (1995) "Event Structure and the Meaning of Verbs," in P. Bærentzen, ed., *Aspekte der Sprachbeschreibung*, Niemeyer, Tübingen, 37–41.

—— (1999) "Punctuality and Verb Semantics," *Proceedings of the 23rd Annual Penn Linguistics Colloquium*, Working Papers in Linguistics 6.1, Department of Linguistics, University of Pennsylvania, Philadelphia, PA, 127–40.

—— (2000a) "The Magic of the Moment: What It Means to Be a Punctual Verb," *BLS* 25, Berkeley Linguistics Society, Berkeley, CA, 109–21.

—— (2000b) "Verb Meaning as Event Structure," *LACUS Forum* 26, 257–68.

Erteschik-Shir, N. (1979) "Discourse Constraints on Dative Movement," in T. Givón, ed., *Syntax and Semantics 12: Discourse and Syntax*, Academic Press, New York, 441–67.

Erteschik-Shir, N. and T. R. Rapoport (1996) "Focussing on Lexical Nuclei," *IATL 3: The Proceedings of the Eleventh Annual Conference and of the Workshop on Discourse*, 87–103.

—— (2004) "Bare Aspect: A Theory of Syntactic Projection," in J. Guéron and J. Lecarme, eds. (2004), 217–34.

Evans, N. (1997) "Role or Cast," in A. Alsina, J. Bresnan, and P. Sells, eds. (1997), 397–430.

Everaert, M. and E. Anagnostopoulou (1997) "Thematic Hierarchies and Binding Theory: Evidences from Greek," in F. Corblin, D. Godard, and J.-M. Marandin, eds., *Empirical Issues in Formal Syntax and Semantics*, Peter Lang, Berne, 43–59.

Fagan, S. M. B. (1992) *The Syntax and Semantics of Middle Constructions*, Cambridge University Press, Cambridge.

Fellbaum, C. (1987) "On Nominals with Preposed Themes", *CLS 23, Part 1: Papers from the General Session*, Chicago Linguistic Society, Chicago, IL, 79–92.

Fiengo, R. W. (1980) *Surface Structure: The Interface of Autonomous Components*, Harvard University Press, Cambridge, MA.

Filip, H. (1989) "Aspectual Properties of the *An*-Construction in German," in A. von Werner and T. Janssen, eds., *Tempus-Aspekt-Modus: Die lexikalischen und grammatischen Formen in den germanischen Sprachen*, Niemeyer, Tübingen, 259–92.

—— (1993) "Aspect, Situation Types and Nominal Reference," Doctoral dissertation, University of California, Berkeley, CA.

—— (1996) "Psychological Predicates and the Syntax-Semantics Interface," in A. Goldberg, ed., *Conceptual Structure, Discourse and Language*, CSLI Publications, Center for the Study of Language and Information, Stanford University, Stanford, CA.

—— (1999) *Aspect, Eventuality Types and Nominal Reference*, Garland, New York. (Revision of Filip 1993.)

Fillmore, C. J. (1965) *Indirect Object Constructions in English and the Ordering of Transformations*, Mouton, The Hague.

(1968) "The Case for Case," in E. Bach and R. T. Harms, eds., *Universals in Linguistic Theory*, Holt, Rinehart, and Winston, New York, 1–88.

(1970) "The Grammar of *Hitting* and *Breaking*," in R. Jacobs and P. Rosenbaum, eds. (1970), 120–33.

(1971a) "Some Problems for Case Grammar," in R. J. O'Brien, ed., *Report of the 22nd Annual Roundtable Meeting on Linguistics and Language Studies*, Georgetown University Press, Washington, DC, 35–56.

(1971b) "Types of Lexical Information," in D. Steinberg and L. Jakobovits, eds., *Semantics*, Cambridge University Press, Cambridge, 370–92.

(1977a) "The Case for Case Reopened," in P. Cole and J. M. Sadock, eds. (1977), 59–81.

(1977b) "Topics in Lexical Semantics," in R. W. Cole, ed., *Current Issues in Linguistic Theory*, Indiana University Press, Bloomington, IN, 76–138.

(1986) "Pragmatically Controlled Zero Anaphora," *BLS* 12, Berkeley Linguistics Society, Berkeley, CA, 95–107.

Firbas, J. (1966) "Non-Thematic Subjects in Contemporary English," *Travaux Linguistiques de Prague* 2, University of Alabama Press, Tuscaloosa, AL, 239–56.

Foley, W. A. and R. D. Van Valin, Jr. (1984) *Functional Syntax and Universal Grammar*, Cambridge University Press, Cambridge.

Folli, R. and G. Ramchand (to appear) "Prepositions and Results in Italian and English: An Analysis from Event Decomposition," in H. Verkuyl, H. de Swart, and A. van Hout, eds., *Perspectives on Aspect*, Kluwer, Dordrecht.

Fowler, G. (1996) "Oblique Passivization in Russian," *Slavic and East European Journal* 40, 519–45.

Fraser, B. (1971) "A Note on the *spray paint* Cases," *Linguistic Inquiry* 2, 603–7.

Freed, A. F. (1979) *The Semantics of English Aspectual Complementation*, Reidel, Dordrecht.

Freidin, R. (1975) "Review of R. S. Jackendoff: *Semantic Interpretation in Generative Grammar*," *Language* 51, 189–205.

Fried, M. (1992) "What's in a Causative: The Semantics of Kannada *–isu*," *CLS 28, Part 1: Papers from the Main Session*, Chicago Linguistic Society, Chicago, IL, 171–85.

Fukui, N. and P. Speas (1986) "Specifiers and Projections," *Papers in Theoretical Linguistics*, MIT Working Papers in Linguistics 8, Department of Linguistics and Philosophy, MIT, Cambridge, MA, 128–72.

Garey, H. B. (1957) "Verbal Aspect in French," *Language* 33:2, 91–110.

Gary, J. O. and E. L. Keenan (1977) "On Collapsing Grammatical Relations in Universal Grammar," in P. Cole and J. M. Sadock, eds. (1977), 83–120.

Gee, J. P. (1974) "Jackendoff's Thematic Hierarchy Condition and the Passive Construction," *Linguistic Inquiry* 5, 304–8.

Gentner, D. (1978) "On Relational Meaning: The Acquisition of Verb Meaning," *Child Development* 49, 988–98.

(1981) "Some Interesting Differences Between Nouns and Verbs," *Cognition and Brain Theory* 4, 161–78.

(1982) "Why Nouns Are Learned Before Verbs: Linguistic Relativity Versus Natural Partitioning," in S. A. Kuczaj, ed., *Language Development: Language, Cognition and Culture* II, Erlbaum, Hillsdale, NJ, 301–34.

Ghomeshi, J. and D. Massam (1995) "Lexical/Syntactic Relations without Projection," *Linguistic Analysis* 24, 175–217.

Giorgi, A. (1983–84) "Toward a Theory of Long Distance Anaphors: A GB Approach," *The Linguistic Review* 3, 307–61.

Giorgi, A. and G. Longobardi (1991) *The Syntax of Noun Phrases*, Cambridge University Press, Cambridge.

Givón, T. (1984a) "Direct Object and Dative Shifting: Semantic and Pragmatic Case," in F. Plank, ed. (1984), 151–82.

(1984b) *Syntax: A Functional-Typological Introduction*, vol. I, John Benjamins, Amsterdam.

(1990) *Syntax: A Functional-Typological Introduction*, vol. II, John Benjamins, Amsterdam.

(2001) *Syntax: An Introduction*, vols. I and II, John Benjamins, Amsterdam. (Second edition.)

Gleitman, L. R. (1965) "Coordinating Conjunction in English," *Language* 41, 260–93.

Gleitman, L., H. Gleitman, C. Miller, and R. Ostrin (1996) "Similar, and Similar Concepts," *Cognition* 58, 321–76.

Godard, D. (1992) "Extraction out of NP in French," *Natural Language and Linguistic Theory* 10, 233–77.

Goldberg, A. E. (1992) "The Inherent Semantics of Argument Structure: The Case of the English Ditransitive Construction," *Cognitive Linguistics* 3, 37–74.

(1995) *Constructions: A Construction Grammar Approach to Argument Structure*, University of Chicago Press, Chicago, IL.

(1997) "The Relationships between Verbs and Constructions," in M. Verspoor, K. D. Lee, and E. Sweetser, eds., *Lexical and Syntactical Constructions and the Construction of Meaning*, John Benjamins, Amsterdam, 383–98.

(1998) "Patterns of Experience in Patterns of Language," in M. Tomasello, ed., *The New Psychology of Language*, Lawrence Erlbaum, Mahwah, NJ, 203–19.

Goldberg, A. E. and R. Jackendoff (2004) "The English Resultative as a Family of Constructions," *Language* 80, 532–68.

Goldsmith, J. (1980) "Meaning and Mechanism in Grammar," in S. Kuno, ed., *Harvard Studies in Syntax and Semantics*, Department of Linguistics, Harvard University, Cambridge, MA, 423–49.

Green, G. (1972) "Some Observations on the Syntax and Semantics of Instrumental Verbs," *CLS* 8, Chicago Linguistic Society, Chicago, IL, 83–97.

(1973) "A Syntactic Syncretism in English and French," in B. Kachru, R. B. Lees, Y. Malkiel, A. Pietrangeli, and S. Saporta, eds., *Issues in Linguistics*, University of Illinois Press, Urbana, IL, 257–78.

(1974) *Semantics and Syntactic Regularity*, Indiana University Press, Bloomington, IN.

Grimes, J. E. (1975) *The Thread of Discourse*, Mouton, The Hague.

Grimshaw, J. (1981) "Form, Function and the Language Acquisition Device," in C. L. Baker and J. McCarthy, eds., *The Logical Problem of Language Acquisition*, MIT Press, Cambridge, MA, 165–82.

(1987) "Unaccusatives: An Overview," *NELS* 17, Graduate Linguistics Student Association, University of Massachusetts, Amherst, MA, 244–59.

(1989) "Getting the Dative Alternation," *MIT Working Papers in Linguistics* 10, Department of Linguistics and Philosophy, MIT, Cambridge, MA, 113–22.

(1990) *Argument Structure*, MIT Press, Cambridge, MA.

(1993) "Semantic Structure and Semantic Content in Lexical Representation," unpublished ms., Rutgers University, New Brunswick, NJ.

Grimshaw, J. and A. Mester (1988) "Light Verbs and Theta-Marking," *Linguistic Inquiry* 19, 205–32.

Grimshaw, J. and S. Vikner (1993) "Obligatory Adjuncts and the Structure of Events," in E. Reuland and W. Abraham, eds. (1993), 143–55.

Gropen, J., S. Pinker, M. Hollander, and R. Goldberg (1991) "Affectedness and Direct Objects: The Role of Lexical Semantics in the Acquisition of Verb Argument Structure," *Cognition* 41, 153–95.

Gruber, J. S. (1965) "Studies in Lexical Relations," Doctoral dissertation, MIT, Cambridge, MA. (Reprinted in Gruber 1976: 1–210.)

(1976) *Lexical Structures in Syntax and Semantics*, North-Holland, Amsterdam.

Guéron, J. (1980) "On the Syntax and Semantics of PP Extraposition," *Linguistic Inquiry* 11, 637–78.

Guéron, J. and J. Lecarme, eds. (2004) *The Syntax of Time*, MIT Press, Cambridge, MA.

Guerssel, M. (1986) "On Berber Verbs of Change: A Study of Transitivity Alternations," Lexicon Project Working Papers 9, Center for Cognitive Science, MIT, Cambridge, MA.

Guerssel, M., K. Hale, M. Laughren, B. Levin, and J. White Eagle (1985) "A Cross-Linguistic Study of Transitivity Alternations," *Papers from the Parasession on Causatives and Agentivity*, Chicago Linguistic Society, Chicago, IL, 48–63.

Guilfoyle, E. (1995) "The Acquisition of Irish and the Internal Structure of VP in Early Child Grammars," *Proceedings of the 20th Boston University Conference on Language Development*, Cascadilla Press, Somerville, MA, 296–307.

(2000) "Tense and N-Features in Modern Irish," in A. Carnie and E. Guilfoyle, eds., *The Syntax of Verb Initial Languages*, Oxford University Press, Oxford, 61–73.

Gundel, J. K. (1978) "Stress, Pronominalization and the Given-New Distinction," *University of Hawaii Working Papers in Linguistics* 10:2, Department of Linguistics, University of Hawaii, Honolulu, HI, 1–13.

(1985) "'Shared Knowledge' and Topicality," *Journal of Pragmatics* 9, 83–107.

Haiman, J. (1985) *Natural Syntax: Iconicity and Erosion*, Cambridge University Press, Cambridge.

Hale, K. (1996) "Universal Grammar and the Roots of Linguistic Diversity," *MIT Working Papers in Linguistics* 28, Department of Linguistics and Philosophy, MIT, Cambridge, MA.

Hale, K. L. and S. J. Keyser (1987) "A View from the Middle," Lexicon Project Working Papers 10, Center for Cognitive Science, MIT, Cambridge, MA.

(1992) "The Syntactic Character of Thematic Structure," in I. M. Roca, ed. (1992), 107–43.

(1993) "On Argument Structure and the Lexical Expression of Syntactic Relations," in K. L. Hale and S. J. Keyser, eds., *The View from Building 20*, MIT Press, Cambridge, MA, 53–109.

(1994) "Constraints on Argument Structure," in B. Lust, M. Suñer, and J. Whitman, eds., *Heads, Projections, and Learnability*, Lawrence Erlbaum, Hillsdale, NJ, 53–72.

(1997a) "The Limits of Argument Structure," in A. Mendikoetxea and M. Uribe-Etxebarria, eds., *Theoretical Issues at the Morphology-Syntax Interface*, Euskal Herriko Univertsitatea, Bilbao, 203–30.

(1997b) "On The Complex Nature of Simple Predicators," in A. Alsina, J. Bresnan, and P. Sells, eds. (1997), 29–65.

(1998) "The Basic Elements of Argument Structure," *MIT Working Papers in Linguistics* 32, Department of Linguistics and Philosophy, MIT, Cambridge, MA, 73–118.

(1999) "Bound Features, Merge, and Transitivity Alternation," *Papers from the UPenn/MIT Roundtable on the Lexicon*, MIT Working Papers in Linguistics 35, Department of Linguistics and Philosophy, MIT, Cambridge, MA, 49–72.

(2002) *Prolegomenon to a Theory of Argument Structure*, MIT Press, Cambridge, MA.

Hall, B. (1965) "Subject and Object in English," Doctoral dissertation, MIT, Cambridge, MA.

Halliday, M. A. K. (1970) "Language Structure and Language Function," in J. Lyons, ed., *New Horizons in Linguistics*, Penguin, Harmondsworth, Middlesex, 140–65.

Harley, H. (1995) "Subjects, Events, and Licensing," Doctoral dissertation, MIT, Cambridge, MA.

(1997) "If You *Have*, You Can *Give*," *WCCFL* 15, Stanford Linguistics Association, Stanford, CA, 193–207.

(2003) "Possession and the Double Object Construction," in P. Pica and J. Rooryck, eds., *Linguistic Variation Yearbook* 2, John Benjamins, Amsterdam, 31–70.

Harley, H. and R. Noyer (2000) "Formal versus Encyclopedic Properties of Vocabulary: Evidence from Nominalizations," in B. Peeters, ed., *The Lexicon-Encyclopedia Interface*, Elsevier, Amsterdam, 349–74.

Harris, A. C. (1984a) "Case Marking, Verb Agreement, and Inversion in Udi," in D. M. Perlmutter and C. Rosen, eds. (1984), 243–58.

(1984b) "Inversion as a Rule of Universal Grammar: Georgian Evidence," in D. M. Perlmutter and C. Rosen, eds. (1984), 259–91.

Haspelmath, M. (1993) "More on the Typology of Inchoative/Causative Verb Alternations," in B. Comrie and M. Polinsky, eds., *Causatives and Transitivity*, John Benjamins, Amsterdam, 87–120.

(2002) "Explaining the Ditransitive Person-Role Constraint: A Usage-based Approach," unpublished ms., Max-Planck-Institut für evolutionäre Anthropologie, Leipzig.

Hawkins, J. A. (1981) "The Semantic Diversity of Basic Grammatical Relations in English and German," *Linguistische Berichte* 75, 1–25.

(1982) "Syntactic-Semantic Generalizations: Uniting Contrasting Rules in English and German," in W. F. W. Lohnes and E. A. Hopkins, eds., *The Contrastive Grammar of English and German*, Karoma, Ann Arbor, MI, 196–231.

(1985) *A Comparative Typology of English and German: Unifying the Contrasts*, University of Texas Press, Austin, TX.

(1994) *A Performance Theory of Order and Constituency*, Cambridge University Press, Cambridge.

(1995) "Argument-Predicate Structure in Grammar and Performance: A Comparison of English and German," in I. Rauch and G. F. Carr, eds., *Insights in Germanic Linguistics, I: Methodology in Transition*, Mouton de Gruyter, Berlin, 127–44.

Hawkinson, A. K. and L. M. Hyman (1974) "Hierarchies of Natural Topic in Shona," *Studies in African Linguistics* 5, 147–70.

Hay, J., C. Kennedy, and B. Levin (1999) "Scalar Structure Underlies Telicity in 'Degree Achievements,'" *SALT 9*, Cornell Linguistics Circle Publications, Cornell University, Ithaca, NY, 127–44.

Heim, I. (1982) "The Semantics of Definite and Indefinite Noun Phrases," Doctoral dissertation, University of Massachusetts, Amherst, MA.

Hermon, G. (1986) *Syntactic Modularity*, Foris, Dordrecht.

Higginbotham, J. (2000) "Accomplishments," *Proceedings of GLOW in Asia* II, Nagoya, Japan.

Hinrichs, E. (1985) "A Compositional Semantics for Aktionsarten and NP Reference in English," Doctoral dissertation, The Ohio State University, Columbus, OH.

Hoekstra, T. (1984) *Transitivity*, Foris, Dordrecht.

(1988) "Small Clause Results," *Lingua* 74, 101–39.

(1992) "Aspect and Theta Theory," in I. M. Roca, ed. (1992), 145–74.

(2000) "The Nature of Verbs and Burzio's Generalization," in E. Reuland, ed., *Arguments and Case: Explaining Burzio's Generalization*, John Benjamins, Amsterdam, 57–78.

Hoekstra, T., H. van der Hulst, and M. Moortgat, eds. (1980) *Lexical Grammar*, Foris, Dordrecht.

Hoekstra, T. and R. Mulder (1990) "Unergatives as Copular Verbs: Locational and Existential Predication," *The Linguistic Review* 7, 1–79.

Holisky, D. A. (1987) "The Case of the Intransitive Subject in Tsova-Tush (Bats)," *Lingua* 71, 103–32.

Hoop, H. de (1992) "Case Configuration and Noun Phrase Interpretation," Doctoral dissertation, Rijksuniversiteit Groningen, Groningen.

Hopper, P. J. and S. A. Thompson (1980) "Transitivity in Grammar and Discourse," *Language* 56, 251–95.

Hout, A. van (1996) *Event Semantics of Verb Frame Alternations: A Case Study of Dutch and Its Acquisition*, Tilburg Dissertation in Language Studies, Katholieke Universiteit Brabant, Tilburg.

(2000a) "Event Semantics in the Lexicon-Syntax Interface: Verb Frame Alternations in Dutch and Their Acquisition," in C. Tenny and J. Pustejovsky, eds. (2000), 239–81.

(2000b) "Projection Based on Event Structure," in P. Coopmans, M. Everaert, and J. Grimshaw, eds. (2000), 403–27.

Huddleston, R. (1970) "Some Remarks on Case Grammar," *Linguistic Inquiry* 1, 501–11.

Hudson, R. (1992) "So-Called 'Double Objects' and Grammatical Relations," *Language* 68, 251–76.

Hust, J. R. and M. K. Brame (1976) "Jackendoff on Interpretive Semantics: A Review of *Semantic Interpretation in Generative Grammar* by R. Jackendoff," *Linguistic Analysis* 2, 243–77.

Inoue, K. (2001) "Verb Meaning vs. Construction Meaning: The Cases of *hit*, *spray*, and *load*," *English Linguistics* 18, 670–95.

Iwata, S. (1998) *A Lexical Network Approach to Verbal Semantics*, Kaitakusha, Tokyo.

Jackendoff, R. S. (1972) *Semantic Interpretation in Generative Grammar*, MIT Press, Cambridge, MA.

(1975) "Morphological and Semantic Regularities in the Lexicon," *Language* 51, 639–71.

(1976) "Toward an Explanatory Semantic Representation," *Linguistic Inquiry* 7, 89–150.

(1983) *Semantics and Cognition*, MIT Press, Cambridge, MA.

(1987) "The Status of Thematic Relations in Linguistic Theory," *Linguistic Inquiry* 18, 369–411.

(1990a) "On Larson's Treatment of the Double Object Construction," *Linguistic Inquiry* 21, 427–56.

(1990b) *Semantic Structures*, MIT Press, Cambridge, MA.

(1992) "Mme. Tussaud Meets the Binding Theory," *Natural Language and Linguistic Theory* 10, 1–31.

(1996a) "Conceptual Semantics and Cognitive Linguistics," *Cognitive Linguistics* 7, 93–129.

(1996b) "The Proper Treatment of Measuring Out, Telicity, and Perhaps Even Quantification in English," *Natural Language and Linguistic Theory* 14, 305–54.

(1997) "Twistin' The Night Away," *Language* 73, 534–59.

(2002) *Foundations of Language*, Oxford University Press, Oxford.

Jacobs, J., A. von Stechow, W. Sternefeld, and T. Vennemann, eds. (1993) *Syntax: An International Handbook of Contemporary Research*, vol. 1, de Gruyter, Berlin.

Jacobs, R. A. and P. S. Rosenbaum, eds. (1970) *Readings in English Transformational Grammar*, Ginn, Waltham, MA.

Jaeggli, O. A. (1986) "Passive," *Linguistic Inquiry* 17, 587–622.

Jakobson, R. (1962) "Morfologicheskie nabludenija nad slavjanskim skloneniem" [Morphological Observations on Slavic Declension], in R. Jakobson, *Selected Writings* 2, Mouton, The Hague, 154–83. (First published in 1958.)

Jeffries, L. and P. Willis (1984) "A Return to the *spray paint* Issue," *Journal of Pragmatics* 8, 715–29.

Jelinek, E. and A. Carnie (2003) "Argument Hierarchies and the Mapping Principle," in A. Carnie, H. B. Harley, and M. Willie, eds., *Formal Approaches to Function in Grammar: In Honor of Eloise Jelinek*, John Benjamins, Amsterdam, 265–96.

Jelinek, E. and R. A. Demers (1983) "The Agent Hierarchy and Voice in Some Coast Salish Languages," *International Journal of American Linguistics* 49, 167–85.

(1994) "Predicates and Pronominal Arguments in Straits Salish," *Language* 70, 697–736.

Johns, A. (1992) "Deriving Ergativity," *Linguistic Inquiry* 23, 57–87.

(1997) "Ergativity: Working Through Some Recent Hypotheses," *GLOT International* 6:2, 3–8.

Johnson, D. E. (1979) *Toward a Theory of Relationally-Based Grammar*, Garland, New York.

Jolly, J. A. (1993) "Preposition Assignment in English," in R. D. Van Valin, Jr., ed. (1993a), 275–310.

Joppen, S. and D. Wunderlich (1995) "Argument Linking in Basque," *Lingua* 97, 123–69.

Joshi, S. (1993) "Selection of Grammatical and Logical Functions in Marathi," Doctoral dissertation, Stanford University, Stanford, CA.

Kaplan, R. M. and J. Bresnan (1982) "Lexical-Functional Grammar: A Formal System for Grammatical Representation," in J. Bresnan, ed. (1982), 173–281.

Katz, J. J. and P. M. Postal (1964) *An Integrated Theory of Linguistic Descriptions*, MIT Press, Cambridge, MA.

Kaufmann, I. (1995) "O- and D-Predicates: A Semantic Approach to the Unaccusative-Unergative Distinction," *Journal of Semantics* 12, 377–427.

Kaufmann, I. and D. Wunderlich (1998) "Cross-linguistic Patterns of Resultatives," unpublished ms., Heinrich Heine Universität, Düsseldorf.

Kay, P. (2000) "Argument Structure Constructions and the Argument-Adjunct Distinction," First International Conference on Construction Grammar, University of California, Berkeley, CA.

(2002) "Patterns of Coining," unpublished ms., University of California, Berkeley, CA.

Kayne, R. S. (1984) *Connectedness and Binary Branching*, Foris, Dordrecht.

Kearns, K. (2000) *Semantics*, St. Martin's, New York.

(2003) "Durative Achievements and Individual-level Predicates on Events," *Linguistics and Philosophy* 26, 595–635.

Keenan, E. L. (1976) "Towards a Universal Definition of 'Subject,'" in C. N. Li, ed. (1976), 303–33.

Keenan, E. L. and B. Comrie (1977) "Noun Phrase Accessibility and Universal Grammar," *Linguistic Inquiry* 8, 63–99.

Kennedy, C. and B. Levin (2001) "Telicity Corresponds to Degree of Change," handout, 75th Annual Meeting of the Linguistic Society of America, Washington, DC.

Kenny, A. (1963) *Action, Emotion, and Will*, Routledge and Kegan Paul, London.

Keyser, S. J. and P. M. Postal (1976) *Beginning English Grammar*, Harper and Row, New York.

Kim, M. (1999) "A Cross-linguistic Perspective on the Acquisition of Locative Verbs," Doctoral dissertation, University of Delaware, Newark, DE.

Kiparsky, P. (1985) *Morphology and Grammatical Relations*, unpublished ms., Stanford University, Stanford, CA.

(1993) "Structural Case," unpublished ms., Stanford University, Stanford, CA.

(1997) "Remarks on Denominal Verbs," in A. Alsina, J. Bresnan, and P. Sells, eds. (1997), 473–99.

(1998) "Partitive Case and Aspect," in M. Butt and W. Geuder, eds. (1998), 265–307.

(2001) "Structural Case in Finnish," *Lingua* 111, 315–76.

Kisala, J. (1985) "Review of Chapter 1 of Ostler's Thesis, *Case-linking: A Theory of Case and Verb Diathesis Applied to Classical Sanskrit*," in B. Levin, ed., *Lexical Semantics in Review*, Lexicon Project Working Papers 1, Center for Cognitive Science, MIT, Cambridge, MA.

Klaiman, M. H. (1980) "Bengali Dative Subjects," *Lingua* 52, 275–95.

Koenig, J.-P. and A. R. Davis (2001) "Sublexical Modality and The Structure of Lexical Semantic Representations," *Linguistics and Philosophy* 24, 71–124.

Kolliakou, D. (1999) "*De*-Phrase Extractability and Individual/Property Denotation," *Natural Language and Linguistic Theory* 17, 713–81.

Koopman, H., and D. Sportiche (1991) "The Position of Subjects," *Lingua* 85, 211–58.

Kratzer, A. (1996) "Severing the External Argument from its Verb," in J. Rooryck and L. Zaring, eds. (1996), 109–37.

 (2004) "Telicity and the Meaning of Objective Case," in J. Guéron and J. Lecarme, eds. (2004), 389–423.

Krifka, M. (1986) "Nominalreferenz und Zeitkonstitution. Zur Semantik von Massentermen, Individualtermen, Aspektklassen," Doctoral Dissertation, University of Munich.

 (1989a) "Nominal Reference, Temporal Constitution and Quantification in Event Semantics," in R. Bartsch, J. van Benthem, and P. van Emde Boas, eds., *Semantics and Contextual Expression*, Foris, Dordrecht, 75–115.

 (1989b) *Nominalreferenz und Zeitkonstitution. Zur Semantik von Massentermen, Individualtermen, Aspektklassen*, Wilhelm Fink Verlag, Munich. (Revision of Krifka 1986.)

 (1992) "Thematic Relations as Links between Nominal Reference and Temporal Constitution," in I. A. Sag and A. Szabolcsi, eds. (1992), 29–54.

 (1996) "Review of H. J. Verkuyl: *A Theory of Aspectuality*," *Studies in Language* 20, 443–54.

 (1998) "The Origins of Telicity," in S. Rothstein, ed., *Events and Grammar*, Kluwer, Dordrecht, Holland, 197–235.

 (1999) "Manner in Dative Alternation," *WCCFL* 18, Cascadilla Press, Somerville, MA, 260–71.

 (2001) "Lexical Representations and the Nature of the Dative Alternation," handout, Conference on the Lexicon in Linguistic Theory, Düsseldorf.

Kuno, S. (1987) *Functional Syntax: Anaphora, Discourse and Empathy*, University of Chicago Press, Chicago, IL.

Kural, M. (1996) "Verb Incorporation and Elementary Predicates," Doctoral disseration, University of California, Los Angeles, CA.

 (2002) "A Four-Way Classification of Monadic Verbs," in A. Alexiadou, ed. (2002), 139–63.

Kuroda, Y. (1988) "Whether We Agree or Not," *Lingvisticae Investigationes* 12, 1–47.

Ladusaw, W. A. and D. R. Dowty (1988) "Toward a Nongrammatical Account of Thematic Roles," in W. Wilkins, ed. (1988), 62–73.

Laffut, A. (1997) "The *spray/load* Alternation: Some Remarks on a Textual and Constructionist Approach," *Leuvense Bijdragen* 86, 457–87.

 (1998) "The Locative Alternation: A Contrastive Study of Dutch vs. English," *Languages in Contrast* 1, 127–60.

 (1999) "Agnation as a Heuristic Tool: An Application to the 'Locative Alternation,'" *Leuvense Bijdragen* 87, 315–35.

Lakoff, G. (1966) "Stative Adjectives and Verbs in English," in A. G. Oettinger, ed., *Mathematical Linguistics and Automatic Translation*, Report NSF-17, Aiken Computation Laboratory, Harvard University, Cambridge, MA, I-1–I-16.

(1968) "Some Verbs of Change and Causation," in S. Kuno, ed., *Mathematical Linguistics and Automatic Translation*, Report NSF-20, Aiken Computation Laboratory, Harvard University, Cambridge, MA.

(1970) *Irregularity in Syntax*, Holt, Rinehart, and Winston, New York.

(1977) "Linguistic Gestalts," *CLS* 13, Chicago Linguistic Society, Chicago, IL, 225–35.

Lakoff, G. and S. Peters (1969) "Phrasal Conjunction and Symmetric Predicates," in D. A. Reibel and S. A. Schane, eds., *Modern Studies in English*, Prentice-Hall, NJ, 113–42.

Lambrecht, K. (1994) *Information Structure and Sentence Form*, Cambridge University Press, Cambridge.

Langacker, R. W. (1987) *Foundations of Cognitive Grammar 1: Theoretical Prerequisites*, Stanford University Press, Stanford, CA.

(1990) *Concept, Image, and Symbol*, Mouton de Gruyter, Berlin.

(1991) *Foundations of Cognitive Grammar 2: Descriptive Application*, Stanford University Press, Stanford, CA.

(1993) "Clause Structure in Cognitive Grammar," *Studi Italiani di Linguistica Teorica e Applicata* 22, 465–508.

Larson, R. K. (1988) "On the Double Object Construction," *Linguistic Inquiry* 19, 335–91.

(1990) "Double Objects Revisited: Reply to Jackendoff," *Linguistic Inquiry* 21, 589–632.

Lee, G. (1971) "Subjects and Agents: II," *Working Papers in Linguistics* 7, Computer and Information Science Research Center, The Ohio State University, Columbus, OH, L-1–L-118.

Lee, H. (2003) "Prominence Mismatch and Markedness Reduction in Word Order," *Natural Language and Linguistic Theory* 21, 617–80.

Leek, F. van der (1996) "The English Conative Construction: A Compositional Account," *CLS 32, Part 1: Papers from the Main Session*, Chicago Linguistic Society, Chicago, IL, 363–78.

Lees, R. B. (1966) *The Grammar of English Nominalizations*, Mouton, The Hague.

Legendre, G. (1989) "Inversion with Certain French Experiencer Verbs," *Language* 65, 752–82.

Legendre, G., W. Raymond, and P. Smolensky (1993) "An Optimality-Theoretic Typology of Case and Grammatical Voice Systems," *BLS* 19, Berkeley Linguistics Society, Berkeley, CA, 464–78.

Levin, B. (1983) "On the Nature of Ergativity," Doctoral dissertation, MIT, Cambridge, MA.

(1989) "The Basque Verbal Inventory and Configurationality," in L. Maracz and P. Muysken, eds., *Configurationality: The Typology of Asymmetries*, Foris, Dordrecht, 39–62.

(1993) *English Verb Classes and Alternations: A Preliminary Investigation*, University of Chicago Press, Chicago, IL.

(1999) "Objecthood: An Event Structure Perspective," *CLS 35, Part 1: Papers from the Main Session*, Chicago Linguistic Society, Chicago, IL, 223–47.

Levin, B. and S. Pinker (1991) "Introduction," *Cognition* 41, 1–7.

Levin, B. and T. R. Rapoport (1988) "Lexical Subordination," *CLS 24, Part 1: Papers from the General Session*, Chicago Linguistic Society, Chicago, IL, 275–89.

Levin, B. and M. Rappaport (1986) "The Formation of Adjectival Passives," *Linguistic Inquiry* 17, 623–61.

(1988) "Non-event –er Nominals: A Probe into Argument Structure," *Linguistics* 26, 1067–83.

(1989) "An Approach to Unaccusative Mismatches," *NELS* 19, Graduate Linguistics Student Association, University of Massachusetts, Amherst, MA, 314–28.

Levin, B. and M. Rappaport Hovav (1991) "Wiping the Slate Clean: A Lexical Semantic Exploration," *Cognition* 41, 123–51.

(1995) *Unaccusativity: At the Syntax-Lexical Semantics Interface*, MIT Press, Cambridge, MA.

(1999) "Two Structures for Compositionally Derived Events," *SALT 9*, Cornell Linguistics Circle Publications, Cornell University, Ithaca, NY, 199–223.

(2002) "What Alternates in the Dative Alternation?," handout, Conference on Role and Reference Grammar: New Topics in Functional Linguistics, Universidad de La Rioja, Logroño, Spain.

(2003) "Roots and Templates in the Representation of Verb Meaning," handout, Department of Linguistics, Stanford University, Stanford, CA.

(2004) "The Semantic Determinants of Argument Expression: A View from the English Resultative Construction," in J. Guéron and J. Lecarme, eds. (2004), 477–94.

Levin, B., G. Song, and B. T. S. Atkins (1997) "Making Sense of Corpus Data: A Case Study of Verbs of Sound," *International Journal of Corpus Linguistics* 2, 23–64.

Levin, B. and C. Tenny, eds. (1988) *On Linking: Papers by Richard Carter*, Lexicon Project Working Papers 25, Center for Cognitive Science, MIT, Cambridge, MA.

Levin, L. (1986) "Operations on Lexical Forms: Unaccusative Rules in Germanic Languages," Doctoral dissertation, MIT, Cambridge, MA.

(1987) "Towards a Linking Theory of Relation Changing Rules in LFG," Report CSLI-87–115, Center for the Study of Language and Information, Stanford University, Stanford, CA.

Levin, L., M. Rappaport, and A. Zaenen, eds. (1983) *Papers in Lexical-Functional Grammar*, Indiana University Linguistics Club, Bloomington, IN.

Li, C. N., ed. (1976) *Subject and Topic*, Academic Press, New York.

Li, Y. (1990) "On V-V Compounds in Chinese," *Natural Language and Linguistic Theory* 8, 177–207.

McCarthy, J. J. (2002) *A Thematic Guide to Optimality Theory*, Cambridge University Press, Cambridge.

McCawley, J. D. (1968) "Lexical Insertion in a Transformational Grammar without Deep Structure," *CLS* 4, Chicago Linguistic Society, Chicago, IL, 71–80.

(1971) "Prelexical Syntax," *Report of the 22nd Annual Roundtable Meeting on Linguistics and Language Studies*, Georgetown University Press, Washington, DC, 19–33.

(1976) "Remarks on What Can Cause What," in M. Shibatani, ed. (1976), 117–29.

McClure, W. T. (1994) "Syntactic Projections of the Semantics of Aspect," Doctoral dissertation, Cornell University, Ithaca, NY.

(1995) "Aspect and Direct Objects in Japanese," *WECOL* 94, 164–80.

(1998) "Morphosyntactic Realization of Aspectual Structure," *Japanese/Korean Linguistics* 7, 445–61.

Macfarland, T. (1991) "Thematic Hierarchies: An Overview," *Northwestern University Working Papers in Linguistics* 3, Department of Linguistics, Northwestern University, Evanston, IL, 105–28.

McKercher, D. A. (2001) "The Polysemy of *with* in First Language Acquisition," Doctoral dissertation, Stanford University, Stanford, CA.

Mahajan, A. (1991) "Clitic Doubling, Object Agreement and Specificity," *NELS* 21, Graduate Linguistics Student Association, University of Massachusetts, Amherst, MA, 263–77.

Maling, J. (2001) "Dative: The Heterogeneity of the Mapping Among Morphological Case, Grammatical Functions, and Thematic Roles," *Lingua* 111, 419–64.

Manning, C. D. (1994) "Ergativity: Argument Structure and Grammatical Relations," Doctoral dissertation, Stanford University, Stanford, CA.

Marantz, A. P. (1984) *On the Nature of Grammatical Relations*, MIT Press, Cambridge, MA.
(1993) "Implications of Asymmetries in Double Object Constructions," in S. A. Mchombo, ed. (1993), 113–50.
(1997) "No Escape from Syntax: Don't Try Morphological Analysis in the Privacy of Your Own Lexicon," *University of Pennsylvania Working Papers in Linguistics* 4(2), Department of Linguistics, University of Pennsylvania, Philadelphia, PA, 201–25.
(2003) "Subjects and Objects," handout, New York University, New York.
Markantonatou, S. and L. Sadler (1995) "Linking Indirect Arguments," *Working Papers in Language Processing* 49, Department of Language and Linguistics, University of Essex, Colchester.
Martínez Vázquez, M. (2001) "Delimited Events in English and Spanish," *Estudios Ingleses de la Universidad Complutense* 9, 31–59.
Masica, C. P. (1976) *Defining a Linguistic Area: South Asia*, University of Chicago Press, Chicago, IL.
Massey, V. W. (1992) *Compositionality and Constituency in Albanian*, MIT Occasional Papers in Linguistics 23, Department of Linguistics and Philosophy, MIT, Cambridge, MA.
Mateu, J. (2002) "Regaining the Direct Object Restriction on English Resultatives," handout, 12th Colloquium on Generative Grammar, Universidade Nova de Lisboa, Lisbon.
Matsumoto, Y. (1996) *Complex Predicates in Japanese: A Syntactic and Semantic Study of the Notion 'Word'*, CSLI Publications, Center for the Study of Language and Information, Stanford University, Stanford, CA.
Mchombo, S. A., ed. (1993) *Theoretical Aspects of Bantu Grammar*, CSLI Publications, Center for the Study of Language and Information, Stanford University, Stanford, CA.
Mel'čuk, I. A. (1979) *Studies in Dependency Syntax*, Karoma, Ann Arbor, MI.
Michaelis, L. A. and J. Ruppenhofer (2000) "Valence Creation and the German Applicative: The Inherent Semantics of Linking Patterns," *Journal of Semantics* 17, 335–95.
(2001) *Beyond Alternations: A Constructional Model of the German Applicative*, CSLI Publications, Center for the Study of Language and Information, Stanford University, Stanford, CA.
Michotte, A. (1963) *The Perception of Causality*, Methuen, London.
Mithun, M. (1984) "On the Nature of Noun Incorporation," *Language* 62, 32–37.
Mittwoch, A. (1991) "In Defense of Vendler's Achievements," *Belgian Journal of Linguistics* 6, 71–86.
Moens, M. and M. Steedman (1987) "Temporal Ontology and Temporal Reference," *Computational Linguistics* 14, 15–28.
Mohanan, K. P. and T. Mohanan (1994) "Issues in Word Order in South Asian Languages: Enriched Phrase Structure or Multidimensionality?," in M. Butt, T. H. King, and G. Ramchand, eds., *Theoretical Perspectives on Word Order in South Asian Languages*, CSLI Publications, Center for the Study of Language and Information, Stanford, California, 153–84.
Mohanan, K. P., T. Mohanan, and L. Wee (1999) "Introduction," in T. Mohanan and L. Wee, eds. (1999), 1–21.
Mohanan, T. (1994) *Argument Structure in Hindi*, CSLI Publications, Center for the Study of Language and Information, Stanford University, Stanford, CA.
Mohanan, T. and K. P. Mohanan (1999) "On Representations in Grammatical Semantics," in T. Mohanan and L. Wee, eds. (1999), 23–75.

Mohanan, T. and L. Wee, eds. (1999) *Grammatical Semantics: Evidence for Structure in Meaning*, CSLI Publications, Center for the Study of Language and Information, Stanford University, Stanford, CA.

Moore, J. and David M. Perlmutter (2000) "What Does It Take to Be a Dative Subject," *Natural Language and Linguistic Theory* 18, 373–416.

Morgan, J. L. (1969) "On Arguing about Semantics," *Papers in Linguistics* 1, 49–70.

Moritz, L. and D. Valois (1994) "Pied-Piping and Specifier-Head Agreement," *Linguistic Inquiry* 25, 667–707.

Morolong, M. and L. M. Hyman (1977) "Animacy, Objects and Clitics in Sesotho," *Studies in African Linguistics* 8, 119–218.

Mourelatos, A. P. D. (1978) "Events, Processes and States," *Linguistics and Philosophy* 2, 415–34.

Mufwene, S. S. (1978) "English Manner-of-speaking Verbs Revisited," *Papers from the Parasession on the Lexicon*, Chicago Linguistic Society, Chicago, IL, 278–89.

Mulder, R. (1992) *The Aspectual Nature of Syntactic Complementation*, Holland Institute of Generative Linguistics, Dordrecht.

Murasugi, K. G. (1992) "Crossing and Nested Paths: NP Movement in Accusative and Ergative Languages," Doctoral dissertation, MIT, Cambridge, MA.

Murphy, G. L. (2002) *The Big Book of Concepts*, MIT Press, Cambridge, MA.

Nemoto, N. (1998) "On the Polysemy of Ditransitive *Save*: The Role of Frame Semantics in Construction Grammar," *English Linguistics* 15, 219–42.

Newmeyer, F. (2002) "Optimality and Functionality: A Critique of Functionally-based Optimality-Theoretic Syntax," *Natural Language and Linguistic Theory* 20, 43–80.

Nichols, J. (1975) "Verbal Semantics and Sentence Construction," *BLS* 1, Berkeley Linguistics Society, Berkeley, CA, 343–53.

(1982) "Ingush Transitivization and Detransitivization," *BLS* 8, Berkeley Linguistics Society, Berkeley, CA, 445–62.

(1984) "Direct and Oblique Objects in Chechen-Ingush and Russian," in F. Plank, ed. (1984), 183–209.

Nilsen, D. L. F. (1973) *The Instrumental Case in English: Syntactic and Semantic Considerations*, Mouton, The Hague.

Nishigauchi, T. (1984) "Control and the Thematic Domain," *Language* 60, 215–60.

Nunberg, G., I. A. Sag, and T. Wasow (1994) "Idioms," *Language* 70, 491–538.

Oehrle, R. T. (1976) "The Grammatical Status of the English Dative Alternation," Doctoral dissertation, MIT, Cambridge, MA.

(1977) "Review of G. M. Green: *Semantics and Syntactic Regularity*," *Language* 53, 198–208.

(1983) "The Inaccessibility of the Inner NP: Corrections and Speculations," *Linguistic Analysis* 12, 159–71.

O'Grady, W. (1998) "The Syntax of Idioms," *Natural Language and Linguistic Theory* 16, 279–312.

Olsen, M. B. (1994) "The Semantics and Pragmatics of Lexical Aspect Features," *Studies in the Linguistic Sciences* 24, 361–75.

(1997) *A Semantic and Pragmatic Model of Lexical and Grammatical Aspect*, Garland, New York.

Ono, N. (1992) "Instruments: A Case Study of the Interface between Syntax and Lexical Semantics," *English Linguistics* 9, 196–22.

Ostler, N. D. M. (1979) "Case-linking: A Theory of Case and Verb Diathesis Applied to Classical Sanskrit," Doctoral dissertation, MIT, Cambridge, MA.

Parsons, T. (1990) *Events in the Semantics of English*, MIT Press, Cambridge, MA.

(1995) "Thematic Relations and Arguments," *Linguistic Inquiry* 26, 635–62.

Penhallurick, J. (1984) "Full-Verb Inversion in English," *Australian Journal of Linguistics* 4, 33–56.

Pereltsvaig, A. (1999) "Cognate Objects in Russian: Is the Notion 'Cognate' Relevant for Syntax?," *Canadian Journal of Linguistics* 44, 267–91.
  (2000) "On Accusative Adverbials in Russian and Finnish," in A. Alexiadou and P. Svenonius, eds., *Adverbs and Adjunction*, Linguistics in Potsdam 6, Institut für Linguistik, Universität Potsdam, 155–76.
Perlmutter, D. M. (1978) "Impersonal Passives and the Unaccusative Hypothesis," *BLS* 4, Berkeley Linguistics Society, Berkeley, CA, 157–89.
  (1983a) "Introduction," in D. M. Perlmutter, ed. (1983b), ix–xv.
  ed. (1983b) *Studies in Relational Grammar 1*, University of Chicago Press, Chicago, IL.
  (1984) "Working 1s and Inversion in Italian, Japanese, and Quechua," in D. M. Perlmutter and C. Rosen, eds. (1984), 294–330.
  (1989) "Multiattachment and the Unaccusative Hypothesis: The Perfect Auxiliary in Italian," *Probus* 1, 63–119.
Perlmutter, D. M. and P. M. Postal (1983a) "The Relational Succession Law," in D. M. Perlmutter, ed. (1983b), 30–80.
  (1983b) "Towards a Universal Characterization of Passivization," in D. M. Perlmutter, ed. (1983b), 3–29.
  (1984) "The 1-Advancement Exclusiveness Law," in D. M. Perlmutter and C. Rosen, eds. (1984), 81–125.
Perlmutter, D. M. and C. Rosen, eds. (1984) *Studies in Relational Grammar 2*, University of Chicago Press, Chicago, IL.
Pesetsky, D. M. (1982) "Paths and Categories," Doctoral dissertation, MIT, Cambridge, MA.
  (1987) "Binding Problems with Experiencer Verbs," *Linguistic Inquiry* 18, 126–40.
  (1995) *Zero Syntax*, MIT Press, Cambridge, MA.
Pinker, S. (1989) *Learnability and Cognition: The Acquisition of Argument Structure*, MIT Press, Cambridge, MA.
Plank, F., ed. (1984) *Objects: Towards a Theory of Grammatical Relations*, Academic Press, London.
  (1985) "Verbs and Objects in Semantic Agreement: Minor Differences Between English and German that Might Suggest a Major One," *Journal of Semantics* 3, 305–60.
Platzack, C. (1979) *The Semantic Interpretation of Aspect and Aktionsarten: A Study of Internal Time Reference in Swedish*, Foris, Dordrecht.
Polinsky, M. (1996) "A Non-Syntactic Account of Some Asymmetries in the Double Object Construction," in J.-P. Koenig, ed., *Discourse and Cognition: Bridging the Gap*, CSLI Publications, Center for the Study of Language and Information, Stanford University, Stanford, CA, 403–22.
  (1999) "Review of K. Lambrecht: *Information Structure and Sentence Form*," *Language* 75, 567–82.
Polinsky, M. and I. Kozinsky (1992) "Ditransitive Constructions in Kinyarwanda: Coding Conflict or Syntactic Doubling?," *CLS 28, Part 1: Papers from the Main Session*, Chicago Linguistic Society, Chicago, IL, 426–42.
Pollard, C. and I. A. Sag (1987) *Information-Based Syntax and Semantics 1: Fundamentals*, CSLI Publications, Center for the Study of Language and Information, Stanford University, Stanford, CA.
Pollock, J.-Y. (1989) "Opacity, Genitive Subjects, and Extraction from NP in English and French," *Probus* 1, 151–62.
Postal, P. M. (1966) "Review of R. M. W. Dixon: *Linguistic Science and Logic*," *Language* 42, 84–93.
  (1971) *Cross-Over Phenomena*, Holt, Rinehart, and Winston, New York.
Potter, B. (1991) "Dative Compounding and the Prominence Theory of Theta Assignment," *ESCOL '91*, 289–300.

Primus, B. (1993) "Syntactic Relations," in J. Jacobs, A. von Stechow, W. Sternefeld, and T. Vennemann, eds. (1993), 686–705.

(1998) "The Relative Order of Recipient and Patient in the Languages of Europe," in A. Siewierska, ed., *Constituent Order in the Languages of Europe*, Mouton de Gruyter, Berlin, 421–73.

(1999) *Cases and Thematic Roles: Ergative, Accusative and Active*, Niemeyer, Tübingen.

Prince, A. and P. Smolensky (1993) "Optimality Theory: Constraint Interaction in Generative Grammar," Technical Report, Rutgers University Center for Cognitive Science, Rutgers University, New Brunswick, NJ.

Prince, E. (1979) "A Comparison of *Wh*-Clefts and *It*-Clefts in Discourse," *Language* 54, 883–906.

(1981) "Towards a Taxonomy of Given-New Information," in P. Cole, ed. (1981), 223–55.

(1985) "Fancy Syntax and 'Shared Knowledge,'" *Journal of Pragmatics* 9, 65–81.

Pullum, G. (1988) "Citation Etiquette beyond Thunderdome," *Natural Language and Linguistic Theory* 6, 579–88.

Pustejovsky, J. (1991a) "The Generative Lexicon," *Computational Linguistics* 17, 409–41.

(1991b) "The Syntax of Event Structure," *Cognition* 41, 47–81.

ed. (1993) *Semantics and the Lexicon*, Kluwer, Dordrecht.

(1995) *The Generative Lexicon*, MIT Press, Cambridge, MA.

Pylkkänen, L. (2000) "On Stativity and Causation," in C. Tenny and J. Pustejovsky, eds. (2000), 417–44.

Quirk, R., S. Greenbaum, G. Leech, and J. Svartvik (1985) *A Comprehensive Grammar of the English Language*, Longman, London.

Ramchand, G. C. (1997) *Aspect and Predication*, Clarendon Press, Oxford.

Randall, J. H. (1988) "Inheritance," in W. Wilkins, ed. (1988), 129–46.

Ransom, E. N. (1979) "Definiteness and Animacy Constraints on Passive and Double-Object Constructions in English," *Glossa* 13, 215–40.

Rapoport, T. R. (1990) "Secondary Predication and the Lexical Representation of Verbs," *Machine Translation* 4, 31–55.

Rapp, I. and A. von Stechow (1999) "*Fast* 'Almost' and the Visibility Parameter for Functional Adverbs," *Journal of Semantics* 16, 149–204.

Rappaport, M. (1983) "On the Nature of Derived Nominals," in L. Levin, M. Rappaport, and A. Zaenen, eds. (1983), 113–42.

Rappaport, M. and B. Levin (1988) "What to Do with Theta-Roles," in W. Wilkins, ed., 7–36.

Rappaport, M., B. Levin, and M. Laughren (1988) "Niveaux de représentation lexicale," *Lexique* 7, 13–32. (An English translation appears as "Levels of Lexical Representation," in J. Pustejovsky, ed. (1993), 37–54.)

Rappaport Hovav, M. (2002) "Review of C. Tenny and J. Pustejovsky, eds.: *Events as Grammatical Objects: The Converging Perspectives of Lexical Semantics and Syntax*," *Journal of Linguistics* 38, 696–703.

Rappaport Hovav, M. and B. Levin (1996) "Two Types of Derived Accomplishments," in M. Butt and T. H. King, eds., *Proceedings of the First LFG Conference*, Grenoble, France, 375–88.

(1998a) "Building Verb Meanings," in M. Butt and W. Geuder, eds. (1998), 97–134.

(1998b) "Morphology and Lexical Semantics," in A. Spencer and A. Zwicky, eds. (1998), 248–71.

(2000) "Classifying Single Argument Verbs," in P. Coopmans, M. Everaert, and J. Grimshaw, eds. (2000), 269–304.

(2001) "An Event Structure Account of English Resultatives," *Language* 77, 766–97.

(2002) "Change of State Verbs: Implications for Theories of Argument Projection," *BLS* 28, Berkeley Linguistics Society, Berkeley, CA, 269–80.

Ravin, Y. and C. Leacock, eds. (2000) *Polysemy: Theoretical and Computational Approaches*, Oxford University Press, Oxford.

Reinhart, T. (1982) "Pragmatics and Linguistics: An Analysis of Sentence Topics," Indiana University Linguistics Club, Bloomington, IN.

(1996) "Syntactic Effects of Lexical Operations: Reflexives and Unaccusatives," *OTS Working Papers in Linguistics*, Utrecht Institute of Linguistics, University of Utrecht.

(2000) "The Theta System: Syntactic Realization of Verbal Concepts," *OTS Working Papers in Linguistics*, Utrecht Institute of Linguistics, University of Utrecht.

(2001) "Experiencing Derivations," *SALT 11*, Cornell Linguistics Circle Publications, Cornell University, Ithaca, NY, 365–87.

(2002) "The Theta System – An Overview," *Theoretical Linguistics* 28, 229–90.

Reuland, E. and W. Abraham, eds. (1993) *Knowledge and Language II: Lexical and Conceptual Structure*, Kluwer, Dordrecht.

Rice, S. A. (1987a) "Towards a Cognitive Model of Transitivity," Doctoral dissertation, University of California, San Diego, La Jolla, CA.

(1987b) "Towards a Transitive Prototype: Evidence from Some Atypical English Passives," *BLS* 13, Berkeley Linguistics Society, Berkeley, CA, 422–34.

Richards, N. (2001) "An Idiomatic Argument for Lexical Decomposition," *Linguistic Inquiry* 32, 183–93.

Ritter, E. and S. T. Rosen (1996) "Strong and Weak Predicates: Reducing the Lexical Burden," *Linguistic Analysis* 26, 29–62.

(1998) "Delimiting Events in Syntax," in M. Butt and W. Geuder, eds. (1998), 135–64.

(2000) "Event Structure and Ergativity," in C. Tenny and J. Pustejovsky, eds. (2000), 187–238.

Roberts, I. G. (1987) *The Representation of Implicit and Dethematized Subjects*, Foris, Dordrecht.

(1988) "Predicative APs," *Linguistic Inquiry* 19, 703–10.

Roca, I. M., ed. (1992) *Thematic Structure: Its Role in Grammar*, Foris, Berlin.

Rochemont, M. S. (1986) *Focus in Generative Grammar*, John Benjamins, Amsterdam.

Rohdenburg, G. (1974) *Sekundäre Subjektivierungen im Englischen und Deutschen*, Cornelsen-Velhagen and Klasing, Bielefeld.

Rooryck, J. and L. Zaring, eds. (1996) *Phrase Structure and the Lexicon*, Kluwer, Dordrecht.

Rosch, E. H. (1973) "On the Internal Structure of Perceptual and Semantic Categories," in T. E. Moore, ed., *Cognitive Development and the Acquisition of Language*, Academic Press, New York, 111–44.

Rosch, E. H. and C. B. Mervis (1975) "Family Resemblances: Studies in the Internal Structure of Categories," *Cognitive Psychology* 7, 573–605.

Rosen, C. (1981) "The Relational Structure of Reflexive Clauses: Evidence from Italian," Doctoral dissertation, Harvard University, Cambridge, MA.

(1984) "The Interface between Semantic Roles and Initial Grammatical Relations," in D. M. Perlmutter and C. Rosen, eds. (1984), 38–77.

Rosen, C. and K. Wali (1989) "Twin Passives, Inversion and Multistratalism in Marathi," *Natural Language and Linguistic Theory* 7, 1–50.

Rosen, S. T. (1996) "Events and Verb Classification," *Linguistics* 34, 191–223.

(1999) "The Syntactic Representation of Linguistic Events," *GLOT International* 4:2, 3–11.

Ross, J. R. (1972) "Act," in D. Davidson and G. Harman, eds. (1972), 70–126.
  (1974) "Three Batons for Cognitive Psychology," in D. Palermo and W. Weimar, eds., *Cognition and the Symbolic Processes*, Winston, Washington, DC, 63–124.
Rothstein, S. (1983) "The Syntactic Forms of Predication," Doctoral dissertation, MIT, Cambridge, MA.
  (1992) "Case and NP Licensing," *Natural Language and Linguistic Theory* 10, 119–39.
  (2000) "Secondary Predication and Aspectual Structure," in E. Lang, D. Holsinger, K. Schwabe, and O. Teuber, eds., *Approaching the Grammar of Adjuncts*, ZAS Papers in Linguistics 17, Zentrum für Allgemeine Sprachwissenschaft, Typologie und Universalienforschung, Berlin, 241–64.
Rozwadowska, B. (1988) "Thematic Restrictions on Derived Nominals," in W. Wilkins, ed. (1988a), 147–65.
  (1989) "Are Thematic Relations Discrete?," in R. Corrigan, F. Eckman, and M. Noonan, eds., *Linguistic Categorization*, John Benjamins, Amsterdam, 115–30.
Runner, J. T. (1993) "Quantificational Objects and Agr-O," *Student Conference in Linguistics* 5, MIT Working Papers in Linguistics 20, Department of Linguistics and Philosophy, MIT, Cambridge, MA, 209–24.
  (1995) "Noun Phrase Licensing and Interpretation," Doctoral dissertation, University of Massachusetts, Amherst, MA.
Ryle, G. (1949) *The Concept of the Mind*, Hutchinson, London.
Sadler, L. and A. Spencer (1998) "Morphology and Argument Structure," in A. Spencer and A. M. Zwicky, eds. (1998), 206–36.
Sag, I. A. and A. Szabolcsi, eds. (1992) *Lexical Matters*, CSLI Publications, Center for the Study of Language and Information, Stanford University, Stanford, CA.
Salkoff, M. (1983) "Bees Are Swarming in the Garden," *Language* 59, 288–346.
Sanz, M. (1999) "Aktionsart and Transitive Phrases," in E. Treviño and J. Lema, eds., *Semantic Issues in Romance Syntax*, John Benjamins, Amsterdam, 247–61.
  (2000) *Events and Predication: A New Approach to Syntactic Processing in English and Spanish*, John Benjamins, Amsterdam.
Sasse, H.-J. (2002) "Recent Activity in the Theory of Aspect: Accomplishments, Achievements, or Just Non-Progressive State," *Linguistic Typology* 6, 199–271.
Schachter, P. (1992) "Comments on Bresnan and Kanerva's 'Locative Inversion in Chicheŵa: A Case Study of Factorization in Grammar,'" in T. Stowell and E. Wehrli, eds. (1992), 103–10.
Schlesinger, I. M. (1979) "Cognitive Structures and Semantic Deep Structures: The Case of the Instrumental," *Journal of Linguistics* 15, 307–24.
  (1989) "Instruments as Agents: On the Nature of Semantic Relations," *Journal of Linguistics* 25, 189–210.
  (1992) "The Experiencer as an Agent," *Journal of Memory and Language* 31, 315–32.
  (1995) *Cognitive Space and Linguistic Case*, Cambridge University Press, Cambridge.
Schmitt, C. (1995) "Types, Tokens, AgrO and Aspect," *ESCOL '94*, 282–93.
  (1996) "Aspect and the Syntax of Noun Phrases," Doctoral dissertation, University of Maryland, College Park, MD.
  (1999) "Against VP Aspect as a Formal Feature," *WCCFL* 16, Stanford Linguistics Association, Stanford, CA, 383–97.
Schütze, C. T. (1995) "PP Attachment and Argumenthood," *Papers on Language Processing Acquisition*, MIT Working Papers in Linguistics 26, Department of Linguistics and Philosophy, MIT, Cambridge, MA, 95–151.
Schwartz, L. (1986) "Levels of Grammatical Relations and Russian Reflexive Controllers," *BLS* 12, Berkeley Linguistics Society, Berkeley, CA, 235–45.
Schwartz-Norman, L. (1976) "The Grammar of 'Content' and 'Container,'" *Journal of Linguistics* 12, 279–87.

Sells, P. (1988) "Thematic and Grammatical Hierarchies: Albanian Reflexivization," *WCCFL* 7, Stanford Linguistics Association, Stanford, CA, 293–304.

Shibatani, M., ed. (1976) *Syntax and Semantics 6: The Grammar of Causative Constructions*, Academic Press, New York.

(1996) "Applicatives and Benefactives: A Cognitive Account," in M. Shibatani and S. A. Thompson, eds. (1996), 157–96.

(1999) "Dative Subject Constructions Twenty-Two Years Later," *Studies in the Linguistic Sciences* 29, 45–76.

Shibatani, M. and S. A. Thompson, eds. (1996) *Grammatical Constructions*, Clarendon Press, Oxford.

Shopen, T. (1972) "Logical Equivalence Is Not Semantic Equivalence," *CLS* 8, Chicago Linguistic Society, Chicago, IL, 340–50.

(1986) "Comments on 'The Semantics of 'Internal Dative' in English' by Anna Wierzbicka," *Quaderni di Semantica* 7, 151–54.

Siewierska, A. (1988) *Word Order Rules*, Croom Helm, London.

(1991) *Functional Grammar*, Routledge, London.

(1993) "On the Interplay of Factors in the Determination of Word Order," in J. Jacobs, A. von Stechow, W. Sternefeld, and T. Vennemann, eds. (1993), 826–46.

(1998) "Languages With and Without Objects: The Functional Grammar Approach," *Languages in Contrast* 1, 173–90.

Silverstein, M. (1976) "Hierarchy of Features and Ergativity," in R. M. W. Dixon, ed., *Grammatical Categories in Australian Languages*, Humanities Press, Atlantic Highlands, NJ, 112–71.

Simpson, J. (1983) "Resultatives," in L. Levin, M. Rappaport, and A. Zaenen, eds. (1983), 143–57.

Singh, M. (1992) "An Event-Based Analysis of Causatives," *CLS 28, Part 1: Papers from the Main Session*, Chicago Linguistic Society, Chicago, IL, 515–29.

Slabakova, R. (1998) "L2 Acquisition of an Aspect Parameter," *Journal of Slavic Linguistics* 6, 71–105.

(2000) "L1 Transfer Revisited: The L2 Acquisition of Telicity Marking in English by Spanish and Bulgarian Native Speakers," *Linguistics* 38, 739–70.

(2001) *Telicity in the Second Language*, John Benjamins, Amsterdam.

Slobin, D. I. (1987) "Thinking for Speaking," *BLS* 13, Berkeley Linguistics Society, Berkeley, CA, 435–45.

(1991) "Learning to Think for Speaking: Native Language, Cognition, and Rhetorical Style," *Pragmatics* 1, 7–25.

(1996) "Two Ways to Travel: Verbs of Motion in English and Spanish," in M. Shibatani and S. A. Thompson, eds. (1996), 195–219.

(1997) "Mind, Code, and Text," in J. Bybee, J. Haiman, and S. A. Thompson, eds., *Essays on Language Function and Language Type*, John Benjamins, Amsterdam, 437–67.

(2000) "Verbalized Events: A Dynamic Approach to Linguistic Relativity and Determinism," in S. Niemeier and R. Dirven, eds., *Evidence for Linguistic Relativity*, John Benjamins, Amsterdam, 107–38.

(2003) "Language and Thought Online: Cognitive Consequences of Linguistic Relativity," in D. Gentner and S. Goldin-Meadow, eds., *Language in Mind: Advances in the Study of Language and Thought*, MIT Press, Cambridge, MA, 157–91.

Smith, C. S. (1970) "Jespersen's 'Move and Change' Class and Causative Verbs in English," in M. A. Jazayery, E. C. Polomé, and W. Winter, eds., *Linguistic and Literary Studies in Honor of Archibald A. Hill*, vol. 2, *Descriptive Linguistics*, Mouton, The Hague, 101–09.

(1991) *The Parameter of Aspect*, Kluwer, Dordrecht.

Smyth, R. H., G. D. Prideaux, and J. T. Hogan (1979) "The Effect of Context on Dative Position," *Lingua* 47, 27–42.

Snell-Hornby, M. (1983) *Verb Descriptivity in German and English*, Carl Winter, Heidelberg.

Snyder, K. M. (2003) "The Relationship between Form and Function in Ditransitive Constructions," Doctoral dissertation, University of Pennsylvania, Philadelphia, PA.

Snyder, W. (1995) "A Neo-Davidsonian Approach to Resultatives, Particles, and Datives," *NELS* 25 (1), Graduate Linguistics Student Association, University of Massachusetts, Amherst, MA, 457–71.

Soames, S. and Perlmutter, D. M. (1979) *Syntactic Argumentation and the Structure of English*, University of California Press, Berkeley, CA.

Song, G. (1996) "Adicity, Causation, and Lexical Aspect," *ESCOL '95*, 299–307.

Speas, M. J. (1990) *Phrase Structure in Natural Language*, Kluwer, Dordrecht.

Spencer, A. and A. Zwicky, eds. (1998) *Handbook of Morphology*, Blackwell, Oxford.

Sportiche, D. (1988) "A Theory of Floating Quantifiers and its Corollaries for Constituent Structure," *Linguistic Inquiry* 19, 425–49.

Spreng, B. (2001) "Verb Classes in Inuktitut and the Transitivity Hierarchy: 'Aspects' of the Antipassive," *Proceedings of the Sixth Workshop on Structure and Constituency in Languages of the Americas*, University of British Columbia Working Papers in Linguistics 6, Department of Linguistics, University of British Columbia, Vancouver, 89–106.

Sridhar, S. N. (1979) "Dative Subjects and the Notion of Subject," *Lingua* 49, 99–125.

Starosta, S. (1978) "The One Per Sent Solution," in W. Abraham, ed.,*Valence, Semantic Case and Grammatical Relations*, John Benjamins, Amsterdam, 459–576.

Stechow, A. von (1995) "Lexical Decomposition in Syntax," in U. Egli et al., eds. (1995), John Benjamins, Amsterdam, 81–118.

(1996) "The Different Readings of *Wieder*: A Structural Account," *Journal of Semantics* 13, 87–138.

Stockwell, R. P., P. Schachter and B. H. Partee (1973) *The Syntactic Structures of English*, Holt, Rinehart, and Winston, New York.

Stolz, T. (1996) "Some Instruments Are Really Good Companions – Some Not: On Syncretism and the Typology of Instrumentals and Comitatives," *Theoretical Linguistics* 23, 113–200.

Stowell, T. (1981) "Origins of Phrase Structure," Doctoral dissertation, MIT, Cambridge, MA.

Stowell, T. and Wehrli, E., eds. (1992) *Syntax and Semantics 26: Syntax and the Lexicon*, Academic Press, New York.

Stringer, D. (2003) "Acquisitional Evidence for Universal Syntax of Directional PPs," in P. St. Dizier, ed., *ACL-SIGSEM Worshop: The Linguistic Dimensions of Prepositions and their Use in Computational Linguistics Formalism and Applications*, IRIT, Toulouse, France, 44–55.

Stroik, T. (1996) *Minimalism, Scope, and VP Structure*, Sage Publications, Thousand Oaks, CA.

Sybesma, R. (1992) *Causatives and Accomplishments: The Case of Chinese ba*, Holland Institute of Generative Linguistics, Dordrecht.

Talmy, L. (1975) "Semantics and Syntax of Motion," in J. P. Kimball, ed., *Syntax and Semantics 4*, Academic Press, New York, 181–238.

(1976) "Semantic Causative Types," in M. Shibatani, ed. (1976), 43–116.

(1985) "Lexicalization Patterns: Semantic Structure in Lexical Forms," in T. Shopen, ed., *Language Typology and Syntactic Description 3: Grammatical Categories and the Lexicon*, Cambridge University Press, Cambridge, 57–149.

(1988) "Force Dynamics in Language and Thought," *Cognitive Science* 12, 49–100.

(1991) "Path to Realization – Via Aspect and Result," *BLS* 17, Berkeley Linguistics Society, Berkeley, CA, 480–519.

(2000) *Towards a Cognitive Semantics II: Typology and Process in Concept Structuring*, MIT Press, Cambridge, MA.

Taylor, J. R. (1989) *Linguistic Categorization*, Clarendon Press, Oxford.

(1996) "On Running and Jogging," *Cognitive Linguistics* 7, 21–34.

Tenny, C. (1987) "Grammaticalizing Aspect and Affectedness," Doctoral dissertation, MIT, Cambridge, MA.

(1992) "The Aspectual Interface Hypothesis," in I. A. Sag and A. Szabolcsi, eds. (1992), 1–27.

(1994) *Aspectual Roles and the Syntax-Semantics Interface*, Kluwer, Dordrecht. (Revision of Tenny 1987.)

(1995) "How Motion Verbs are Special: The Interaction of Semantic and Pragmatic Information in Aspectual Verb Meanings," *Pragmatics and Cognition* 3, 31–73.

Tenny, C. and J. Pustejovsky, eds. (2000) *Events as Grammatical Objects*, CSLI Publications, Center for the Study of Language and Information, Stanford University, Stanford, CA.

Testelec, Y. G. (1998) "On Two Parameters of Transitivity," in L. Kulikov and H. Vater, eds., *Typology of Verbal Categories: Papers Presented to Vladimir Nedjalkov on the Occasion of his 70th Birthday*, Niemeyer, Tübingen, 29–45.

Thompson, S. A. (1990) "Information Flow and Dative Shift in English Discourse," in J. A. Edmondson, C. Feagin, and P. Mülhäusler, eds., *Development and Diversity: Language Variation Across Time and Space*, Summer Institute of Linguistics, Dallas, TX, 239–53.

(1995) "The Iconicity of 'Dative Shift' in English: Considerations from Information Flow in Discourse," in M. E. Landsberg, ed., *Syntactic Iconicity and Linguistic Freezes*, Mouton de Gruyter, Berlin, 155–75.

Tomlin, R. S. (1986) *Basic Word Order*, Croom Helm, London.

Travis, L. (1984) "Parameters and Effects of Word Order Variation," Doctoral dissertation, MIT, Cambridge, MA.

(1991) "Inner Aspect and the Structure of VP," *Cahiers de Linguistique de l'UQAM* 1, 132–46.

(2000a) "Event Structure in Syntax," in C. Tenny and J. Pustejovsky, eds. (2000), 145–85.

(2000b) "The L-syntax/S-syntax Boundary: Evidence from Austronesian," in I. Paul, V. Phillips, and L. Travis, eds., *Formal Issues in Austronesian Linguistics*, Kluwer, Dordrecht, 167–94.

Trithart, L. (1975) "Relational Grammar and Chicewa Subjectivization Rules," *CLS* 11, Chicago Linguistic Society, Chicago, IL, 615–24.

(1979) "Topicality: An Alternative to the Relational View of Bantu Passive," *Studies in African Linguistics* 10, 1–30.

Tsunoda, T. (1981) "Split Case-marking Patterns in Verb-types and Tense/Aspect/Mood," *Linguistics* 19, 389–438.

(1985) "Remarks on Transitivity," *Journal of Linguistics* 21, 385–96.

Ullmann, S. (1962) *Semantics: An Introduction to the Science of Meaning*, Basil Blackwell, Oxford.

Ura, H. (2000) *Checking Theory and Grammatical Functions in Universal Grammar*, Oxford University Press, Oxford.

Uszkoreit, H. (1987) *Word Order and Constituent Structure in German*, CSLI Publications, Center for the Study of Language and Information, Stanford University, Stanford, CA.

Vainikka, A. (1993) "The Three Structural Cases in Finnish," in A. Holmberg and U. Nikanne, eds., *Case and Other Functional Categories in Finnish Syntax*, Mouton de Gruyter, Berlin, 129–59.

Vallduví, E. (1992) *The Informational Components*, Garland, New York.

Vallduví, E. and E. Engdahl (1996) "The Linguistic Realization of Information Packaging," *Linguistics* 34, 459–519.

Van Valin, R. D., Jr. (1990) "Semantic Parameters of Split Intransitivity," *Language* 66, 221–60.

ed. (1993a) *Advances in Role and Reference Grammar*, John Benjamins, Amsterdam.

(1993b) "A Synopsis of Role and Reference Grammar," in R. D. Van Valin, Jr., ed. (1993a), 1–164.

(1999) "Generalized Semantic Roles and the Syntax-Semantics Interface," in F. Corblin, C. Dobrovie-Sorin, and J.-M. Marandin, eds. *Empirical Issues in Formal Syntax and Semantics 2*, Thesus, The Hague, 373–89.

(2002) "The Role and Reference Grammar Analysis of Three-Place Predicates," unpublished ms., University at Buffalo, SUNY, Buffalo, NY.

(in press) "Semantic Macroroles in Role and Reference Grammar," in R. Kailuweit and M. Hummel, eds., *Semantische Rollen*, Narr, Tübingen.

Van Valin, R. D., Jr. and R. J. LaPolla (1997) *Syntax: Structure, Meaning and Function*, Cambridge University Press, Cambridge.

Van Valin, R. D., Jr. and D. P. Wilkins (1996) "The Case for 'Effector': Case Roles, Agents, and Agency Revisited," in M. Shibatani and S. A. Thompson, eds. (1996), 289–322.

Vanden Wyngaerd, G. (2001) "Measuring Events," *Language* 77, 61–90.

Vendler, Z. (1957) "Verbs and Times," *Philosophical Review* 56, 143–60. Reprinted in Z. Vendler (1967), 97–121.

(1967) *Linguistics in Philosophy*, Cornell University Press, Ithaca, NY.

(1984) *The Matter of Minds*, Clarendon Press, Oxford.

Verkuyl, H. J. (1972) *On the Compositional Nature of the Aspects*, Reidel, Dordrecht.

(1989) "Aspectual Classes and Aspectual Composition," *Linguistics and Philosophy* 12, 39–94.

(1993) *A Theory of Aspectuality*, Cambridge University Press, Cambridge.

(1999) *Aspectual Issues: Studies on Time and Quantity*, CSLI Publications, Center for the Study of Language and Information, Stanford University, Stanford, CA.

Verma, M. K. and K. P. Mohanan, eds. (1990) *Experiencer Subjects in South Asian Languages*, CSLI Publications, Center for the Study of Language and Information, Stanford University, Stanford, CA.

Verspoor, C. M. (1997) "Contextually-Dependent Lexical Semantics," Doctoral dissertation, Center for Cognitive Science, University of Edinburgh, Edinburgh.

Vlach, R. (1981) "The Semantics of the Progressive," in P. Tedeschi and A. Zaenen, eds. (1981) *Syntax and Semantics 14: Tense and Aspect*, Academic Press, New York, 271–92.

Voorst, J. van (1988) *Event Structure*, John Benjamins, Amsterdam.

(1993) "A Localist Model for Event Semantics," *Journal of Semantics* 10, 65–111.

(1995) "The Semantic Structure of Causative Constructions," *Studies in Language* 19, 489–523.

(1996) "Some Systematic Differences Between the Dutch, French, and English Transitive Construction," *Language Sciences* 18, 227–45.

Ward, G. and B. Birner (2004) "Information Structure and Non-Canonical Syntax," in L. R. Horn and G. Ward, eds., *The Handbook of Pragmatics*, Blackwell, Oxford, 153–74.

Washio, R. (1997) "Resultatives, Compositionality and Language Variation," *Journal of East Asian Linguistics* 6, 1–49.

Wasow, T. (1977) "Transformations and the Lexicon," in P. Culicover, T. Wasow, and A. Akmajian, eds. (1977), 327–60.

(1980) "Major and Minor Rules in Lexical Grammar," in T. Hoekstra, H. van der Hulst, and M. Moortgat, eds. (1980), 285–312.

(1985) "Postscript," in P. Sells, *Lectures on Contemporary Syntactic Theories*, CSLI Publications, Center for the Study of Language and Information, Stanford University, Stanford, CA, 193–205.

(1997) "Remarks on Grammatical Weight," *Language Variation and Change* 9, 81–105.

(2002) *Postverbal Behavior*, CSLI Publications, Center for the Study of Language and Information, Stanford University, Stanford, CA.

Wechsler, S. (1995) *The Semantic Basis of Argument Structure*, CSLI Publications, Center for the Study of Language and Information, Stanford University, Stanford, CA.

(1997) "Resultative Predicates and Control," *Texas Linguistic Forum 38: The Syntax and Semantics of Predication*, Department of Linguistics, University of Texas, Austin, TX, 307–21.

(2001) "An Analysis of English Resultatives Under the Event-Argument Homomorphism Model of Telicity," *Proceedings of the 3rd Workshop on Text Structure*, Department of Linguistics, University of Texas, Austin.

Wechsler, S. and Y.-S. Lee (1996) "The Domain of Direct Case Assignment," *Natural Language and Linguistic Theory* 14, 629–64.

Whitney, R. (1983) "The Place of Dative Movement in a Generative Theory," *Linguistic Analysis* 12, 315–22.

Wienold, G. (1995) "Lexical and Conceptual Stuctures in Expressions for Movement and Space: With Reference to Japanese, Korean, Thai, and Indonesian as Compared to English and German," in U. Egli et al., eds. (1995), 301–40.

Wierzbicka, A. (1980) *The Case for Surface Case*, Karoma, Ann Arbor, MI.

(1986) "The Semantics of 'Internal Dative' in English," *Quaderni di Semantica* 7, 121–35.

Wilkins, W. (1987) "On the Linguistic Function of Event Roles," *BLS* 13, Berkeley Linguistics Society, Berkeley, CA, 460–72.

ed. (1988) *Syntax and Semantics 21: Thematic Relations*, Academic Press, San Diego, CA.

Wilks, Y. (1987) "Primitives," in S. C. Shapiro, ed., *Encyclopedia of AI*, vol. 2, Wiley, New York, 759–61.

Williams, E. (1981) "Argument Structure and Morphology," *The Linguistic Review* 1, 81–114.

(2003) *Representation Theory*, MIT Press, Cambridge, MA.

Wojcik, R. (1976) "Where Do Instrumental NPs Come From?," in M. Shibatani, ed. (1976), 165–80.

Wolff, P. (2003) "Direct Causation in the Linguistic Coding and Individuation of Causal Events," *Cognition* 88, 1–48.

Wolff, P., G. Song, and D. Driscoll (2002) "Models of Causation and Causal Verbs," *CLS 37, Part 1: Papers from the Main Session*, Chicago Linguistic Society, Chicago, IL, 607–22.

Wunderlich, D. (1987) "An Investigation of Lexical Composition: The Case of German *be-*Verbs," *Linguistics* 25, 283–331.

(1996) "Models of Lexical Decomposition," in E. Weigand and F. Hundsnurscher, eds., *Lexical Structures and Language Use*, vol. 1, *Plenary Lectures and Session Papers*, Niemeyer, Tübingen, 169–83.

(1997a) "Argument Extension by Lexical Adjunction," *Journal of Semantics* 14, 95–142.

(1997b) "Cause and the Structure of Verbs," *Linguistic Inquiry* 28, 27–68.

(2000) "Predicate Composition and Argument Extension as General Options – A Study in the Interface of Semantic and Conceptual Structure," in B. Stiebels and D. Wunderlich, eds., *The Lexicon in Focus*, Akademie Verlag, Berlin, 247–70.

Zaenen, A. (1993) "Unaccusativity in Dutch: An Integrated Approach," in J. Pustejovsky, ed. (1993), 129–61.

Ziv, Y. and G. Sheintuch (1979) "Indirect Objects – Reconsidered," *CLS* 15, Chicago Linguistic Society, Chicago, IL, 390–404.

Zubizarreta, M. L. (1987) *Levels of Representation in the Lexicon and in the Syntax*, Foris, Dordrecht.

Zwicky, A. M. (1971) "In a Manner of Speaking," *Linguistic Inquiry* 2, 223–32.

Index of topics

Index of authors

Note: Since this book has such an extensive list of references, we have indexed authors only when the work cited is the source of an idea which figures prominently in the discussion in the text.

Index of languages